The End of the World

The End of the World

CULTURAL APOCALYPSE
AND TRANSCENDENCE

Ernesto de Martino

Translated by Dorothy Louise Zinn

The University of Chicago Press CHICAGO AND LONDON

The University of Chicago Press, Chicago 60637
The University of Chicago Press, Ltd., London
© 2023 by The University of Chicago
Published 2023
Printed in the United States of America

32 31 30 29 28 27 26 25 24 23   1 2 3 4 5

ISBN-13: 978-0-226-82055-2 (cloth)
ISBN-13: 978-0-226-82057-6 (paper)
ISBN-13: 978-0-226-82056-9 (e-book)
DOI: https://doi.org/10.7208/chicago/9780226820569.001.0001

Originally published in Italian as *La fine del mondo*, © 2002 and 2019,
Giulio Einaudi editore S.p.A., Torino.

Support for this publication was provided by the Autonomous Province of
South Tyrol, Department 34, Innovation, Research, University Museums.

AUTONOME PROVINZ BOZEN - SÜDTIROL PROVINCIA AUTONOMA DI BOLZANO - ALTO ADIGE

PROVINZIA AUTONOMA DE BULSAN - SÜDTIROL

Library of Congress Cataloging-in-Publication Data

Names: De Martino, Ernesto, 1908–1965, author. |
Zinn, Dorothy Louise, translator.
Title: The end of the world : cultural apocalypse and transcendence /
Ernesto de Martino ; translated by Dorothy Louise Zinn.
Other titles: Fine del mondo. English | Cultural apocalypse
and transcendence
Description: Chicago : The University of Chicago Press, 2024. |
Includes bibliographical references and index.
Identifiers: LCCN 2023007858 | ISBN 9780226820552 (cloth) |
ISBN 9780226820576 (paper) | ISBN 9780226820569 (ebook)
Subjects: LCSH: Civilization, Modern—20th century. | End of the world. |
History—Philosophy. | History—Religious aspects—Christianity. |
Personality and culture.
Classification: LCC CB425 .M4213 2023 | DDC 909.82—dc23/eng/20230221
LC record available at https://lccn.loc.gov/2023007858

♾ This paper meets the requirements of ANSI/NISO Z39.48-1992
(Permanence of Paper).

Contents

Translator's Preface VII
Introduction XI

Overture: Will There Be a World Tomorrow? *1*

1: Mundus *17*

2: Psychopathological Apocalypses *61*

3: The Drama of Christian Apocalypse *123*

4: Apocalypse and Decolonization *169*

5: The Apocalypse of the West *191*

6: Anthropology and Marxism *237*

7: Anthropology and Philosophy *277*

Glossary *325*
Notes *331*
References *349*
Index *359*

Translator's Preface

My two previous translations of de Martino's monographs (de Martino 2005a, 2015) have been an excellent preparation for translating *La fine del mondo*, much in the way that a mountain climber who wants to tackle Mount Everest starts by training on lower peaks. This work presents numerous challenges, all of which I will not detail here; my aim is simply to make some crucial choices transparent for readers so that they will be able to understand my approach, if not share it completely, for translation is inevitably a subjective endeavor.

As with my other translations of works by de Martino, I have remained very close to the original without many flights of literary fancy, although there are some parts of the text that do have a truly elegant prose. Because this book was a work in progress that remained unfinished at the time of de Martino's death, I have felt it all the more necessary to try to respect what he has left us rather than creatively reelaborate his text, even at the cost of some fluidity. One of the principal challenges with de Martino's writing is his peculiar lexicon. This book is no exception, but its heavy incorporation of philosophical language exacerbated the difficulty in no small measure. For Heideggerian terminology—notoriously difficult to translate—I have cherry-picked from solutions I found in the Macquarrie and Robinson and Stambaugh translations of *Sein und Zeit*. I have dealt with some items in the annotations to the text, which are either a reworking of the annotations by the French and Italian editors and translators (left unmarked) or else my own contributions (noted with "[trans.]"). Bracketed ellipses in the text indicate where the editors (Charuty, Fabre, and Massenzio) performed cuts from de Martino's original writings or de Martino himself omitted text from sources he cites. I did not make any additional cuts to the text except where de Martino included parenthetical citations of references that now appear in the list of references; because of their abbreviated and/or fragmentary nature, they have been deleted and replaced by author-date style citations in the notes. Because many terms crop up in different chapters throughout the volume, I have created a glossary that readers can use as a reference: it includes expressions appearing in bold type for the first time in the book. This glossary is meant to help the reader—especially the de Martino neophyte—to get a handle on his lexicon, but it is in no way meant to offer an exhaustive treatment of each entry. Indeed, the annotations and glossary have been kept to a bare minimum in order to respect the word count limits imposed by the press.

It is important to bear in mind that the book is a reconstruction from the copious notes that de Martino left behind, not a polished text. For this reason, here and there readers will find some repetitions and ungrammatical forms—missing articles, incomplete sentences: these are part and parcel of de Martino's original telegraphic notes and reflect the work's unfinished quality.

A few words about sources. De Martino cites widely in German and French, and for the text's economy in some cases I have translated directly into English. Where he translates his sources into Italian, to the greatest extent possible I retranslated from the original texts and consulted extant English translations. In some cases I have noticed divergences between de Martino's own Italian translation and the French or German original, and where it has some significance, I have indicated this to the reader. Again, because of limited space, I could not linger on such issues, fascinating as they are. All biblical citations are from the New Revised Standard Version of the Bible.

De Martino often uses verbs as nouns, and I have chosen to respect this in most instances by rendering them in English as gerunds. Not only is this usage typical of a certain academic Italian style of days gone by but it also adds a dynamic, processual quality to the writing that I have tried to retain even where I could have used an equivalent noun. Other issues of word choice have more to do with gender politics: in the middle of the twentieth century, the "universal male" in academic Italian writing was prevalent, just as it was in English. To me this usage makes de Martino appear anachronistic; at the risk of being accused of pinkwashing him, I have changed *man* in most places to *humanity* or *humankind*, or else I have made it plural with *they/their* or *people*. Where de Martino discusses Marx and other authors who have used *man*, however, I have kept it, especially as it appears in current English translations. Additionally, I have translated de Martino's references to *padri* and *patria* as "ancestors" and "homeland" (not "fathers" and "fatherland"). A final political point is the translation of *primitivi* as "primitives" with reference to some non-Western peoples, a term that de Martino sometimes put in quotes or prefaces with "socalled" but at other times does not. I have respected his usage, again with the consideration that these were his notes and not a definitive text: as will be clear from the book's content, de Martino's political position was wholly respectful of Indigenous peoples.

La fine del mondo was my inseparable travel companion for one year and some fifty thousand kilometers. I toted the book with me everywhere like a security blanket during the year in which I worked on the project, reluctant to part with it even for a weekend. Working on the translation as I was during the second year of the COVID-19 pandemic, I was probably not the only person thinking about the end of the world on a constant basis. I actually conceived of this translation in 2019, well before the virus made headlines, when the new Italian edition was published, but it did not get off the ground until my sabbatical year from October 2021 to September 2022. If the pandemic were not enough, the outbreak of the Russian invasion of Ukraine in February 2022 resuscitated long-buried risks of nuclear conflict after thirty years of post–Cold War détente. Whether or not it was this current context that has made more people sympathetic to my project, I do not know, but I do owe a great deal of thanks to the multitude of individuals and institutions who have supported my work.

First and foremost, I thank the Free University of Bozen-Bolzano for allowing me to take this sabbatical year, which has given me the precious time to fully concentrate on the project. This was made possible by my colleagues within the Faculty of Education, in particular Federico Corni, Dario Ianes, Monica Parricchi, Johannes van der Sandt, and Renata Zanin. The second major set of thanks goes to the Autonomous Province of South Tyrol, which generously supported two research periods abroad in Germany and the US. The first stay in autumn 2021 was at the University of Cologne's Erich Auerbach Institute for Advanced Studies, where I was welcomed as an associate fellow by Anja Lemke, Semra Mägele, Martin Roussel, and their kind staff. Martin Zillinger of the Department of Anthropology was my host, and I was grateful for exchanges with him and other colleagues during my stay in Cologne: Augustine Agwuele, Jutta Lauth-Bacas, Anna Brus, Michaela Pelican, Eckhard Pistrick, Erhard Schüttpelz, Ulrich van Loyen, and Thomas and Dagmar Widlok. My other research stay was in New York City as a visiting scholar at Columbia University. There, thanks to Naor Ben-Yehoyada's invitation, I was able to make extensive use of the libraries and discuss de Martino with various colleagues: Maria José de Abreu, Matthew Engelke, Rosalind Morris, Elizabeth Povinelli, and David Scott. Thanks to Rosalind and Naor, Jasmine Pisapia and I entered into an exciting dialogue on translating de Martino.

This sabbatical year also gave me the opportunity to talk about de Martino and this project in other venues: the folks at the University of Heidelberg's CAPAS (Center for Apocalyptic and Postapocalyptic

Studies)—Robert Folger, Thomas Meier, Rolf Scheuermann, and Joshua Schuster—were very welcoming and showed me how a good sense of humor is an indispensable tool in apocalypse studies; Hande Birkalan-Gedik had me speak at the University of Frankfurt workshop on Traveling Theory. Francesco Vacchiano and João de Pina Cabral invited me to talk about de Martino and "presence" with colleagues at Venice's Ca' Foscari University, and both have been very generous with their input on the translation, as has Fabio Dei of the University of Pisa.

Sandro Duranti and Steve Feld gave me a great deal of encouragement from the start, and I am grateful to Mary Al-Sayed of the University of Chicago Press for taking on the project and helping make it viable. Also at Chicago, I benefited from the help of Fabiola Enríquez Flores, Stephen Twilley, and Dylan Montanari, and I hope I did not make the valiant Steve LaRue suffer too much over the copyediting. My dear friend Cynthia Karalla has generously loaned her art to the book's cover. For smaller questions, I must thank a number of people: Liz Baer, Roberto Beneduce, Marina Della Rocca, Andre Gingrich, Helene Harpman, Amy Oden, Odile Panetta, Gianni Pizza, Francesco Pompeo, Daniela Salvucci, Simona Taliani, Elisabeth Tauber, and Lisa Wolf.

I cannot acknowledge enough the bountiful and patient support I have received from Marcello Massenzio and Sergio Fabio Berardini throughout my work on this translation: *grazie infinite* to both for helping me to navigate difficult waters and resolve thorny translation questions. Any errors of interpretation or explication that appear despite their good offices are fully my own responsibility.

Special thanks are also due to my family, especially Antonio for taking care of Numa during my travels.

I dedicate this translation to the memory of Lia de Martino (1936–2019) and George Saunders (1946–2020), both of whom preceded me in promoting the work of the great *maestro*.

Matera, September 2022

Introduction

The End of the World is one of those monumental volumes that in turn generates multiple levels of discourse. Much has already been written in Italian and French on the long and complicated history of its creation. Certainly discussion of the book can deal directly with its contents, which appear outwardly fragmentary but are richly flowing in so many suggestive rivulets, each promoting further speculation. There is much to be said, too, about the work's relevance today, both as a commentary on the state of the world and as a contribution to current discussions in several disciplines. Other levels of discourse might consider this book's relationship to the rest of de Martino's oeuvre or treat the history of its reception, principally in Italy and France. The task of writing an introduction to such a book is truly daunting since it could foresee any or all of these levels, but the present essay will only deal with the first three, and very concisely at that.

In Italian *La fine del mondo* was published posthumously for the first time in 1977, twelve years after de Martino's death, due to the Herculean effort of the late Clara Gallini, a former student of de Martino's who worked from the abundant notes, drafts, and other materials the *maestro* had left behind. A massive tome of over seven hundred pages, the 1977 edition—framed by Gallini's monumental but rather ambivalent introduction, itself spanning over eighty additional and very dense pages—has inspired yet also perplexed generations of Italian students and scholars, rendering the book an object of much debate and rethinking. After its first appearance, the book disappeared into a "phantom" existence (as Giordana Charuty has put it) until Gallini and Marcello Massenzio published a new edition in 2002 with the same content and layout but with a wholly new introduction by the editors that reconsidered many of Gallini's previous analyses. The idea to make this book available in English followed the 2016 publication in French of a wholesale revision of the text by Giordana Charuty, Daniel Fabre, and Marcello Massenzio, based on their meticulous work in the de Martino Archive and featuring extensive editorial commentary and annotations. A new Italian edition following the same structure was published by Einaudi in 2019, and the translation presented here has fundamentally worked from that text.[1] It is, of course, a new reconstruction of the author's unfinished project, and therefore the reader must bear this in mind with a degree of tolerance but also appreciation: while the book is still composed of dozens and dozens of sections of varying length, the editors have produced a work that is much more cohesive than the 1977 and 2002 editions, allowing de Martino's voice to better emerge from under the mass of fragments. They have jettisoned some portions of the earlier editions, reorganized clusters of text, and incorporated relevant documents from the Archive, principally de Martino's notes published by Roberto Pàstina in 2005 as *Scritti filosofici* (Philosophical Writings). All in all, there is still a rough quality of the ensemble that gives the reader a partial insight into what the new editors have described as de Martino's "laboratory."

Ernesto de Martino (1908–1965) defined himself as a religious historian and ethnologist. As this volume makes evident, though, he was also very much a philosopher: indeed, Paolo Virno (2006) has called him "one of the most important and original philosophers of twentieth-century Italy." From his early training in Naples in the history of religions, he gravitated to the circle of Benedetto Croce, whose idealist historicism dominated Italian humanities throughout the last century. De Martino was also a political activist and public intellectual, and when he was working on *La fine del mondo*, the world lived in the shadow of a not-so-distant Holocaust, a very present nuclear threat,[2] and various decolonization struggles: all of this influenced his thinking in the mid-1960s. And yet in some ways parallel to the spirit of the Second Vatican Council that was ongoing during his work on the book, de Martino's engagement held out the desire to construct a better future of peaceful planetary coexistence. In her introduction to the first edition of this volume, Clara Gallini defined the work as the "culmination of de Martino's thought," and indeed through the lens of apocalypse de Martino treats a host of themes he was already developing throughout his career: religious history, "presence" and its crisis, ritual and symbol (and more broadly the status and role of culture), a reflexive epistemological critique, humanistic pathos, political commentary, psychological anthropology and ethnopsychiatry, phenomenology, and a rethinking of Marx. He engages all of these themes with his characteristic interdisciplinary vision. What does make *The End of the World* appear to be a more "philosophical de Martino" than previous works is the fact that, to a much greater extent, the text is suffused with a Heideggerian language. Yet the reader should not be lured into thinking that de Martino adopts this lexicon uncritically and wholesale: he puts a new twist on it (or as Bakhtin might say, a double voicing) informed by his own thinking as well as by that of Croce and Italian "positive" existentialism.

The book's original subtitle, "Contribution to the Analysis of Cultural Apocalypses," only hints at de Martino's ambitious comparative project of drawing together heterogeneous material from different apocalyptic "documents" in space and time. De Martino has gathered diverse categories of apocalyptic thought under the heading of "cultural apocalypse." First, as a religious historian de Martino saw beliefs and rituals of world renewal in the ancient world as a form of cultural apocalypse, and he explores the ancient Roman *Mundus patet* in this light as well as cyclical time in other civilizations (chap. 1). We begin to see here the relationship between ritual and cosmogony in human cultures, navigating the tension between world ending and world refoundation. Second, apostolic Christian apocalypse introduced a new sense of historicity with the end already having taken place (chap. 3). The decisiveness of placing Jesus as the center of time, so that the end begins with him—his birth, death, resurrection—and gets projected into an indefinite future of his second coming, thereby discloses the field of present temporality for Christian action in the now. This is an apocalyptic orientation that does not paralyze the believer but instead opens up human, Christian agency. Next, as an ethnologist, and drawing especially from the scholarship of his friend Vittorio Lanternari,[3] de Martino saw millenarian and prophetic movements in non-Western settings as another type of cultural apocalypse, a reaction to the brutal impact of colonial oppression (chap. 4). De Martino reads such millenarianisms in their political dimension of what we would now call globalization and decolonization. These movements are a way of resolving the contradictions of colonialism's legacy in those societies, giving a mythical-ritual horizon for dealing with individual crises of presence but also a collective hope for a new, better world. Returning to the West, Marxist apocalypse was another vision of world ending—that of bourgeois capitalism in favor of the workers' paradise (chap. 6).[4] The cultural apocalypse that appears to have the greatest urgency, however, is "the apocalypse of the West" as manifested in contemporary art and literature (chap. 5). Here de Martino considers above all existentialist literature (chiefly Sartre's *Nausea*) but also modernist poetry and prose. Unlike the other types of cultural apocalypse, which in one way or another featured an *eschaton*—the end of *a* world in final days that would usher in redemption, a renewed world—this latter apocalypse without eschaton describes the threat of an end to *the* world tout court. In this perspective, the nuclear threat of total annihilation is only the latest, though deadliest, manifestation of a longer trend in Western culture.

Among the various cultural apocalypses, it is this latter one of the modern West that bears the closest resemblance to another type of apocalypse, "psychopathological apocalypse" (chap. 2), and in effect de Martino's original project was to draw the forms of cultural apocalypse into a comparison not only among themselves but above all with psychopathological apocalypse. As a founding figure of Italian ethnopsychiatry and medical anthropology, de Martino was steeped in the literature of existentialist and phenomenological psychology and psychiatry (e.g., Karl Jaspers, the school of Ludwig Binswanger). In particular de Martino was struck by *Weltuntergangserlebnis*, the lived experience of the end of the world as a dimension of some forms of mental illness. In the opening section of chapter 1, de Martino dwells at length on the memorable case of the schizophrenic peasant of Bern, which in many regards epitomizes the category of psychopathological apocalypse. De Martino's interest in psychopathology had its roots in his previous studies of magic and religion, in which he developed his notion of "presence," sometimes used interchangeably with Heidegger's Dasein (being-there) as a conception of being. De Martino's presence is not a wholly metaphysical construct but has a historical and cultural rootedness, and it is in the course of history and historical conditions that presence faces challenges or "critical moments" throwing it into crisis. And, as de Martino notes, crisis of presence is "a permanent anthropological risk." This dimension of crisis particularly engrossed de Martino, and from it he elaborated his highly original analysis of "ritual dehistorification," appearing in various moments in the book, to explain how myth and ritual bring about protection, healing, and recovery of presence. Put very succinctly, through the mythical-ritual apparatus of culturally shared symbols, the presence in crisis in history latches on to a metahistorical time of myth, and the ritual repeats a parallel crisis already successfully resolved on the level of myth in a timeless past. This mythical-ritual resolution accompanies the presence back into history, where it can resume its course, effectively getting "unstuck."[5] De Martino's monographs on magic (1948, 1959), funeral lament (1958), and tarantism (1961) demonstrate how culturally defined and practiced rituals protect presence from an uncertain future, restore human agency poached by possession, or assist presence in overcoming critical moments such as bereavement. Without such cultural mechanisms, presence risks drowning in the mire of psychopathology.

With his comparative exploration de Martino seeks to understand the conditions in which apocalypse—as mythical-ritual symbol—can be considered redemptive, as in the cultural apocalypses with eschaton, and when instead it veers toward psychopathology, as in the West's current crisis of "no future" expressed in visual arts and literature. Throughout the book, de Martino focuses on "world" as phenomenologically experienced. He reads the experience of loss or collapse of world in psychopathological apocalypse—the *Weltuntergangserlebnis*—in dialectical relation to cosmogony, the ordering of world.[6] This cosmogonic process, on both individual and collective levels, leads de Martino into a rethinking of the concept of culture itself as a palimpsestic concretion of human action over the *longue durée*, solutions developed within individual cultural groups for the constant reaffirmation of human presence in the face of their given historical conditions (chap. 7). De Martino's specific concept describing this is *appaesamento*, translated here with the gerund "settling," a process of domesticating the world, rendering it ordinary and familiar, that lies in diametric opposition to *spaesamento* (unsettling), associated with alienation and uncanniness. In relation to settling, de Martino writes of "cultural homelands" (*patrie culturali*), not to be understood as *Heimat* in its noxious blood-and-soil connotation but as a way of expressing the phenomenological rootedness of settling that gives a horizon to presence and mutually founds "world."[7] The passage on "the bell tower of Marcellinara" (chap. 5) has become iconic in de Martino studies for its poignant recounting of an episode in de Martino's fieldwork that concisely vivifies the meaning of cultural homeland and unsettling.

In the process of carrying out this phenomenological exploration, de Martino elaborates two concepts arising from his original synthesis of idealist, existentialist, and Marxian philosophy: the "ethos of transcendence" and "communitarian project of things at hand" (chaps. 6, 7). The repeated expression of these concepts in different guises throughout the book testifies to their in fieri status: we really have the concrete sensation of de Martino hammering out his ideas in various attempts. In forging his concept of the ethos of transcendence, de Martino draws from Croce's idealism as well as Heidegger's existentialism and several other influences: it is a transcending value, a will to be in history that moves the impulse of presence (Dasein) in every moment, founding human Being as a "duty-to-be" (*dover esserci*) and with it, further transcendences that give expression to the "useful" (economic) and cultural forms. De Martino posits the ethos of transcendence as an ontological basis that precedes the economic sphere, a kind of missing link in Gramsci's own contestation of vulgar materialist versions of Marxist thought that explains how praxis and sensible activity come to be. He also underlines the social quality of the ethos of transcendence in that it is called to transcend in *intersubjective value*. The propelling dynamic of the ethos of transcendence, however, does not advance through the world in a rudderless, flailing movement, and this is where the communitarian project of things at hand enters the picture, that is, culture. With this latter expression, de Martino takes Heideggerian

Entwurf throughout the volume as project, projecting, projectability, as a horizon for the potential for being, at the same time capturing the collective nature of human culture. That is, individual Being is inexorably rooted in culture, which takes on the concretion of transcendences received from prior generations.

Another key thread that weaves throughout the book is de Martino's epistemological critique. As early as his first monograph, *Naturalismo e storicismo nell'etnologia* (1941), de Martino drew attention to the need for epistemological reflexivity, and he continued to emphasize this throughout his work. This point crops up on several occasions throughout *The End of the World*, for example in relation to the Christian historiography (chap. 3) or the faults of certain Marxist analyses (chaps. 6, 7). But it is within some striking lines in chapter 4 ("Apocalypse and Decolonization") that de Martino lays out his famous notion of "critical ethnocentrism."[8] Critical ethnocentrism was de Martino's proposal to resolve the dilemma between adopting a straightforward, "dogmatic" ethnocentrism and unbridled relativism. Acknowledging the fact that ethnology is science that developed within Western thought, de Martino argues that Western scholars cannot renounce their own perspective and pretend to "go native," as we might say in Anglophone anthropology, but must critically reappropriate their own epistemology through the ethnographic encounter with cultural difference. Of course, since de Martino's time, we need to recognize that the range of critical ethnocentrism would have to extend to "Westernized" scholars, or "halfies" in Abu-Lughod's terminology, where the picture becomes even more complex, but the fundamental idea nonetheless remains of a necessary, critical epistemological self-awareness in the act of studying the "other."

The examination of apocalypse in *The End of the World* shuttles between individual and collective levels: the individual pole is clearer in psychopathological apocalypse and in the artistic expression of the West's crisis, while the collective pole appears more prominently in the assorted historical and ethnographic examples of millenarianisms. Does this imply a correspondence whereby the individual level is closer to apocalypse without eschaton and the collective level is aligned with eschaton? Not necessarily. As Amalia Signorelli (1997) has noted, de Martino did not thoroughly articulate the relationship between individual and collective levels of presence and therefore also the crisis of presence. Of course we do not know what de Martino would have developed in a final version of his opus, but we can say that he viewed culture itself, through the mythical-ritual apparatus first and foremost, as an antidote to sliding into the pole of psychopathology. And it is therefore no coincidence that the contemporary West, which has "lost its religion," has developed a widespread *Stimmung* of crisis. But this is also the heart of his comparative questions circling around Western crisis as his central concern: what is the relationship between the art of the crisis and psychopathology, and what is the relationship between psychopathology—which would seem to have its own forms of "magic"—and "religion" and culture? De Martino's intellectual project holds interesting resonances with some of the scholarship coming under the rubric of affect theory in contemporary anthropology and across the humanities.

The relationship between these two axes, the individual-collective dimension and that of apocalypse with or without eschaton, remains intriguing. As presented in this book, however, the various apocalypses appear a bit static in space and time, whereas a shifting of apocalypses among these dimensions is an empirical realty. Consequently, the rise of ultraconservative religious currents and fundamentalisms around the globe could be analyzed according to this framework. How is it that a "normal" Muslim shifts into a pathologically destructive jihadist mode, as with the apocalypse of the September 11 attacks? How does the millenarianism of a charismatic Reverend Jim Jones in Guyana shift into the total self-annihilation of a community of believers?[9] What should we make of the shift from "everyday" white racism to white supremacist movements, some of whose adherents have committed the most heinous racist and anti-Semitic mass murders in numerous tragic episodes over the last several years? And yet apocalyptic thinking is not only this kind of pathology, or we would fall into the trap of the former-Nazi ethnologist Wilhelm Mühlmann, criticized by de Martino for writing off millenarian movements as psychopathological (chap. 4). A shifting apocalypse can also potentially work in a positive direction, moving toward collective and eschaton-bearing dimensions. We could then interpret movements like Greta Thunberg's Fridays for Future as shifting the menace of environmental apocalypse into cultural agency to overcome the crisis; or, from outside the North Atlantic, the decolonial praxis of many Indigenous movements as shifting the oppressive weight of an apocalypse introduced with "modernity" into a reaffirming *re-existence* (Mignolo and Walsh 2018). Or, as de Martino might put it in his abstruse language, transcending in value according to communitarian projection. Seen in this light, de Martino's questions take on particular urgency for our contemporary world since they speak to many issues we are facing at present. We can only regret that he did not have more time to formulate his answers.

Will There Be a World Tomorrow?

The Problem of the End of the World

When Professor Prini announced the subject of my talk, there was a reaction in the room that old parliamentary proceedings used to describe with the word *sensational.*[1] Among other things, it must have seemed to many that in a conference on the prospects of tomorrow's world, it is at the very least impertinent (in the dual sense of not being pertinent and naughtily provocative) to take the floor to remind the audience that "tomorrow" the world, as a human cultural world, can end; that any reply whatsoever to how the world could and should be "tomorrow" entails the preliminary question of whether or not there will be a world "tomorrow"; and whether there is the risk today that at least some forces are conspiring to make it end. Still others in the audience may even have thought that merely posing a problem of this sort is slightly jinxing, in the Neapolitan sense of the term.[2] Bringing attention to such an extreme possibility has the sole effect of depressing spirits with ominous evocations and of inducing defensive reactions between the serious and the facetious that make up the gestures to ward off evil that are used in such circumstances.[3] I must however invite the audience to get over these immediate reactions, at the same time reassuring everyone that my talk has no intention of depressing spirits but simply to make a contribution, however modest, to the correct framing of a problem that—precisely if it is ignored or lightly set aside—can entail catastrophically negative consequences for humanity as a whole.

A preliminary problem regarding the "world of tomorrow" is that of humankind's relationship to the world as it appears in modern cultural awareness. I believe that this relationship is articulated in two distinct and united moments of which the contemporary world demonstrates having a particularly acute perception. In one sense the world—that is, human society filled with human values and practicable according to these values *must* not end, even if—and indeed, precisely because—single individuals have a finite existence. In another sense the world *can* end, and not so much in the naturalistic sense of a cosmic catastrophe that can destroy the earth or render it uninhabitable but precisely in the sense that human civilization can self-destruct, lose the sense of intersubjective values of human life, and employ the very powers of technological domination over nature in a way that is quintessentially senseless: to annihilate the very possibility of culture. If I had to identify the fundamental character of our epoch, I would say that perhaps more than ever before in history it lives in the dramatic awareness of this *must* and this *can*: in the alternative that the world *must* continue but that it *can* end, that life *must* have a sense but that it *can* also lose it for everyone and forever, and that humanity, only humanity, bears the entire responsibility of this must and this can, not being guaranteed by any level of universal history operating independently of the real decisions of people in society.

In the cultural consciousness of our epoch, the relation between what we may call life's **ethos of transcendence** in intersubjective values and what instead represents the collapse of this ethos—with a corresponding loss of the world's sense and practicability—undoubtedly presents a great variety of concrete manifestations that a systematic study should highlight and subject to evaluation. The extreme manifestation, in which the risk appears in the most radical way, takes on clearly psychopathological features, as for example in schizophrenic *Weltuntergangserlebnis*. But even without arriving at these extreme cases, we perceive plentiful pathological undertones in the collapse of artistic languages, just as in certain existentialist trends and in certain lifestyles. When Heidegger in *Sein und Zeit* theorizes the *Geworfenheit* of being-there; when Sartre in *La nausée* illustrates the unbearable world opening up to nothingness; when D. H. Lawrence complains that we have lost the sun, the planets, and the Lord with the seven stars of the Bear, receiving in exchange the "poor, paltry, creeping little world of science and machinery";[4] when Moravia in *Boredom* describes "a malady of objects": although they are so diverse, we recognize a common *Stimmung* in these cultural expressions. This is the mark of the same radical risk: the possibility of a world that collapses in that the very cultural ethos that conditions and supports it collapses. Furthermore, cultural expressions as heterogeneous as the death drive in Freud or the decline of the West in Spengler seem to point in the same direction.

It is not improbable that such an acute cultural consciousness of the end of the world in the modern period has been fomented by the possibility of nuclear war or the terrifying episodes of genocide in the Nazi death camps. But already the fact that we needed the two hundred thousand people of Hiroshima or the six million Jews who perished in the extermination camps indicates how deep the roots of our crisis are. The image of a single human face that bears the signs of violence and offense at the hand of another should be enough to put into motion the dramatic tension of a world that "can" but "must not" end in the person looking at that face. That the faces lost through human guilt are two hundred thousand or six million does not add anything to the scandal of that single face, and nothing else is needed but that single face to call into question the world and to mobilize the human cultural ethos that again and again is summoned to render the planet more inhabitable and familiar for all. But apart from Hiroshima and the extermination camps, there are other aspects of the modern world that have made our perception of the risk of the end particularly acute. The very rapid transformation in ways of life introduced by the spread of technological progress; migratory flows from the countryside to the city and from underdeveloped regions to industrial regions; the sudden leap of more or less backward economies or even tribal societies to economies and societies by now part of the Western world: this all has led to the crisis of a great number of traditional cultural homelands without an integration into a new cultural homeland having had the time to develop. The rapid processes of transition, the lacerations and empty spaces that they entail, the loss of cultural models in a situation that can no longer utilize the familiar ones: all this induces enormous crises and reproposes in the most dramatic way the elementary problems of our relationship to the world. Only in this context can we manage to understand, for example, the reflection of a French worker like Navel, who in his *Travaux* recounts in an autobiographical form the passage from his peasant origin to the condition of a worker, among other things expressing, in a recurrent way, the recovery of the world and his own body that life in a modern factory had radically placed in question. In the evening the worker Navel returns to his room and prepares his supper, and it is here that he catches himself in the act of opening the door to the cupboard and taking the saltcellar to add salt to his soup:

> I marvelled at my hand's successive perceptions of the wood of the cupboard, the iron of its lock, the glass of the salt-cellar, and the pinch of salt that I took from it. I was astonished to find so much knowledge in the mere skin of the fingers. I endeavoured to live in complete wakefulness, always aware of the moment, the object, the gesture. Childhood alone lives on discoveries; the adult slumbers among his habits. It's always good to learn what life is—and suddenly I was learning, in the green wood of direct contact. The only life worth living is a life of wonder.
>
> Whilst my hand held the small crystals of the pinch of salt, I was aware that it resembled the hand of all the earth's grandmothers, when they make the gesture of removing the lid to put salt in the soup—the gesture

that I'd seen my mother make. I conversed with her, at dream-like speed: "I'm putting salt in my soup, my hand is your hand, you're not dead."

But, further back than my mother, I was aware of all the dead, all the beings that had given me this hand just like other hands. Man lives with his hands. Mine had belonged to generations of serfs. It had often oc-cupied its solitude by closing on the hot bowl of a pipe at the day's end, on the helve of an axe in forests full of snow. Life is what one touches: similar sensations give rise to similar imaginings. By bequeathing me their hands, the woodcutters, vinedressers and farm-labourers had also bequeathed all that had passed through their heads, under their blonde or rufous locks.[5]

It once happened to me, traveling by car along a road in Calabria, to ask an old shepherd directions to a certain crossroad that I was looking for, and since his directions were not very clear, I suggested that I take him by car to the crossroad in question, to then take him back to the point where we met. The old shepherd accepted my invitation with extreme suspicion, and during the ride he looked out the window with growing agitation, as if he were looking for something very important. All of the sudden he cried out, "Where is the bell tower of Marcellinara? I don't see it anymore!" In effect, the bell tower of this village had disappeared from the horizon, but with this, the ancient shepherd's familiar world—his domestic space—was profoundly altered, and because of this disappearance he had the agoniz-ing experience of the collapse of his very limited cultural homeland with the habitual landscape that was the everyday scenario of his movements with the herd. It happened this way that it was no longer possible to go any farther in the company of this shepherd, and it was necessary to take him back to the starting point, where he greeted the reappearance of the lost bell tower with joy. This is an extreme example, almost a caricature, of the connection with a cultural homeland as the condition for the world's practicability: but this connection is well known to the scholar of human civilizations, and it stands out in ancient civilizations in particular.

What can happen when, in a colonial situation, a certain migratory flow suddenly changes its habitat and passes from tribal conditions of living to an industrial type of civilization, has been reported several times. Here, I will recall the case that the ethnologist Rouch had the opportunity to study in Accra on the Gold Coast when it was still under British colonial rule. It is a particularly interesting case, among other things documented in a film by Rouch himself, which was screened a few years ago at Florence's international ethnographic film festival.[6] The case deals with a migratory wave of the Bambara from middle Niger[7]—where they lived from fishing and agriculture—to the more civilized regions of the coast. The Bambara were attracted by the prospect of fabulous earnings in the nascent industrial civilization of the coast, where they indeed found material conditions of life that were certainly much better than those of their tribal homeland. But in the new setting a twofold fact came about: on the one hand, all of the cultural mechanisms that the emigrants had available at home to deal with critical moments of their life as farmers and fishermen—that is, their pantheon, their rituals, their ceremonies—were no longer usable in the new setting, bound as they were to a now-abandoned habitat, to critical moments that had lost their sense, and to tribal relations now broken up. On the other hand, the Bambara were struck by a series of traumatizing episodes in their life as emigrants. The English governor, the army, the police, the bureaucracy, cars, trains, and so forth, all formed a totality of elements that they could not manage to insert into any cultural horizon and that represented the end result of a historical process to which they were substantially foreign. In this situation, quite soon a host of very serious mental disorders arose in the Bambara community of Accra characterized by the rise of unconscious drives that could neither be controlled nor sublimated in certain cultural horizons. The community of Accra was thus struck by a veritable epidemic of mental illnesses that alarmed the authorities, so much so that doctors and psychiatrists were unable to efficaciously intervene in the situation, which escaped the nosological frameworks of European medicine and psychiatry. One Bambara, who was a man with extensive experience and greater abilities than other emigrants, managed to solve this situation. He took some elements of the old cultural apparatus—for example, the cone-shaped altar at the center of a clearing—modifying them on the basis of the new situation. He then divided the traditional altar in various sections, the highest of which hosted the governor as a new divinity in the industrial and colonial pantheon, and then came the doctor, the police chief, the doctor's wife, and so forth. At the base of this cone-shaped altar, which in a certain sense represented a mythical image of the colonial situation, there was a storage space for sacrificial offerings. But what made this readaptation of tribal religion to the new situation particularly interesting were the rituals and ceremonies. The Bambara, keeping the old rituals of possession that are typical of their magical-religious tradition, let themselves get possessed by the divinities of the new pantheon: so in the course of the ceremonies held at the altar, they were possessed by the spirit of the English governor, the police chief, or the train engineer; and as liturgical formulas, they used the bureaucratic formulas that formed another traumatizing element in their new city life. In this way, the traumas and conflicts accumulated on a daily basis, and which previously exploded in outright mental disorders, were now released through the ritual order of possession, and they received a horizon in specific mythical figurations. In this way the new cultural apparatus could carry out a rebalancing and reintegrating function, and the mental disorders found a most appropriate means of control.

This singular episode inspires a few observations. Western science and technology, born within a particular cultural ethos that is the result of a long history, undoubtedly form values that are not only universal but universalizable. However, they are universalizable values only to the extent that they do not remain beyond the human worlds that are entering into the process of Westernization at a growing pace and also to the extent that science and technology fully develop an ethos suited to the type of integral humanism and integral democracy that they certainly contain, at least potentially. In this regard, we should not forget that a long road lies ahead of us, and just as there is black magic, there is also a way of understanding science as a morally indifferent technicism, and thus compatible, for example, with the atomic secret and nuclear war. The central problem of the *world of today* thus appears to be the foundation of a new cultural ethos that is no longer suited to the "bell tower of Marcellinara" but to the entire planet, which the astronauts now contemplate in cosmic solitude and that is in fact becoming—if through contradictions and resistance— our fundamentally unitary cultural homeland, with all of the wealth of its memories and perspectives. To the extent that this new ethos will become truly operative and unifying, it will manage to gather the original dispersion and division of peoples and cultures into an ecumene of commonly acknowledged values. A world that "must not" end will emerge victorious over the recurrent temptation of a world that "can" end, and the end of "a world" will not mean the end of "the world" but simply, "the world of tomorrow."

Third World Apocalypse and European Apocalypse

As has been authoritatively stated in this conference, a fuller understanding of African prophetic movements—although they make up an identifiable subject area because of their variety of conditionings, geneses, structures, and functions—requires a wider comparative perspective that includes similar American, Oceanian, and Asian movements.[8] This is not only because similar events require comparison but also because in our case there is a common historical moment that groups together and qualifies all of these movements, lending a unity of perspective to the comparative study. This moment is their uncoincidental burgeoning and multiplying in the epoch of the crisis of colonialism and the society that expressed it, that is, the epoch of the formation of the Third World. Yet the comparison suggests an even broader perspective. Mediated during the colonial period by missionary activity, especially that of Protestant sects and churches, the Judeo-Christian eschatological tradition has exercised a preeminent influence on Third World prophetic movements. In certain cases this filiation is explicitly recognized by the Indigenous prophetic movements (e.g., Russellism in Africa). On the other hand, the relationship is inverse in the case of the Mormon sect, because Mormonism was influenced by the Indigenous Ghost Dance movement that emerged among the Paiute on the Nevada-California border. By virtue of these connections, a broader ethnological analysis—which in a traditional ethnological sense is aimed above all at measuring the degree of reshaping of Indigenous cultural traditions within the new prophetic and eschatological formations—is propelled in an entirely natural way toward the comparison of Indigenous prophetic movements with those that have blossomed on the trunk of the Judeo-Christian prophetic, millenarian, and eschatological tradition, a tradition that runs through the whole of Western history from the Middle Ages to today. In the context of this wider need for comparison, we should consider some recent monographic collections, such as numbers 4 and 5 of the *Archives de Sociologie des Religions*, respectively from July–December 1957 and January–June 1958; the volume *Millennial Dreams in Action,*[9] which gathers the contributions of various scholars from a symposium held at the University of Chicago in April 1960; and the volume *Religions de Salut*, published in 1962 by the Institute of Sociology of the Free University of Brussels.[10] The first two collections in particular establish precisely the need for comparative study that is not restricted to Indigenous prophetic and eschatological movements of relatively limited diachronic depth and still observable today by the ethnographer but that instead encompasses in a systematic way also the almost bimillenary Christian eschatological tradition. I would like to observe that if on the one hand this tradition fosters the burgeoning of sects and millenarian movements, at the same time it makes its constant influence felt on Western theological and philosophical thought itself, getting transformed in terms that are at least potentially secular and civic in Marxian philosophy and in Marxist movements.

The need to broaden the comparative perspective in relation to our topic has thus already been noted, and it will certainly be productive to the extent that it finds an inner form of control in an ethos of comparison between different cultural-historical developments. Until now these have been corporative, incoherent, divergent, and dispersed, but they are now virtually forced to enter into dialogue and relate to one another under the drive of an ecumenical tension that, in the present historical moment of humanity, has taken root like never before—despite all appearances—in the very heart of things, moving souls and reflecting itself in minds.[11] In his project for an interdisciplinary study in the field of human sciences, Georges Gusdorf recently wrote that "the time has come to pass from a comparison of cultures to a culture of comparison."[12] Which, if I understand correctly, seems to mean that it is not just a matter of showing the value of a generic interdisciplinary need for collaboration as complementary to the need for specialist work but to participate in a unifying ethos that time and again, and in a deliberate and methodical way, relates the sciences of humankind to the human that we are here and now in the context of a cultural-historical situation that is our own. I would nonetheless like to avoid a misunderstanding. This comparative and unifying ethos, in my view, does not employ a perspective-free cultural relativism whose ideal seems at times to be a rather frivolous fashion show of models of culture driven forward on the catwalk by the anthropological science of an aestheticizing presenter in front of a public that is open to all purchases. What Lévi-Strauss let slip rather imprudently in a recent interview given to *Aut-Aut*[13] is even less helpful to the establishment of this ethos: his ideal of a man of science is one who takes on "God's point of view," that is, "understanding mankind as if he were completely out of the picture"; indeed, "as if the observer were from another planet and had an absolutely objective and complete perspective." In this way the expert of social sciences has to take on the perspective of an aesthete who examines people "as if they were ants." The truth seems to me to be something else; that is, since the researcher has grown up and been raised within Western civilization, he can only be willing to deliberately place into question the corporativisms and fetishisms that he may have absorbed from this upbringing, and he can and must do this according to the lines of development of a critical, open ethnocentrism that is fostered by the ethos of comparison of the cultural history of the West with others that until now have been unrelated, divergent, and dispersed, in view—as already stated—of a very humbly human, and very historically determined, task of unification. Without this being intended as a critique of the instruments of analysis utilized by structuralism in anthropology, it seems to me that the pretense to "place oneself out of the picture," to "look at people as if they were ants from another planet" and to take on "God's point of view" actually leaves the field open to certain dubious abdications of which moreover we find traces in the aforementioned interview with Lévi-Strauss, where among other things, we read,

> I see humanity evolving not in the sense of a liberation, but I would surely say, of a progressive and increasingly complete subjugation to natural determinism. It seems to me that what we can reconstruct from the ancient eras of humanity, as well as what we can still study in so-called

primitive societies, demonstrates that these are societies that are still largely free with respect to natural determinism, in the sense that man and the conditions of his existence are still essentially determined by his dreams, his speculations; and that because of his low economic level, man enjoys an autonomy with respect to nature that is much broader than what subsequently occurs. Subsequently, indeed, we witness the progressive restraining of humanity through a series of intermediaries described by dialectical materialism, and it seems to me that what is happening and what will happen more and more is the "direct drive" with which humanity is regulated by the great determinisms of a biological and demographic nature. The future of humanity will be one of an increasingly complete slavery to the "fatality" of nature.[14]

It seems to me here that the scientific ideal of considering people as ants is transformed into a prophetic message that humanity will inevitably be reduced to a sort of anthill, that humanity fatally approaches an apocalypse without **eschaton,** the total ruin of humanity. This is actually no longer even a prophetic message but a cold scientific prediction that now obliges us to adapt to the event, just as it is necessary in autumn to adapt oneself to the coming and inevitable winter. I would be tempted to counter the structuralist anthropologist's prophecy with an opposite and complementary prophecy contained in a passage from Dostoevsky's *Notes from Underground*:

Now I ask you: what can be expected of man since he is a being endowed with such strange qualities? Shower upon him every earthly blessing, drown him in a sea of happiness, so that nothing but bubbles of bliss can be seen on the surface; give him economic prosperity, such that he should have nothing else to do but sleep, eat cakes, and busy himself with the continuation of his species, and even then out of sheer ingratitude, sheer spite, man would play you some nasty trick. He would even risk his cakes and would deliberately desire the most fatal rubbish, the most uneconomical absurdity, simply to introduce into all this positive good sense his fatal fantastic element. It is just his fantastic dreams, his vulgar folly, that he will desire to retain, simply in order to prove to himself—as though that were so necessary—that men still are men and not the keys of a piano, which the Laws of Nature threaten to control so completely that soon one will be able to desire nothing but by the calendar. And that is not all: even if man really were nothing but a piano-key, even if this were proved to him by natural science and mathematics, even then he would not become reasonable, but would purposely do something perverse out of simple ingratitude, simply to win his point. And if he does not find

means he will contrive destruction and chaos, will contrive sufferings of
all sorts, only to win his point! He will launch a curse upon the world,
and as only man can curse (it is his privilege, the primary distinction
between him and other animals) it may be by his curse alone he will
attain his object—that is, convince himself that he is a man and not a
piano-key! If you say that all this, too, can be calculated and tabulated—
chaos and darkness and curses, so that the mere possibility of calculating
it all beforehand would stop it all, and reason would reassert itself—then
man would purposely go mad in order to be rid of reason and win his
point! [. . .] Now the ants have quite a different taste. They have a mar-
velous edifice of that pattern which endures for ever—the ant-heap.[15]

Thus, from a discourse that seemed headed in a general methodological direction, and therefore only indirectly related to my topic, we find
ourselves unexpectedly led into the sphere of apocalypse, but this time a
nonreligious apocalypse without eschaton in which no small part of Western culture is variously involved. The problem of prophetic and eschatological movements in the Third World thus leads us afar if Western
ethnologists in the ethnological relationship are truly willing to place into
question the cultural world to which they belong; in other words, if the
analysis of the elements connected to Third World prophetic and eschatological movements must necessarily involve a coming to awareness of and
focus on the current Western cultural climate itself. In the last instance,
in order to know what Third World apocalypses are and "where they're
headed," it is also necessary to focus on the apocalypses in which we, as
Westerners, are involved. The aim of this is to reach—as far as possible—a
higher perspective, one that indirectly discloses a projectable being-in-
the-world and being-together for everyone. It will therefore not be enough
to compare Third World prophetic and eschatological movements with the
Judeo-Christian prophetic and apocalyptic tradition and whatever else
more or less directly follows it. The comparison also necessarily entails
that insidious Western apocalypse that is characterized by the loss of sense
and of domesticity in the world, the failure of intersubjective human relations, the ominous shrinking of any horizon whatsoever of a future that
is practicable in a communitarian way according to human liberty and
dignity; and finally, by the risks of alienation we perceive to be embodied
in, if not in technological progress, certainly in technicisms and in the
fetishization of technology. As is well known, this is a condition of crisis
whose genesis dates back to the second half of the nineteenth century;
but it is only today, in a time that includes the last two postwar periods,
that it has taken on particular significance and diffusion. By now the common reference to those philosophies of history that contain predictions of

the death of the West is not enough; nor is the reference to certain themes of negative existentialism: through the arts and literature the theme of apocalypse without eschaton appears fully as a matter of mores that needs to be analyzed. Sartre's "nausea," Camus's "absurd," Moravia's "malady of objects," Beckett's plays: these not only reflect this particular apocalyptic custom of our epoch but also the "success" of these literary projects testifies the extent to which they resonate with the disposition of people's spirits and therefore how widespread is the sensibility to which they refer. On another cultural level, Euro-American science-fiction literature, which is so rich with dark social prophesies and predictions of the degeneration and extinction of humankind and its world, of a regression to the inchoate, in turn gives evidence of how the theme of apocalypse without eschaton has taken on the character of an orientation that is to a certain degree collective, utilizing among other things all the power of the so-called mass media to spread itself.

Especially beginning with the period after the First World War, attempts multiplied to describe and interpret this apocalyptic disposition of minds and spirits in the contemporary West, mostly oriented in a sociological or cultural-historical direction. Sticking to the most recent literature, it is sufficient to recall, as examples, the lectures held by Emmanuel Mounier from 1946 to 1948 during the "Rencontres internationals de Genève" and the "Semaine de sociologie" (lectures contained in the third volume of Mounier's works under the title *La petite peur du XX*ᵉ *siècle*);[16] the report by Franklin Le Van Baumer on the twentieth-century version of the apocalypse, published in *Cahiers d'histoire mondiale;*[17] the essay by Franz Altheim, "Apokalyptik Heute," published in *Die Neue Rundschau;*[18] the works of Hans Sedlmayr on art in the modern world;[19] the book by Helmuth Petriconi, director of the Romanesque Seminar of the University of Hamburg, *Das Reich des Untergangs: Bemerkungen über ein mythologisches Thema;*[20] and the collection of articles "Apocalisse e Insecuritas" in an issue of *Archivio di filosofia.*[21] Finally, I should mention, but only as a document of the point of view of two Soviet sociologists on the recurrent theme of apocalypse in Euro-American science fiction, an essay by E. Brandis and V. Dmitrevskij that appeared in translation in the last issue of the journal *Comunicazione di massa*, published by the Center for the Sociology of Mass Communication of the University of Rome's Pedagogical Institute.[22]

I must nonetheless note that the fundamental limit of these essays (above and beyond limits that could result from their scientific quality, the greater or lesser breadth of information, and the particular interpretative orientation with which they have been executed) is that they remain substantially closed within an analysis of modern Western apocalypse without any opening to a systematic intercultural comparison with Third World eschatological apocalypses. This prevents these essays from taking advantage of the liberatory power that, in a subject like this, emerges from the comparison of cultural histories that are certainly different but not unrelatable; on the contrary, they are susceptible to a unifying comparative evaluation if it is true that the Western apocalyptic-eschatological tradition has profoundly influenced the prophetic movements of cultures subject to the impact of white colonization; if, moreover, it is true that the spread of an ethnological theme that is no longer compatible with the schemes of Tylorian or Frazerian evolutionism has contributed to the crisis of a providential and unitary plan of history; and finally, if it is true that the crisis of the colonial epoch and the society that founded this epoch are at the root and condition both of the eschatological apocalypse of the Third World and of the apocalypse without eschaton of a part of contemporary Euro-American culture. On this last point it is necessary to note that the growing spread of the West's technological conquests, together with the colonialist exploitation whose traces and legacy are still so obviously noticeable, have exposed traditional Indigenous cultures to the risks of a catastrophe from which those cultures and those societies have defended themselves through, among other things, prophetic, apocalyptic, and eschatological movements. Moreover, within Western culture itself technological fetishism, complicated by the internal contradictions of traditional bourgeois society, has in turn fomented risks of human alienation and disintegration from which the apocalypse without eschaton has been, if not actually a means of defense, certainly the most desperate and dramatic cultural expression. As different as they are in their features, their conditioning, and their functioning, the two apocalypses—the eschatological one of the Third World and the one without eschaton of the West in crisis—thus ultimately have their roots in a common situation: the same threat of dehumanization of the human which characterizes the present time. This reaffirms the legitimacy of a comparative study that is the scientific equivalent of that vast effort of defense and human reintegration that today, on our planet, is trying to make its way on the most immediate social and political level with so much difficulty.

But the comparative study of cultural apocalypses in the present historical conjuncture can also advance in another direction that, in my view, has considerable heuristic value. I am referring to the psychopathological documentation on the collapse of the world and intersubjective relations, a documentation that is by now abundant and that can be used by social scientists thanks to existential analysis in psychopathology. But in our case, what heuristic value are we dealing with? Psychopathological documentation exposes with particular clarity the human, worldly catastrophe that is carried out in the experiences of a radical alteration and uncanniness of the world, in states of derealization, the delusions of negation, in the *Weltuntergangserlebnis* of incipient schizophrenia, or in certain epileptic auras, and finally, in that psychotic state that Schiff has called "paranoia of destruction," smugly adorning it also with the biblical destination of the "Samson's reaction"[23] (in a more up-to-date, though less scientific way, we could call it "Dr. Strangelove's reaction"). To the extent that cultural apocalypses are functional in a concrete historical or social context—that is, to the extent that they carry out a real reintegrating and mediating function that produces intersubjective values—we should undoubtedly distinguish them clearly from psychopathological apocalypses, which are typically disintegrating and unproductive. Nonetheless, the crisis-reintegration dialectic in those cultural apocalypses that are most clearly reintegrating and productive can benefit considerably from the heuristic indication coming from the psychopathological documentation, where the risk of a nude crisis without a horizon appears. Moreover, it is within the dramatic nature of religious apocalypses that they can tip over toward bare crisis from one moment to the next, and in fact there are many intermediate nuances between integrating religious apocalypses and patently psychopathological apocalypses that manifest the collapse of a society and a culture, or simply the psychic collapse of a so-called prophet. As Lommel[24] has underlined, the Unambal of Kimberly (North West Australia), exposed to a white colonial influence that completely devastated their socioeconomic regime as seminomadic hunters, experienced a type of apocalypse without eschaton that reflects—together with a number of other signs—a psychic collapse that needs to be examined not only on the cultural-historical or sociological level but also on an ethnopsychiatric level. Even for the apocalypses of agrarian societies mostly oriented toward a culturally reintegrating and productive eschatological moment, we must continuously deal with certain psychopathological risks that threaten the prophet's personality as well as the followers' behavior. Finally, the heuristic value of the psychopathological document lies not only in the examination of eschatological, religious apocalypses of the Third World or millenarian sects in the Euro-American world but also in the examination of the apocalypse without eschaton that feeds into such a large part of the cultural life of the contemporary West. It is certainly no coincidence that the psychological adventure of the protagonist of Sarte's *Nausea* is in many respects suited to a comparison with experiences of uncanniness in the everyday world, the loss of objects and of one's own **being-there**, a sinister **being-acted-upon** and a tension of things toward the deformed and monstrous that characterizes the psychotic experience of a looming catastrophe of **being-in-the-world** itself.

I would now like to specify the sense and limits of this talk, necessarily too brief for the complexity of the problem that it raises, and therefore subject to misinterpretation. First of all I would like to clarify that it is not a matter here of the simple framing of a problem or possible research project. In other words, I propose considering Third World prophetic and apocalyptic movements within the wider context of cultural apocalypses in the modern and contemporary world. This entails a systematic comparison of different traditions, a comparison in which the West itself enters into the comparison and not only with regard to the Judeo-Christian apocalyptic-eschatological tradition, the problematic of relations between history and eschatology, and the overturning of this tradition in Marxian philosophy and in Marxist movements. Indeed, the comparison must also include the apocalypse without eschaton in which such a great part of Euro-American culture appears caught up. I have also underlined that psychopathological documentation takes on a considerable heuristic value in light of this comparison.

This project of a broader comparative study on cultural apocalypses constitutes an ethnological problem in a general sense—or, if you will, a problem of cultural anthropology. The theme of cultural apocalypses in fact enters in an elective way into a science of comparison of the cultural history of different *ethne* in an epoch in which the spread of technological developments of Western culture, the crisis of colonialism and the society that expressed it, the formation of the Third World, the encounter and relationality of different cultures, and the perspective of an ecumenical civilization all renew the traditional "social sciences," especially ethnology. A project of this sort no doubt requires that the ethnologist weave a continuous dialogue with other specialists; this, moreover, is part of a need that is increasingly felt in the present cultural climate, which not only faces pressing problems of relations among different cultural traditions but also no less pressing problems of collaboration between distinct specialistic traditions, especially when "unifying" themes of research are touched that reveal "no-man's-lands": aspects of being human that are lacking a scientific status.

It is probable that the research project outlined in this talk will raise reservations and skepticism in many quarters with regard to the legitimacy of the proposed problem and the methodology to follow. It will seem to some that the cultural products introduced into the comparison are too heterogeneous for the comparison to be legitimate and conclusive; that there is an obvious stretch in wanting to understand within the same comparative connection eschatological apocalypses in the Third World, the Judeo-Christian apocalyptic tradition, the apocalypse without eschaton of Western culture in crisis, and psychopathological apocalypses; that broadening to this point the tasks of ethnological research means making it lose the solid specialistic ground on which it has moved until now; that the preparatory studies are not yet sufficient to carry out a project of this sort; and finally, that the modes of interdisciplinary dialogue among various specialists, which the breadth of the topic necessarily requires, are not clearly understood. To these, or to other similar reservations and skepticisms, I could reply exhaustively if the available time allowed for it. Here, by way of a conclusion, I will limit myself to imploring the most uncharitably disposed to have at least a certain indulgence for a project that, despite all of the dangers and difficulties that lie ahead of it, still reflects the need to promote on scientific ground that ethos of encounter and discussion, relation and unification that humanity, today perhaps more than ever, is experiencing so dramatically.

1

Mundus

1. The Case of the Bernese Peasant

1.1. Toward the end of 1947, a young peasant, age twenty-three, was admitted to the canton hospital of Münsingen (Bern) exhibiting a typical schizophrenic delusion of the end of the world. The subject of this delusion was a detrimental and sinister alteration of the world, a radical upset of the cosmic order and community relations. The world—which the patient represented to himself in the way that was closest to his experience as a farmer, as what man produces with his work and nature generates through its seasonal rhythms—had entered into a radical crisis beginning the previous spring, when it happened that the patient had uprooted some shrubs, and with this guilty act of his started off a process of breakdown. But blame for the ominous alteration was even more attributable to the fact that in autumn, his father had uprooted an oak tree in order to sell it: from the hole in the ground left after the uprooting, water flowed that spilled on the ground. Another guilty act that had thrown the world into disorder, according to the patient, was the redoing of the entrance to his father's farm, whose door's shape and color were changed, thereby introducing a dangerous alteration in the relations between the paternal home, the door, and the rest of the world. In particular, the sun no longer struck the old door in moving along its daily path, and this altered the sun's regular course, the normal passing of the day, and the lighting up of the paternal home. The collapse of the world—the falling apart of its order, domesticity, and inhabitability—was also manifested in the total **unsettling** of the landscape and in the unbreathable quality of its air: the sinking of a mountain, the flattening of the earth, the transformation of the air in a smelly blue gas completed the catastrophic picture of the interruption of plant and animal life and the suspension of productive human labor. This menacing precipitation of the world toward an impracticable chaos not only involved heaven and earth but also the subsoil. Again, starting with the uprooting of the oak and the remodeling of the door to his father's farm, the ground—which was once the stable support and fertile nourishment of the vegetation—began to sink as if it had become cavernous in length and width. And into this subterranean space, depicted as a realm of the dead, living people tumbled in search of firm ground underneath their feet but instead sank deeper and deeper into the void. The uprooting of the oak tree had also altered the order of the waters, and water gushed from the hole left by the uprooted oak, corroding the ground and rendering it less and less stable; this dug an ever-widening abyss. As for what was moving on solid ground, there were some living people, but they were already a minority whose numbers were dwindling: the majority, continuously increasing, were people who had or were about to fall into the hollow underground world. Finally, the disarticulation of the cosmic, terrestrial, and subterranean order was accompanied by a profound change in community relations: the living people on the earth or those fallen into the underground cavity, relatives or strangers, all distanced themselves from the patient. They became hostile and remote or were even designated as "foreign peoples." At the center of this catastrophe was the patient, who participated in it partly as a victim and partly as one who bore the responsibility for it.

> When asked what he means by "demise" [*Untergang*], he says "When people are no longer in the right place." But it is not only people who are no longer in the right place but also trees, houses and above all "things." A "change" has taken place. People [he alludes to the people lost in the underground cavern[1]] no longer have their things with them, and now they are looking for them. "They always speak only about me [as the cause of the disaster]. They want their things back and their homeland [*Heimat*]. It is not possible to restore the beautiful world to make it right. "The world, the beautiful world that was there before, is no longer here." (So how is it now?) "Changed." (What has changed?) "People are no longer in the same place, things, houses, paths. The globe is smaller, no mountains. They no longer know where the borders are passing. The world is flat. People are no longer home. I, too, am no longer in the right place." (What is the right place?) "Where one is at home." (When will the world get better?) "When [the people] have their things back, when they are home again in the right place. When everything is in order again." [. . .] (How will the people down there manage that?) "When I am home again."[2]

The patient had attempted to deal with the catastrophe by becoming the savior of the people who had fallen into the hollow subterranean world. He had tried to stop the disorderly flow of water from the hole left by the oak tree's uprooting; he had tried to bring onto solid ground the people who had fallen into the hollow and unstable underground space. But since the savior himself was not "on solid ground," his rescue operation achieved only limited and precarious results, and his intention of placing an end to the evil spell of this gaping, consuming tomb, in order to recompose life's **settled** scenario, had essentially failed.

1.2. [. . .] Alfred Storch[3] and Caspar Kulenkampff,[4] who report this case, outline the salient features of the patient's biography as follows[5]:

> This young farmer, who had always been quiet, reclusive and a bit savage, had never felt entirely at ease with the rest of the world. In his childhood he had suffered from a "bad" mother—who hit him and who later turned to drink—and from a conflict with his coarse father, to whom it nonetheless seemed he submitted with great docility; from his parents' disunity; from his meek character and awkward body; and he must have suffered greatly from the lack of sufficient ties with others, and later socially with the opposite sex. Despite all this, his love for nature and his connection with it made the world in which he grew up the center of his existence.
>
> This farming world of his was characterized by concrete natural events, like growth and ripening, vegetation, the land's fertility and infertility; by light, sunrise and sunset. The spatiality of this world was determined by the house and the landscape as a safe existential home [*Heimat*]. Even the temporality of his existence took its character from the immediately visible, from the sun's course that regulates day and night and determines the course of the world. His connection with the localization of shrubs and trees, especially the mighty oak tree that made up part of this homeland horizon, is part of the concrete transparency of an existence centered on home and hearth[6] [. . .]

1.3. The *Weltuntergangserlebnis*, the experience of the end of the world, is an alteration in the form and structure of the **Dasein** in its entirety. As Wetzel says, the experience of the end of the world is immersed in the "instantiation of an *Unheimlichkeitsstimmung*":[7] that is, a humoral disposition of an ominous nondomesticity in which a total, decisive threat moves in a hidden and inexpressible way.[8] The single delusional images can be understood starting with this fundamental experience (Storch and Kulenkampff 1950, 102). In the experience of the end of the world, being is manifested as "an at least partial, yet radical 'detachment' from the shared world and into a private world."[9]

Here we cannot better express the experience of the end of the world as an experience of losing the intersubjectivity of values that make a world possible as a human world. The inner sign of **worldhood**, what makes up its fundamental character of normality, is its **projectable** intersubjectivity based on a practicability that is socially and culturally conditioned. And it is no coincidence that the most pertinent term for designating the normality of the world comes from associational life, where the normal world is *domestic, familiar, mine,* in that it is communicable to "others" (even if it is only a group of socially and culturally conditioned others: to those others who are with us in the same house, who live in the same landscape, who live in the same village, the same homeland, who participate in the same group, who speak the same language or dialect, who share our memories, institutions, customs, perceptions, aversions).

The loss of the world's "normality" is a loss of its historicity, its exit from the path that leads from the "private" to the "public." This happens because what is "private," intimate, extremely personal has an embodied meaning when it is opened up to the public realm, when it is inserted as a moment in a dynamic of intersubjective valorization, when it sooner or later becomes a word and communicating gesture. The idolization of incommunicability takes on an almost morbid character unless it becomes a polemic against the rigidification of socialized and commonly accepted values and when it is a sign of a new effort of recovery of the human in view of a more profound communication. This idolization of incommunicability assumes the morbid dimension of a manifest egotism, of a collapse of the ethos of **presence**, and an abdicating love that retreats from its inexhaustible worldly task. And we are not amiss in looking suspiciously or with dismay or pity on all those who spend their days exalting the ineffable that they carry within, the treasure they hide in their chest, of which they are usually miserly for others, except when they break their silence and offer highly enigmatic products on written pages, colored canvases, and plied materials.

In the experience of the end of the world, the loss of the ordinary world reflects the loss of **presentification**, the reversal of the movement that leads from the private to the public, a collapse in the capacity to transcend the situation of value, the reduction of leeway for value attribution along the whole gamut of possible situations of valorization. This in turn implies the collapse of the everyday process of worlding that is constantly taking place, being preserved and reshaped thanks to humanity's primordial "communitarian" impulse.

If the loss and destruction of the patient's world—until now domestic, familiar, and safe—becomes understandable thanks to identifiable biographical facts, the identification of such biographical connections appears essential for the comprehension of everything. "It's just that it is not enough to make understandable the 'wholly other'[10] understandable that happens with the onset of the schizophrenic end-of-the-world

Stimmung. This opens up only with an existential understanding" (Storch and Kulenkampff 1950, 102).

It is no coincidence that the terms for designating the "normality" of the world have been drawn from the vocabulary of associational life, where the "normal" world is the domestic, familiar world of ancestors or homeland.

1.4.

Caspar Kulenkampff[11]

I am deeply interested in the interdisciplinary study of religious-historical phenomena and in particular in the collaboration of cultural historians with the psychiatrists and ethnopsychiatrists. In the context of a study of cultural apocalypses and their differentiation from psychopathological ones that my institute has been conducting for some years with the help of psychiatrists in clinical neuropsychiatry of the University of Rome (in particular with Prof. Bruno Callieri and Dr. Giovanni Jervis), my attention was attracted to the case of the twenty-three-year-old peasant whom you, together with the late Prof. Storch, wrote about in an article that appeared in *Der Nervenarzt* 21[12] (1950), pp. 102ff. This case is of significant interest for our study because the fundamental themes that appear in it (the end of the world connected to the uprooting of an oak tree, the water gushing from the hole left open, the falling of living people into the realm of the dead, and the loss of all cosmic life due to this uprooting) all superficially recall ideologies that are widely held in peasant culture (the tree of the world, the tree of life, the end of the world due to the uprooting of a cosmic oak tree, water, access to the realm of the dead, etc.: think of the ancient Roman *mundus*, of *Yggdrasill*,[13] etc.). This reference, which is superficial but certainly not coincidental, offers a propitious opportunity for analyzing the relationship between cultural and psychopathological apocalypses and to define their different structures. For the purposes of comparison, however, there are some gaps in the information in the case you have described, and perhaps you can help us to fill them. Here is the information that we would like:

—the patient's canton and town of origin;

—the family's economic history (are they, as it seems, smallholding farmers?);

—Is it possible to obtain a schematic drawing or map from which one can see with sufficient clarity the position of the farmhouse, the oak, the door exposed to the noon sun whose substitution had contributed, according to the patient, to causing the sun's repositioning?;

—in the peasant world of the region from which the patient comes, are there common folktales about the tree of the world, the tree of life, etc.?

I thank you sincerely, also on behalf of my colleagues, for any assistance you might give us.

Ernesto de Martino
Professor of the History of Religions
University of Cagliari

1.5. Case no. 1.

Our patient is a young farmer, age twenty-three, with asthenic traits; a gaunt face; curly, dark blonde hair; sunken, pensive eyes; a slightly stiff, curved bearing. He walks slowly, with a shuffle. The expression on his face is fixed. Only occasionally a hint of a smile around the edges of his mouth. He gazes fixedly, as if looking through one. The stiffness of his expression does not allow one to decide whether it is anxiety or unease. [. . .] He speaks little, slowly, hesitantly, often in a truncated manner. [. . .]

The patient's father is a small man already in his seventies who married late: he is closed and inaccessible. His mother is only forty-seven and has for some time been an alcoholic. [. . .] [Belligerent and quick to violence. The patient is on good terms with his father[14]] The patient also has an eighteen-year-old sister and twin siblings that are only five and a half. (Storch and Kulenkampff 1950, 102–3)

First a brief crisis at age nineteen, in 1945, and then ill again at the beginning of May 1947. The illness, which brought him to a private clinic, began when a military plane crashed in Switzerland. He thought that the airplane had been shot down, and he held himself responsible for the incident. He could no longer sleep; he went wandering about, suffering from a growing anxiety. He was especially anxious about an approaching end of the world, an end that above all struck nature's vegetation, the sun's radiance, and so forth. Released from the clinic after a treatment with insulin and electroshock (the end of August 1947) and a diagnosis of "second catatonic crisis in a weak young farmer," a year later (the end of December 1948) he was admitted to the canton hospital of Münsingen near Bern, after a period in which he had worked as a farmer's hired hand: now he exhibited acute catatonic symptoms.

The theme of airplanes: "no more airplanes have risen up to make air" (Storch and Kulenkampff 1950, 103); "since they were 'shot by the planes,' there are no more snowy peaks or mountains" (103); "The pilots have been saying for a while now that they can no longer fly because of me"; "The airplanes can no longer fly well, because the world doesn't run right" (104).

In all of the examinations of the patient, the central point was the alteration of the world, its riskiness and its threatening destruction. The world is "the creator of man, the growth of trees and plants, and air that the airplanes have made." He himself and his father are responsible for the alteration of the world. In spring he had uprooted some shrubs and feels guilty about it. In autumn, however—and this is what is now in the foreground—his father chopped down a large oak in order to sell it: he should not have done it. (Why?) "I found out about it, I noticed it." Water began to spout from the hole left in the ground, running over one side and spreading onto the soil. As another cause of the demise of the world, he describes his father's remodeling of the farmhouse door. The door, located on the sunny side of the house, previously acute-angled and made of black wood, was now redone square and with yellow wood. This, too, should not have been done. Because of this remodeling the sun could no longer pass through the door, and for a while it had to remain in a different place than before. [. . .] "The sun is no longer right [*richtig*], it is always in the same place. The world's course is no longer right." "The course of the day is no longer right, slower. The globe is no longer right." "No more lakes. The water has all converged." The rhythm of day and night has changed. The evening sun does not set properly. Since they were "shot" by the pilots, the snowy peaks and mountains of Switzerland are no longer there. The earth is flat.

"The globe has become smaller." No more airplanes have risen up to produce air. The composition of the air itself has changed. It has become thinner. He calls it "gassy blue air." It has an unpleasant odor. "Everything in the air is blue: before, it was not like this." "One cannot live in such air for long. The growth of plants has stopped, as has people's productivity. Even all the buildings have changed." "The world has become wider, but there are hardly any houses left."

The growth of trees and plants can no longer take place because the ground is hollow. The soil has become cavernous far and wide. And so it happened that people in search of solid ground dug themselves in and continue to dig underground in the realm of the dead, where they only find dead people and pieces of clothing. (How did the people end up down there?) "Because of the demise [*Untergang*]." In this underground space, water poured in from the hole of the oak tree that his father had cut down and sold. You can drown there and must sometimes swim. Since animals have also gone down, living people must suffer from hunger here. The patient distinguishes generically between living people who are underground and represent the majority from a small group of the resurrected. People other than himself he calls "the others," those who are foreign "the people" or even "the foreign peoples." He himself belongs to the living people.

From the hollow space underground he received news that the world will collapse in the future. This news came from an unspecified "evil power." He is in contact with the people lost underground. Through a transmitter they hear everything he says, and he listens when they speak. They are ill disposed to him because they want to return home to take their things, and they cannot. The people no longer want to reappear, they don't want to see me anymore." When asked what he means by "demise" [*Untergang*] he says, "When people are no longer in the right place." But it is not only people who are no longer in the right place but also trees, houses and above all "things." A "change" has taken place. People no longer have their things with them and now they are looking for them. "They always speak only about me. They want their things back and their homeland. It is not possible to restore the beautiful world to make it right." "The world, the beautiful world that was there before, is no longer here." (So how is it now?) "Changed." (What has changed?) "People are no longer in the same place, things, houses, paths. The globe is smaller, no mountains. They no longer know where the borders are passing. The world is flat. People are no longer home. I, too, am no longer in the right place." (What is the right place?) "Where one is at home." (When will the world get better?) "When [the people] have their things back, when they are home again in the right place. When everything is in order again. Up high, in the air, to slide home." (How will the people down there manage that?) "When I am home again." While he himself and everything else is thus no longer in the right place, his paternal home has moved afar. "You can't see our home anymore. It's far from here. I don't know where it is." As a result he has lost contact with his relatives and neighbors. "They don't want to see me anymore. The people have persecuted me, they no longer want me. Father didn't believe it, because of the demise of the world. For this reason I am persecuted." "They sent me away. Lately they've been bad to me. I don't want to see them anymore, either." (103)

On his part the patient has managed to block a definitive demise in the same way that he was previously co-responsible for the threat of this demise. Once he did it by stopping the water's power by turning a switch: following this, the water ceased to flow. Another time he sought to save the people down in the underground space, bringing them to solid ground. He could do this since he was on relatively stable ground. He saved many, but since he, too, was in a wrong place, he could not save any more. His salvational action took place through a magnetic power that the patient has in the area of his larynx. He thus "up-lifted" (*herauf-gelupft*) people from the ground, especially Swiss soldiers. Related to the magnetic area of his neck, he suffered from problems swallowing, and at times he struggled to swallow potatoes or beans. For some time he has had this magnetic power in his larynx, and this power developed when he swallowed a large apple with its whole stem, and this apple got stuck in his neck, damaging his larynx. Since then he has not been able to swallow properly. The area became magnetic, and it also became a place through which he related with the people. "For a while the pilots already said that they could no longer fly because of me. They are pulled down by the magnet. It's an illness that causes attraction." "The planes can no longer fly well, since the world no longer runs right." (Do the people want the buildings to return to their right place?) "The houses are so close. They should be farther away. Because of the water down there, the earth slid away, there's been an attraction. They got close to that side." The patient has not tried to do anything about the alteration in the air. The airplanes have not gotten in the air again. Everything is now suspended. The demise of the world has certainly been blocked, but that does not mean that the world has been repaired. He feels alone and abandoned. "They want to be on steady ground, these true people, whose place is solid ground. The ones who do not deserve it are down there, and earlier they lost consciousness. Because the oak and the shrubs are no longer standing." (But some are on solid ground?) "The living, because of the salvation. I saved them. But since I have no longer been in my father's house (in his birthplace, his homeland), things are not like they were before, and my father did not follow my advice, he uprooted the oak. Due to the oak being cut down, people and things fell down there. Since there were no longer shrubs (*Stauden*), the ground was no longer solid. The people tumbled down and the water gushed. It is no longer the right place, where it was before. The right people, the living, were also down there before." (And were you also there?) "I was always up here, never below, but not on steady ground." (Why?) "An earthquake. The rabble down there certainly struck a blow. I felt it." (104)

1.6. The commentary by Storch and Kulenkampff (1950, 104ff.) opens with the description of the patient's Dasein: the young farmer, a bit savage, reclusive, quiet, "had never felt quite at home in the world (*ganz heimisch*)"[15] (104). His aggressive and alcoholic mother, his coarse and authoritarian father, his parents' disunity, his poor school marks and sense of inferiority toward his classmates, his scant relations with the latter and subsequently with the opposite sex: all this gives depth to the course of his life from infancy to adolescence. The natural world in which he grew up became the center of his existence, his fundamental tie. This farmer's world of his was shaped "by concrete conditions and natural events; growth and vegetation, fertility and infertility of the soil; the light, the rising and setting of the sun."

His world's spatiality is determined by the domestic, native home and landscape. The temporality of his existence likewise takes on the character of being immediately visible: from the course of the sun that regulates day and night and determines the course of the world. This existence centered on home and homeland is reflected in an intuitive way in the trees and shrubs, especially in the mighty oak that belongs to his domestic horizon. Through the removal of this oak, the image of his world underwent a decisive transformation, full of misfortune . . . When the patient says, "The world I was in until a short time ago is no longer there, the beautiful world," it becomes apparent that the existence of our patient, the modality of his being-in-the-world, has suffered from a radical destruction in the course of his psychosis . . . The patient's expressions, like the earth being flatter, the mountains have collapsed, the seas are no longer there, hint at the loss of the variety of perceivable forms and a general leveling. The terrestrial globe, altered in its very form, contains a landscape in which there is no longer a difference between hills and valleys, between earth and water. Since farther on, as the patient says, growth has ceased, we may speak of a process of devastation and solitude to which the entire terrestrial-spatial horizon of his world has been sacrificed. In such a world lacking in vegetation, similar to a desert, devoid of differences, it becomes difficult to find signs of orientation, reference points for an orderly division. This is what the patient means when he says that he no longer knows where boundaries lie. A leveling fall into ruin and a loss of boundaries thus go hand in hand. An existence abandoned to the lack of delimitation of this spatiality without internal limits of articulation no longer finds its here and there, a certain location and place in which things situate themselves and to which they belong. In his expressions, therefore, the patient continuously refers to the fact that people, houses, things, streets, are not "in the right place." These become for him an unfamiliar "elsewhere," alien, foreign, strange, even in their composition and structure. The world's devastation and solitude and an absence of limits thus go together with a "loss of domesticity," an "alienation" of the world 404). In a world like this, we should not be surprised if he does not feel *heimisch* and if he defines the previous world as "beautiful" (in the sense of well ordered) in opposition to the present one (405).

The existential analysis of the patient's spatiality now extends to another aspect of his experience: even the "ground" has been destroyed. It is not firm under his feet, it gives way from under his feet, it is empty, collapses or sinks, and so forth. People and things sink down as a consequence of the world's collapse; they have gone into the subterranean world. This general downward tendency clearly reflects that "everything has lost solid ground." He himself perceives the abyssal nature of his world as an "earthquake" caused by the living underground train wreck. This abysmal sinking of the ground effectively represents a new form of existence: the emptiness beneath the ground, on which standing is insecure and roots can neither take hold nor find nourishment, and therefore nothing can grow. This is the complete reversal of the living's direction, of "upward" to "downward" (from which we see the "subterranean hollow" feature of the ground, its being not only a gaping abyss but like an irresistible undertow that threatens to drag everything into the realm of the dead); all this is organic form and existential unity. People with their things, and the animals, are swallowed up by this engulfing abyss, and likewise all the forces of plant life, all of the vital lymph emerging upward and now broken off from below. In such a project of the world,[16] becoming gets lost along the gamut of the possible: every form of production ceases, the sun stops and the strength of its light diminishes, and so forth. The loss of becoming gives rise to the rigidification of the cosmos (which finds its expressive equivalent in the patient's physiognomic rigidity); and furthermore, the loss of becoming gives rise to chaotic disorder.

Chaotic disorder—the designation that can encompass all of these individual states of deprivation—and the loss of becoming that spreads along the whole front of actual or possible existence appear here not only in close relationship to belonging but also as structural moments of that fundamental *Weltentwurf* of the gaping abyss, in which in our case the Dasein has been submerged (105).

It is not only in the telluric environment—that is, what involves the earth—that we find an alteration in the structure of being-there: the ethereal sphere has also undergone a profound change. The air has changed, it has become thinner, rarefied. The patient describes this altered air as gassy blue air, unpleasant and in which one cannot live for long. The destruction of the ethereal world is not a random, delusional image: it is a version that corresponds to the telluric world, which confirms that the Dasein has been struck in its entirety. The air, as an element of the ethereal with which we have a relationship through breathing, because its nature belongs to the pneumatic living world, to the spiritual. The air of the end of the world is precisely an air from which the living pneumatic essence has been removed: it has been reduced to a dead gas (the air of life degrades into a gas air) (105).

Now we understand what the uprooting of the tree means for the patient. The uprooting of the oak tree marks the beginning of the end of the world for him. All of the world's becoming was as if it had been jolted by the uprooting of this oak, and its stricken roots get identified with the very roots of life. The tree as a symbol of rooting on Earth and of the ascent toward ethereal and pneumatic areas, as a symbol of life that renews itself, etc. (cf. Nikolaus Lenau[17] and Klages 1932[18]). Mythologically, the cosmic tree, the tree of life, the tree at the center of the world.

The space of life becomes the catatonic realm of the dead; the living pneuma in the air of live reduces itself to gas (105).

Entering the schizophrenic landscape, the patient must have experienced the cutting down and uprooting of the oak as "his Dasein becoming baseless and rootless" (106). At the center of this cosmic collapse stands the patient. Meanwhile, as the others, the people, "foreign peoples," sink down into the abyss with their things and animals, the patient remains the midpoint of events, in solitude, in a desolate, insecure, immobile and chaotic world. What is clinically called the autistic feature of schizophrenia is here lived as being isolated, and it is to be interpreted as a modality "of being in the world." The Dasein, destroying itself, gets stripped of its "ontological character of *Mitsein*" (106).

The house, the domestic world, is far. I don't know where it is.

The patient loses his homeland: *Heimatlosigkeit*.

The alienation of the world is the loss of homeland.

In a Dasein without a homeland, the patient and the world's things "are no longer in the right place." People "reject" him not only in distancing themselves but by taking on an appearance of avoidance that is hostile for the patient. Isolation, loss of boundaries, alienation—in other words, chaotic disorder—loss of becoming, loss of foundation, of homeland, and so forth (105). A downward tendency, to the realm of the dead, in the engulfing abyss.

1.7. How did our patient come to be dominated by nothingness, death, and illness? Two moments belong to man simultaneously: we are beings tied to the earth, to terrestrial gravity, and at the same time we belong to air and light. As an ascending existence we participate in liberty, we breathe within the possibilities of the future. If, however, man can no longer live this emerging existence for the future, "la vie ascentionelle et surgissante"[19]—precisely as in the case of our patient—then his Dasein loses its solid basis. The maternal terrestrial element appears in its fearsome guise of death as a gaping abyss. Man falls prey to the Spirit of Gravity and of the Shadows, he plummets, and he abandons himself to the abyss of nothingness. "Tout ce qui s'abaisse participe au néant."[20] Resting exposed to the call of the abyss turns into a loss of **potentiality of being** (*poter essere*) and a falling into an isolation untied from all relations with the world. In order to save oneself from this abyss, a superhuman strength is necessary. Only an absolute power beyond time and history can overcome this destruction of historical and finite existence. Man cannot do it unless he claims to be a being equal to God, "eritis sicut Deus."[21] The patient attributes himself with precisely this divine omnipotence, becoming savior of the world. This is exactly the meaning of the sense of omnipotence of schizophrenic delusions: that it provides the appearance of stability in the absolute to a lack of consistency and presence of the destroyed Dasein (107ff).

In this regard, Storch and Kulenkampff recall the opposition of light and gravity in Schelling,[22] the "steigendes und sinkendes Dasein" (rising and falling Dasein) of L. Binswanger[23], and G. Bachelard, *L'air et les songes*: participation in the rising movement of our aerial freedom with our perfection and purification.[24] On the lethal aspect of the maternal terrestrial element: E. Neumann, *Ursprungsgeschichte des Bewusstseins;*[25] "The Spirit of Gravity," in Nietzsche, *Also sprach Zarathustra* (*Thus Spake Zarathustra*); "[E]verything that falls . . . becomes a part of the void": G. Bachelard, *L'air et les songes;*[26] No-longer-being-able-to-be-there in M. Heidegger, *Sein und Zeit* (*Being and Time*).[27]

(1) An end of the world for which the patient feels responsible.

(2) In the delusion, the end has a central symbolic motivation in the uprooting of an oak tree on the part of the father, who cut it down and sold it. The alteration of the door.

(3) Water gushing from the hole or opening left by the uprooted oak spreading across the ground.

(4) The ground became unstable, and people were excavating underground, in the realm of the dead, in search of solid ground. In this subterranean space, the water burst forth through the hole of the uprooted oak.

(5) He is in communication with the underground people. He tries to save them, but since he himself is not on solid ground, he only partly succeeds.

(6) The sinking of the living into the underworld and the unstable ground occur together with the alteration of all things, which are no longer in the right place; with the loss of growth of all living things, plants, etc.; with the transformation of the air in a blue gas; the shrinking of the world, its becoming flat, without boundaries, etc.

1.8.

Unfathomable *nothingness* does not necessarily present only negative features. In the vast, boundless abyss of "nothingness" there is also the "soul" that lives in the absolute fullness of its essence in that it is embraced and preserved in the fullness and deepness of the divine, in the boundless unfathomableness of the divine. For the soul that has lost its homeland in the divine, this bottomless divine abyss alone is transformed into an annihilating and engulfing abyss, just as Goethe's Werther faced "instead of prospects of eternal life, the abyss of an ever-opened grave." What the patient experienced as the specific loss of being—confused as he is in his schizophrenic disassociation—has its historico-cultural parallel in our world in the historically demonstrable transformation of the abyss of the divine primordial depth in its incommensurable richness—the abyss of Augustine and the mystics—into the engulfing chaotic and vacuous abyss, the *giuffre* of Pascal and Baudelaire. This historico-cultural transformation (Walther Rehm, "Tiefe und Abgrund in Hölderlins Dichtung," 1943) reveals a specific threat to the humanity of our time, detached as it is from the connection with the divine and with other people, who thus fall into isolation. (108n1)

Once again we see the connection that existentialist psychiatry perceives between crisis and the sphere of the sacred. But if every interpretative perspective aimed at reducing the sacred to the phenomenology of mere existential crisis is radically mistaken, the perspective of existentialist psychiatry is likewise radically mistaken in that it values the thesis of the sacred, the divine, the mythical-ritual as a cultural horizon necessary to deal with the crisis. This necessity is historically conditioned, but today, "in the modern world," those conditions are increasingly lacking (the agony of the sacred) without this necessarily being connected to a "threat" that looms over humanity. What is important is the "intersubjectivity of values" maintaining an opening to this intersubjectivity, the always self-renewing will to communicate our private world to others and to embrace time and again, deep down, the communicating voices of other people, the messages they are sending us. But the metahistorical horizon of the sacred is not, as metahistorical, an indispensable horizon in all times and places, in all periods, to carry out this making public of the self and this interiorization of others. In order to "do good" (that is, wanting the private that opens to the public instead of the private that closes itself) it is not necessary to do it through Christ or God: one can simply do it for the people of his own epoch without having to turn to a detour to reach them through Christ or God. Today the path leading from person to person is becoming short, while the one that passes through the divine increasingly appears long and inaccessible. In the past our ancestors traveled it profitably, and only in this way, through this detour, did they know how to connect with each other. But now what in the past was "way, truth, and life" really appears as an obstacle, as an interruption of relations, as escape and death. And we need to gain awareness of this true necessity in order to build a new regime of encounter and communication within it.

One says, "But the criterion of good is given by Christ and God: if you lose it, you will also lose the good to be done to mankind." And Buddha? And the gods of Olympus? And the supreme being of the primitives? Is it not possible to do them good? Have not other civilizations realized the human encounter through other horizons of the sacred? "Perhaps, but our horizon embraces higher values." And so let us consider these values, first of all: if symbolic life is indispensable for us to protect us from existential risk, then our symbols should be in full agreement with these values, containing their development and expansion. They should be symbols in which, by virtue of such an agreement, we can believe and not symbols that oblige us to divide our souls between opposing masters:

> What is the source of this interpellation that we experience in the encounter with the metaphysics of schizophrenic images of the end of the world? What speaks to us is not only the metaphysical content of apocalyptic and eschatological images, of threats and promises of the end-time and the millenarian Kingdom. Precisely, in our case, we do not come to consider otherworldly contents, but we remain in a dull surrender to the mere event of the collapse of the world event as such. If in the process we are deeply touched by a human element, relative to the destiny of humanity, it is because the essential ontological structure of our existence is revealed in numinous images[28] in which the fall and salvation of humanity are represented. In the encounter with such patients we are struck by a sense of surprise and astonishment, since we are lost in the familiarity of our doings and in all spheres of things that regard us and that we busy ourselves with daily—we have forgotten being and nothingness. The reason for this is that the very occurrence of the patients' unfree **duty-to-be** [*Seinmüssen*], looking out onto nothingness, reminds us of our "forgetfulness of being," so to speak, and it makes present its "belonging" to nothingness . . . etc.[29]

2. *Mundus patet*

2.1.
Plutarch, *Romulus* 11.2:

> A circular trench was dug around what is now the Comitium, and in this were deposited first-fruits of all things the use of which was sanctioned by custom as good and by nature as necessary; and finally, every man

brought a small portion of the soil of his native land, and these were cast in among the first-fruits and mingled with them. They call this trench, as they do the heavens, by the name of "mundus." Then, taking this as a centre, they marked out the city in a circle round it.[30]

Ovid, *Fasti*, bk. 4, 819–26:

A suitable day was chosen on which he should mark out the line of the walls with the plough. The festival of Pales was at hand; on that day the work began. A trench was dug down to the solid rock; fruits of the earth were thrown into the bottom of it, and with them earth fetched from the neighbouring soil. The trench was filled up with mould, and on the top was set an altar, and a fire was duly lit on a new hearth. Then pressing on the plough-handle he[31] drew a furrow to mark out the line of the walls: the yoke was borne by a white cow and snow-white steer.[32]

Festus, *De verborum significatu* 144L:

The *mundus*, as Capito Ateius relates in the sixth book of *Pontifical Law*, would open three times a year, on these set days: the day after the Vulcanalia, the third day before the nones of October, and the six that before the ides of November. In his *Commentaries* on civil law, Cato reports as follows: "The name mundus derives from that world (*mundus*) that is above us: its form, indeed, as I was able to learn from those who have had access, is similar to the latter's form. The ancestors believed that its lower part must be closed all the time, as if it had been consecrated to the Manes gods, except on the aforementioned days. Furthermore, they believed these days to be permeated with a religious scrupulousness due to the fact that, in that period, things that were occult and secret in the religion of the Manes gods were brought, so to speak, to the light and openly manifested, and therefore they did not want anything that regarded the affairs of state to be dealt with in that period. Thus on those days enemies were not fought, one did not enlist in the army, assemblies were not convened, one did not deal with anything regarding the operations of the state that were not impelled by extreme necessity.[33]

Macrobius, *The Saturnalia*, 1.16–18

Now when the Latiar, that is, the celebration of the Latin Festival, is proclaimed, and during the days of the Saturnalia, and also when the entrance to the underworld is open [. . .], religion forbids the joining of battle [. . .], and when the entrance to the underworld is open, this being a sacred occasion dedicated to Father Dis and Proserpine, and men deemed it better to go out to battle when the jaws of Pluto are shut. And that is why Varro writes: "When the entrance to the underworld is open, it is as if the door of the grim, infernal deities were open."[34]

2.2. Excerpt from the report by Gustav Glaesser[35]

With this we have arrived at the brief section entitled "Il *Mundus Cereris*," entirely based on the premises presented by the author and which we summarize briefly.[36] It is undoubtedly the book's greatest merit that it highlights, with vast documentation, the chthonic-infernal aspect of Cereris, the Italic deity, that has been neglected by almost every other prior scholar. *The* presantanea *sow and the* praecidanea *sow*[37] *are offered to Ceres, a sacrifice reserved for the underworld; Ceres is in some way a deity of the dead, who (together with Terra) watches over the exact execution of the funeral rites. It is Ceres, goddess of the* mundus, *who is connected to this mouth of hell that puts the world of the living in contact with the Manes.*[38] *When the spirits of the dead are irritated, they come out of this grave under the appearance of* larvae. *The author sees no reason to attribute to Greek Demeter's influence these dark powers attributed to Ceres: according to his opinion, it is "an ancient popular superstition, inseparable from the belief in ghosts."*

According to our author, the attribution of this mouth of hell to Ceres (*Cereris qui mundus appellatur*, etc. Festus, 126L) is very ancient, while according to others it is late and false [. . .]. It appears to be confirmed by the famous inscription of Capua where we read *the name (damaged) of a priestess of Ceres, qualified by* Mundalis. This is an inscription that even Mommsen, in his *Corpus*,[39] described *litteris magnis et antiquioribus*,[40] therefore relatively ancient. In another passage, Festus (144L) puts together various reports provided by different ancient sources regarding the *mundus* itself, moreover designating the same three days (August 24, October 5, November 8) as those in which the *mundus* opens [*patet*]. In this second passage, however (based in part on a treatise by Ateius Capito, a jurist at the time of Augustus), Ceres is not mentioned; the author does not believe that this omission authorizes us to cast doubt on the attribution of the mundus to Ceres, which is *expressly underlined in the first passage*. Other well-known citations follow, taken from all of the authors who have dealt with the *mundus* (cf. our summaries). This is not the place to go into the technical and philological details for the umpteenth time at the expense of broad religious-historical outlines. In any case, and despite the scantiness and the often contradictory character of the ancient sources, the author believes that he can draw some conclusions from them: for example, as to the shape of the *mundus*. It was equipped with a vault; the lower part in which, it appears, one could not enter, must have consisted of an excavated pit in the ground covered with a lid that was raised only three times a year. *The rites connected to the* mundus *aimed at establishing direct contact between the Manes and the living*; although Festus does not say it explicitly, it is understood that the souls of the dead could come out of the underworld using *the mundus to spread through the upperworld*. This is what the ancient etymology of the word manes suggests, which the ancients derived from *manare* (Festus, 115L: *Manalem lapidem putabant esse ostium Orci, per quod animae inferorum ad superos manarent, qui dicuntur manes*).[41] Even so, the only ritual connected to mundus that we know of is that of the opening of the pit: it is evidently on that occasion that it was possible to penetrate the *upper* part of the *mundus*. It is likely that in this circumstance a sacrifice was offered, as Weinstock also believes[42] [. . .]. If the mundus can be interpreted as a place of worship of the ancient Roman Ceres (and this is precisely the author's thesis), the vague description by Cato—*qui intravere*—cannot but mean that such access was reserved to the *flamen Cerealis*[43] and his assistants [. . .]. Nonetheless, we are lacking pertinent clarification in the sources, from which, however, the decisively chthonic nature of the worship emerges in all of its attractive clarity (cf. Macrobius, 1.16–18, a passage abundantly cited by all authors). The expression *tristes atque inferi* used by Varro applies well to the *di manes* of Festus, but in its most generic meaning it can also bring together the other underworld divinities. The list of forbidden activities in those days agrees in two points with that provided by Festus: prohibition to begin a battle and to recruit troops. *Varro adds that one does not even have the right to make the troops march, but he omits the prohibition on holding assemblies*. And while Festus's list is limited to official activities, Varro's even prohibits raising anchors or getting married. But the expression *religiuosum est* leaves no doubt that the three days are essentially *religious* for both Varro and Festus. The two texts thus agree on the essential things, but in any case the differences are such that we can exclude that Varro's text was Festus's direct source: it may be that the latter had available a lost text from an ancient source.

Before advancing the aforementioned citation from Varro, Macrobius gave an interesting hint, moreover without indicating his source: religious law forbids combat during the Latin festivities, during Saturnalia, and therefore also *mundus patet—quod sacrum Diti patri et Proserpinae dicatum est, meliusque occlusa Plutonis fauce eundum ad proelium putaverunt*.[44] There is thus an important disagreement between the first text by Festus, which makes Ceres the goddess of *mundus*, and that of Macrobio who says it is consecrated to Dīs Pater/Pluto and Proserpine.

At this point, the author poses the question: which *mundus* are we talking about? In this regard, he cites the study by Weinstock [. . .] that distinguishes two groups in the ancient accounts regarding *mundus*: a) a tradition represented by Ovid (*Fasti*, 4.821ff.) and Plutarch (*Romulus*, 11) that situates the notion by relation to the rites of Rome's founding by Romulus; b) the rest of the texts that deal with another *mundus* that has nothing in common with the first. Neither mundus can be identified with the Roma *Quadrata* nor with the so-called Palatine *mundus* [. . .]. The differences are fundamental: the mundus connected to Rome's foundation is filled and cannot be reopened; *Romulus's* mundus *is situated on the* Comitium—*the location of Ceres' mundus is unknown, but it may be supposed that it was in the immediate vicinity of the goddess's temple, that is, near the Circus Maximus* [. . .]. The famous Bernese scholiast (cf. our various summaries) offers an interesting indication in reference to this: *Alii mundum in sacro Cereris et caelum pro mundo positum dicunt,*[45] along with the clarification that the *mundus* had a very narrow opening, a bit more than 1.3 meters. On the other hand, the expression *in sacro Cereris* confirms Festus's testimony that attributes the *mundus* to Ceres. Weinstock (loc. cit.) suggests that the *sacrum* was "a small room built as an addition to the evidently original pit": the mundus in his view belongs to a well-known type of altar equipped with "Grubenkammern," pit chambers, a hypothesis considered by the author to be the product of an "archaeological imagination." The author agrees with Deubner ("Mundus," in *Hermes*, 283n68, an article we have summarized[46]) in rejecting Weinstock's interpretation of the scholium under discussion, although he admits that we may conclude from it that the *mundus* was found in Ceres's "sacred perimeter." On the whole, however, even Le Bonniec has been forced to recognize that "the data regarding the *mundus* are too fragmentary and uncertain for us to be able to arrive at an unquestionable solution."[47] Indeed, none of the solutions proposed by the previous authors can be considered entirely satisfactory. These are interpretations that we have already summarized above, and thus there is no need for repetition. Moreover, one author is against the other, and we do not have supporting evidence to weigh in favor of either one or the other. As for Fowler's thesis,[48] which is considered "appealing" by Piganiol (*Recherches sur les jeux romains*, 1923[49]) and by Turchi (*La religione di Roma antica*[50]) but rejected by Weinstock, not even this seems acceptable to our author: in fact, no text alludes to the supposed agricultural function of the *mundus*, and the ancient sources describe it as an extremely narrow pit and by no means a *Kornkammer*. Moreover, the days it is open are religious, a fact that excludes all agricultural activity, and so forth. In any case, the author credits Fowler with at least having attempted to explain the choice of those three dates, but the weak point of his argument is the opposition he proclaims between the date of sowing of spelt and that of the *triticum* [wheat]. [...]. Above all, Fowler's theory would assume that the third day of the opening of the *mundus*, November 8, was not original but tacked on as an addition. In fact, this date could only have been adopted at least three centuries after the first two, since—if we are to believe Verrius and Pliny—during this long period ancient Latium only ate spelt (recall that the sowing of *triticum* had to take place, for example according to Virgil and Columella, at the beginning of November). Moreover, like Rose (loc. cit.)[51] the author does not exclude the idea that the *mundus*, even if it was not necessarily a true container for wheat seed—as Fowler would have it—could have been used for certain agricultural rituals, it could for example hold small quantities of wheat, not so much as early produce as instead to be blessed by the powers of the underworld, thereby bringing luck—according to the principle of *pars pro toto*, universally valid in the realm of agricultural magic—to the community's entire stock of cereal (Rose). The author also agrees with Rose on the other reasons that lead us to attribute an agricultural meaning to this ritual: the first day of opening falls on the eve of the Opiconsivia festival of August 25, the second the day after the *ieiunium Cereris* of October 4. For the date of August 24, the explanation Fowler advances seems acceptable to the author, though with the modification proposed by Rose. As for the *ieiunium Cereris*, it is a late institution belonging to Hellenized worship, as the author shows in other parts of his work: the Greek rite was grafted onto the ancient ritual of the opening of the *mundus*. Between the two festivities there was a close connection: the fast day of October 4 has the meaning of a normal purification on the eve of a religious holiday, that of October 5. It is natural that days reserved for such an important ritual were considered religious, in which any agricultural work whatsoever was ruled out.

[...]

Again regarding the agricultural interpretation of the *mundus*, the author cites, critically, the theories and etymologies formulated by M. H. Wagenvoort ("Initia Cereris," in *Medelingen van de koniklijke Vlaamse Aacademie van België, Kl. De. Letteren*, X, 4, 1948, also translated in English in his collection *Studies in Roman Literature: Culture and Religion*, Leiden, 1956), an author who—developing an etymology proposed by Kretschmer that *mundus* means "mouth"—believes that *mundus* Cereris must have had, at least originally, another meaning: that it refers to soil favoring the growth of plants, given that for this etymologist, *cereris* (lowercase!) is none other than the genitive of a hypothetical neutral *cerus*, *cereris* would mean growth—in other words, the "soil-mana," of *numen*, the object of magical rites (Wagenvoort is one of the most eminent representatives of the interpretation of Roman religious matters in a "Melanesian" key, as his critics rebuke him (G. Dumézil, etc.), starting from the notion of *numen-mana*). The Bernese scholium thus preserves the memory of a magical rite that had the aim of controlling and stimulating the soil's fertility. Even the part that children played in ancient magic and religious ceremonies is well known, and thus the descent of a boy into the *mundus* is nothing extraordinary. Nor is it surprising that such magic would be practiced precisely on the eve of sowing. But the belief in the specters that emerge from the mundus, though ancient, would be secondary, because *mundus cereris* (again lowercase!) would have had the meaning of "the opening of growing power," "the pit of the soil-mana," and so forth (from the English translation of the aforementioned work by Wagenvoort).

Our author does not seem convinced regarding the exactness of the etymology under discussion or the conclusions that the professor from the University of Leiden draws from it. Kretschmer's Indo-European etymology appears especially problematic, given that the most authoritative linguists consider the word *mundus* to be of non-Indo-European origin [. . .]. Besides the authoritative etymological dictionary by Walde and Hofmann, the one by Ernout and Meillet[52]—no less important—declares: "It is quite possible that the infernal *mundus* has nothing in common with the celestial *mundus* and is of Etruscan origin" (cf. also A. Ernout, *Philologica*[53]). Moreover, the presumed existence of a neutral *cerus, cereris*, is purely hypothetical, while the "soil-mana" is perhaps nothing more than a modern, "primitivist" invention. After all, as the author justly notes, we do not understand how, at least for the date of August 24, an agricultural ritual can "stimulate or control growth," seeing as in that moment of the year the harvest is already over, while sowing only begins a month later. In conclusion, among the various "agricultural" interpretations, the most acceptable one seems to be that of Fowler, although with the modifications proposed by H. J. Rose. For the dates of October 5 and November 8, this is certainly in agreement with the aforementioned scholiast, and so forth. In any case—the author reminds us—we should not lose sight of the fact that the most reliable and ancient sources describe the *mundus* as an infernal pit consecrated to the worship of the Manes. It is thus above all Ceres's chthonic nature that gets manifested in these rituals. The goddess receives the sacrifice of a *praecidanea* sow offered by an heir that has not carried out burial rites: alongside Tellus, she thus protected the *ius manium*,[54] so much so that every transgression of this was an insult to Ceres. It is no wonder then if the *mundus* consecrated to the Manes was designated as the *mundus* of Ceres as a matter of course. The ascertained ancientness of the *praesentanea* sow and the *praecidanea* sow, sacrifices that put the goddess into direct contact with the dead, leads us to consider the patronage exercised by Ceres over the *mundus* to be equally ancient.

[. . .] It was on this chthonic ritual, the original feature of the *mundus*, that the Hellenized cult of the underworld divinities was grafted, Dīs Pater/Pluto and Proserpina-Persephone—divinities of the *mundus*, as Macrobius calls them. But this can only be a late attribution, as even Wissowa admits (1912, 194).[55] In this new cycle, Ceres seems dispossessed in turn by this infernal couple, an effect of that accelerated Hellenization of Roman worship that took place after the *ludi Tarentini* of 249 BCE, which marked the official adoption of Pluto and Proserpina into the Roman pantheon. Considering Proserpina to be a divinity of the *mundus*, a connection was imagined between the myth of her abduction and that subterranean pit, a connection familiar to the scholiasts of Virgil. But these are coincidences without any religious-historical value.

As we see from the whole formulation of his work, the author reconnects the rituals of *mundus* to the more ancient cult, accessible to us, of the "indigenous" Cerere, in opposition to Wissowa, Altheim,[56] etc. The author certainly admits that this ritual has a dual nature already in its original form, simultaneously agricultural and chthonic, so that Fowler's interpretation retains its relative substance, although it illuminates only one of the two aspects of the *mundus*. Such an agricultural interpretation is not at all incompatible with one that also considers the chthonic side intimately connected to the *mundus*, the worship of the Manes, etc. It is a well-known fact throughout religious phenomenology, even that which is far from the Roman world, that the divinities of the soil and the earth can at the same time be infernal and agricultural (Consus, for example, seems to have been simultaneously an infernal divinity and god of stored harvests). The cult of Ceres, connected to *mundus*, probably presented the same dual nature and ambivalence.

3. Eternal Return and Mythical-Ritual Symbolism

3.1. The end of the existing terrestrial order can be considered in two distinct senses: *as a historically determined cultural theme*, and *as a permanent anthropological risk*. As a historically determined cultural theme, it appears in the context of certain mythic configurations that make explicit reference to it: for example, the theme of the periodic destructions and regenerations of the world in the myth of the eternal return, or the theme of a terminal catastrophe of history in its unilinear and irreversible course. As a permanent anthropological risk, ending is simply the risk of not being able to be in any possible cultural world; the loss of the possibility of making oneself practicably present in the world; the shrinking—to the point of total annihilation—of any horizon whatsoever of worldly practicability; the catastrophe of any communitarian projecting according to values. Human culture in general is the solemn exorcism against this radical risk no matter which exorcistic technique—so to speak—has been adopted. And if the cultural theme of the end of a certain existing world order makes up one of the historical means of recovery and redemption with respect to this risk, even where the theme is absent or unimportant, the corresponding risk is always present, and culture establishes itself precisely in dealing with and controlling it, no matter how the dramatic event is reflected in a historically determined cultural consciousness.

3.2. Irreversibility, crisis, mythical-ritual repetition of the origins.

We should interpret the cyclical consciousness of time—which expresses itself religiously in the ritual repetition of a myth of origin and foundation and cosmologically in the theory of the eternal return—in its most fruitful cultural-historical moment, as a protective system for mediating the historicity of human becoming, defending it from the risk—which is always present as a temptation—of annihilating it in the great indolence of the repetition of the identical and the pure cyclicity of returning-to. The mythical-ritual symbol of the repetition of a myth of origins marks a sort of *imitatio naturae*: the return-to is taken up, culturally reshaped, and resolved in a horizon that discloses being-in-the-world. Human becoming that rises above the indolence of subhuman becoming continues to be tormented by this very indolence: the irreversibility of human time risks becoming reversible. Reversibility regained and overturned: that is the mythical-ritual symbol of repetition in the myth of origins.

The duty-to-be in the cultural world, the risk of not being (*non poterci essere*) in any possible cultural world: the primordial ethos of presentification lives in this tension.

The reversibility of time as the risk of annihilation is regained and overturned; in other words, it is launched anew toward the irreversibility of cultural-historical becoming, open to valorizing duty-to-be: this is the meaning of the ritual repetition of a myth of origins. Judeo-Christian tradition allows historical consciousness of irreversible becoming to enter into mythical-ritual consciousness itself: the emphasis moves from the exemplariness of the origins to the exemplariness of the center of becoming, from the divine to the divine incarnate (Christ), from the repetition of the origins to the repetition of the center (the death and resurrection

of Christ), from the cyclicity of catastrophic events to waiting for a unidi-
rectional end (the Kingdom [of God]). The repetition of the divine origins
of history is now followed by the repletion of the divine-human center of
history, with the problem of individual salvation in the single end-time
announced. The great problem of our era is the salvation of the individual
in human society, in a socialization of the individual that is not a massifica-
tion, bureaucratization, automation, technicism, state idolatry, diviniza-
tion of the leader, and so forth.

3.3. Cyclical time.

Cyclical time, implicit in the liturgical repetition of the same myth of
origin and foundation and made explicit as a theory in the metaphysics
of eternal return, is a cultural time in which the risk of a "return backward" to the crisis—with its typical neurotic and psychotic forms of
destructuring—gets recovered and opened up to the time of valorizing
irreversibility. In the cyclical time of these mythical-ritual symbolisms,
the returning time of the crisis gets imitated, but imitated in order to redeem it in the time of valorizing transcendence and presentification. Redemption takes place offering an institutional horizon in which what risks
returning in the alienation of a ciphered symptom—that is, an extreme
situation in which the being-there risks not being-there—is sought out
and made to return in order to be recovered in the process of valorization and thereby reintegrated in the historical and cultural time of decision. But the cyclical time of myths of origin and foundation is not only
a horizon of recovery and reintegration of the wretched past that returns
in an incoherent, ciphered, unrecognizable way; it is also a time that is
protective of the historicity of becoming, in that it resolves the critical
moments of existence in exemplary solutions that have already taken place
in illo tempore by means of the numina. The historical re-presentation
of those moments is thus *dehistorified*,[57] concealed in its historicity and
in the fully human responsibility that historicity entails. In this way the
human decision of those moments takes place within the protection of
the already-occurred decision on the mythical level. This amounts to
saying that, through the *pia fraus* of being in history as if one were not
there, the actual being-there of secular agency gets opened up, guaranteed in its results and prospects by what has already been decided *in
illo tempore*.

Cyclical time is the time of predictability and security: its model is offered by the astronomical and seasonal cycle. But in the context of human
history nature's tendency becomes a risk because human history is precisely that which must not repeat and must not return, since this repeating

and returning is catastrophic for valorizing irreversibility. For history, the time of predictability and security is the time of indolence, the risk of the naturalization of culture.

3.4. The risk of the catastrophe of the world and being-in-the-world itself is all the greater the more restricted and precarious is the sphere of the world **at hand** and the technical and mental tools of **handiness** (that is, in the last instance, the more it is possible to perceive the limits of the ordered and orderable[58] within a certain communitarian project of economic life). This risk finds in mythical-ritual symbolism its horizon of recovery toward valorization, whether economic or of another type. The wholly other of the world, the chaotic passing of perceptive spheres into each other, the insubstantiality of each of these spheres, the elimination of distances, the irruption of the wretched past in ciphered symptoms, the outflow of the ego in the world, the plurality of simultaneous or subsequent psychological existences, the impracticability of becoming and the refusal to choose, and so forth: all this finds in mythical-ritual symbolism its horizon of recovery and reintegration. The risk of the wholly other corresponds to the numinous configuration and the relationship of ritual reappropriation; the catastrophe of the world order corresponds to mythical metamorphoses; and with the return of the wretched past, the liturgical makes certain "origins" return, and so forth.

3.5. The horizon of the eternal return (cf. Pavese, *Diario*[59]). Nature tends to the eternal return because it is lazy, because the return of the identical is the most economical way of becoming, and because it is untamed.[60] But in humanity and culture, with the separation from nature as a problem, the tendency to the eternal return has become a risk, a risk that threatens freedom. Culture is indeed a dramatic separation from the indolence of nature, the introduction in nature of a force in which pure and immediate repetition is now an extreme danger: the compulsion to repeat—undramatic in nature—takes the name of regularity (the regularity of the starry sky); in man it becomes mental illness, a disarticulation and loss of presence in the world, a death drive. Culture has introduced into nature the force that we call the primordial ethos of presence as a will to human history that opposes the temptation of the eternal return. In this struggle in which culture is engaged against the eternal return, nonetheless, the eternal return has been reshaped and subjected to human ends in at least two ways. First of all, as a mythical-ritual symbol, that is as *imitatio naturae*. Through religious dehistorification history has been able to unfold in a sort of protected regime, founded precisely on the "as if" of ritual repetition of a same myth of origins: culture got founded in an exemplary way in a mythical era, and in this era the historical proliferation of becoming could get continuously reabsorbed, concealing history in the repetition of the identical. Meanwhile, however, behind the mask of history's dehistorification, and precisely thanks to such a gigantic institutional hypocrisy, infant humans were able to take their first steps in the world and cultivate an agency that, as human and historical, could not be repeating but deciding. One was in history "as if he were not in it," but since this *pia fraus* was necessary for being in it, the *imitatio naturae* did not reproduce the natural eternal return but reshaped it into a dynamic that liberated consciousness from the human situation and disclosed being-in-the-world.

There is a second way that the natural eternal return has been incorporated into culture with science that controls it and subjects it to human ends. In order for the natural eternal return to become an object of experimentation and reshaped into operative law, it was necessary for the human risk of being overwhelmed by the indolence of returning to no longer constitute the central cultural problem.

A. The mythical-ritual symbol is the consciousness of culture as the eternal return of the identical, according to the natural model. The reduction of culture to nature.

B. Science is the reduction of nature to culture. The reduction of human history to the natural eternal return takes place in metahistory, and moreover the metahistory of myth rediscloses human history, the *Einmaligkeit* [uniqueness] of this historical decision. The dialectic of "religious consciousness."

"Men make their own history, they do not know they are making it."[61] This is certainly the quintessential perspective in which religious consciousness moves. But historians cannot limit themselves to pointing out this unaware consciousness time and again, offering a gallery of "reflections" in which one indicates again and again precisely what is being reflected. Another point is important: to determine the historical reasons of that knowledge, the rationality of that incoherence, the positive existential function of such an apparent absentmindedness or forgetfulness, and in the last instance the protective charge and mediating power of "being in history as if one were not in it." Religion (mythical-ritual symbolism) has been—and in part, still is—a cultural institution that has disclosed being-in-the-world for humanity threatened by the risk of not being there; moreover the problem of defending oneself from this risk is certainly not excluded even for those humans who make the effort to take on a consciousness of the entirely human genesis of all human history. Yet it is precisely this consciousness that now prevents turning to religious-cultural institutions (to mythical-ritual symbolism) to carry out reintegration in good faith.

Nature tends to the eternal return because it is the most economical mode of becoming, because it is "lazy," and because the Spirit has not yet detached itself from it. With the Spirit[62]—that is, with humanity and culture—the tendency toward the eternal return becomes a risk against which humanity and culture are called to fight. The Spirit is detachment from the indolence of nature, the introduction into it of a force in which pure and immediate repetition now appears as a threat, of a force that is called the primordial ethos of presence, which generates human history as the struggle against the eternal return. Even so, in this struggle culture has incorporated the eternal return, reshaping it into a cultural product: it is mythical-ritual symbolism, an *imitatio naturae* as a protection from the natural eternal return, from the risk of not being in the world and of losing presence through the anxiety of freedom.[63] But the *imitatio naturae* of mythical-ritual symbolism has been employed for mediating the coming to awareness of human and worldly values. Through being in history "as if one were not in it," history began to appear to consciousness because the very "as if" of the not being in it was a historical decision; it lived in history. Finally, history began to appear in mythical-ritual consciousness itself; this happened in an eminent way in the Christian symbol. But with this the agony of religion also began, and the problem that is so profound today began to be posed, that of a symbolism that no longer uses the meta-history of myth, a symbolism aligned with the recognition that "men make their own history, and they fully bear responsibility for it."

3.6. Identity is nostalgia for the identical, returning to the indistinctness of origins, resisting the proliferation of historical becoming, the death drive, disappearing in a situation in place of transcending it, the annihilation of being-in-the-world. It is the original sin that offends and at the same time gives sense to the primordial ethos of making oneself present. Or, when nostalgia for the identical becomes aware of the approaching void, identity takes on the form of being that repeats, of nostalgia for cyclical becoming, imitating astronomical order, the succession of seasons, and natural law. The symbolic order takes on this risk and indirectly discloses being-there's commitment to transcending situations according to cultural values that humanity generates and that are addressed to humankind. The symbolic order includes, in an intuitive and highly emotional context, origin and perspective: the symbolic mythical-ritual order periodically recollects an absolute origin of history and its absolute fulfillment; the political-symbolic order recalls the origin and perspective of the epoch to which it belongs.

3.7. As much as a psychoanalyst can consider the homology established between the ritual repetition of myth in religious life to be superficial and hasty and abreaction to be a fundamental moment in psychoanalytic therapy; and as much as the ethnologist and historian of religion, no less than the psychologist, would like to have meticulous, detailed analyses that would highlight the differences as well as the similarities, there is no doubt that the problem of the relationship between the myth-ritual nexus and psychoanalytic technique is one of the most productive themes of the most recent movement renewing religious studies. Indeed, we can already benefit from the first differential analyses of this sort carried out in a field that, due to the quantity and quality of ethnological material available, appears in a certain sense to be elective.

To play, as in children's games (to play mother and child, cooking, train, thieves, Indians, etc.) means instituting a "dehistorified" relationship with the real that one does not yet possess, by virtue of which all of the elements are possessed and controlled, if only on a metahistorical level. Such a relationship anticipates the period in which all things now played will become less malleable historical events, not entirely dependent on one's own mastery and endowed with all of the seriousness, commitment, and uncertainty of hard reality. (The real child that the mother will have one day cannot be planned as wished like a doll or the playmate who is playing along, etc.). The impact with revealed reality is softened in its harshness by getting transposed into a domesticated, dreamy, symbolic reality—above all one that is maneuverable according to rules that are already known and gradually put into action by the player as he carries out his game. What does not have importance in play, however, is myth— the image of primordial, foundational times carried out by numina and repeated ceremonially. This feature does not get expressed in the lightness of play, which is a simple, immediate abandonment to a dreamy demiurgic relationship to the real.

Animals play to anticipate the world of prey to be hunted but with more docile and predictable objects than real prey.

3.8. Archaic man's "step back."

> Archaic man, [Thomas Mann] said, stepped back a pace before doing anything, like the toreador poising himself for the death-stroke. He sought an example in the past, and into this he slipped as into a diving-bell in order to plunge, at once protected and distorted, into the problems of

the present. In this way his life achieved its own expression and meaning. For him the mythology of his people was not only convincing, that is, possessed of meaning, but explanatory, that is, an assigner of meaning.[64]

From the point of view of **hierogenetic** analysis, this "step back" forms the central problem. Why the "step back"? What actually was the reason that a sense of security and protection came from it? On the other hand, since every person acts with models inspired by certain traditions in mind, what is the peculiarity of the mythical model or tradition? Now, the mythical "step back" is a technique of dehistorification through which the historical initiative of here and now (with its concrete responsibility) got concealed or disguised, and in this way disclosed, as if it were the repetition of a primordial initiative: on the level of ritual the same myth returned, one whose exemplary result was reabsorbed in the historical proliferation of becoming. The sense of myth is in the security that derives from its technicism and likewise the sense of things that emerges from the myth. To be in history as if one were not in it, that is what the step back of ritual repetition of myth expresses. However, if the myth attenuates, conceals, reduces, and disguises the historicity of becoming (and thus protects from time that moves forward), it forms a horizon of configuration, of stopping and recovery in relation to the incoherent return of the past, from repetition as a fundamental aspect of the **crisis of presence**. Myth therefore performs a dual protective function: from the historical proliferation of becoming, and from repetition of a past that has not been overcome and which returns as an indomitable psychic estrangement. Myth is a model of reabsorption in relation to the historical proliferation of becoming, a model of recovery in relation to the return of a past that has not been overcome. It attenuates historicity, it obscures it, and at the same time it reopens toward historicity; it reintegrates alienations operating in the unconscious. With this we have a dual symbolic "disguising" of myth: to conceal historicity, and as a technique for recovering of a past that has not been overcome. Myth is the technique of concealing historicity to be overcome and a technique of configuration and recovery of reintegration of a historicity that has not been overcome. Myth as a protected existence.

3.9. Gerardus van der Leeuw, "Urzeit und Endzeit," *Eranos Jahrbuch* 17, 1949.[65] [. . .] 324ff. Cyclical time, linear time: but to these two we must add ethical time, the time of presence that—prodded by current problems— retraces, choosing the history of Western civilization. This time compares this history with that of other civilizations and advances a human proposition of planetary unification in order to render it worthy of the conquest of cosmic spaces and the new history that will come of it. It is a human proposition, like all cultural propositions (even if they were held to be divine), and in full awareness of its human origin and destination it cannot count on any destiny written in the stars but only on mankind living in society.

Myth is metahistory, a metahistorical horizon. It is the myth of origins that the ritual repeats and renews, reabsorbing within it the historical proliferation of worldly becoming and representing the world ever anew according to the exemplary power of the first time, when the world began through the inaugural decision of the numina. Preserving the world, sustaining life, means ritually repeating its foundation myth. The myth is the myth of the end announced as imminent or near or far and in any case already prefigurable and anticipatable in a ritual experience. It is an end that is nonetheless in turn a beginning either of a repetition of the cycle or liberation from the worldly and the human. Finally, the myth is a myth of the center, of a privileged event that gives sense to sacred history in its entirety, both in terms of the past and the future: through that event history enters into the perspective of ending, and nothing decisive can happen anymore, except for the end and the continuous sacramental repetition of the central event that has made the decision once and for all.

This is myth in the consciousness that mythical-ritual practitioners have of it. But this metahistorical consciousness of history is nonetheless in history and falls under historiographic judgment, which discovers in it the passage from a minimum to a maximum of historical consciousness. The minimum is certainly in the myth as the myth of origins and continuous reabsorption in the historical proliferation of becoming in the *exemplum* of the primordial foundation decided by the numina. Here, human deciding is recognized as such, for what it is, almost entirely outside of mythical consciousness and in substantial subordination with regard to it. To the myth of origins generally corresponds the tendency to "be in history as if you were not in it," provided that the myth conceals the tendency within the mythical consciousness that one has of it. Furthermore, profane activities take place not only in the shadow of this consciousness but are protected, mediated, and disclosed by it. Already in the myth of eternal return, history makes its first appearance in mythical consciousness because the return of the cycles is indeed the negation of history, but the cycle is a temporal series of events, ages of the world, and in the last instance becoming, no matter how mystified. In the myth of the center of history one passes to a wider recognition of historicity in the sphere of mythical consciousness, since it appears a datable event, incomparably privileged, that redistributes the phases from beginning to end. When consciousness of history appears in mythical consciousness itself, however, the seed of an irreconcilable contradiction appears that marks, as it advances, the agony of mythical consciousness and in general of religious symbolism as mythical-ritual symbolism. Today we are immersed at the height of this agony, and we are faced with the choice between history and metahistory, between concealment and recognition of the humanity of becoming.

> Sometimes this end [of the world] is the conclusion of a slow degenera-tion, just as the Golden Age was a climax. But much more characteristic is the conception of a final time that irrupts suddenly and puts an end to everything, slashing the fabric of time like a sword. Here it can really become an experience. Its advent is expected shortly, as we know from the New Testament. As late as the second century, a Syrian bishop led his whole community, including children, into the desert to meet the Lord.[66]

Cyclical, reversible time connected to the ritual repetition of a mythi-cal metahistory, characterized by the reabsorption of the proliferation of becoming in primordial and beginning time and by the concealment of the very history of becoming; the negation of lived time. To this is coun-terposed lived time included in the horizon of an absolute beginning and end: the irreversibility of time, its processual nature, but not the endless-ness of human history. The world has begun, it will end, history is sacred history, and yet the eternal return imposes itself within this framework as a calendrical eternal return in the liturgical year (a dehistorified year).

In the cycle of cyclical time, a decisive event is missing: each event decides nothing but repeats what has already been decided in the begin-ning; whereas in eschatological time,

> at a certain point in the cycle someone appears who proclaims a defini-tive event, the day of Yahweh, the last judgment, the ultimate salvation, or the final conflict as in Iran. The images used are all borrowed from the course of nature: day and night, summer and winter. But the ethos has changed; a hiatus has been made, a *tempus* in the strict sense, which changes everything. Thus the prophet Zacharias can say that it will be light at eventide[67]. This final time revolutionizes the course of the world. (van der Leeuw 1957, 339)

[...]

3.10. Mircea Eliade, *Mythes, rêves et mystères* (Paris: Gallimard, 1957).[68]
    "[T]here is no mythic motif or scenario of initiation which is not also presented, in one way or another, in dreams and in the working of the imagination. In the oneiric universe we find again and again the symbols,

the images, the figures and the events of which the mythologies are con-stituted. Upon this discovery, due to the genius of Freud . . ." (14). None-theless, it is not possible to explain myths with dreams, to reduce myths to processes of the unconscious (14).

The myth "*reveals* something as having been *fully manifested*, and this manifestation is at the same time creative and exemplary" (14, emphasis Eliade's). All myths take part in some way in the cosmogenic type of myth: they narrate how the world was founded or created *in illo tempore*, and this narration is a how that is also a why (15). Myths "disclose *true* stories, concern themselves with the *realities*" (15). This means that myths cannot be reduced to oneiric life. A dream is particular, private, personal; it is not experienced by the whole person but only by the oneiric consciousness; it is lacking universality and exemplariness: it is a closed, ciphered symbol and remains as such until the key to it is found. Myth, instead, has a value that transcends the individual: it is lived by the whole person, it is univer-sal and exemplary; it is an open symbol (16).

The resemblances are nonetheless undeniable. Like myth, dream abol-ishes space and time (16) (and many oneiric mechanisms recall those of myth; moreover, the affinity between dream and myth is noted in the his-tory of religions, which is familiar with formations—like Alchera[69]—that are both dream and mythical era, provoked dreams-revelations, incuba-tion,[70] dreams interpreted on the level of magical-religious life, etc.).

Regarding the religious aura of certain contents of the unconscious. The unconscious is the result of immemorial critical situations, the pre-cipitate of countless extreme situations; it is experience that founds the world, that draws the cosmos out of chaos (17). Now, transcendence and the exemplarity of religion and myth "[compels] the religious man to come out of personal situations, to surpass the contingent and the particu-lar and to comply with general values, with the universal" (18). Religious experience is "a total crisis of existence and the exemplary solution of that crisis" (18). "The religious solution lays the foundation for an exemplary behavior, and, in consequence, compels man to reveal himself as both the real and the *universal* (18, emphasis Eliade's). "It is the religious vision of the world and the ideology derived from it which have enabled the man to bring his individual experience to fulfilment, to 'open' it towards the universal" (19).

Example: The Tree of the World is a religious symbol "bound up with the ideas of periodic and unending renewal, of regeneration, of 'the source of life and youth,' of immortality, and of absolute reality" (19). Like every other religious symbol, it does not save if it is not experienced by the man in his entirety.

By emerging into his dreams, the image of the Tree has "saved" the man only in part from his individual predicament—has made him able, for example, to integrate a crisis in the depths and to recover his psychic balance, which was more or less seriously menaced. But, not having been accepted in its symbolic sense, the image of the Tree has not succeeded in revealing the universal, and therefore has not lifted the man up to the plane of the Spirit, as religion, however rudimentary, always does. (19–20)

Mircea Eliade, *Myths, Dreams, and Mysteries*, trans. Philip Mairet (New York: Harper and Row, 1960), 39ff., "The Myth of the Noble Savage."

The aspiration for paradise, nostalgia for an Edenic condition, in the myth of the savage.

Savages also, after all, have their myths of paradise. "For the savage, too, perfection had existed at the beginning" (44). But "[p]eriodically he re-memorised the essential events which had placed him in the position of 'fallen' man" (44). For the primitive, there are two types of time, irreducible to one another: the time of events *in illo tempore* (cosmogonic myths, myths of origin), to be repeated periodically, and those without a model, which are of no interest and are "forgotten" (45). Examples drawn from the lunar civilization of Jensen, 45.[71] The *regressus ad originem*, reintegration in the original plenitude (48). The recitation of the cosmogonic myth as a therapeutic means: the patient, through such a recitation, returns to the past and is rendered contemporary to creation: the patient's memory is thus not only called to preserve the memory of origins but to project itself ritually into mythical time, when the world was formed as it is.

The *return to the past*, the possibility of *undoing time*, does not belong solely to archaic thought. The research thus widens. "[T]he importance allowed to Time and to History in contemporary thought, as well as the findings of depth-psychology, may shed further light upon certain spiritual dispositions of archaic humanity" (49).

It is scarcely fifty years since the problems of Time and History came to occupy the centre of Western philosophical thought. This, moreover, is why we have today a better understanding of the behaviour of the primitives and of the structure of Indian thought than we had in the latter half of the nineteenth century. In the one case as in the other, the key is to be found in their peculiar conceptions of temporality. It had long been known that primitives, as well as the Indians and other ancient peoples of Asia, shared a cyclic conception of Time, but that was all: we had not noticed that cyclic Time itself was periodically annulled; and that, consequently, even those who held that view of Time were manifesting their desire to *escape from duration*, their *refusal to assume it*. (49n, emphasis de Martino's)

For the Buddha, *karma* is the power of proliferation of temporal becoming, the eternal return to existence and suffering. The Buddha announces his message of liberation from karmic law, an end to be pursued through certain techniques. "Now, one of the methods of 'burning up' the karmic residua is a technique for 'returning to the past,' becoming conscious of one's previous lives" (49–50). We find this technique, which is pan-Indian, in the *Yogasūtra* (III, 18)[72] and is based on "retracing time backwards" (*pratiloma*, against the grain). With such a *regressus ad originem* one arrives at "the point where existence first 'burst' into the world and unleashed Time" (50): once even this first existence is surpassed, one is immersed in nontime.

In other words, it is possible, starting from any moment of temporal duration, to exhaust the duration by retracing its course to the source and so come out into the Timeless, into eternity. But that is to transcend the human condition and to regain the nonconditioned state, which preceded the fall into Time and the wheel of existences (50).

(The conception of historiography as a list of examples and the Platonic theory of knowledge as anamnesis of a world of ideas has a *mythical* origin: 51–2.)

Even psychoanalysis as a technique entails a *return backward*.

But, within the horizons of modern spirituality, and in conformity with the Judæo-Christian conception of historic and irreversible Time, the "primordial" could mean only one's earliest childhood, the true individual initium. Psychoanalysis, therefore, introduces historical and individual time into therapeutics. [. . .] The patient [. . .] is also suffering the after-effects of a shock sustained in his own temporal duration, some personal trauma that occurred in the *illud tempus* of childhood—a trauma that has been forgotten or, more exactly, has never come to consciousness. And the cure consists precisely in a "return to the past"; a re-tracing of one's steps in order to re-enact the crisis, to re-live the psychic shock and bring it back into consciousness. (53)

In other words, while archaic thought and Indian thought return to cosmogony by virtue of their cyclical conception of time, psychoanalysis returns to childhood. In both cases, we have a *return that cures* (or saves). The psychoanalytic paradise is the period from the prenatal stage to weaning, followed by a rupture that is traumatic.

Jung, in turn, discovers the collective unconscious, a place of archetypes or psychic structures that have never been individual and aware (54).

What all mythical formulas have in common is that "the decisive deed took place before us, and even before our parents" and that we repeat the primordial, we are a continuous echo of the origins (54–55). For psychoanalysis the foundation of the illness took place in childhood: the difference is fundamental. Psychoanalysis recognizes that the symptom is a closed symbol of a crisis that returns, and it operates technically to reinsert that symbol into the flow of consciousness, thereby explicitly theorizing recovery and reintegration. Mythical-ritual dehistorification instead foregrounds the return to the origins and being in history as if one were not: the recovery takes place but is not theorized at all; on the contrary, the condition of the mythical-ritual technique's functioning is that the agent is unaware or forgets that it is a technique of recovery.

3.11. Mircea Eliade [in "The Morphology and Function of Myths," *Traité d'histoire des religions* (Paris: Payot, 1949),[73] 338ff.] views the paradox "historical event = hierophany" and "historical time = mythical time" to be "apparent." He thinks that to dispel it, "it is sufficient that we place ourselves in the particular conditions of the primitive mentality" that has conceived such equivalencies. Primitive man is interested in human actions and finds them significant "to the extent that they repeat gestures revealed by the divinity, civilizing heroes and ancestors." Anything that does not have a metahistorical model has no importance. Here we should note that any attempt at hierogenetic reconstruction is avoided: to understand primitive paradoxes means simply relocating oneself in the particular conditions of the primitive mentality, placing the conception of history as a system of metahistorical models that history repeats *next* to our conception of history, and *next* to irreversible series of single events the reversible series of events that repeat the metahistorical model. The logical fallacy is precisely in that *next* because an encompassing discourse is never formed by discourses that are placed next to one another in a sort of relativistic indulgence and in a morphological descriptivism that is complicated by calls for an immediate reliving of the parts that are *next* to. The encompassment is in a unitary, genetic discourse that improves what we are today, making this "ours" of today ensue from what we were then. We can succeed in understanding the other only with autobiographical clarity.

To say that for primitive man only events that have a metahistorical (mythical) model are significant, and that an event is insignificant for primitive man because it has no mythical precedent (339), is to declare that things are this way because they are this way. It is describing the primitive mythical consciousness in its limitation. But the real hierogenetic problem is to make that limitation prove to be necessary, understanding its existential function, its cultural quality. For an understanding of this sort, however, the point of departure is that bit of humanistic consciousness that in every person cannot be lacking no matter how restricted it is. Humanistic consciousness is the recognition of a sphere of actions that depend on humankind, the knowledge that if man does not take the initiative, does not elaborate certain techniques, does not avoid certain obstacles, he does not obtain the corresponding results. In a chipped stone; in hunting traps; in a hunt; in transplanting, sowing, harvesting; in the passage from a digging tool to the hoe or from the hoe to the plow: all of these contain an undeniable humanistic consciousness, finding oneself as a person who must decide on present situations, inventing techniques or instruments, or making good use of traditional techniques or instruments.

[. . .]

Comments.

The protective (and thus technical) function of the myth-ritual nexus is dual: from one point of view this nexus protects the individual presence from the incoherent return of situations that have not been overcome and from the current crisis of alienation. From another point of view, it protects the presence from the historicity of the human condition. The myth-ritual nexus carries out this dual function thanks to the institution of a metahistorical level that operates as a horizon for configuration and recovery regarding the incoherent return of the past and at the same time as a level of dehistorification of the proliferation of social becoming. In myth-ritual as a horizon of configuration and recovery, the closed symbols (i.e., the symptoms) are reshaped into open symbols (the images of the myth), and the incoherent return of the past is transformed into a ritual "made to return." [. . .]

The protective function of the myth-ritual nexus is carried out in the institution of a metahistorical level that configures, gives horizon to, and shapes the incoherent return of the past and that—at the same time—operates as a level of reabsorption and concealment of historical becoming and of the historicity of the human condition. The mythical-ritual symbol thus displays a dual character because it presents itself as "the undecided that decides" and at the same time, as "the decidable that gets connected to the already decided." Its character lies in the dynamic whereby the undecided is recovered and reopened to decision, and the actually decidable is resolved in the exemplary decision of the beginning.

[. . .]

The alienation of presence is configured in the mythical-ritual horizon: but what in this horizon is formed as a figure is human presence itself but not recognized as human. In the mythical event, presence poses itself as a transcendental task: but this task, as much as it is transcendent, invites a relationship, a path of reappropriation, an outcome of recognition and finding the self again. The mythical events of the numina narrate the numina, not people: but we can read in this the history of people who lose themselves, look for themselves, and to a more or less restricted extent, dramatically find themselves again (find the passage in van der Leeuw again).

[...]

3.12. Indian symbolism of time.

In *Images et symboles* (Paris: Gallimard, 1952), 57ff.,[74] Mircea Eliade considers Indian symbolism of time a "theory" of eternity arising from the anxiety of history[75] and from which the Indian draws the logical consequence of renouncing the world. At the same time it is a second path to salvation, "the renunciation of the fruits of action," fulfilling one's own vocation in the world without pride or delusion, carrying out one's duty in historical time, and constantly preserving in spirit the perspectives of Great Time through the periodic recitation of the founding myths of a certain metaphysical, ethical, and social order. It should be noted that Mircea Eliade only gives us a very generic analysis of anxiety of history, which in reality is the risk of losing presence, with all of the ciphered symptoms of such a loss. We should moreover note that the two paths—one of renouncing the world and the other of being in history as if one were not in it—are respectively like a pedagogy of the transcendence of value and of reintegration into value, a pedagogy that takes place within the horizon of transcendence. Religious life gives a metahistorical horizon to the crisis, recovering the risk of not being-there in history and mediating the reintegration in cultural values. It is this real movement that we need to reconstruct, even with its limits and its dramatic contradictions, if we do not want to repeat the religious experience in a sort of edifying sermon. Evaluating solely the claim to abandon the world, the historian or phenomenologist is forced either to recognize that this claim is exposed to failure or to not realize the fact that Indian spirituality, despite this claim, created a functioning cultural-historical world (and not the annihilation of culture) or, finally, to admit one alongside the other as "two" paths to salvation, the rigorous one of mysticism and the one of compromise of being in history as if one were not in it. But when we consider the movement that from the crisis crosses the mythical-ritual horizon of dehistorification, we in fact disclose a certain history imbued with certain values (even if they are not actually recognized as wholly human value), crisis and mystical impulse, abandonment of the world and cultural life in the world, dehistoricization and integration into history, transcendental horizon and readings that regain cultural values in such a horizon—all these are composed into a new coherence that illuminates the genesis, structure, function, and conditioning of religious life in the context of a civilization or period.

In his essay on the Indian symbolism of time and eternity, Mircea Eliade falls into the fundamental methodological aporia of describing the metachronic *claim* of religious life without explaining the genesis, function, and value of this claim. The escape from time, as it is pursued by the *yogin* and as the *yogin* practices and expresses it, is repeated in the scholar's description, which at most brings more order and coherence to it and makes us aware of a few implications. How and why in cultural life, in the history of human civilizations, the claim to escape the profane civil order was formed and maintained and what function and value are vested in it form problems for the scholar, but his solution basically repeats the religious experience: man aspires to escape history, and through religious experience Great Time is really opened. Now, the difficulty lies precisely here, and precisely here begins the real problem for historical knowledge, which places in doubt the very possibility of a history of religious life. Indeed, if the claim of escape from history is real in the sense that the escape from history actually ensues and enters into a relation with the metatemporal and the supramundane, the history of religion can only narrate about relatively secondary aspects in which it inheres to deals with the unreality of the world: the claim as such *eludes historical narrative*, and at most it is possible to compete with the religious man to describe what he has experienced. History of religion and religious life get confused precisely in the decisive moment, and a more or less dissimulated apologetics creates disruption precisely when an option for scientific consideration is most needed. Genetic (hierogenetic) problems thus become secondary and are treated reluctantly, and in any case, just to the extent necessary to illuminate what interests the most: the relationship between religious life and the archetypes.

3.13. Ritual behavior repeats the mythical model, and through this periodic reabsorption of becoming on the exemplary level of metahistory, the character of ritual behavior is defined. Even so, as a behavior that repeats metahistorical models, it could appear to be a historical behavior, declare itself to be a merely human initiative of repetition. This is why—in order to avoid this—ritual in turn has a mythical foundation and is included in the category of *exempla* instituted *in illo tempore*. The ritual not only *repeats*, for example, the death and resurrection of Christ but it repeats them in a form, the last supper, founded by Christ himself. In this way, the repetitive rituality concerns both the existential order founded *in illo tempore* and the ceremonies that *in illo tempore* were founded to allow humankind to interact with the mythical order.

The movement that began with the publication of Rudolf Otto's *Das Heilige* (1917) obviously did not arise out of the blue.[76] In the fifty years before 1917 we can find preparatory themes strewn here and there, and it is possible to identify certain cultural currents that were already ongoing that would then converge in the "movement" in question. However, only with the publication of *Das Heilige* does a period begin in European cultural history (or, if one prefers, Euro-American) in which a level of development is established of relationship, convergence, and at least potential unification of what previously either participated in independent traditions or was only in a state of mention or outline. This level is given by the sacred, ritual, myth, the primitive, the magical, by the wealth of varieties of religions of the ecumene, living or extinct as they were. Precisely on this level the seeds of cultural "relativism" already present in the work of Dilthey[77] moved as if on a soil particularly suited to bearing fruit. It was here that the interest in the dark side of humanity found an environment that was, in a certain sense, elective, and the irrationalistic ferments that in philosophy and in literature—as well as in the visual arts—had already for some time given ample evidence of themselves, now found a place of connection, confirmation, and growth. In all this the progress of religious ethnology, and in general of the history of religions, had a preponderant part: an Otto and a Hauer[78] are in fact historians of religion, just as Kerényi or an Eliade are. But even when it is neither ethnologists nor historians participating in this *Stimmung* of the period but sociologists like Lévy-Bruhl, philosophers like Bergson or Jaspers, psychologists like Freud and Jung, or writers, artists, or even National Socialist fanatics like Rosenberg (*The Myth of the Twentieth Century*),[79] the works of religious history were revelation and stimulus of something that was already deep in one's heart.

3.14. What is myth? This question first arose within Western civilization with Plato and the Sophists as a polemic of philosophical reason against the irrationality of mythopoeisis and subsequently, with the advent of Christian civilization, as a polemic of faith against false and impostor gods. The question has taken on particular importance in the current cultural climate with all probability in connection to the decisive choices in which our epoch is engaged. This renewed interest has seen the participation of ethnologists and anthropologists alongside historians of religion;

philosophers, historians, and critics of contemporary literature have participated with various perspectives; and even political ideologists like Sorel (whose echo raised by the "myth of the general strike" has certainly not died out). In it, the word *myth* has come to cover the most diverse cognitive contents in such a way that today the greatest confusion and danger of misinterpretation prevails.

The situation is somewhat embarrassing for the historian of religion and the ethnologist, for the folklorist and the cultural anthropologist—that is, for those who are called again and again to use this cognitive category in the course of their studies and who should possess certain criteria both to circumscribe mythic products in the mass of cultural facts and to identify in this or that myth its genesis, structure, dynamics, its varied fortune and function, and finally, to return to model the cognitive category of "myth" itself on the basis of results of one's own philological, ethnographic, or archaeological research. The question "what is myth" will thus be dealt with in relation above all to the work of the historian of religion called to recognize concrete myths and thus to treat "problems of method" to recognize it and conduct continuous tests of current opinions or "theories" regarding myth.

Mythical-ritual symbolism

(a) as a socialized (communitarian) level of arrest and configuration with regard to risks of possible radical alienations of individual existences (i.e., as a level of active search for and recovery of risks pertaining to the loss of life's valorizing presentification and as a level of defense from risks of retreating to a total impracticability of the world);

(b) as a level of attenuation and concealment of the wholly human responsibility in actual operative decision (reabsorption of such deciding in the ritual repletion of an identical mythical model of foundation of the practicable communitarian order);

(c) as a level of active recovery with regard to the risk of the incoherent return of the critical past that was never really overcome;

(d) as a level of prefiguration of the critical unpredictability of the future and thus as an attenuation and concealment of the historicity of possible future occurrence;

(e) as a level of distancing from and postponement of the end in such a way as to give a horizon to practicable worldly testimony.

3.15. "Initially," or rather "at the top," means "in the beginning," just as in fables, "once upon a time" does not mean "a single time" but "once and for all." Myth is not a poetic invention in the sense that we give to this word today. On the contrary, because of the very fact of its universality, myth can be expressed, and with equal authenticity, according to a number of different perspectives (Coomaraswamy, *Hindouisme et bouddhisme*, French trans. [Paris: Gallimard, 1949],[80] 19).

Once and for all: the primordial event that happens once and for all, and which can be repeated ritually, appears as a horizon of dehistorification of historical becoming characterized precisely by events in which the "each time" of their taking place counts for itself and not others, still less for all. In history we must begin each time ever anew: the myth of origins offers a level in which to absorb this proliferating "ever anew" in a privileged, metahistorical time that stands for all time and dehistorifies becoming in the repetition of unchanging metahistorical permanence itself. With this, historical becoming is concealed; in fact it appears as a disguise, appearance, nonvalue, and through this *pia fraus* one is in history "as if" one were not in it. This does not mean, however, that one is not in it, that one does not act and decide each time (and how could one?), but that the consciousness that accompanies the historical agency is subordinate, protected and disclosed by the hegemonic mythical-ritual consciousness of a divine work that has already been completed in that time that counts for every time and can be reactivated each time.

3.16. The fluidity of becoming simply means that presence does not remain without a leeway of practicability and projectability of that very becoming. If a critical situation resists the decision of presence, if it is not clear what needs to be done to undo a knot in one's existence, one continues to decide for all other situations, and even the critical situation receives an adequate response in one way or another, in a more or less long time. We can consider, for example, the crisis of mourning that accompanies the loss of a loved one: even if, faced with the motionless body, one experiences the tremendous event in the face of which there is nothing that can be done, in reality people continue their doing, their operating. Whether stronger people in their silent, huddled interior pain or the weaker in desperation, they carry out the work of mourning that marks the extremely slow and painful passage from a living person who communicated with us in a dialogue of words and affection to the deceased person with whom we can only monologue, recalling his works and committing ourselves in a certain faithfulness to them ("my father taught me . . ."). The work of mourning commands us to go beyond the situation of grief: for if this situation truly imprisons us, and the death of a loved one does not transform itself into a choice of ours regarding his death, in our making him die within us that contains the best things of his life, then we ourselves begin to die along with what has passed away. In the unsuccessful alternative we render historical time reversible, ending up losing the very moral power that, deciding the alternatives, renders being-in-the-world possible. One who does not overcome a critical situation remains its prisoner and is subjected to its tyranny. Presence remains without leeway in the face of a grieving situation, losing the fluidity, the practicability, the projectability of worldly becoming; in every situation it tends to repeat the grieving situation, to become the deceased and our desperation or terror. The dead who are not made to die by the living tend to return in an unresolved way, perhaps in a disguise that makes them unrecognizable and contaminating the whole gamut of possible situations in real life.

End of the world and death.

The thought that a single individual will inevitably end up dying risks becoming a pathological symptom to the extent that it isolates itself within consciousness, invading it and paralyzing it. Those who close themselves in this thought begin to die from it, and this is a death that is the worst of all since it announces itself as a void in thinking, as a useless fantasizing, and as a growing terror of the moral nothingness that approaches. Precisely this is death's medicine: the renewed commitment to act according to intersubjective values, communicate with others through these values, and in this way ceaselessly transcend mere biological individuality, raising it in every instant toward the permanence of life "that matters." The death of an individual is a strictly private moment of the individual himself, the most clamorous sign of egoity:[81] it is the incommunicable par excellence, so much so that the very word *death* is the only necessary sound but nonetheless does not have a message to transmit; the only enunciation that gathers all of the possible insignificance of what is humanly speakable. But individuals, who are human, found and maintain themselves as such through this valorizing emerging of the presence, through this disclosure of the private to the public, through this world of others in which one listens and responds, in a discourse that has only scant respite in restful, dreamless sleep (since even in the nightly dreaming, the discourse continues, although in a form that is ciphered to waking consciousness). In this perspective and in this dynamic, death as a terminal condition of the biological individual transforms itself into a death that is being born in the intersubjectivity of values: in other words, the biological dying of an individual, which in a certain sense begins at birth, is remodeled into a "making someone die in value, operating in the concreteness of a historical society," which the divine Plato already knew in his own way when he declared the life of every instant to be the discipline of death: "Die and become." Do these famous formulations not hint at the very medicine against death?[82] If people do not manage to make their dear, highly private "I" die again and again in value, then the death that terrorizes and alarms does indeed threaten: in the retreat of valorizing presentification, the terrible experience of Teresa of Avila takes place: "I die because I do not die."[83]

Analysis, in this perspective, of death and dying in psychopathology.

2

Psychopathological Apocalypses

1. Lived Experiences of the End of the World

1.1. Alfred Storch, "Tod und Erneuerung in der schizophrenen Daseins-
Umwandlung" [Death and renewal in schizophrenic Dasein conversion],
Archiv für Psychiatrie und Nervenkrankheiten, 181, no. 3 (1949): 275–93.[1]

The experience of *being-acted-upon*.

In the case reported on page 276ff., a woman feels subjugated to her
husband, dispossessed, that her life has been snatched from her. "She can
no longer live through her own power," because her husband (and her
mother) have taken it away from her (278). The destruction of her Dasein
is experienced in the form of atrophy of her chances for maternity, and
this atrophy is perceived as a *Lebensraub*, a theft of life. "With their gaze
they can take away my ego just like my coat" (a reference to the working
energy used by the nurses by exploiting her own) (279). Men can use
her as an inert instrument for their sexual needs: their simple "hypnotic
gazes" force her to prostitute herself (278). Natural affective values have
been snatched from her so that she is "empty and without interests." The
nurse interrupts and upsets the train of her thoughts. Her thoughts are
"scattered," "conversation exhausts her." "I lose myself in others, as if I
were sacrificing myself" (279).

The hostile world has a diabolical power over her because "a part of my
life is too strongly connected to the lives of others." She is forced to hate
and defend herself. She no longer possesses a defined being for herself.
"I can no longer have any thoughts to myself and hide them from others."
The others "compensate" for what she is thinking; they listen and reply
to her. Storch speaks of magical participation in relation to her altered
structure of existence.

A discharge of the ego into the world: she is forced to transform herself
into something else; she finds her own existence again "outside" (herself),
in men, animals, things. Her *joie de vivre* is "outside in the cows"; "instead
of the children" that she should have had, "little chickens are running

around outside." This continuous projection in the other that she is exposed to empties her, and her living existence becomes "a bare figure." "I am no longer fully human, only a minimum, entirely given over to the benefit of other useless subjects." "The most primitive feeling of 'finding oneself' has gotten lost, the original sensation no longer exists outside of anger." "I am no longer inside life, but beyond."

The loss of self, "the negation of Dasein" proceeds in a dual direction of reification of the spiritual and of a dematerialization of the corporeal. Reification acts as a splitting into parts: the reified ego is dispossessed, it becomes inexistent, a "conglomerate." The closed unity of her previous existence has been lost. Even other people are conglomerations. And as she partly passes through into another, the others pass into her. Atomization, disarticulation of the real. She is a "nonthing that gets remodeled every day" (279).

The dematerializing evaporation serves as a dissolution of her body in the air, in breath, in anything that flutters. Men are specters, the specters are visible. The phenomena permeate each other like breaths, those of others go through her, and she goes through them. She is out in the wind. The magical reconstruction: multipresence, and so forth. Force, and so on. Drawings that create: not imitations, but models of the real. Catasterisms[2] of the person (283). But all her attempts to uplift herself, bodily or with her thoughts, upward to the stars are futile. The basic direction of her life struck by this illness is falling downward. What she "thinks upward" is again "pulled down," unthought (*abgedanken*); it is "stuffed into the mountain." Since she is exposed to reification and distribution, "the star's power has waned." "The sun no longer warms; the moon no longer shines. The image of the star, that is my life." Only for some instants can she carry out her always renewed striving of being unreachable by the material destruction of the world of the stars (283). Instead of resting in God, she is "dissolved into nothingness" (286).

> For human existence the schizophrenic process means a progressive loss of Dasein, a "negation of Dasein"—as our patient puts it—an obliteration of the being able to be oneself and with others, a being set outside living becoming. This loss of self (*Selbstverlust*) can take various forms: in the case at hand—very typical of a certain group of schizophrenics—obliteration is experienced as destruction deriving from an overpowering, hostile counterworld; a no-longer-having-oneself as dispossession; powerlessness as disempowerment; being exposed in separation as displacement and possession by those counterforces; being removed and torn away from oneself appears as a denial of one's existence and being caught up in and overpowering, counterworldly Dasein. The decrease

in Dasein's abundance appears here as a drainage, an emptying out, and theft of Dasein. The social world and material environment are no longer experienced as living but rather as lifeless. Being together is disintegrated into being against; taking part in each other disintegrates into a thieving taking part from the other. The counterforces have the power to seize individual corporeal and spiritual actions. This all means a disassociation of the living existence that becomes thinglike and breaks down into interchangeable, removable parts to be assembled in new conglomerates. This also means an evaporation that dissolves the corporeal Dasein in a mutual interpenetration, as with air or breath. [. . .] This entire Dasein transformation takes place as the breakdown of lived time; the continuity of becoming is shattered in the discontinuity and fluidity of continuous metamorphoses in which the Dasein no longer arrives at an actual presence but only momentary images incessantly arising and passing. In such a world, a living, historical development ceases; the Dasein has lost its historicity. In the continuous loss of being experienced over and over, Dasein can become neither future nor past. (286–87)

Through this form of Dasein loss we can recognize a forfeit to an overpowering, hostile world, a coerced exteriorization, a dispossession of one's own. "Consciousness is shifted outside." The patient is separated from herself, her fulfilled Dasein is been taken from her and is injected into the hostile world. In this *Gegenwelt* lies everything that has remained unfulfilled, unshaped, the not-experienced and the not-lived-out, what has remained excluded from her Dasein. This alienation and exteriorization is carried out as a dematerialization and evaporation, as materializing embodiment and as evaporating spiritualization. [. . .] The unfulfilled aspect, life historically, of her Dasein confronts her from outside her *Umwelt* and *Mitwelt*.[3] It is her own inner contradictions that early on destroyed the equilibrium in the development of her life and impeded the possibility of unity, of finding her own center. As she put it, again and again she searched in vain to "elaborate" a center between *Selbstbehauptung* and *Selbsthingabe*. (287)

The patient continually experienced herself as dead, transferred to the realm of the dead and spirits and returning again. She had a brief terrestrial and cosmic renewal through the entrance into a superterrestrial world of light (289ff.). The patient's condition of existence recalls in many respects the metamorphosis of mysteries, mystical "initiations," in which there is an experience of passing through death. It also recalls descriptions of the after-death condition, of the "intermediate condition" laid down in *The Tibetan Book of the Dead* (cf. Jung's commentary).[4] [. . .] This is also true of initiations among [so-called[5]] primitive peoples, in which the youth, who is about to become a man and must sacrifice his boyhood, is made to participate in a renewal. (290)

But while in initiations we are dealing with an event that is illuminated by knowledge of ancient traditions, an event through which the individual reaches a wider and fuller life, in the patient the numerous deaths take place as a violent and obligatory destiny that obliterates the new terrestrial and cosmic births again and again. The formation of a higher self is not reached [. . .]; instead of "resting in God," the patient "breaks down more and more into nothingness."[6] (290)

The patient is like an alchemist who cannot carry out the *solve et coagula*: the path toward the "center" is lost, even if it is sought again and again. The patient is engaged in struggle that resembles the process of alchemy's metamorphosis and renewal: but in the patient this process stops at the intermediate steps and, so to speak, always turns back. As in the intermediate situation spoken of in *The Tibetan Book of the Dead*, in the after-death condition, or "between death and new embodiment," the patient does not know whether she is dead or alive, if she is returning to her old body or taking on the new one. In *The Tibetan Book of the Dead*, at this point in this condition a mentally shaped "body of desire" arises that, when it does not reach the final end of union with the primordial light, gives way and falls back into new embodiment "in the circle of births," in our apparent world, and to the encounter with frightful demons and spirits that must be recognized as the creation of one's own psychic condition. Here, too, the relation to the patient's condition is evident (291).

Did not the patient herself become a demon, hungering for Dasein, fulfillment, abundance, and light, always outside herself while hungering for herself, unresolvingly tied to herself and yet no longer really coming to herself (292)? "I struggled to the point of mortal fatigue to hold on to the higher life of faith and devotion" (Hölderlin) (Storch 1949, 293).[7]

1.2. Jaspers, Primary Delusional Experiences, Miscellaneous. Karl Jaspers, *Allgemeine Psychopathologie*, 6th ed. (Berlin: Springer, 1953; first published 1913; 5th ed. 1946; 6th ed. unchanged), "Primäre Wahnerlebnisse" [Primary delusional experiences], 93–108.[8]

Jaspers begins with the observation that delusion has always been considered the fundamental phenomenon of madness, although it is not easy to circumscribe the concept of delusion. Assuming that "der Wahn ist ein Urphänomen" (delusion is a primary phenomenon), and that the experience in whose context delusion takes place is the experiencing and thinking of reality (93), Jaspers analyzes the two interpretative theories of delusion, the first of which—presented by Westphal[9]—argues that we should not speak of a veritable primary delusional experience and that all delusional ideas are derivative. According to Westphal the point of departure is the awareness of an alteration in personality from which delusional ideas derive secondarily. Jaspers notes, however, that if this serves to understand paranoid developments and secondary delusional ideas in general, it does not regard the basics of veritable delusion. We can say as much for the derivation of delusional ideas from affect, for example from mistrust. The second interpretative theory holds that the cause—or the condition—of delusion is a weakness of intelligence (*Intelligenzschwäche*): but Jaspers observes that the paranoiac is no less intelligent than the healthy person, and his critical facility is not obliterated but only "put into the service of the delusion" (97). This means that what delusion is, and what distinguishes it from a healthy mind, remains to be identified. In reality, Jaspers says, "We have to assume some specific alteration in psychic function, not a failure of intelligence," is at the basis of the delusional belief. It is therefore necessary to analyze these primary delusional experiences phenomenologically.

Sensations, experiences, *Stimmungen*, and awarenesses emerge in the patient:

> "Something is going on; do tell me what on earth is going on," as one patient of Sandberg[10] said to her husband. When he asked what she thought was going on, the patient said, "How do I know, but I'm certain *something is going on*." Patients feel uncanny[11] and that there is something suspicious afoot. Everything gets a *new meaning*. The environment is somehow different—not to a gross degree—perception is unaltered in itself but there is some change which envelops everything with a subtle, pervasive and strangely uncertain light. A living-room which formerly was felt as neutral or friendly now becomes dominated by some indefinable atmosphere. Something is in the air which the patient cannot account for, a distrustful, uncomfortable, uncanny tension invades him (Sandberg). [. . .] [W]ith this delusional atmosphere we always find an "objective something" there, even though quite vague, a something which lays the seed of objective validity. This general delusional atmosphere with all of its vagueness of content must be unbearable. Patients obviously suffer terribly under it and to reach some definite idea at last is like being relieved from some enormous burden. Patients feel "as if they have lost grip on things, they feel gross uncertainty which drives them instinctively to look for some fixed point to which they can cling. The achievement of this brings strength and comfort, and it is brought about only by forming an idea, as happens with healthy people in analogous circumstances. Whenever we find ourselves depressed, fearful or at a loss, the sudden

clear consciousness of something, whether false or true, immediately
has a soothing effect. As judgment gains in clarity, the feelings loosed
by the situation will (ceteris paribus) dwindle in their force. Conversely
no dread is worse than that of danger unknown" (Hagen[12]). Experiences
such as these give rise to convictions of persecution, of having committed
crime, of being accused, or by contrast, of some golden age, transfigura-
tion, sanctification, etc. (98)

Let us now try to imagine what the psychological significance is of
this delusional experience of reality in which the environment offers *a
world of new meanings*. All thinking is a thinking about meanings. [. . .]
Perceptions are never mechanical responses to sense-stimuli; there is
always at the same time a perception of meaning. A house is there for
people to inhabit; people in the streets are following their own pursuits.
If I see a knife, I see a tool for cutting. If I look at an unfamiliar tool from
another culture, I may not see its precise meaning but I can appreciate
it as a meaningfully shaped object. We may not be explicitly conscious
of the interpretations we make when we perceive but nevertheless they
are always present. Now, *the experiences of primary delusion are analogous to this seeing of meaning*, but the awareness of meaning undergoes
a radical transformation. There is an immediate, intrusive knowledge
of the meaning and it is this which is itself the delusional experience.
If we distinguish the different sense-data in which meaning of this sort
can be experienced, we can speak of delusional perception, delusional
ideas, delusional memories, delusional awarenesses etc. In fact there is
no kind of experience with a known object which we could not link with
the word "delusion" provided that at the level of meaning, awareness of
meaning has become this experience of primary delusion (Kurt Schneider, G. Schmidt).[13] (99)

Among delusional experiences (*Wahnerlebnisse*), Jaspers distinguishes
delusional perceptions, delusional representations (*Wahnvorstellungen*),
and delusional awarenesses (*Wahnbewusstheiten*). Delusional perceptions
range from experiences of unclear meanings to clear delusions of observation and relation. Things suddenly begin to signify something that is
suddenly different. For example, men in the street dressed in uniform are
"Spanish soldiers." Another uniform: "Turkish soldiers." All soldiers from
all armies are thronging the streets. This delusion appeared during the war
of 1914. Another man seen in the street, with a dark jacket, is the resurrection of Archduke Ferdinand. In these perceptions, fully normal in terms of
sensory perception, the delusional meaning is immediately experienced.

In other cases a clearly expressed delusional meaning is not yet present:
"Objects, persons and events are simply eerie,[14] horrifying, peculiar, or

they seem remarkable, mystifying, transcendental. Objects and events signify something, but nothing definite."

> A patient noticed the waiter in the coffee-house; he skipped past him so quickly and uncannily. He noticed odd behaviour in an acquaintance which made him feel strange; everything in the street was so different, something was bound to be happening. A passer-by gave such a penetrating glance, he could be a detective. Then there was a dog who seemed hypnotized, a kind of mechanical dog made of rubber. There was such a lot of people walking about, something must surely be starting up against the patient. All the umbrellas were rattling as if some apparatus was hidden inside them. (100)

But the alteration, in the preceding dysphoric case, can also take on euphoric features that mix together with the dysphoric ones:

> In other cases patients have noticed transfigured faces, unusual beauty of landscape, brilliant golden hair, overpowering glory of the sunlight.[. . .] [A] new era is starting. Lights are bewitched and will not burn; something is behind it. A child is like a monkey; people are mixed up, they are imposters all, they all look unnatural. The house-signs are crooked, the streets look suspicious; everything happens so quickly. The dog scratches oddly at the door. "I noticed particularly" is the constant remark these patients make, though they cannot say why they take such particular note of things nor what it is they suspect. (100)

In delusions of reference, the perceived contents are experienced in an evident relation to the patient himself, they are allusive. The phrases of interlocutors, even the most banal ones, allude to something else that regards the patient. Nothing is coincidental, but is aimed at the patient.
Jaspers, Changes.

> At the beginning of a mental illness some persons undergo an uncanny feeling of change (as if they had been bewitched, enchanted or there may be an increase in sexuality, etc.) All of this adds to the awareness of impending madness. It is difficult to say what this awareness really is. It is the outcome of numerous, individual feelings, not a mere judgment but a real experience.
> A woman who suffered from periodic insanity described how this feeling arose even when the psychosis itself was not at all unpleasant. "The illness itself does not frighten me but only the moment when I begin the experience again and do not know how it will turn out." Another patient

who suffered from brief, florid psychoses wrote: "The most frightening moments of my life are when I pass from my conscious state into confusion and the anxiety which goes with it." Referring to prodromal phenomena, the same patient said: "The uncanny aspect of the illness is that its victim cannot control the passage from healthy to morbid activity." (415)

Jaspers distinguishes the primary delusional experience, underivable from other psychological elements, from the delusional perception that concerns the recognition of a particular meaning of the world. *Wahnstimmung* is the experience of an unclear, but radical, change that intervenes in perceiving and in the perceived; *Wahrnehmung* is already the interpretation of the sense of that change.[15] The delusional state experiences that "there is something"; the delusional perception is already oriented to establishing what exactly it is. At times the preamble does not occur, and the delusional idea bursts forth "already fully armed." Moreover, this delusional perceiving presents very different nosological aspects and meanings if it is based on elaborations that are very near to real experience and in immediate relation with it; if it instead is based on metaphorical "as ifs" in which cultural influences, education, or one's environment play a variable role; or finally, based on an unengaged, random, coarse and fleeting formulation of discourse.

As much as they may be appropriate in the sphere of the psychiatrist's professional activity, these distinctions nonetheless present the danger of losing the organic connection among phenomena for which precisely that connection is important when a cultural-historical and religious-historical perspective prevails. While from a clinical point of view, for diagnostic and therapeutic ends it is necessary to highlight the difference between delusional state and delusional perception, and between this and that modality of delusional perception (in particular, between this and that modality of "the end of the world"), in an analytical-existential perspective the accent falls on the generic unity of all psychopathological phenomena, on the logical generating of distinctions in which such a phenomenology gets articulated starting from a fundamental hermeneutic principle: the crisis of presence and the restraint on **cultural reintegration**. Since the risk of crisis is no stranger to the healthy man, comprehension is determined as the relationship between the victorious and the defeated in the same battle: aside from the document of clinical experience, to track down this genetic unity of comprehension, we need the assistance of the internal document of the common human drama; otherwise, the accumulation of clinical data turns out to be unproductive for that very understanding (think of the chaos of psychiatric classifications, of that sort of "indifference" [*qualunquismo*] of distinguishing that so often neglects fundamental distinctions and arbitrarily unifies very different things!).

1.3. Beyond the "vague" phase of alteration of meaning (there is something) and feeling unsettled in a world that is getting alienated from its domestic meanings, that is losing the foundation of "domesticity" within which it is possible to face even those things that one does not yet know what they are, the moment of perceived alteration gets logically delineated with the following delusional features:

(a) The alteration has an extraordinarily weighty meaning for the person experiencing it; it indicates something regarding the experiencer in a direct and radical way (*tua res agitur*);[16] at the alteration's center is the person having the experience.

(b) The alteration is perceived in the most banal occurrence of daily life: the reflection of the sun in the street, some lines of a newspaper, some chairs placed in a row, and so forth are no longer the usual reflection of the sun, the usual printed lines in which a newspaper is written, the chairs placed in a row, and so on, but in an obscure way they allude to something, as though a semantic aura were afflicting them; they go beyond their domestic and obvious limits to become indicators of an indeterminate beyond. And furthermore: things lose their usual practicability, their memory of possible behaviors for us (the reflection of the sun on the street that indicates the behavior of a sunny day, or good-weather days, or a bothersome heatwave, and so forth: the lines of a newspaper that get read or skipped over on the basis of whether or not the news interests us; the chairs lined up that are necessary to avoid running into or that indicated the possibility of sitting down, and so forth); and because of this emptying out of their everyday and obvious practicability, they start to go beyond in an incoherent way. Things are *too* semantic.

(c) Perceived in the most banal everyday occurrence, since it is the collapse of the beyond of the obvious practicability of things, the alteration defines their strangeness and *Unheimlichkeit* in the sense of their being *too little* (artificiality, theatricality, lethal stiffness, mechanicalness, insubstantiality, flaccidity, loss of the resistance— manageable and at hand—that renders them practicable in the horizon of possible practicable projects).

(d) Even if it takes a cue from this or that extremely obvious or banal thing, the alteration perceived in overall everyday occurrence tends to take on a cosmic significance precisely because this or that is not in question as such, but their being signs of an alteration that affects the **worldly** perceivable in its entirety. "I went into a café and there were three white tables; it seemed to me that this might mean the end of the world" (Mayer-Gross, *Clinical Psychiatry* [London: Cassel, 1954], 238).[17]

(e) Given the catastrophic-cosmic nature of the alteration that strikes perceived things along the whole gamut of perception, we can understand how perceptions of day and night, heaven and earth, the sun and the sky take on a particular significance of catastrophic alteration: in other words, the most remote backdrop to cultural domesticity (the regularity of nature), the backdrop through which other, more circumscribed domesticities take shape (the street, the houses, people, one's own home, family members, etc.). Daylight has lost intensity, the sun is weak and does not set, stars fall from the sky, the earth is flat, the air that we breathe becomes an unbreathable gas, plant life withers, the rain is a deluge: everything exceeds its order, precipitating to its own means of destruction, incompatible with existing.

(f) The too much or too little of the perceived things along the whole gamut of perception ensure that every perceived thing contains a scandal: it is something incoherent, out of place, a futile search for the beyond in the emptiness of the domestic beyond. Because of this futile search for its beyond, every perceived thing is in tension: its obscure semantic aura is experienced as a catastrophic wait, the universe is a universe in tension. In the futile search for its beyond, each perceived thing can become anything whatsoever; it is chaotically all allusive: the beyond of every perceived thing wanders in search of its horizon of perceptibility. This wandering gets deformed into the monstrous: it becomes maliciously alive with a life that is full of hostile intentions, of secret intrigues, of deceitful traps, of destructive intentions, in a continuous hinting at the perceiver as the center to which the chaotic message of the "ending" is inexorably addressed.[18]

(g) The too much or too little of the perceived things along the whole gamut of perception is—as stated—a manifestation of the collapse of the beyond: a collapse that loses the domestic-cultural beyond (where every perceived thing is too little and maliciously weak) and that seeks its beyond in vain (where each perceived thing is too much, is maliciously strong). Now, the loss of the transcendental ethos, with its loyalty and its cultural initiatives, with its "backdrop" of domesticity taken on again and again in the here and now of a valorizing decision-making, with its living intersubjectivity of a unique projecting, not only places the world at risk but also triggers the obliteration of the very leeway of valorizing presentification: the leeway with regard to which the world exists and that forms being-in-the-world. The catastrophe of the world and the catastrophe of being-there in it form a single catastrophe that—in this perspective—is manifested above all as a loss of *distance* with respect to an object, resting "on this side" of intentional presentification in regard to a "beyond" of the intended object. In this loss of distance the world is experienced as too far or too near to presence, a world lost in a radical, unreachable alterity or menacingly irrupting within presence itself. Moreover, presence is felt either to be detached from the world, isolated, without a possible relation; or else it is flowing into the world without being able to hold itself back in any privacy. With regard to the presence-world relationship, the too much/too little antinomy gets repeated here, threatening the whole gamut of possible within-the-world perception in the sense that one's own corporeality at times becomes a too hard barrier, separating from the world without the possibility of meaningful communication, and at times it becomes a too weak barrier, chaotically penetrated by the worldly, without respect for a private sphere preserved as such. In other words, either the world distances itself, leaving an empty inwardness, one that is highly private, incommunicable, frozen, sunk into a miserable solitude; or else it irrupts without leaving leeway for the slightest possibility of recovery, appropriation or valorizing choice. Or further: the public character of being-in-the-world either retires, burning bridges behind it, or else it attacks the presence in its last fragment of intimate self-possession.

(h) In the context of the perception of "self" or "oneself," the catastrophe of the ethos of transcendence is manifested in the feelings of depersonalization, the loss of privacy in the experience of the publicness of one's thoughts and movements of the soul, dispossession, being-acted-upon (too little), or emptily making oneself commensurate to the magnitude of the risk (magical power, delusions of grandeur, etc.) (too much).

(i) The too much or too little semanticity that threatens the whole gamut of possible within-the-world perception; the too much or too little distance of the world with respect to the presence and of the presence with respect to the world; the too much or too little semanticity of presence and the nature of the insolubility of the antimony that presides over this vicissitude—all this is coherently

connected to the syndrome of refusing to become or act (the catatonic syndrome), to the paradox of the "no" that opposes every
"yes," to mirrorlike imitation, to echolalia, to stereotypies.[19]

1.4. Power.
Lévi-Strauss (in his introduction to the collection of writings by Marcel
Mauss, *Sociologie et anthropologie*, 2nd ed. [1950; Paris: Presses universitaires de France, 1960, 1950], xlix, l) mentions an interpretation of *mana*[20]
and more or less similar representations:

> [I]n man's effort to understand the world, he always disposes of a surplus
> of signification (which he shares out among things in accordance with
> the laws of the symbolic thinking which it is the task of ethnologists and
> linguists to study). That distribution of a supplementary ration—if I can
> express myself thus—is absolutely necessary to ensure that, in total, the
> available signifier and the mapped-out signified may remain in the rela-
> tionship of complementarity which is the very condition of the exercise
> of symbolic thinking. I believe that notions of the *mana* type, however
> diverse they may be, and viewed in terms of their most general function
> (which, as we have seen, has not vanished from our mentality and our form
> of society) represent nothing more or less than that *floating signifier* which
> is the disability of all finite thought (but also the surety of all art, all poetry,
> every mythic and aesthetic invention), even though scientific knowledge
> is capable, if not of staunching it, at least of controlling it partially. . . . In
> other words . . . I see in *mana, wakan, orenda*, and other notions of the
> same type, the conscious expression of a *semantic function*, whose role is
> to enable symbolic thinking to operate despite the contradiction inherent
> in it. That explains the apparently insoluble antinomies attaching to the no-
> tion of mana, which struck ethnographers so forcibly, and on which Mauss
> shed light: force and action, quality and state; substantive, adjective and
> verb all at once; abstract and concrete; omnipresent and localized. And,
> indeed, *mana* is all those things together, but is that not precisely because it
> is none of those things, but a simple form, or to be more accurate, a symbol
> in its pure state, therefore liable to take on any symbolic whatever? In the
> system of symbols which makes up any cosmology, it would just be a *zero
> symbolic value*, that is, a sign marking the necessity of a supplementary
> symbolic content over and above that which the signified already contains,
> which can be any value at all, provided it is still part of the available reserve
> and is not already, as the phonologists say, a term in a set."[21]

This *floating semanticity* that goes beyond the single signified and is
the basis of notions like *mana*, this *semantic aura* of perceiving beyond

perceptible and denominable spheres nonetheless remains a simple ascertainment in Lévi-Strauss's interpretation, or at least the analysis stops at a superficial level. The floating signifier and the semantic aura of the perceived thing find their expression in *mana*; but *mana, wakan, orenda*, and so forth, establish a horizon of possible representations that—because of its socialized, interpersonal, and culturally conditioned character and open to value—carries out the function of recovery and reversal with regard to the universe in tension of crisis. The floating semanticity of *mana* circumscribes a horizon that reverses the perceptive spheres that risk going beyond incoherent motion: the semantic aura of *mana* indicates the cultural task of transforming the individual, incoherent, and incommunicable crisis into an interpersonal and public reintegration. Through *mana* the universe "goes beyond," getting accepted in its "beyondness," but this "beyondness" is disclosed to an order of relations that is valid for everyone, prescribing the ways of restoring being-in-the-world.

1.5. Jaspers, *Allgemeine Psychopathologie*, 280ff.[22]
[. . .]

The concrete world of the individual always develops *historically*. It stands within a tradition and always exists in society and community. Therefore any inquiry into how a human being lives in the world and how different he may find it must be of an historical and social nature. We are presented with a wealth of complicated structures which we may call after the particular human manifestation prevailing at the time: e.g. man as a creature of instinct, economic man, man in power, professional man, the worker, the peasant, etc. The world which objectively exists provides the space in which the individual takes his ways and byways and is the material from which he currently builds his personal world.

It is not the task of psychopathology to investigate all this but it is important for any psychopathologist to have some orientation here and be factually informed about the concrete worlds from which his patients come.[23]

The question arises whether there may be transformations in a *psychopathological* sense, whether there are *specific "private worlds"* in the case of psychotics and psychopaths (personality disorders). Or whether all "abnormal" worlds are only a particular realization of forms and components which are essentially universal and historical and have nothing to do with being sick or well. In this case it is only the mode of their realization, and the singular way in which they are experienced, which could be called abnormal. (280–81)

Jaspers reports the interest that the study of these "abnormal worlds" holds, and specifically, the identification of their *structure*, which in a unitary way allows us to understand behaviors, actions, modes of thinking, and opinions that derive from those "transformations" of the world. Nonetheless the *genetic* problem of these abnormal worlds remains underappreciated. Jaspers then refers to the problem of the structures of psychotics' abnormal worlds, which was outlined by von Gebsattel, E. Straus, von Baeyer, L. Binswanger, and Kunz. For the genetic-constructive part, compare page 540.

Two distinctions have to be made: there is the constant metamorphosis of all human worlds through the processes of culture, the *historical manifold*, and there is an *unhistorical variety* of psychopathological possibilities. L. Binswanger reminds us that Hegel's thesis still holds: "Individuality is its own world." But we can investigate it either as a cultural, historical phenomenon or as a psychological or psychopathological one. Whether and when psychopathological world-pictures, in themselves unhistorical, have had any relevance for history and culture is a matter for historical research but no unequivocal answers have yet been found. (280–81)

When does a "personal world" become abnormal? The normal world is characterized by objective human ties, a mutuality in which all men meet; it is a satisfying world, a world that brings increase and makes life unfold. We can speak of an abnormal personal world: (1) if it springs from a specific type of event, which can be empirically recognized, e.g. the schizophrenic process, even though the products of this world may be thoroughly positive. (2) if it divides people instead of bringing them together. (3) if it narrows down progressively, atrophies, no longer has any expanding or heightening effects. (4) if it dies away altogether, and the feeling vanishes of "being in secure possession of spiritual and goods, the firm ground in which the personality roots and from which it gains the heart to achieve its potentialities and enjoy its growth" (Ideler).[24] (281–82)

[W]hy is schizophrenia in its initial stages so often (though not in the majority of cases) a process of cosmic, religious or metaphysical revelation? It is an extremely impressive fact: this exhibition of fine and subtle understanding, this impossible, shattering piano-performance, this masterly creativity (van Gogh, Hölderlin), these peculiar experiences of the end of the world or the creation of fresh ones, these spiritual revelations and this grim daily struggle in the transitional periods between health and collapse. Such experiences cannot be grasped simply in terms of the psychosis which is sweeping the victim out of his familiar world, an objective symbol as it were of the radical, destructive event attacking him. Even if we speak of existence or the psyche as disintegrating, we are still only using analogies. We observe that a new world has come into being and so far that is the only fact we have. (284)

2. It Is Necessary to Begin with the Ethos of Transcendence

2.1. Observations.

In the cultural-historical perspective of the subject of the end of the world and eschaton as salvation, it is first of all necessary to analyze the end or collapse as a psychopathological risk. The psychopathological document of the end and collapse holds a unique methodological value of laying bare such a risk in this extreme and exasperated form so as to better shed light—through the force of contrast and through polar opposition—on those cultural reintegrations, those variously religious symbols, that have fought against this risk and that—if in extremely mediated ways—have redisclosed the signifying and practicable world. As Ey says, "The miracle of psychic life is precisely that bringing madness within us, deep within us, immanent in our nature, we do not abandon ourselves to it" (263n31 list[25]). And he says further: "Between the physical and the moral, there is life" (74); "Psychism . . . envelops and contains the organism from which it emanates and which it exceeds" (75); "It is necessary to see in the organism as a form of existence not only an architecture but a becoming, a movement that makes us pass from the order of vitality to that of humanity" (157). Elsewhere he appeals to Janet's concept of psychological tension (179ff.) and defines psychiatry as a pathology of freedom (77). Now, in this tension, this psychism that exceeds the organic, this movement that goes from **vitality** to humanity, this force that can falter (Janet's *la force et la faiblesse psychologiques*) is not life, the *élan vital*, as we might seem to deduce from some of the author's passages (between the physical and the moral there is life, etc.), but the ethos of transcendence, the primordial and underivable task that actually makes the order of vitality pass to that of humanity, of the intersubjective valorization of life. Life as such is incapable of distancing itself from itself by transcending into culture: the transcending energy that founds humanity is thus in a primordial *élan moral* without which the vital basis itself, individuals as bodies, could not subsist intact as individual human bodies. The collapse of this impulse—whatever may be the hereditary or acquired somatic events that can enter into conditioning when we consider this loss from a medical-operative perspective—is that pathology of freedom of which Ey speaks: the retreat of the power of transcendence for the whole gamut of the valorizable, the catastrophe of the valorizing impulse.

Psychopathological states as a movement of dissolution of existing functions and as the freeing up of underlying elements (161); the conception of a "force" or a system of forces organized through time that, wavering, entail the various forms of mental regressions (170), and so forth: these only have an illusory interpretative meaning if we do not start from the ethos of transcendence, from an analysis of intersubjective valorization as foundational for humanity, and from a cultural-historical appreciation of the dominant levels of valorization and the corresponding risks of regression, wavering, of collapse. Here we see the positive element represented by cultural relativism and ethnopsychiatry precisely in the recommendation to judge integration and disintegration within a culture and not on the basis of an abstract model of "human nature" inferred from contemporary Western civilization and dogmatically held to be valid for all possible cultures. The danger of the concept of structure is that a Parisian or Melanesian youth, or one from ancient Greece, the primitive adult, the neurotic and the psychotic from the Viennese bourgeoisie, and the illiterate peasant from Southern Italy, and again—from Moreau to Ey—dream and mental illness (and even the dreaming of the contemporary, cultured European and the dreaming of the Australian Aranda, etc.) are removed from their cultural-historical context, equated and confused in a single structure that makes us lose the exact sense of their respective experiences, their dynamic-integrating or regressive-pathological character.

Integration and regression: but with respect to what? To measure both, it is necessary for there to be a conception of what permanently belongs to humankind and to its cultural power in every era and in every place as well as an evaluation of the concrete cultural solutions that have taken place in human history: in other words, we need a historical philosophy of culture.

2.2. According to Ey, page 170,[26] melancholy (like mania) constitutes a first degree of dissolution of consciousness since it is a drama of the moral consciousness. In my perspective melancholy is established first and foremost as a monstrous, radical, unmotivated guilt that extends along the whole gamut of the practicable, and that because of this extending converts the practicable into the impracticable. The problem is nonetheless this: what guilt does the melancholic bear without knowing it? The only satisfactory reply is this: the melancholic does not bear guilt for this or that (the delusional motives that emerge in consciousness are secondary) but for living the collapse of the ethos of transcendence, of being conquered by the overturning of his duty-to-be-in-the-world, of not ever being able to place himself, in any moment of living, as a center for decision and choice according to intersubjective values. Precisely because the duty-to-be-in-the-world according to such values grounds both the being-there and the world, the risk of not being able to be there in any possible world (i.e., in no world that is worth it) grounds the *radical guilt*, necessarily unmotivated because it consists in not being able to give motives that disclose values. This means that the melancholic consciousness is inherently destined to finding only artificial reasons for its own melancholy, precisely because it is, intrinsically, a loss of reason on every front of the reasonable. It bears the guilt of this loss; it is this losing oneself as a pure guilt that coincides with life, which is the collapse of the ethos of transcendence that grieves over its own collapse and never being able to halt the catastrophe with the buttress of a single authentic motive.

Just as in melancholy one experiences the collapse of the ethos of transcendence as a monstrous and unmotivated guilt of moral nonreason along the whole gamut of the morally reasonable, in experiences ranging from derealization to the end of the world, that collapse is manifested as a catastrophe of **entities within-the-world**: that is, as a disintegration of the communitarian project of things at hand. It is necessary to judge mania and melancholy within the context of the catastrophe of the duty-to-be-in-the-world, and schizophrenia in that of the catastrophe of the world.

Being-acted-upon and radical alienation (*Unheimlichkeit*, the **ganz Andere**) from what is acting upon one make up the two fundamental moments of the experience of alienation. This experience reflects the collapse of the ethos of valorizing transcendence: a collapse that takes place along the whole gamut of the valorizable and that also involves that inaugural valorization that is the communitarian project of things at hand (the entities within-the-world, their obvious worldhood, one's own body, the unfolding of psychic life in affects, volitions, thoughts). Experiences of derealization and depersonalization germinate in this soil. But in this soil all of the other pathological experiences also germinate: the radical guilt of this collapse of the ethos, and diametrically opposed, empty transcendence, the secondment of the total permissiveness unleashed by this emptying out of transcendence: feeling oneself to be the object of conspiracies, scheming, hexes, and so forth, or sheltering oneself from dangers of this sort through an artificial exaggeration of the person according to a model of absolute and definitive grandeur or through the effort to evade radically the historicity of becoming and the choices that such historicity entails; and so forth.

2.3. Ethos of transcendence = duty-to-be-in-the-world.

The fact that Dasein is *in-der-Welt-sein* is a fundamental theme in Heideggerian existentialism. But *being-there* as being-in-the-world refers to the true transcendental condition of the *duty*-to-be-in-the-world. Nevertheless, presence is thinkable inasmuch as it unleashes presentifying energy, the valorizing emerging of the immediacy of life. This means that precisely this energy, this "beyond," constitutes the true transcendental condition of existence. The worldhood of being-there relates to the duty-to-be in worldhood, to the duty-to-be according to a communitarian **project** of being, according to distinct ways of projecting and intersubjectivity. Humankind is always *inside* the need to transcend and in the distinct ways of this transcending: only through valorizing transcendence does human existence establish itself and find itself as a presence in the world; experience situations and tasks; found a cultural order, participating in it and modifying it. It is never given to humanity to transcend this very energy of transcendence, which operates in it whether or not it is aware of it, whether it recognizes it as such or not: humankind can only exercise it by redisclosing itself again and again to its imperative or variously suffer its crisis, up to the point of obliteration that, for the individual, is madness or death, and for communities, decline or collapse of their vision of the practicability of the world. But whether this energy laboriously opens the way to its impulse or collapses back on itself, this unfolding and risk of collapse always take place *within* it; they are part of its internal dialectic without it ever being able to skip over itself or reach a "nature" per se before any human valorization—or to "pure spirit," according to an ultimate and definitive transcendence. This nontranscending energy of intersubjective, valorizing transcendence is quintessentially transcendental—that is, it is the ultimate and underivable condition of thinkability and practicability of existing. As it time and again calls to going beyond the immediacy of living, it is not *élan vital*, but ethos that is so hardly reducible to biological fact that the biological conditioning makes its unfolding perceptible inside, not outside, and prior. Furthermore, it by no means exhausts itself in cultural-historical mores, in customs, in individual "morals," in this or that ethic; but mores, customs, individual morals or ethics all proceed from the way and the limits within which the ethos creates awareness of itself and exercises itself in historic morals. Language, political life, moral life, art and science, philosophy, mythical-ritual symbolism in religious life—all proceed from this ethos. Anthropology is only the systematic awareness of this ethos, the definition of the distinct modes of its historical manifestation; the identification, in the transcendence of transcending, of the coherences that preside over single ways of the beyond; of what belongs to the universal structure of existence and what instead refers solely to individual, transient cultural-historical formations.

[...]

Background domesticity; horizon of domesticating practicability; presentifying emergence of the existing valorization repeating itself again and again, though without ever exhausting the ideal totality of being: these three moments form the concrete articulating of the ethos of transcendence in life. The presentifying emergence takes place in the domesticity of a background: in other words, in the assumption of an obvious givenness, preserved in anonymity, and yet it is not problematic precisely because it is a concretion of pasts or very remote transcendences that were "once" presentifications in the history of an individual, as in that of humanity. In such a background of presentification and cultural domestications that have occurred once and that now figure as an obvious, anonymous, unindividuated given, the current presentification according to value becomes leeway and gives itself a concrete horizon of qualified, practicable domestication. In other words, it emerges according to orientations that are each time hegemonic, according to this or that *telos*. Now, this immense "entrusting to" through "gathering in" begins over and over with the communitarian project of things at hand, in which life itself, "needing this or that . . . ," stands as a human order that produces life, needs, and the means for satisfying needs, and in which loyalty to the handy domestications that have already once occurred acts as a conditioning background to the adaptation of practicable technical traditions, innovation, invention, and so forth, which are concentrating in a certain well-defined current handiness, in various shades of a more or less mechanical and methodical "application."

3. Sociology, Cultural Psychiatry, Ethnopsychiatry

3.1. Sociology and history of psychoses and psychopathologies.

Jaspers, *Allgemeine Psychopathologie*, 709ff.,[27] "The Abnormal Psyche in Society and History (Social and Historical Aspects of the Psychoses and Personality Disorders)."

While somatic medicine deals with humans as natural beings, and therefore the human body as an animal body, psychopathology has to reckon with the fact that besides being natural beings, humans are culturally conditioned beings. There is no doubt that human life as a natural being *inherits* its bodily and psychic dispositions, but as a more properly cultural life it is not heredity, but handed-down *tradition* of society that characterizes human life. Jaspers nonetheless notes that the distinction between natural heredity and cultural tradition is not as clear as we sometimes suppose. First, we should note that tradition is transmitted not only through language but that everything has a language, so to speak, and transmits cultural messages: the instruments we use, a dwelling, ways of working, the landscape, forms of social relations, gestures, attitudes and behaviors, customs and habits, fashions, ceremonial etiquettes, and so forth. Jaspers furthermore recalls the polemics regarding the Jungian collective unconscious as a reserve of myths and symbols common to humankind surfacing in the unconscious of dreaming, psychoses, and in magical and religious beliefs. The historical or biological nature of this phenomenon remains extremely ambiguous: if the collective unconscious is a historical fact—indeed the content of symbols has a historical sense harkening back to a cultural-historical human origin—the problem arises of the biological hereditariness of culturally and historically acquired features. If instead we consider the collective unconscious a biological fact, then in establishing this ahistorical and generically human heritage, we would need to disregard human cultural history. But this is impossible, even if the operation would appear to succeed through the expedient of considering what has actually—inasmuch as it has a significant symbolic content—arisen from a certain cultural-historical conditioning to instead be original, an extreme image, not coming from history. If, finally, we consider the collective unconscious as a name for the material necessities of man, which in several places on Earth can have given rise to—independently of any transmission—identical inventions, instruments, thoughts, and so forth, the discussion is entrusted to the polemic of what belongs to *Elementargedenken* and what instead is due to historical diffusion, and in the last instance the polemic over monogenesis or polygenesis of human cultural life on Earth. However, according to Jaspers, even if it is harder in practice to draw the limits between heredity and tradition than it is conceptually, there is a dual influence that man is subjected to: that of biological heredity and that of cultural tradition. Heredity anchors itself in man no differently from in animals, unconsciously and according to causal necessity, sometimes remaining idle if lacking corresponding environmental stimuli, but becoming visible again after many generations when the environment brings it into play (hereditary relationship is not "forgotten"). What gets historically established instead needs tradition and some degree of appropriation on the part of consciousness; it is not universally human but only historically conditioned, and when it is forgotten and is not memorable through documentary traces, it gets transformed—that is, it is simply lost.

Observations on heredity and tradition.

Humanity is *detachment* from the immediacy of living; this *detaching* is valorizing transcendence, and this transcendence is in turn not transcendable toward mere naturalness of living (abstract nature without the human) or toward fully realized Spirit[28] (the abstract being now delivered from the task of going beyond). This means that the human condition always lies in transcending life in value and that one of these valorizations—the first, inaugural valorization—is that of the communitarian projecting of things at hand within which an inside is constructed in relation to an outside; one's own body in relation to other bodies; a series of strengths and abilities; individual existence in the context of a communitarian world; an institutional order in the production of material goods (the economic order) and in the codification of the communitarian relationship (the social order); and finally, in a science of handiness founded on the practical principle of observation and experiment and on the as-if of the absolute legality of nature.

In this perspective heredity is a practical operational concept that alludes to the moment of natural conditioning, while tradition is an operational concept that alludes to social and cultural conditioning and to the margin of liberty, initiative, choice, of valorizing "transcendence" that tradition leaves the individual:

> The transmission of culture like the entire life of man is accomplished within a community. The individual reaches his fulfilment and finds his place, meaning and field of activity in the community in which he lives. The tensions between himself and the community are one of the understandable sources of his psychic disturbances. Every moment of the day the community is effectively present for every individual. Where the community has become consciously rationalized, organized and has taken a specific shape we speak of society. (710)

Society and culture model the predisposition to psychic pathology as well as single psyches. Social and cultural anamnesis is obviously indispensable. Research on psychopathological phenomena in society and history; the analysis of the importance of psychic abnormality for society, for historical mass phenomena, for the history of culture, for significant individual historical personalities, and so forth. This research has a meaning for a realistic comprehension of humanity as a whole but also for psychopathology in that it indicates the importance of social conditions, the cultural cycle, situations according to type and the onset of abnormal psychic life. The "historical-sociological" horizon (713). As for the methods of this research, alongside the critical methods of the historical material, [Jaspers] considers comparisons of peoples, cultural forms, and population groups. The importance of statistics (713).

The division of psychic disorders according to regions, peoples, cultures; sex, age; town and country; family; religious confessions (denominations); professions and jobs; situations of cultural contact (colonial situation, immigration, etc.); collective situations of crisis (war, epidemics, revolutions, famines).

Abnormal psychic conditions change according to the way spiritual life is conceived. There is a great difference between whether I deem my passionateness to be subject to natural *passiones animae,* or whether I interpret my doing and feeling to evil or sin; whether I think I am exposed to the action of gods and demons, possessed, or whether I believe that other people can harm me magically, hex me, and so forth. "In the same way there are basic differences in the conduct which individuals follow when they try to master their psychic disturbances; this may be variously interpreted as doing penance, attempting a philosophical self-education, engaging in rituals, taking to prayer or seeking initiation into mysteries" (728).

[...]

Comparison between contemporary psychotic states and archaic, primitive, or mythical mentality, and so forth (732ff.):

> The kind of thinking found in a primitive state of consciousness is something essentially different from psychotic disorder. It results from a collective development and serves the actual community, whereas schizophrenic thinking isolates the individual and separates him from the community. The pictorial thinking[29] of the primitive takes place within a cultural community which so far as rational thinking goes is still but little developed; that of the schizophrenic takes place in spite of a preserved capacity for rational thought, in terms of the civilization to which he belongs. Comparison which finds an analogy between primitive people and schizophrenics would only be fruitful if we could use it to demonstrate what is specific not only to the two conditions but also to whatever it is that characterizes every act of pictorial thinking and its content. One would then not only recognize the heterogeneity of the conscious state of the schizophrenic, the primitive and the dreamer—which in any case is quite clear to us—but would also get to know the distinctiveness of the psychic contents and acts. But nothing has been achieved in this respect. Here enumeration of similarities is initially quite impressive but it soon becomes rather boring, particularly as in the given case one always feels at the same time the dissimilarities as well.
>
> Therefore we have to ask: (1) Were schizophrenic experiences a source of primitive notions and ideas? This question cannot be answered. (2) How does primitive thought stand in comparison with that of schizophrenics? It is obviously "healthy" thought and does not have the characteristics of a schizophrenic primary experience or of a schizophrenic psychic event. (3) What is meant by the "re-emergence" of buried archaic images long lost to civilization, of buried myths, symbols, possibilities and powers? (739–40). [According to Japers, this is a problem of highly dubious formulation].

The psychopathological in different cultures (739–40).

3.2. Cultural psychiatry studies mental disorders in relation to their social-cultural conditioning: in other words, in relation to social stratification, occupation, ethnic group, particular communities, the positive or negative influence of the hospital environment in therapeutic processes. Incidentally, in this field of study one has come to describe the problem of the relationship between mental disorders and mythical-ritual symbolism, not in the banal sense commonly accepted in classic psychiatry—that certain mental disorders can variously combine with magical-religious interpretations and with mystical ideologies—but in the sense that in particular cultural conditionings, mythical-ritual symbolism is responsible for a real cathartic, rebalancing, reintegrating—and in the last instance, therapeutic—function. Thus, while in classic psychiatry religious life was of interest only to the extent that certain mythical-ritual symbolisms could take on a psychopathological meaning and they served to depict certain abnormal behaviors that were more or less reducible to the nosological frameworks of Eurocentric psychiatry, in cultural psychiatry the need has begun to be felt to establish in what conditions, within what limits, and above all, through what dynamics mythical-ritual apparatuses perform a normalizing function within the context of particular cultures or subcultures. In this new perspective, a whole host of problems take on importance that in classical psychiatry were totally nonexistent. First, the very concept of normal and abnormal, of psychic order and disorder, is called into question, because if it is true that certain mental illnesses are universal, it is also true that there is a different cultural modeling of the abnormal, and the frameworks of Eurocentric psychiatry are not exactly applicable to all cultures of the ecumene. Second, it has become increasingly clear that in certain non-European cultures or in some European subcultures, in assessing "abnormality" Eurocentric psychiatry has risked misunderstanding what in reality contained a dynamic from crisis to reintegration, from the abnormal to normalization, from disorder to order, if only in terms of cultural relativism. In this way, cultural psychiatry has initiated a revision of nosographic classifications, a widening of diagnostic criteria, and a more unbiased appreciation of therapeutic efficacies that classical psychiatry has tended to deny, or at least neglect, grouping them all in categories of "folk medicine," "superstition," and the like. But above all, cultural psychiatry has felt the need—with the assistance of anthropologists, cultural historians, and social science scholars in general—to return to the problem of the genesis, structure, and functioning of mythical-ritual symbolism. Similarly, anthropologists, cultural historians, and social scientists have realized that in the study of religious life, they cannot limit themselves to the level of normality, since religious life actually fulfills a function of "normalization": this entails the analysis of the abnormal, for which it represents "a normalization apparatus."

Psychic "disorder" is characterized by a disintegrative dynamic in relation to any cultural order or system of intersubjective values. Every culture is called to intersubjectively resolve the problem of detachment from nature, of the protection of conscious life, of the deployment of forms of cultural coherence that stand as rules for that detachment and that protection. And finally, every culture is such to the extent that it assures the possibility of initiatives, innovations, readaptations, or remodeling on the part of single individuals who are more talented than others. Moreover, every culture is constantly threatened—both as a whole and in each of the individuals that take part in it and in every moment of the biographical trajectory of each individual—by the risk of reversing this dynamic, making itself incapable of detachment from nature, the protection of conscious life, the deployment of forms of cultural coherence, and ultimately of an expert intersubjectivity of its proceeding through time.

The struggle between this task and that threat is precisely culture: when it is threatened, it isolates itself, breaks its dialectic nexus with the task, and presents the sign of culture's negation: one has a psychic "disorder." This implies (1) that to judge a behavior as disordered or abnormal, it is necessary for it to be incompatible with any culture whatsoever; (2) that such an ascertainment cannot disregard knowledge of the social-cultural environment in which the behavior in question is taking place, just as it cannot disregard the assessment of a single case in a dynamic sense; (3) it is not possible to separate the "diagnostic" problem from the problem of the reintegrating efficacy of mythical-ritual symbolism; that is, from the problem of the conditioning, limits, and modus operandi of this efficacy.

3.3. Needs.

It is necessary to draw together in an organic unity and give a common discourse to the needs that have recently been expressed in various cultural moments of our era in crisis. First, we need to follow the existentialist current Husserl-Heidegger-Binswanger, in which the concept of "presence" as "being-in-the-world" opens itself to the concept of the "crisis of presence" and the risk of "not-being-in-any-possible-world." Second, we need to keep in mind the problem of method in order to free ourselves from Western ethnocentrisms in the judgment that Western science gives of non-Western cultures, a problem that arises in cultural anthropology and that in ethnopsychiatry (or comparative psychiatry or the cross-cultural study of mental illnesses) takes on particular signifi-cance for the distinction between the psychically normal and abnormal, or for the definition of an anthropological criterion of psychic "risk" in any human culture, and for the culturally conditioned forms that this risk takes on in human cultural history. Third, we need to highlight themes of individual history that psychoanalysis sheds light on, those of social and cultural conditioning of that history, which the American culturalists insist on so much. Fourth, we need to utilize studies of myths, symbol (with an assessment of the limits and needs expressed in Jungianism), ritual, the sacred, and so forth. Finally, it is necessary to give energy, ex-ecution, and unity to all of these topics by appealing to a renewal of the historicist tradition and freeing it from theological vestiges of the "plan" of universal history.

3.4. Normal and abnormal.

The evaluation of psychic normality or abnormality is a historical eval-uation. Indeed, the norm or the deviation from the norm, contact with reality or the loss of this contact, entail in the evaluator an assessment of the history of the individual and knowledge of the social and cultural world in which he is inserted. Only in this way is it possible to penetrate lived behavior, the quality of *Erleben*. There is undoubtedly a fundamental criterion of judgment, and that is the decision if, in the specific case, the presence is moving from the risk of crisis toward reintegration into the level of culture to which it belongs and in the values that flow through this level (in that case, behavior is normal), or if, on the contrary, the movement has inverted: it moves toward the crisis of presence, gradu-ally losing contact with its own individual or group history, with the val-ues (with the reality) of its own society and culture. But to decide about this "inversion" of movement—if it is a matter of regression or progress in transcendence; of detachment from cultural reality or redemption in this reality; the absolutization of the private or the dissolving of the private into the universality of communicable values—it is necessary to grasp the cultural history of the person being evaluated and evaluate the normality or abnormality of individual behavior within this history. In European psychiatry all this has taken place in an implicit way, because in one way or another we already know, or we think we know, what the features of our culture are. But leaving aside the fact that even in European psychiatry evaluation can become much more precise when that implicit knowledge is subjected to methodical verification, in ethnopsychiatry the missing explication of historical knowledge has led to a host of seriously mistaken assessments, as when, for example, shamanism was reduced to Arctic hysteria.

3.5. Types of problems to keep clearly distinct:

> Reports on non-Western, and particularly primitive, medical beliefs, with special reference to beliefs regarding mental illnesses.
> Studies on mental illnesses among non-Western populations on the cultural conditioning of mental illnesses, etc.
> Studies of the relationship between illness, therapy, and cultural reintegration through magical-religious symbolism.

3.6. It is not a matter of "explaining health with illness": an attempt of this sort would already be illness. Instead, it is a matter of understanding health in its concrete reality, that is, in making itself healthy *beyond* the risk of falling ill. In this perspective, the use of psychopathological experiences takes on a significant heuristic value. These lay bare the moment of risk with particular clarity, in that in falling mentally ill, what in the healthy person stands as a risk of a continuous overcoming is transformed into a psychic occurrence characterized by not being able to overcome that risk and by unproductive attempts at defense and reintegration. Psychopathological experiences gain more heuristic value because that concrete dynamic making itself healthy over and over, characterizing health, forms the most protected moment for cultural consciousness immediately engaged in making itself well. As a consequence it feigns an abstract health and leaves aside an equally abstract illness, which would interest only the insane and their specialized doctors, the psychiatrists. This is a double falsehood that introduces a host of misunderstandings, distortions, and mistaken interpretations into anthropology. Furthermore, a whole range of cultural products in which becoming healthy appears to have a specific connection to the risk of falling ill are either nimbly *reduced* to pathological manifestations or are dangerously removed from an awareness of the pathological moments and the healthy ones that struggle with varying outcomes in them. Once, this was the way that mystical states, possessions, and certain aspects of magic tended to be judged, in an essentially pathological perspective (superficial or specialized: from the declamatory *tanto potuit religio suadere malorum*[30] to the various diagnoses of hysteria among mystics, etc.). And furthermore, in a whole movement of cultural life and custom in the contemporary world that seems to be increasingly prominent—politics, literature, visual arts, theater, philosophy—pathological moments are not clearly known as such, lacking any criterion for analysis; hence, much of the pathological passes for healthy, and much of the healthy passes for pathological.

[. . .]

Yet the understanding of psychopathological experiences here does not at all mean dealing with diagnostic, etiological, and therapeutic problems of psychiatry. Such problems are left undecided even if the philosophical and cultural-historical perspective adopted with regard to the theme of the end of the world does not deal with *patients to be treated* but with particular orientations of contemporary culture that, even if they manifest a connection to the pathological, are far from being able to be reduced to it. Psychiatry starts from the model of the healthy in order to treat the ill: the present study moves within the sphere of cultural life, and it uses the pathological to shed light on the very procedure of "getting healthy" that characterizes culture, at least as long as it manages to function.

[. . .]

3.7. The end of the existing world order can be considered a *cultural theme* in the context of determining mythical figurations that make express reference to it, for example as a theme of periodic destructions and regenerations of the world in the context of the myth of eternal return or as a theme of the final catastrophe in the context of a unilinear and irreversible eschatological course of human history. As an explicit cultural theme, the end of an existing world order should be considered a historical product of varying diffusion and significance, and with different meanings: a historical product that the research on cultural apocalypses has the task of analyzing each time in the concreteness of a given society and particular periods. But even before facing any research on cultural apocalypses, it is necessary from the outset to assess the end of the existing world order in its universal meaning of permanent anthropological risk: as a risk of not being able to be-there in any possible world. This second meaning of "end" must, however, now be justified and clarified.

3.8. Danilo Cargnello,[31] "Dal naturalismo psicoanalitico alla fenomenologia antropologica della 'Daseinanalyse,'" in *Filosofia della alienazione e analisi esistenziale*, Archivio di filosofia (Padua: CEDAM, 1961), 127–89.

The investigation of the ways in which human presence reveals itself in its indissoluble globality is a proposition of anthropoanalysis. Thus, it is the study of the different manners of its factual transcendence independently of whether we are dealing with a "healthy" presence or one that is "mentally ill." On the contrary, the healthy-ill antinomy, which is of central necessity in the clinical field, remains entirely extraneous to the interest of anthropoanalyst, who is interested in humankind independently of a judgement of health or "pathology." Precisely because he is a person, even the psychotic cannot avoid projecting himself in a world and remains in any case *weltbildend.*[32] (166)

We should reject this proposition of anthropoanalysis. Presence is worlding, presentification is worlding presentification, intersubjective valorization of life, the primordial ethos of valorizing transcendence. But this ethos is an impulse that is threatened by a collapse, by a radical crisis that allows modes of depresentification and **deworlding** to emerge. Only in relation to a certain cultural-historical world, to the dynamic of its valorizing ethos, is it possible to judge the annihilating temptation that wracks it and of which it—as a cultural-historical world—represents a continuously renewing redemption. Therefore, anthropoanalysis cannot disregard cultural-historical and ethnopsychiatric analyses, and it cannot avoid the continuous obligation to decide, when faced with a human product or behavior, whether and to what extent a "healing" is achieved that is the cultural valorization of life or whether the "risk" of falling ill appears.

Cultural anthropology, psychoanalysis, existential analysis, and comparative psychopathology all contribute to facing and resolving cultural-historical and religious-historical problems pertinent to the theme of "world ending" in the current Western climate, in apostolic Christianity, and in developing Third World messianic, apocalyptic, and millenaristic movements. If, until today, the psychiatrist has been dealing with the "unhealthy" mind and the cultural historian with the "healthy" mind, today we perceive the need for a common ground of interdisciplinary research, since every "unhealthy" person becomes ill within a society and culture and within the horizon of a certain cultural history, just as every cultural-historical world, every period, and every civilization struggle with varying degrees of success against risks of crisis, and they therefore require an understanding on the historian's part that engages judgment of illness and health. The incoherent gap of competences, methods, and ends between the psychopathologist and the historiographer has neglected the dialectic relationship between mental health and illness, favoring a dualistic imagination of two worlds, one healthy and one ill, according to the boundary marked by neuropsychiatric hospitals and within the limits in which the clinical, diagnostic, and therapeutic relationship between the psychiatrist and patient takes place. Now, the distinction between health and illness, the struggle of health against illness, events of falling ill and recovering, not only takes place beyond these borders and limits but concerns humankind in general: indeed it is inherent in human culture as such and affects all of its historical creations. If culture is the struggle against the radical crisis of the human—in other words, against becoming mentally ill—how can the historian reconstruct cultural life disregarding the meaning this struggle takes on in each case, and how can the psychopathologist understand his patients without a systematic awareness of culture's norms and history?

3.9. "Daseinanalyse."[33]

Taking Heideggerian Dasein as the presence that is *Sein-können* and *Gewesen-sein, Daseinanalysis* (or anthropoanalysis) aims to be the analysis of the ways of this Dasein "independently of whether we are dealing with a healthy presence or one that is ill." In this way, the *in-der-Welt-sein* of presence is analyzed in its various psychopathological modes; in other words, in the "worlds" of psychotics (e.g., the world of the schizophrenic), since the mentally ill person—as a human being—"cannot avoid projecting a world" and therefore remains "a *weltbildend* being." Now, we should note that in following this route, one undoubtedly manages to learn about the world of the psychotic from the analysis of available clinical material. But the structure we obtain confusedly includes the world of the primitive, the mystic, the religious person, the sorcerer, and the poet (or perhaps even the child), and therefore we do not understand the usefulness of the framework: the human possibility resulting from it is totally vague if we group together the healthy and the ill, religious people and children, shamans and poets. Or else, the analysis turns to underlining the differences between the world of the healthy and that of the ill, mystics, children, and so forth, and so it lacks a criterion of distinction, or it needs to borrow it from somewhere else, or it abandons itself to gratuitous and banal affirmations regarding the differences.

[. . .]

In reality, being-in-the-world is identified with the very life of culture, and the "worlds" of psychotics become relatively comprehensible only as an experienced risk of not being able to be in any possible human cultural world. Such "worlds" are anthropologically important in that they denounce a temptation immanent in the cultural order itself, the temptation of annihilating itself: this is a temptation that draws attention to the cultural battle and defines culture itself in its fundamental quality, that of being-in-the-world through the decisions and choices of individuals, of single "presences."

Existential analysis in psychopathology, which has been theorized by Binswanger and Minkowski,[34] aims to study the world in which people suffering from mental alienation live: being ill becomes, in this perspective, a different way of being. But is this contemplation of the structure really legitimate if one neglects, if only temporarily, judgments regarding health and illness, abnormality and the abnormality of humankind? As long as we are talking about a specific cultural-historical world within Western history, from the Greeks to today, and we seek to identify the *Weltanschauung* of Apostolic Christianity, the Middle Ages, or the Renaissance, the attempt appears totally legitimate. Similarly, with the necessary methodological caution, it is legitimate when Western scholars try to reconstruct cultural worlds that do not belong to the development of their own civilization, as is the case, for example, of Vedic India or Confucian China, or the totemism of the Aranda. But when we speak, on the same basis from a structural point of view, of a world of the alienated, we run into a fundamental aporia: while the worlds of the Apostolic Christian, the medieval or Renaissance person, the Vedic Indian or Chinese at the time of Confucius, and the Aranda totemist constitute certain modalities of human cultural life and are effectively "worlds" in which intersubjective communication and the work of humans in society have taken place (so much so that these civilizations have existed), the "world" of alienation presents features that are not compatible with any cultural life and mark the collapse of culture itself as a possibility. This is true for any civilization and any epoch: all have their ill people and all fight in their own way against the risks of an experiencing that gets endlessly privatized and impedes communication. In other words, if being-in-the-world constitutes the norm of presence, the condition of its emerging and engaging itself time and again in the process of presentification, how can the presence that risks not being in any possible cultural world still be called a "world"? And how can we assess how "a" world—the experiencing that arises from one's own historical world getting lost; the connection with one's own culture; the relationship with others, with the cosmos and with oneself; the meaning of action; the disarticulation of the dialectic of time; the radical dispossession of the human—and everything else that makes up the panorama of the psychopathological? The coherence of worldhood is always in the opening to intersubjective meaning, to communicability, to plannability: but the process of deworlding that establishes itself in the psychic "disorder" as such has a coherence only in the sense that the symptoms are organically comprehensible once we admit the fundamental incoherence of not-being-in-the-world: that is, once we suppose worldhood as a constant reference point.

3.10. That "worlds" can be delusional is an error of interpretation that generates numerous misunderstandings. The delusional world has precisely the character of not being a world, of arising from a fundamental experience of deworlding and depresentification. The "delusional world" is delusional precisely because it is lacking cultural communicability, because it isolates the risk or disarticulates the dialectic of risk reintegration. It remains defined by the sense of its dynamic, which is recessive: from the public to the private, more and more private, up to total silence and radical unconsciousness.

The delusional world has its roots in a fundamental experience of deworlding and depresentification and an "autistic effort at reintegration." The term *effort* indicates an unauthentic exertion destined to failure, but the judgment of inauthenticity refers to the autistic, private, socially and culturally nonsignifying nature of the "delusional world." This assessment of inauthenticity, which is "diagnosed," can only take place in relation to the cultural-historical world in which presence participates: it is within this relationship with a world of historically determined values that the negative or positive sense of the exertion of worlding gains prominence. In each specific case, we may be dealing with a private world that takes on a public sense, or a public cultural order that privatizes to the limit of the total incommunicability of **anxiety**, increasingly isolating itself from every effort at reintegration.[35] Which of the two possibilities is, in the specific case, the real one—if it is for example a delusion of religious life that mediates values, of a schizophrenic "end of the world," or the Book of the Apocalypse—is a judgment that can only be cultural-historical, formulated in connection to parameters of a society and epoch. Existential analysis, ethnopsychiatry, ethnology, and historiographic thought all imply domains of knowledge that contribute to formulating the judgment in question, and the limit of each of these domains is manifested when only one of them presumes to judge as if the others did not exist.

In what way is it possible to distinguish the normal from the abnormal in human behavior? For such a distinction it is necessary to analyze the "sense" of the behavior, and this analysis can only take place in relation to the "sense" of universal culture and to the "sense" of the specific civilization in which the behavior in question is historically located. The judgment of normality or abnormality is therefore extremely difficult, since it entails, first, the concept of culture as transcendence of the situation and as transcendence according to values; second, it entails recognition of the values operating in a particular historical civilization. Third, it entails recognition of the dynamic in which the behavior is inserted: that is, if in the given cultural-historical context it means regression or progress, ciphered symptom or open symbol, disintegration toward a private reality or reintegration into social reality, a protective moment that opens the existential crisis to qualified agency; or an attempt at defense that fails, an impulse toward the communication with others or loss in an isolation that becomes increasingly total and incommunicable. Precisely due to the historical subtlety of the judgment of normality, there is a particularly frequent error when recognition concerns the behavior of individuals belonging to civilizations that are foreign to the Euro-American or Western world, as it is called: it is very easy indeed to consider, for example, shamans to be neurotics or psychotics. But in the heart of Western civilization itself errors of judgment are frequent between "true" and "false" mystics, between the ecstasy of a Saint Teresa of Avila[36] and a simple psychic disorder to be variously assessed in a medical setting. Furthermore, the lack of distinction between Western culture and its "peasant" subcultures can induce erroneous evaluations: consider, for example, Apulian tarantism.[37]

We need to pay attention to the fact that, with reference to "sense," the same behavior can appear twice in the same individual: as a symptom of a crisis and as a symbol of reintegration during the regular functioning of a specific cultural institution.

3.11. Delusion of influence.[38]

The delusion of influence's feature of historical inauthenticity, as compared to analogous magical beliefs organically inserted in a specific primitive civilization, seems to me to be evident, and it offers a criterion for distinguishing the illness from concrete forms of cultural life. When Suzanne V., Mme P., the countess of Monté, Chaby, Victor and the other "influenced" persons mentioned by Dumas[39] speak of electricity, Jesuits, or Jews, they are utilizing concepts for the purposes of their delusion that have a completely different history and function in the present society: lacking a tradition that is coherent with their psychic drama, they turn to what, because of a wholly superficial resemblance, seems to simulate such a coherence. Or else they speak of sorcerers, spells, sects of sorcerers, and the like, invoking what, in other times and in other historical environments, constituted an effective tradition that was still alive, publicly accepted and respected. But in this case, the inauthenticity lies in the fact that in the patient's environment, sorcerers, sects, and spells do not make up living tradition, and there is a very lively contrast between the historical reality of this environment, its institutions, possible behaviors, and so forth, and the delusion. The "magical expedition" among the Aranda is a reality an operating institution: the *arungquilta* is an effective institution, and so on: the entire culture is, so to speak, prepared to traditionalize and redeem a certain experience of influence. But if a Milanese businessman faced with an economic setback begins to feel "influenced," for example, by the Jesuits, and he believes himself to be the victim of their magical "expeditions," there is no doubt that it is a matter of a "delusion," because—and only because—it is an anachronistic drama in relation to historical Milan, to the world of its industrialists, and so forth. If instead a

Lucanian peasant woman believes that her breast milk was stolen by her
neighbor, or she believes that she is the victim of the evil eye or binding
(*fascinatura*) and turns to appropriate practices, we can no longer speak
of delusion of influence; because the cultural tradition of her historical
world is still prepared for her experience, it keeps institutions alive that
are suited to battling it.[40] Pathological delusion's "rift" with historical reality arises precisely from its anachronism, and thus its inauthenticity, and
hence also the delusion's tendentially private character, without public
cultural resonance. And precisely from this arises the impossibility of a
cultural redemption from the risk of the delusion, its disintegration in relation to the environment, the impossibility of inserting it into the sphere
of socially acceptable behavior, and so forth.

3.12. The adaptation of reality.

The flaw of theories constructed on the concept of "adaptation to reality" lies in the fact that "reality" is understood in the sense of a naive
reality, as a given order that the object reflects in thought or in which the
subject is organically inserted with action. This naive realism can certainly
suffice for the purposes of the pragmatic doctor, though even in psychotherapy sooner or later one ends up perceiving its limit. But as soon as we
leave the strictly psychiatric sphere and attempt to compare clinical data
with religious-historical data, the realistic philosophy more or less explicitly contained in the expression "adaptation to reality" generates a host
of confusions and especially the impossibility of distinguishing between
delusions and historically defined cultural formations. The resulting absurd consequence is that normal or healthy people as we consider them
in current modern usage represent very rare exceptions in all primitive
civilizations and in all great historical religions; indeed, they do not exist
in more remote stages of human cultural life. Facts of primitive mentality
cataloged in Lévy-Bruhl's vast collection and clinical facts recorded in the
nosographic contexts of psychiatric works all get confused together in
relation to their psychic quality; thus, the conclusion arises that modern
rationalism, taken as the standard of mental health, emerged from the
great collective delusions of past epochs and can be contrasted to current
delusions that guide primitives who are still living in the ecumene.

[. . .]

Every behavior is mentally healthy if it is suited to the historical reality, organically inserted within consciousness in a living, public tradition, and currently executing a specific function within a given cultural
world. What appears in modern France—and is certainly a delusion of
influence—reveals its pathological quality not in the simple feeling of
being "influenced" and in the search for certain influencers but because

in patients' cultural-historical environment their drama does not have a widely recognized and accepted public resonance and corresponding institutions are lacking.

It is not enough, however, to turn to the criterion of cultural coherence with a certain environment to distinguish magical-religious "belief" from delusion. If a Milanese industrialist taking a cue from an economic setback begins to feel malignly influenced by the Company of Jesus, the brusque separation from his cultural environment alone is certainly a sign of a pathological condition. If, however, a Lucanian peasant believes that her breast milk has been stolen through a spell, the participation in a socially widespread tradition and the coherence with a certain cultural level leads us to find it highly probable that the peasant woman in question is not a victim of delusion of influence like the Milanese industrialist. But the diagnostic judgment of "abnormality" and "illness" cannot be held to be valid if we do not consider the "dynamic meaning" that the ideology of influence has in the biography of a single Milanese industrialist or Lucanian peasant woman. If the belief in stolen breast milk becomes the center of all of the Lucanian peasant woman's everyday behavior; if such a belief becomes parasitic and invades her entire psychic life, progressively breaking its relationship with the historical world; if the use of counterspells does not reestablish mental equilibrium but on the contrary contributes to isolating the subject from her environment, multiplies conflicts, and impedes any life of relationship, then we must conclude that it is a mental disorder in the Lucanian environment too. This means that in order to judge mental abnormality, it is necessary to also make reference to the reintegrative efficacy that a given mythical-ritual symbolic horizon actually exercises.

4. In What Conditions Can the Experience of the End of the World Be Defined as Pathological?

4.1. "Can the world end?" Since this is the dominant question in the terror of the end, it constitutes one of the extreme products of alienation, and when it becomes an experience of the end of the world it gets confused with the schizophrenic's *Weltuntergangserlebnis*. "Can the world end?" Someone who asks this and wanders with his terror from one conjecture to another is posing the ending of the world precisely with this; he enters into the course of ending that no longer detains itself in any new beginning; he runs to the end escaping the sole task that is humankind's responsibility, that of being Atlas who holds up the world with his effort and knows that he is holding it up. The world "can" certainly end: but the fact that it ends is its own business, because humanity's only responsibility is to place it in question again and again and begin it again and again.

Humanity cannot play this part, fighting each time as long as it can the battle against the various temptations of an ending that cannot begin again and a beginning that does not include the free assumption of the ending. In order to be productive, thinking about the end of the world must include a life project, it must mediate a struggle against death; indeed, in the last instance it must be this project itself and this struggle itself. The first Christians waited for the Kingdom of God, but if Christian civilization emerged from their wait, this is a result of the fact that Christianity was love, aside from faith and hope: indeed, as we read in the famous hymn of the First Letter to the Corinthians, love was placed even higher than faith and hope. Thinking about the end of the world today in the prophetic cults of colonial and semicolonial peoples is productive to the extent that it mediates the end of an epoch of colonialism and the process of liberation of new national communities. Finally, thinking about the end of the world as an effect of nuclear war is productive today because it mediates the awareness of that extreme form of technicist alienation that is the end of the world as the technical gesture of a hand, as a push-button apocalypse. "And yet, if one day, because of a cosmic catastrophe, no person will be able to begin again because the world is finished?" Well, in ending the world, that last gesture of humankind is an attempt to start all over: this is a death that is worthy of it, and it is worth the lives and works of countless human generations that have succeeded one another on our planet.

4.2. There is nothing pathological about the end of "a" world: on the contrary, it is a beneficial experience, one that is related to the historicity of the human condition. The world of childhood ends, and the one of adolescence begins; the world of adolescence ends, and the one of adulthood begins; the world of adulthood ends, and the one of old age begins. In our society, upon marriage the young couple generally abandons the world of their families and begin a new life that entails the birth of a new world: a mixed sentiment of tenderness and melancholy envelops happiness during the celebration of the new bond and especially in the moment of definitive detachment. When the persons whom we have loved and who were a living, vital part of our world are taken away by death or they are far away because of a separation that is basically equal to death, it seems that not only do they disappear together with their world but also our own, and at times the effort to overcome the crisis of mourning is enormous as well as that of slowly reconstructing a new world without them. An epoch of freedom ends, and one of servitude begins; and as much we might not tolerate the loss of the world in which we were free and death is sought, the crisis is overcome provided that a small margin of recovery remains:

that small, imperceptible margin that, for example, those who managed to survive the German death camps were able to preserve.

The end of "a" world is thus in the order of human cultural history: it is the end of "the" world, as an ongoing experience of the end of any possible world, that constitutes a radical risk.

The animal world "cannot" end, and its "end" is the catastrophe of the species. Humankind, instead, "passes" from one world to another, precisely because it is moral energy that survives the catastrophes of its worlds, regenerating new ones again and again. But this energy is suffused with the risk of collapse, of the experience of the "end of the world" (not "of a world"): such an experience, which signals an end to being there, depresentification, deworlding, the crisis of presence and modes of absence, is *normally* covered in the sense that it must always be covered, and this cover constitutes cultural life. Only in reflection can cultural effort discover the necessity of this negative, eccentric moment that gives importance to one's own exertion and that is laid bare by madness.

4.3. Critical moments of becoming.

Generally, each moment of becoming is new and thus critical for presence. In its extreme, the radical defense of this risk extends indiscriminately to *all* moments of becoming, to *all* of history, consisting in the refusal of any content of the experience, any initiative, any adaptation. It is catatonic stupor, a statue-like immobility, with a characteristic tension that distinguishes it. Another defense is waxy flexibility and specular imitation. By mirroring what happens, one expresses the attempt to transform the process of becoming into the repetition of the identical. A characteristic defense is stereotypy or ritualism, that is, entrusting oneself to the repetition of identical series of acts that are in a certain sense metahistoric. These forms of defense are generally incompatible with civilization. They have a spasmodic and caricature-like character; in other words, they belong to the domain of psychopathology. Culturally meaningful defenses begin when riskiness is socialized, institutionalizing itself in given critical moments of existence, leaving more or less extensive parts of history free—that is, secularly practicable. Culturally meaningful defenses thus begin when the system of guarantees aims at indirectly rendering possible giving way to the risk rather than radically suppressing it: a disclosure—though conditional—to history. Certain historical spheres of reality are disclosed in that one enters into them through the mythical-ritual nexus, that is, since their historicity gets transfigured (in reality, allowed) through the repetition of the identical (the first time, the myth of origins).

All of our strange little rituals—and in general the fragments of ritual behavior—express an elementary way of treating the onset of mental chaos, the collapse of limits, being overwhelmed by becoming. As it gradually flows, the anxiety of becoming accumulates and pressure builds up. And so medicine is a moment of resting in metahistory, an alleviation of becoming thanks to the paradox of suppressing the moment of novelty, in turn thanks to the repetition of the identical or an identical series of acts thanks to ritual and stereotypies. This repetition of the identical, this *momentary killing of history*, this pause or interruption in becoming, generates the representation and experience of a *beginning again from the start*, a history that renews itself, a *second birth*. In any case it constitutes a compensation, a liberation, a relaxation in which one can give himself up to the further course of historical becoming. Naturally the efficacy of a ritual depends on its correct execution, that is, on *exact repetition*, without even the minimum novelty or alteration intruding on it. But the very paradoxicality of the attempt—which is not intrinsically executable (indeed, the attempt to kill history is part of history and generates new history)—and the obscure awareness that one cannot actually get outside of history produce that typical care, that *mania of exactness*, that anxiously induces people to repeat a ritual in the fear that it has not been carried out properly, to have committed errors, and so forth; in other words, to have let that novelty, that individuality intrude that one paradoxically attempts to suppress. The elimination, or at least reduction of this distressing doubt—extremely difficult in the case of the private drama of the modern psychopath—is historically achieved through certain institutions of a public nature and the formation of certain publicly respected traditions (e.g., the ritual is carried out by a special person, and so on).

It is well known how the psychasthenic's ritualistic need often arises in connection with certain critical moments, when the event requires particular *commitment* and *initiative* and in any case underlines a difficult passage. Falling asleep, having to do exams, and so forth leads to a reintensification of the ritualism in psychasthenics. "If I touch this paving stone with my foot three times, everything will go well for me." In other words, this little ritual fragment generates the representation and experience of an interruption of the flow of becoming with the corresponding release of accumulated anxiety, with a supply of energy, and so on.

[...]

4.4. Notes on the *End*.

The end of the world as a psychopathological experience is the experience of a radical risk incompatible with any culture, that is, the experience of not being able to begin any possible world, of not being able to overcome the situation in value. Precisely because one-is-in-the-world as an operative presence, one emerges and maintains oneself in it to the extent that the valorizing energy of transcending the situation is exerted. The risk of not being able to exert this energy, the experience of its collapse takes on the form of a radical risk of final and definitive catastrophe: the impossibility of steering the signifier as a possibility into the signified as a reality is translated in the experience of a charge of indefinite and undefinable semanticity, in a possible that does not find the real, in a force that afflicts every being and in its empty "beyond" reflects the emptiness of the transcending energy. The universe enters into tension, each of its spheres becomes a center of the dissolution of meaning, a dissolution that expands irresistibly and announces itself to more and more spheres: it is the crackling spread of a forest fire and the rapid, inexorable narrowing of the ring of fire around the lost wayfarer. The experience of the universe in agony also takes the form of a universe that is already dead, in which all things are motionless, as if in a coffin, stiffened in their limits without a signified or a beyond: the collapse of transcending energy that valorizes presence is always reflected in this, a collapse that the delusion depicts as an experience of an incoherent beyond, an all-allusive force, a charge of semanticity that distances itself more and more from semanticization. It is a collapse that is an experience of a stiffening of all spheres, of their losing that beyond, that relational horizon, that intersubjective domesticity that makes them spheres of a culturally experienceable world in which tradition and initiative, memories and choices are composed in a lively dialectic.

[. . .]

The world that becomes "motionless," becoming that loses its "fluidity," and life that loses valorization all form a moment experienced by the ethos of transcendence that undergoes an inversion: the other moment is the universe in tension, the all-allusiveness of the various spheres in search of semanticity, the power that afflicts these spheres and pushes them to go beyond their limits in an incoherent way and makes them take part chaotically in everything real and everything possible, ceaselessly, and never offering an effective practicable foothold. The polarity of motionlessness and tension, of rigidity and all-allusive force, of the loss of practicable footholds and incoherent psychomotor discharge: all this bears the sign of radical alterity and being-acted-upon, the sign of alienation in the pathological sense of the world. In all of the experiences arising from it, indeed, precisely what lies at the root of the ego and the world becomes other; there is an obliteration of the valorizing energy of presence, an inability to emerge as presence in the world, and an experiencing of the catastrophic deworlding of the world, its "ending." Precisely because being is always the being-there of valorizing transcendence, the risk of not-being-there experienced in its immediacy gets polarized in the closing up of situations, in their not going beyond themselves, and at the same time, their going beyond in an incoherent way, as blind forces in search of meaning, as roving semanticity charged with everything and nothing and that crushes with its extreme superabundance made up of extreme misery. In this way, in the hardening of the limit and the ciphered tension that afflicts it, the presence that loses itself experiences not being able to transcend its limit in value; it experiences its "death."

The actual experience of the end of the world is pathological: more precisely, the isolation of this experience is more pathological than its complete ending and its becoming the center of disorganization for all psychic life. What gets experienced this way is the loss of overcoming situations and thus not being able to emerge from them as transcending presence. The world then loses meaning, and the entities within-the-world are no longer prolonged in us as being recalling possible behaviors. The entities within-the-world rigidify, they become artificial, their boundaries become too permanent, without a possible "beyond." Or else the consistency of these entities sags and their limits become too flaccid, as if the world were made of rubber. Or the entities are afflicted by an empty "beyond," as an evil force of dissolution: the experience of the universe in tension. Things discharge into each other, becoming all allusive, they transcend in an incoherent way. The catastrophe approaches and surrounds its victim on all sides. Furthermore, even one's psychic life itself becomes a force that discharges, flowing into the world in a diametrically opposed way to the irruption of the world in psychic life.

In the eschatological horizon of myth, the end of the world undergoes an inversion, its risk moves toward reintegration. From the current experience one passes to the imminence or to the indeterminate prospect of the end, thereby giving horizon to expectational behaviors. That is, one passes to the experience of an end that has already taken place and a new world already beginning, giving a horizon to behaviors of the regenerated and to evidence of regeneration provided by these behaviors.

When the universe risks "going beyond," it means that the energy of transcendence is faltering: when one does not manage to "go beyond" the situation and be there as presence by virtue of this "going," the universe begins to lose its character of a practicable situation, and its domestic hither suggests an incoherent beyond, *ganz andere*. To combat this risk, religious life configures a "horizon" of beyond, that is, a socialized level for evoking, provoking and configuring the beyond, and to reappropriate in the form of destinies, tasks, and positive values what in the crisis lies only as the obliteration of presence. Therefore, the beyond of the crisis has its inversion in the beyond of mythical-ritual symbols, and such symbols, when they are operative, represent precisely the method for passing from one beyond to another, in other words, from the universe that goes beyond the beyond that returns to the universe, from the presence that loses itself in the situation to the presence that, even if it is through an intricate path, in the end finds itself and regains possession of itself in the world. So, for example, the crisis of puberty finds its horizon of evocation, discharge, recovery, and valorization in the mythical-ritual symbolism of puberty ceremonies.

Totemism as a socialized, mythical-ritual horizon in a society of hunters and gatherers in which reintegration from the crisis takes place around the animal because it is the center of all of the most critical moments of existence.

The *Weltuntergangserlebnis*—the event of the "catastrophe" (or "collapse") of the world that is a typical experience of incipient schizophrenia, though not specific to it—does not appear determined by the concept of the world nor that of the end: in other words not by the "content" of experience but from the way in which it is experienced (Callieri).[41]

> It is the floating and dreamy mode of existence of a man torn from his domestic world and propelled into a world without horizon or substance; of a man who has no "homeland" or "roots"—neither with regard to being with others nor with regard to being in himself—and who experiences the destruction of his historical existence as the destruction of his sense of worldly life, that is, as the catastrophic collapse of the world. (Storch)[42]

The WUE[43] takes place when the Dasein, being-there in the world, is torn away from "its historical continuity" and is no longer grounded in the ego-here-now; it is strangely insubstantial, fleeting, suspended, fluid (Callieri 1955).

The experience of the world "ending" (giving to "ending" the meaning of a "break down," a "collapse," a "catastrophic annihilation") is pathological if it reflects in the *Erlebnis*, the "break down," the "collapse," the "catastrophic annihilation" of the "there" of being-there. The pathological sense remains defined by the isolation and spread of this experience toward the limit of that nothingness that is the "disappearing world": in other words, the loss of the very possibility of making a world appear and of emerging in it as presence. Naturally the "end" of the world cannot be experienced but only its "ending," its regression toward obliteration, its undoing that reflects the collapse of the energy of presence as a primordial ethos of worlding, and as a primordial will to history (of meanings, values, practicability according to forms of cultural coherence). The pathological gets defined to the extent that this experience of rushing toward an end becomes exclusive, uncontrollable, irresistible, prevailing, private, incommunicable, incapable of configuring itself in a system of signs that exhaust it and of "inverting" through communicable and historically meaningful values of world renewal. The culturally meaningful apocalypse instead defines itself not in order to isolate the *Erlebnis* of ending but because the ending, getting inverted, is a historically meaningful beginning integrated with society and history, a mediator of communicable values. In Christianity this "inversion" is mirrored in the tension between the millenaristic proclamation and love, between the Kingdom of God and the Church, between the experience of a world that enters into "ending" and an "ending" that commands a "beginning," witnessing, being there, to wait preparedly and participate, acting in the context of faith, hope, and love.

In the WUE a moment appears of terrifying obliteration and one of passage to a world that is new, better, absolute, and so forth. But the obliteration constitutes a fundamental, exclusive, prevailing moment, and the passage to the new world takes on the improper character of an exaltation of the very private, empty ego, perhaps borrowing from certain mythical traditions claimed verbally and impoverished of all their real cultural and historical value. If in the moment of annihilation what is about to happen often gets experienced as being an act of meeting "lacking in content" and with feelings of anxiety and foreboding, in the moment of pseudoreintegration the content is artificial precisely because what is getting absolutized is the ego that empties itself of relations with society and history and that exhausts itself in the useless attempt of this absolutization of its own emptiness.

"I constantly feel like I can predict the universe. I am Jesus Christ's wisdom incarnate . . . All these things came into my mind . . . I guided the universe with my mind because I must guide souls: I felt that the Lord has willed that I must save all the souls . . . I must become the Holy Spirit and save all the souls, even the ones damned to hell . . . Even the pope knows who 'I' am," etc.

To all appearances the "contents" of this delusion have been borrowed from Catholic tradition, but in reality the effort of ego expansion only mediates nothingness. What counts is the absolutization of the empty ego that reaffirms its inability to mediate values in the very moment that it extols its proclaimed power.

4.5. The experience of the end of the world in incipient schizophrenia. [. . .]

Psychiatry remains extremely cautious, and justly so, with reference to the end of the world as a delusional theme. Indeed, it denounces the danger of an abstract grouping together, in the genericness of the theme, of processes with different clinical meanings that have distinct pathological dynamics. The end of the world appears in incipient schizophrenia, in oneiroid or confused-oneiroid states with a mystical context; in chronic delusions; in an epileptic hallucinatory state with apocalyptic content; in certain neurotic states; in chronic states with a background of anxiety; in induced psychoses of a collective sort. In each of these nosological frameworks the theme of the end of the world is established in a different way, passing from the primary experience of a radical alteration of the ego and the world to a varied range of secondary interpretations and cultural references, and they therefore present a diagnostic value that is anything but unequivocal. But as much as this caution is justified on the psychiatric level, especially in view of the diagnostic and therapeutic aims, the legitimacy remains of an existential analysis oriented to identifying the experience of the end of the world as a triumphal risk in mental illness and as a risk that opens to reintegration by virtue of eschatologies in culturally conditioned millenarianisms and apocalyptic thinking.

The end of the world is defined as belonging to the physiology of a given cultural life or the psychopathology of a given individual biography according to the dynamic in which it appears: it is a matter of the physiology of cultural life when "the end of the world" denotes a mythical-ritual horizon within which the risk of a private and incommunicable experience, of a world that ends, gets recovered and reintegrated according to intersubjective and communicable values through a practicable leeway for being-there in the world. When, instead, the dynamic moves in the opposite direction, and cultural horizons get disarticulated and collapse, regressing toward a private and incommunicable experience of an "ending" without effective recovery, then we are in the sphere of individual psychopathology. In the former case, judgment is the responsibility of the cultural historian; in the latter, primarily that of the psychiatrist. But due to the organic connection that exists between the end of the world as a risk and the end of the world as recovery, the historian cannot do without the psychiatrist's indications, and the psychiatrist cannot avoid—precisely in his professional practice as diagnostician of mental pathologies—the diligence of a historiographic judgment that reconnects the pathological episode to the individual biography of the patient and the patient's biography to the concreteness of a certain cultural-historical context.

The experience of the world becomes completely other and in deworlding entails a "being-acted-upon," precisely because presence as agency is struck at the roots. And this being-acted-upon also comes to the forefront as a becoming wholly other of the psychic functions themselves, as an alienating of the self to the self, as a dispossession of thinking, wanting, feeling. Worldly becoming not only loses its fluidity, its projectability and practicability, but psychic becoming itself is experienced in the process of getting stuck. Not only do the perceptual spheres enter into a crisis of too much or too little semanticity, but thought itself acquires a dual tension. [. . .]

5. The Religious and the Psychopathological: How to Conceive of Their Interdependence?

5.1. End of the world—schizophrenia and religious psychology. Albrecht Wetzel, "Das Weltuntergangserlebnis in der Schizophrenie," *Zeitschrift für die gesamte Neurologie und Psychiatrie* 78 (1922): 403–28.[44]

Obviously the problems of religious psychology require a further comparative analysis. However, "comparison" is really not the right term for this activity, in touching on the relationship with religious psychology. It is not a matter here of comparing orientations and experiences that, in their quality and their form seemingly appear entirely similar but in reality, with respect to their origin, are of a totally *different* type. What in religious psychology refers to particular tonalities and feelings of a fundamentally euphoric or dysphoric character, to experiences with an apocalyptic accent, to experiences of grace and perdition, no doubt in part belong to the effects of schizophrenia, regardless of other psychopathological connections. Moreover, in this borderland the problem arises of why, very generally, the creation of content in schizophrenic experiences and attitudes has a pronounced tendency to the religious, the cosmic, the metaphysical, to great relations. (410n3, emphasis Wetzel's)

This passage by Wetzel encapsulates the problem—which we are here leaving without a solution and not even correctly formulated—that is at the basis of the planned monograph on the "end of the world" as a cultural symbol. In what does that "totally different" lie that distinguishes the culturally productive apocalyptic experience from the schizophrenic experience of the collapse of the universe? What is the criterion for distinguishing the pathological feature of clinical cases regarding such an experience and the end of the world as it was experienced by apostolic Christianity, by civilizations engaged in the sense of the mythical horizon of eternal return, by the current prophetic movements of colonial or semicolonial peoples, or—finally—the end of the world as it has been presented in Günther Anders's book?[45]

With regard to case 15, Wetzel (425ff.) reproposes the methodological problem of influence, of the coloring and various accentuations of the three stages: experiencing, introspection subsequent to the experiencing, and the reproduction of what is experienced through psychic constitution along with conditionings due to the one's cultural world, education, the orientations of a given epoch, and so forth; or else through general transformations that characterize psychotic life. [. . .]

> Furthermore, it is perhaps also possible to establish types of these particular "colorations." For example, we have the impression that precisely in schizophrenic *Weltuntergangserlebnis* and related psychoses, not only with reference to the way it is displayed but already in the very way it is experienced, we can establish types for patients coming from strongly Catholic places [. . .], and these types differ in a characteristic way from the types coming from the district of Pforzheim, which is interspersed with Protestant churches and which distinguishes itself from other districts from an ethnic point of view.

In this regard, compare note 2 on page 424 dealing with case 13, which refers to the only example of the collection that demonstrates a strong influence from an environment oriented toward millenarian expectation (cult meetings). In the same note, Wetzel mentions the well-known fact of schizophrenias arising in Protestant areas during the cult's common prayer and also in Protestant areas with missions.[46]

[. . .]

The material collected by Wetzel mostly refers to acute and incipient psychoses, in which the end of the world experience appears either in a more or less prolonged form in time or in a totally episodic way. Sometimes, however, it is also a matter of an acute crisis during chronic psychoses (406). In the acute phase of incipient schizophrenia, the experience of the end of the world appears in two principal and opposite types:

(1) End (collapse) of the world as the transition to a newer, grander world.

(2) End (collapse) of the world as a horrifying annihilation.

The first type conceives of the end not as an annihilation of the old world as annihilation per se but as a process in which a new, better, grander world takes the place of the old world in forms that are unfamiliar to date. This first type conceives of the end as the inauguration and introduction to a new world; as "last judgment" with all of its apocalyptic connotations, and it is the most frequent form we encounter in clinical psychiatry. [. . .] The second type is experienced in a pure form as an end, as the horrifying annihilation of the world. Its meaning lies in its psychological relations to sensations and feelings (406–7).

In dysphoric experience the perception of the world does not appear altered; every new impression is registered precisely both in a quantitative and qualitative sense, and yet it is *changed*, everything has become stranger than it ever was before. The designation to which the patient always refers is that everything has become *nondomestic, unsettled* (*unheimlich*). A tormenting uncertainty follows, the suspicion that something is happening of radical importance, something catastrophic and horrifying, and that generally, even if not always, has the patient at its center and has a very specific meaning for his person: "Tua res agitur" (Hagen).[47].

[...]

A Good Friday atmosphere recurs in the patients' descriptions. End-of-the-world motifs can arise in this atmosphere. "It is as if the world were collapsing," and with a greater sense of irreality, "it will be like this when the world collapses." This "as if" is followed by the conjecture that this whole horrifying experience could effectively mean the end of the world and an increasingly specific reinterpretation of all the impressions in this sense.

We are not dealing with a sequence that represents the typical development of the single case. Each nuance can emerge for a longer or only fleeting period, and, starting with each of these modifications, it can follow a path to remission, a retreat to *Verflachung*, to a catatonic condition, to hallucinosis or a concrete delusion, which in reference to its content represents a liberation from the unbearable tension.

From a merely psychological point of view, relief takes place by beating a path to the recognition that the "collapse of the world" means the irruption, the advent of a "New Time." [...] The experience of the end of the world in schizophrenia can be compared:

(a) In its millenarian and eschatological themes, the euphoric experience can be compared to hysteric ecstasies and certain exceptional epileptic states.

(b) The dysphoric experience recalls some experiences of psychasthenic constitution, and especially the nihilistic delusion of the melancholic (the world is gone, it's dead; the patient is gone, he's dead, etc.). The end of the world, when it appears here, is taken on as a symbol, an analogy. (410)

Annihilation in depressions manifests a different tone from that of the end in schizophrenics. It is not an anxiety over what suddenly appears, or experiencing a cosmic catastrophe that is coming about, but rather horror in the face of what already is, terror in the face of the emptiness, exhaustion, and annihilation. A characteristic sense of isolation that we encounter as a feature of the schizophrenic end of the world also appears among such depressives: the patients complain that they have been left in the desert, in ice and snow, and so forth.

Case 5 (415): Obscureness, stiffness, immobility, inertia, collapsing to the ground, earthquake. "I thought an earthquake was coming":

> I read in the Bible that the division is on Earth, and so I thought that *God would come to Earth* to give it a single confession. I saw that it was getting dark, there weren't any clouds. And then, at once everything was so calm, the air no longer moved, the leaves hung inert. Then, when they moved, I thought that there had been an earthquake. [. . .] I didn't feel the earthquake. Already a couple of days earlier I had said to my husband that *there would be an earthquake.*[48]

The end of the world and New Year's Eve.
Case 4 (414ff.), a fifty-two-year-old cloakroom attendant.

Two weeks before she was brought into the hospital, she had left a lamp on every night because she felt anxious. On New Year's Eve her anxiety had become particularly intense, because not long before a girl had told her that the world would end between Christmas and New Year's. The next day she had worked as a cloakroom attendant. When she went out into the street, it was very dark, no stars were shining, no church bells rang. She was gripped by an anxiety that the world was going to collapse [*die Welt würde zusammenklappen*]. Around eight o'clock she headed to church, but she wandered at length in the streets and rang at "the homes of rich people." The houses were submerged in shadows. After she rang, here and there a light appeared in the windows: at the same time, one after another the stars shined again, as did the moon. She was happy about this, thinking that the world would not collapse. She continued hurrying. "I was pushed along. I was dead tired and yet I had to continue to hurry." Finally she returned home. The moon had disappeared again, it was dark, she was again gripped by a great anxiety, she thought that now the airplanes would come (to bomb: however, the war was long over), she went with a lamp to the cellar, she knocked on the doors of the people living on the other floors, and finally she fell to the ground and was taken to the hospital.

"Wholly other," "Last Judgment," to be judged.
"Voices from the sky, from the roof."

Case 6 (415ff.): dysphoric-euphoric, *ganz andere*,[49] guilt, isolation: a twenty-three-year-old postal worker.

On July 14, she saw the Savior sleeping on his throne. It was a dream. The angels were also sleeping. One angel stayed awake. It had power and was vigilant. She saw herself lying down, in a state of disorder as she was presently. When she woke up, she thought it was impossible that the Savior was sleeping. But at 10:30 she experienced a total upheaval. From that day on, everything in the world became murky. She thought she was the only one to notice this. Watching from the windows she saw everything darken, the rain became stormy. It was not a usual rain but a sort of deluge. The children in the streets cried; they were no longer playful and cheerful. A child from the neighborhood who before used to come to her so cheerfully now distanced himself from her and from that day on was in a bad mood; he watched her pitifully. She had a picture of the Savior on the walls of her home; when she used to smile at it, it smiled with her, but now it was sad when she looked at it. Her brother returned home from the shop; [. . .] he was *ganz andere* than before. [. . .] Even her other brother was *komisch* [in the local dialect, strange, surprising[50]]. He could no longer perform his work well. People hurried about the streets so glumly but nonetheless terribly excited. The automobiles drove so slowly. The sun was no longer so bright. [. . .] The colors were as they always were, but they no longer had same life as before.

From that day on, everything remained this way. She thought that she was guilty. She was not able to pray. God would no longer listen to her. And yet a voice always said to her: "You can still be filled with pride and happiness." It was a clear voice. It came from heaven, she knew it. It was not the voice of the Savior or dear God, but it came from heaven. It certainly did not come from the devil. The voice did not come directly from heaven but from the roof. She had been unhappy but not anxious. She could no longer have anxiety, because she was no longer a person like others. She left everything hanging; she was indifferent to everything. She thought, whatever will be will be, and yet she had cried an awful lot: not for herself, but for *children who died of cold, for people who died of hunger.*

Case 7 (417): "Everything was so doubled, as if it were totally different [*ganz andere*][51] in the world." A woman worker, thirty-eight years old: "It was *as if it were a Last Judgment.*"

5.2. Bruno Callieri, "Contributo allo studio psicopatologico dell'esperienza schizofrenica della fine del mondo," *Archivio di psicologia, neurologia e psichiatria* 16, no. 4/5 (1955): 379–407.

In the experience of the end of the world it is "as if" the patient became aware of the anxiety that is the fundamental mode of our existence.

This contentless anxiety is loaded with "intentions" of meaning addressed to the world in which the patient exists. As pure being-there-in-the-world, pure "thrownness" (*Geworfenheit*), he feels the world to be destruction, the world no longer exists for him. Our world, the world of objects that surround us and that we bring into existence daily, "is balancing precariously on a bell tower"; it loses its orderly arrangement in an order of objective values and meanings. It is thus terribly logical and understandable that the intentions of meaning come to rest on abnormal complements of meaning: that is, in our case, objects and people in the surroundings (a brother, a doctor, a red book, meat, a table, a wardrobe) are loaded with inadequate, rigid meanings, weighted down by an ambiguous affective tone.

The hermeneutic perspective of the end of the world becomes more pertinent and profound when our starting point is presence as transcendence of a situation in value, transcendence that is threatened by non-transcendence, and thus by the risk of not-being-there-in-the-world. The "world" develops and is maintained by the duty to transcend in the presence that "overcomes" the situation and that lies wholly in this overcoming, just as worldhood wholly lies in the various results that arise from this movement. The loss of presence, the drop in transcending energy, the loss of transcending as a duty, is thus the collapse of the world: the world heads toward ending because it heads toward the ending of the presence called to begin it and maintain it again and again. The heavens fall because Atlas no longer holds them up. In the "fall" of the worldly, presence lives in anxiety over its abdication; it experiences an intentionality that no longer manages to be fulfilled. This "fall" or "collapse" takes on two diametrically opposed aspects in experience: on the one hand, intentionality roams freely, according to an empty, all-allusive and threatening "beyond" that afflicts single perceptual spheres, charging them with a tension toward an empty, threatening, all-allusive "beyond." On the other hand, because it is "empty," the empty excess of semanticity of the single perceptive spheres involves a lack of semanticity, projectability, practicability of these very spheres, which are experienced as "rigid," "artificial," "inert," "dead," outside of any possible intentionality. Thus on one side lies the terrifying image of the universe in tension, in which every perceptual sphere hints at risky **koinonias** with all of the others, releasing itself according to accidental resemblances that become just as many opportunities for substantial identities; on the other side lies the no less terrifying image of the sclerotic universe, whose perceptual spheres are endowed with a lethal inertia, not participating in any "beyond" that places them in an order, artificial and theatrical in regard to the truth of life, or even arranged in a sort of deathly rigidity. In other words, the experience of the end of the world oscillates between "too much" and "too little" semanticity according to an ambivalence of aspects that cannot be decided: and if in the experience only one of these emerges at times (the universe in tension or the sclerotic universe), the other is always ready to step in by virtue of a polarity that is justified by the very nature of this experience. Furthermore, both of these aspects entail a fundamental experience of "radical alterity." The world is altering or is altered, it is no longer the domesticable domestic world; something absolutely new is about to happen or has already happened, not in the normal sense that the world changes through time and we along with it but in the sense that now the change lies in the experiencing of the very worldhood that winds to an end and that becomes "other" precisely as worldhood, thus "radically other."

The wholly other of the world that gets deworlded reflects the loss of presentifying function of the presence, its becoming other (its "becoming alien") instead of keeping itself as the norm of the identical and the different. The experience of the end of the world reflects this connection in that the alteration or catastrophe of the worldly is experienced as an alteration that has a very personal sense: here more than ever, *tua res agitur*. Something radical strikes at the very roots of the person, regards this person, alludes peremptorily to him, not in the generic sense, which would be normal, of a certain immensely important occurrence in the life of the person but in the specific sense of an alteration of the quality of this occurring as a category of the real so that this occurring—instead of taking the "normal" form of a question that leaves leeway for the response of presentification—is felt to be oriented toward the modality of a being-acted-upon that takes away any leeway for responding and that grips, dispossesses, and threatens through this systematic dispossession. The becoming of the world that ends risks "stealing the soul" of every moment; and indeed, if the world that ends reflects the loss of presence that again and again is called to begin it, that ending is experienced quintessentially as dispossessing, an aggression and a theft, a persecution, and finally as a last, definitive judgment under which one falls because of the immense weight of an extreme guilt.

[...]

5.3. The end of the world in schizophrenic drawings.

The experience and the representation of self and the world in schizophrenic drawings. Volmat, pages 155–59.[52] In the schizophrenic's extemporaneous drawings we note, from a structural point of view, the following elements.

Stereotypy, that is, the repetition of the drawing as a whole. This tendency toward a stereotypic fixation combines with rigidity, deformation, simplification, and mechanization. Stereotypy is associated with iterations, immediate repetitions of a motor or verbal act that, once it has ended, is repeated pointlessly. Iteration in drawing translates into a series of identical features that are more or less close together, concentric circles or sections, zigzags or arabesques.

The horror of emptiness that renders the drawings completely full. The utilization of space to the fullest, its geometrization, in the same way, being horrified of time, of becoming, of the unpredictable, geometrizes time through a tendentially total planning and a schematic simplification of actions to be carried out. The tendency to touch up through overlapping (without erasures, without actual corrections), the unlimited care for "finishing touches," perhaps of the smallest detail. The tendency toward balance and symmetry, the monumental, "improvement," as geometricity. The importance of the frame: its meaning of protecting the composition from the risk of regressing into chaos. The composition's tendency to fragmentariness, to the scattering or dispersion of its elements: the absence of perspective (a world without "depth," in other words, without horizons of dynamic feasibility of possible movement), objects in tension, deformed, "fixed in their getting deformed." Superstition of immobility, immutability, and spatial-temporal fixity.

The transparency of objects (the insubstantiality of objects finds expression in the transparence with which they are drawn); the omission of the objects' real features; the addition of legends, writing, words that underline the representations and to increase their power of persuasion; the multiplicity of points of view of the object. Adherence to the model as a tormented defense reaction in the face of the dissolution of the person and the leaking of the objective world. Conventionalism: or, where its effort to pathological adherence fails, deformation of the world or the projection of self in the world.

Stylization as a result of the tendency to simplification (the concrete as "too many" particulars), repetition (the concrete has too many alterations, becoming is unbearable): geometricized simplification and detemporalizing repletion as elements of stylization. The relationship to "rhythmic tendencies" of our psychomotor life. The conjoining of images (human-animal forms, human-plant, etc.), displacement and concealment (substituting one group of images with another that represents it). The projection of images: deriving from the absence of the distinction between perception and representation, between me and the external world, between idea and action, between word and object, between subjective imitation of an event and the creation of the event ("magical" world).

The space of the schizophrenic is the negation of that experience and its substitution with a primordial, sacred, unchangeable space, unharmed by the chaos of forms.

Time: while the manic tends to live in an abstract present and the melancholic in an abstract past (with a negation of the future that can arrive at suicide), the schizophrenic tends to the "negation" of time, the complete arrest of its living flow, its spatialization: not as a mental instrument of practical control but as an immediate experience and total reduction. Thus, the petrification, the mineralization, the experience of death and the absence of a dynamic meaning of things; their death because they no longer indicate historically possible centers of action socially and historically. Thus, also, the experience of "immortality" as an interpretation of the world that can no longer become, that is "stopped." If one had to represent this time according to an image in the style that is consistent with it, one could draw a face of a clock whose hours are represented by twelve exactly identical skulls. Patients refer to a sacred, mythical time of origins, before the apparition of history, just as they refer to a mythical and sacred space. This negation of history is the negation of lived time . . . Stereotypy, the repetition of actions and forms, can be considered a ritual of periodic abolition of time (Volmat 1956, 168ff.).

Absence of movement: rigidity of the feature; inflexibility; fragmentariness and discontinuity; cold colors, in broad adjacent areas, enhance the impression of immobility, of the "death of passions."

Color symbolism. Symbols and plastic themes:

- Trees, emotional projection of the self, family members or transference relations; mostly exotic trees, never fruit trees: a bare tree, dead, solitary, uprooted, petrified, etc.
- Deserted street, blocked, with no exit, set between mountains, that disappears under vegetation.
- Protective barrier in front of objects that are a projection of myself.
- The mountain as another projection of myself; desolate, immense, far from the clouds, Calvary, with a cavern; in a flat, immense lost horizon.
- House without doors or windows, where you cannot live, where you cannot enter, without a fireplace, without smoke; the house where I died: pitiful, in ruins.
- Ancient ruins; or a castle that is reflected in a lake; with stereotypy of balconies; isolated, or crowded one on top of the other or groups of buildings; geometric, etc.

- Water, sometimes associated with the tree.
- The sun.
- Lightning bolt.
- Symbolic bestiary.
- An eye.
- The scenes.

An escape from time: toward the timeless, toward the *illud tempus*.[53] Either toward imaginary time or an exotic past (or present). Petrifactions of the universe.

Escape from the self, one's own dehumanization: escape in the animal, plant, mineral, the automatic and mechanical. Mask. Petrifaction.

5.4. Schizophrenia is the most philosophical of mental illnesses, obviously not in the sense that the schizophrenic is a philosopher (he is the negation of knowledge and love, the two great forces that make up humankind) but in the sense that the healthy person—that is, capable of healing the existential wound in himself and others time and again—can through the analysis of schizophrenic experiences gain awareness of the extreme risk that human existence is exposed to: the collapse of the transcendental ethos. The struggle against this risk differentiates humans as the founders of cultural life, as heroes of the "rational" intersubjective endeavor, communicable in the face of temptations of disaggregation and chaos. It is the struggle against this risk that defines the human as movement from the private to the public and inner auscultation of public voices that resound in the world in a given historical epoch and in the context of a particular culture. But it is precisely for this reason that schizophrenia, which is the inversion of all this, has a great pedagogical power for every person who has opted for combatant reason, who intends to assess the enemy front in all of its breadth and depth.

Manic-depressive psychosis illuminates us not so much as to the breaking of relations with the world as instead to the self that oscillates between heinous guilt and the acceleration without a horizon of all psychic processes. But should we not perhaps interpret this "heinous guilt" as the radical guilt to someone who loses the very root of choosing according to values?

5.5. The case of the writer Reto Roos, with L. Binswanger's commentary.[54]

The Swiss writer Reto Roos, whose first novel won a literary prize. Hospitalized several times for periods of deep depression, he took his life at age forty-five, hanging himself. In this patient's history we find many references to the problem of the "object loss" in melancholy. [. . .]

According to Binswanger, in the patient's self-descriptions the support, prop, and object of effective attaching (*sich hängen*) are not to be sought upward, in the vertical direction of value, but downward, as "anchoring." Reto Roos's suicide by "hanging" could in my view be interpreted as the only possibility for "tying himself upward," that is, "hanging himself." In this, the loss of valorization consumes its outcome, coinciding with an act in which the material "tying oneself" upward coincides with death. According to Binswanger, this suicide is not to be interpreted as "a pure and simple bankruptcy or avoidance of life, with a sort of resignation [but as] a 'whatabout' [*worüber*], full and without possible alternatives, the last fuel that can be thrown into the furnace of life when the self is almost extinguished, erasing oneself from one's book of household expenditures," according to an expression used by Reto Roos himself. The theme of suicide is "the last and not transcendable" *whatabout* to which here it is possible to hold on to, the full decision and without alternative in which being there can constitute itself in time in the full sense of the word. Such a constituting for a *whatabout*, full and without alternative, takes place with a final effort—as Jarg Zönd would say: compare Binswanger, *Schizophrenie*, 1, 2, and 3 study[55]—and certainly often with an extremely vigorous effort, in fact even brutal.

Reto Roos' self-description:

The depressive states [not sadness] begin this way: things that mean a lot to you are deprived of feeling; you feel an inner weakness, *unstable* [*haltlos*]. You seek some sort of ground with people, things, activities; if the feeling *returns* with such an anchor, the *future* is *easier*, you can even *forget yourself* completely. Yet there still may be an *anxiety* somewhere, the *feeling will disappear again*, you *do not really trust your feelings* and *therefore also the future*. If we do not manage to return to a living *contact*, we struggle like a *drowning man, clinging* to everything that seems to offer hope. You are in the state of Ahasuerus, who does not find rest anywhere. *Thoughts run empty* and are always about the same things. At last you comes to a complete exhaustion of feelings; you are extinguished [= have no more fuel], and that is the hardest thing to bear(!). [. . .] *Surrendering* to this state [still an "object"!], you can walk around like a dead person, waiting and waiting [protentive empty intention]. You have a single need, not to break your *patience* [still an "object" or fuel]. If it goes on too long and the feeling does not change back [the possibility of full intentional structure of temporal objectivity], then *despair* comes. You cannot go backward in life; life has passed you by, too (retentional empty intention); standing still you no longer catch up (protentive empty intention). So you let yourself sink into the *depths*, burrowing into the soul, for the affect of grief, despair, the demoniac is at least *feeling alive*(!), if it also goes in a circle. [Nonetheless even in this empty course the soul's tormenting despair is made of flammable matter, with which "the fire is started."] The *soul wrings its hands*, it is busy, swollen. Compulsions arise, *you do not control yourself*, you are *driven around* [We find here for the first time the loss of self (*Entselbstigung*) and with it the abandonment of self to mere *occurrence*. It must be clear a priori that the "loss of the object" and "loss of oneself" are reciprocally correlative, entailing each other.] If you muster the will to fight against the compulsions, they grow; if you manage for a moment to dominate them, there is *hope*. If you manage a second time, hope *increases* to the point of *ecstasy*. But then you have another relapse. You get discouraged: it has not helped, everything is suddenly as before . . . You are disappointed again, and the *weight presses you into the ground*, deeper and deeper. You *have drowned in yourself, seeking refuge* all around where things are easier, more bearable, if *there is only a little feeling* or *calm without thoughts*, a *dream* a *veil* upon everything [It is not a matter of a specific "whatabout" (*Worüber*) or object, nor an agonizing void in the course of thought, but a sort of intermediate state between both, brought in part by rest, calm affectivity, and in part veiled by dream, or better, by dreaming]. (Binswanger 1957, 53ff.)

A digression follows with attempts at a psychological and psychoanalytic interpretation of suicide: the patient had in fact begun a psychoanalytic treatment that he soon abandoned because of the feeling, reinforced by the analyst, that the treatment in question would have deprived the patient of his artistic abilities.

When you have hardly anything left in the world [no whatabout (*Worüber*) that you can support yourself on, ground yourself on, anchor yourself to] and the *Angst* is still floating, *when you give yourself up and erase yourself from the housekeeping book*, then you really come to the *full and very clear decision of suicide.*

5.6. Crisis of objectivization.
The crisis of the power of objectivization according to values necessarily has a dual aspect: the crisis of the object and that of the subject. The crisis of the object means the loss of the very possibility of constructing a world of objects, that is, to order the situation in a world of values. The situation that does not manage to objectivize itself due to the lack of the very fundamental objectivizing function necessarily translates itself on the level of the presence in crisis in certain experiences that, from a clinical point of view, are symptoms of the illness. The basic experience is that

everything that happens displays hostile intentions toward the subject, and that every sphere of the real becomes all allusive of all the others without ever being able to define the all-allusive impulse in a satisfying way. Each thing alludes to others in a passive and automatic process of identification that takes advantage of superficial resemblances of attributes or simple verbal homonymies to establish unstable, temporary identities in which the all-allusive process nonetheless reopens. The world fills up with "intentions," with responsible acts, and in their indefinite occurrence all of the intentions and responsibilities hint at the subject as a victim, at a darkly wicked plan, a devious machination. In this moment of the crisis what gets objectified is the human responsibility of choice itself, so that instead of defining the other-than-self in a physiological way, as a choice, it becomes other, it alienates the power of choice itself. We can well understand why such a moment can be connected to an experience of radical alterity of the object, to the anxiety of the radically other, since what gets alienated here is the presence: the inalienable presence risks becoming an object, of losing itself. The crisis of the subject essentially entails feeling alien, artificial, mechanical with a host of nuances in the experience of the inefficiency of the self, up to the feeling of a heinous as much as unmotivated guilt and of an equation between doing and being guilty: everything that is done is guilt. Here, too, the guilt's radical, unmotivated character are explainable, because it is the truly radical guilt of not being able to give a motivation to action, of not being able to choose a world of objects according to values. The conspiring of this dual causality of the crisis (each thing is an "untried" cause to the subject as victim, every action is guilty) discloses the inappropriate defensive "reaction" of catatonic stupor.

5.7. Catatonia and ritualism.

The pure anxiety of becoming constitutes a psychopathological experience that involves all moments of that very becoming, independently of their contents. The extreme defense from this pure anxiety is the refusal of any relation with the world whatsoever and thus—if anything—the immobility of catatonic stupor, with its typical tension. A paradox arises from this, a quintessentially contradictory effort consecrated to inanity: the systematic refusal of every relation with the world in fact makes visible a refusal that is irrepressibly inserted in the world. Precisely given that the defense gets radicalized, the paradox intensifies to the breaking point, so that if on the one hand it is the risk of restabilizing a worldly relationship, on the other it is the irruption of a blind fury aimed at suppressing that relation through aggression and material destruction. Despite this paradox, the catatonic defense nonetheless reveals its relative existential coherence once we assume as a point of departure the crisis of anxiety of becoming and the experience of a defense. Because of what it has that is specifically human, the becoming is an irreversible experiencing of ever-new situations in which the memories of analogous situations already experienced and of the respective behaviors already employed never cancel out the novel character of the situations themselves and the obligation to transcend them with original initiatives, with "unique" decisions integrated into society and history. Now the risk of not preserving oneself as presence in becoming, of being overwhelmed by the historical flow of situations, gets expressed in the catatonic defense as a protective effort of reducing the becoming of being, according to a radical dehistorification contained in the refusal of any relation with the world. This same effort is expressed with rigorous coherence in "waxy flexibility": the *alterations* imposed on the body from outside transform themselves into indefinitely protracted *permanencies*. That is, every *new* position of the body and its limbs gets immediately isolated from becoming and preserved, in other words, eliminated in its character as a beginning to which something follows, a question to which an answer follows, or a novelty that manifests in the most elementary and peremptory way the historicity of the human situation. When the alteration instead concerns not one's own body but the external world and appears not in cenesthesia but in vision and hearing, the reduction of the becoming to the permanence of being takes on other forms. As regards vision, the world comes into view as a range of perceptive spheres, the defense of polarization isolates one of these spheres (even if it is tiny or insignificant) and it immerses itself in it as if the world were reduced to it. This expresses the material reduction of the perceptive range to the unit of a single perception and taking refuge in this unit as if in an equipped fortress of permanency. Just as the alteration introduced in the position of the body gets isolated and held indefinitely, so too does the alteration that appears to the vision as a range of possible spheres is not accepted as such but gets reduced to an isolated perception in which one is immersed in an attempt at permanency.

The reduction of the seen or heard alteration to the permanence of being is also manifested in specular imitation: here, the refusal of the question gives rise to the simple repetition of the question itself in the sense that the seen or heard alteration is not the opportunity for a response but the stimulus of a mimetic or phonic repetition that immediately isolates this alteration and suffocates its temptation to becoming through the inertia of repeating. In this way the alteration gets eliminated with a reply that repeats the question, and the threat of a beginning that could reopen becoming undergoes the exorcism of the beginning that begins nothing except the imitation or echo that repeats it, resolving it in permanency.

Catatonia, with its extreme radicalism, can be likened to the defense of the besieged who takes cover behind the last barricade on which, nonetheless, the enemy continues to press, opening here and there dangerous breaches: waxy flexibility, polarization and specular imitation appear—keeping to our analogy—as attempts to close these breaches or institute makeshift defenses. But if we now turn to stereotypies, the most suitable image seems to be that of the besieged who attempts an exit and winds up among the enemy but is protected from his lethal blows to the extent possible. Stereotypies in fact concede something to the alteration, to the world, but on the other hand they reshape behavior, introducing a sign of isolation and nonparticipation into it. The face or head are held in such a way as to sculpt some visible unchangeability, and the alteration is traversed inside of this armor that separates and protects. If being sculpted in some sign of persisting cannot be maintained with all of the rigor possible, if the diabolicalness of alteration brushes and insinuates itself, than the alteration finally gets accepted but reduced to the repetition of the identical, in other words to an alteration that is only apparently such, because in effect it is "eternal return" of the identical series of subsequent alterations, a beginning and a following that systematically cancels itself through the return to the very same beginning. Although becoming can accumulate question upon question and demand reply upon reply, always different in relation to the always different questions, stereotypy as a defense counterposes a sole reply that repeats itself exactly: a reply that in effect does not reply to the world but solely to the need of crossing through it without being brushed by it.

Here we touch an important moment of the function of ritualism. Precisely because it is dominated by that form of permanence that is the exact repetition of the same cycle of actions, and precisely because in this repeating it is not so much the quality of what is repeated that is efficacious as it is the form of the dehistorifying repetition, ritualism contains a seed of a moment of protective separation from the world, of a restorative escape from becoming. In the anxiety of history that does not repeat (and that precisely because it does not repeat, it torments), we retire to the well-equipped fortress of metahistory that repeats (and that restores precisely because it is the realm of repetition, apparent becoming, return of the identical, beginning and succession that annul each other in reproducing the beginning over and over). Moreover, since ritualism separates from becoming, it is essentially separate action, sheltered from any contamination whatsoever of changing, innovating, or altering. The paradox of ritualism lies exactly here, and it reproduces that of catatonia, of polarization, of waxy flexibility and specular imitation: indeed, ritualism is accompanied by the murky awareness that becoming threatens the very heart of ritualistic behavior and that repetition's attempt to escape metahistory by belonging to history that does not repeat does not avoid novelty and initiative. This is where the characteristic attention to exact repetition arises, the *mania of exactness*, the doubt of error in execution, the need to reproduce ritual behavior in the fear of having let some novelty intrude that denounces becoming and coming to terms with the world for just a moment: that moment that makes a breach in repetition's barricade, risking making it fall along its whole gamut!

5.8. Ambivalence. Kranz in *Studium Generale* 8, no. 6 (1955), 373ff.,[56] mentions the polarity of meaning and the polyvalency of mythical figures in relation to schizophrenic ambivalence. With reference to the latter, he recalls quote from Gruhle:

> [One of the most important features of schizophrenic experience is] a simultaneous yes and no, whether it has to do with a motor process, a feeling or a decision.[57] According to Storch, [schizophrenic ambivalence] belongs to "the loss of constancy and certainty of the structure of things," which has its parallel in the prelogical thought and prelogical experience of primitive people.[58]

The resemblance between the ambivalence of schizophrenic experience and the ambivalence of the numinous or myth should certainly not be taken for sameness. First, we need to ask why some features of psychosis (or neurosis) resemble the numinous and mythical-ritual symbolism; second, why the numinous and mythical-ritual symbolism display features that resemble a psychosis (or a neurosis). Second,[59] the problem remains of distinguishing the patient from the healthy person, the psychosis (or neurosis) from the entire complex of magical-religious institutions regularly functioning in historical societies and in the different epochs of those societies. The two questions are conjoined, and it is not possible to solve one without solving the other. With regard to psychotic ambivalence of both the numinous and of mythical-ritual symbolism, we should note that the former presents itself as a risk, while the latter presents itself as the resolution of that risk. Presence is a decision, transcendence of the situation according to intersubjective values: it is thus totally understandable that the risk of losing presence is manifested, in one of its extreme episodes, as ambivalence, an unresolving clash between "yes" and "no" that sweeps throughout psychic life and affects the whole gamut of possible transcendences. This is a clash that has its most dramatic expression in the tension of catatonic stupor, that is, in the systematic contrasting of a "no" to every possible "yes." The horizon of the numinous, the "wholly other," and mythical-ritual symbolism in the process of functioning in a specific culture all *take on this risk* and head it toward a *cultural* solution. To the extent that they take it on, they resemble recovery, but to the extent that they resolve it, they do not resemble it at all. Thus, while in psychoses and neuroses ambivalence bears a negative valence tending toward an unresolving clash that has no outcome—because every attempt to get out of it isolates [the patient] more and more from the inspired decision of communicable and intersubjective relations—in the sphere of magical-religious life, instead, ambivalence is just the beginning moment of a dynamism that opens itself to the progressive distinction of valences, and in recovering the wholly other discloses communicable and intersubjective values that are socially circulatable, culturally conditioned, and oriented in the sense of a world in some way "practicable" and "projectable" *together* with others. This means that the *correspondences* between psychoses and magical-religious life (or mythical, archaic, prelogical, or however else one wants to more or less appropriately call it) arise from an *abstract* comparison between a patient that, as a patient, gets abstracted from the world with various symptomatic modalities and according to different nosological frameworks and an institution that, as an instrument of normal life in a given culture, is oriented to a *reintegration* of this risk of abstraction. We thereby compare two opposing dynamics: in this lies the legitimacy and at the same time the limit of the comparison. No doubt the analysis of the mentally ill has the great methodological importance of laying bare the moment of risk against which the numinous, the sacred, the magical-religious, and mythical-ritual symbolism combat. But while in magical-religious life that risk is a moment of a dynamic of recovery and reintegration, in mental illness it gets increasingly isolated as bare risk without effective recovery and reintegration. Someone climbing a staircase and someone going down it will necessarily meet at a certain step: but their meeting does not signify that, in the moment in which they place their foot on the same step, the respective snapshots of their identical position have the same dynamic meaning because one is going up and the other is going down.

Whether we reduce magical-religious life to mental illness or postulate the difference but insist solely on the correspondences without offering any valid criterion for distinguishing one from the other; or, finally, we assume magical-religious life to be totally independent from psychopathological risk or having merely fortuitous relations with it, we end up in each of these cases with an arbitrary interpretation of the structure and function of mythical-ritual symbolism as a phenomenon of culture. At the same time, we also preclude an understanding of the existential meaning of mental illness.

With reference to the relationship between "myth" and "psychosis," Kranz (1955) writes,

> In any case it would be rash if we sought to reduce the psychotic state—and in particular schizophrenic experience—to the simple, uncontrolled activation of archaic-mythological experience. Archetypical material taken from dreams and fantasies appears not only in the mentally ill[60] and neurotics but also in healthy people. However, this does not prove that "the irruption of the numinous equals psychosis" (G. Adler). We strongly believe instead that the numinous can emerge through an unknown psychic process or disruptive tendencies that have always been a part of humankind, and as in cyclothymic depression, the original anxieties of humanity remain exposed, nonetheless, without their irruption "generating" psychoses or the psychosis "producing" them, or that they "are" psychosis. (374)

The problem, as obscurely as it is posed, emerges here in the psychiatrist's discourse. The numinous is not a psychosis (cf. Gerhard Adler, *Zur analytischen Psychologie* [Zurich: Rascher, 1952]), but constitutes a historically conditioned cultural defense from the risk of an existential crisis. Precisely through this function, which introduces itself into the thick of concrete possibilities of crisis, opening them to reintegration, the numinous (the sacred, magical-religious life, mythical-ritual symbolism) presents uncoincidental resemblances with psychopathological phenomenology, since the modeling and reintegrating forces that it places in motion are necessarily following the character of these possible critical episodes of which it represents the recovery and the inversion. Moreover, precisely the recovery and inversion that the numinous effects in the heart of the existential crisis allow us to clearly distinguish the cases in which the apparatus is efficacious from those in which it is not; in other words, from those which—despite abstract comparative appearances—present the negative valence of a crisis without horizon. This interpretation of the mental illness–numinous relationship offers a certain criterion for not confusing the two terms of the relationship: a magical practice, a form of religious life, a given mythical-ritual symbolism are such when the historian of culture is capable of showing for a civilization, period, or circumscribed manifestation of the sacred, or for a given personality (the founder of a religion, a prophet, a mystic), the positive dynamism that leads from crisis to regeneration, from the ineffable and from the private to the communicable world of intersubjective values, from the anxiety of history to a practicable world and projecting together with others, from being-acted-upon to the active explication of forms of culture coherence, from the "wholly other" that upsets to a process of reappropriation that mediates worldly actions.

A host of new tasks for the scholar of religious historiography derives from this. First of all, the phenomenology of the crisis constitutes a field of research and analysis that have direct interest for this domain of historiographic knowledge. The assistance of existential analysis in psychopathology and the findings of ethnopsychiatry has as much importance here as the philological techniques to which historiography is so closely bound and the techniques of fieldwork aimed at capturing and analyzing living, functioning institutions. Once a certain mythical-ritual symbolism has been identified, full historiographic understanding requires identifying its critical moments of existence whose dynamism functions as a horizon for recovery and reintegration: the historiographer cannot do this without turning to psychopathological phenomenology. The reconstruction must then turn to specifying this horizon's mode of operating, the opening toward values that it permits, the cultural dynamism resulting from it, the limits of this dynamism, the incidents to which history exposes it, the various conditionings through which the apparatus is kept (or keeps itself) effective or falls into ruin, substituted by another. Second, since the degree of intersubjectivity and communicability identifies the efficacy of mythical-ritual symbols with regard to the crisis that isolates and closes, disaggregates and annihilates, the historiography of religious life always entails a sociological dimension of evaluation: a mythical-ritual symbol is a cohesive element endowed with an expansive force that extends to the tribal group, the nation, or a multinational civilization, and it is subdivided in various ways by sex, age, and class, giving rise to specific sacred groupings, such as the initiates society, sects, priests, churches, religious orders, and missions. The psychopathological and sociological dimensions therefore take on particular significance in this complete and dynamic perspective of religious-historical research.

3

The Drama of Christian Apocalypse

1. The Necessities of Historical Reason

1.1. When we say that man "is in history," it is necessary to pay attention to what we mean by "history."

First of all, it is necessary to distinguish the word *history* in a triple sense: of *res gestae*, *historia rerum gestarum*, and *res gerendae*.[1] These three senses are interrelated, since human "history" is always articulated in the three moments of conditioned *res gestae*, of the current memory of the past and the conscious task of *historia condenda*.[2] Second, it is necessary to clarify the relationship between history and awareness, between history and rationality, and between history and intersubjective values.

People make their history (*res gestae*), but the consciousness they have of this making coincides to a certain extent with what they really do. There are unconscious motivations and unconscious ends to human action that are not actually present in its agents but can be gleaned through the analysis of their action from the perspective of an "other" contemporary observer or in the historiographic recollection of posterity. We must note, moreover, that if they are complemented with unconscious motivations and ends, human historical behaviors are always "rational," that is, interpretable according to certain "coherences." Their irrationality arises only because in daily human interaction, unconscious motivations and ends are unseen or because—in the *res gerendae* perspective—it is inevitable that we "choose" the "more rational" over the "less rational" or "irrational." As for intersubjective values, history is dominated by them from within in the sense that it is a movement of valorizing intersubjectivities: this is so in *res gestae* as the past production of cooperative modes of being-in-the-world; this is so in *historia rerum gestarum* as the reconstructive memory of this productivity; and finally, this is so in *res gerendae* as present decision according to value.

Given this, the principle that humankind is in history means that people generate all of their cultural assets, even those bearing an awareness of their divine foundation.

The problem of history constitutes one of the most characteristic themes of the present cultural climate. Western civilization has become increasingly aware it is distinguished by a "sense of history" that gains importance within the Judeo-Christian tradition itself. The work of Cullmann is noteworthy in this respect:[3] furthermore, the need to readapt Christianity to this sense of historical existence—but without losing the Christian message—lies at the center of the problem of demythologizing the New Testament.[4] Besides these relations between history and religious life, history and Christianity, history and myth, there are questions more closely connected to the methodology of historiographic research and to the meaning and value of history in the context of the social sciences. This reconsideration of the problem of history has largely been influenced by the crisis of a narrowly Eurocentric historicism and by the direct assumption of Western history as the model of human history; by the crisis of the concept of unilinear "progress" promoted by ethnology and Orientalist studies; by the de facto constitution, on the ruins of the colonial era, of a "third power" of nations and civilizations whose own history has certainly been extraneous to the historical experiences of the West (the Classical world, early and medieval Christianity, humanism and the Renaissance, the Reformation, the development of the New Science and the Enlightenment, Romanticism and positivism, etc.) but that are nonetheless involved in other historical developments that can in no way be judged as "delayed phases" or "deviations" from Western development. Other significant problems refer to relations between historical research and ethnology, anthropology, sociology, psychology, ethnopsychiatry, and so forth, as well as the place of historical research in interdisciplinary studies concerning specific cultural phenomena.

[Authors to study:]

Oscar Cullmann. *Christus und die Zeit* (Zollikon-Zurich: Evangelischer Verlag, 1946).[5]

Rudolf Bultmann. *Geschichte und Eschatologie* (Tübingen: J. C. B. Mohr, 1958).[6]

Karl Jaspers and Rudolf Bultmann. *Die Frage der Entmythologisierung* (Munich: Piper, 1954).[7]

1.2. Eliade (*Images et symboles*, 1952, 35[8]) says that man opposes history even when he pretends to be nothing but history. But it should be noted that we might also say, antithetically, that man is in history even when he pretends to leave it with mythical-ritual behavior. And we could continue with the antithesis: indeed, adopting the first criterion, historians can only be historians up to a certain point, that is, up to the point at which they encounter extreme situations that manifest their metahistorical destiny, their meaning beyond history. Having reached this point, historians must limit themselves to indicating extreme situations, taking them as revelations that that cannot be derived further: in other words, as archetype-contents that in the last instance confer meaning and reason to the truth of religious-historical modeling. If they adopt the second criterion of historical reconstruction, they do not recognize contents of consciousness (myths, rituals, symbols) that are not generated by historical situations according to reasons and ends—conscious or unconscious—to be traced wholly to the situational character of human existence: what humankind is in the world and what the world is, the human intersubjective valorization of life. The first criterion conceives of the historian's job as a temporary route that leads to religious testimony: here, the historian is the *famulus* of theological knowledge. The second criterion contains a critical instance of all religious pretenses as pretenses of humanity's metahistoric destiny, and it orients itself again and again to reconverting in human, secular, worldly terrains what in individual religious-historical testimony is a relationship with what is beyond human, secular, worldly, "profane" history.

"When the son of God incarnated and became the Christ, he had to speak Aramaic" (Mircea Eliade[9]). The historicity of a religious phenomenon does not only concern the fact that "when the son of God incarnated and became the Christ, he had to speak Aramaic" but the very symbol of the son of God in the sense that the symbol of Christ is comprehendible "through" a certain cultural history. History is a dialectic of crisis (the risk of losing presence), symbol (the technical instrument of recovery), and value (the unifying power of qualified conscious action). The sense of history lies in the passage from mythical-ritual symbols of religion to secular symbols (ethical-political, poetic, scientific).

M. Eliade's misunderstanding lies in the identification of the concept of history with "being in situation." Now, the situation, the precise here and now of individual existence, is an abstraction; in a certain sense a historical person is never in situation but always and in any case in the act of transcending it toward value. Consciousness has a place only in the leeway that presence preserves with regard to the situation, that is, in the leeway for which the situation gains a meaning; it opens to a cultural permanence, to a work that defeats becoming and death.

If the terms of history and the precise situation of the individual really were identified with each other, history would be the synonym of obtuseness and mediocrity, since nothing is more obtuse and mediocre than the little situational world by which we let ourselves live or die. Mircea Eliade is right when he demonstrates that humankind always attempts to escape from the situation in which it finds itself, but the point is that such escape does not take place from the "world" of human values but from the bondage of the situation by virtue of qualified actions.

1.3. Writing with regard to religion in *Essays on the Law*, 277 (Viano,[10] 236), Locke expresses the typical Enlightenment position on superstition as bizarre belief or madness. In reality the task of religious-historical consciousness is to trace religious life—even what is usually designated as "superstitious"—to a particular form of coherence and rationality, at least within the limits of certain historical conditions.

Historical reason has the task of looking for the reasons behind human behaviors. Hence, either religion is irrational, and so it is obviously not possible to find its historical reasons, or else it is a historically conditioned rationality, and only then is it possible to find its historical reasons.

In order to regain the rationality of religion, it is necessary to carry out a set of integrations. First of all, the mythical-ritual symbol manifests its rationality if we consider not only the conscious sphere but also that of the unconscious. Second, if we identify the critical moments for which it acts as a horizon, the profane and worldly values that it discloses and protects. Third, if we manage to establish its sociological dimension, in other words, its way of operating in human groups that make up a specific society.

Religion appears irrational simply because the instruments that we use to analyze it are irrational, inadequate for their object: every time an irrational residue appears in religious life, it is a sign that there is an irrational residue in religious-historical methodology.[11]

1.4. To reconstruct a religion historically, starting from its oral and written traditions, above all means reaching and identifying the *human* motivations (conscious or unconscious) and the human ends (conscious or unconscious) that generate those traditions and their modifications in time. But—and this is a point of decisive importance—it is not possible to limit ourselves to this reduction or the mythical consciousness of history, almost as if the task of the historiographer were only that of "unmasking" the myth. A fundamental moment of research in fact lies in justifying what the reasons are of a certain mythical *disguising* of history, because certain motivations arise in consciousness while others enter with a mythical mask, and because certain ends to be reached were conscious while others appear elaborated mythically—that is, they too were disguised. In religious-historiographic research it is not a matter of "unmasking" myths but of justifying the historical function of mythical disguises, and this as a way of demonstrating that only through a mythically modeled coming-to-awareness according to the particularities established by the document was it possible, for a given society in a given period, to cross through history without being overwhelmed or destroyed by it. To do the history of history's mythical consciousness means reconstructing the coherence that governs its formation and functioning: and this reconstruction entails not only a **catabasis** toward the unconscious motivations and intentions but also an **anabasis** toward the conscious modes of motivations and intentions that are manifested in the myth. Religious-historical research means rendering explicit the implicit coherence of religious behavior: subtracting the myth from its irrational appearance, preventing oneself from "repeating it" exactly as it is, remaining imprisoned by it. But this can be done only in reconstructing the present consciousness of a certain mythic symbol with what lies within (unconscious motivations) as well as with what lies beyond (the unconscious intentions or ends). By virtue of this reconstruction, myth regains its coherence, its function, and its rigorous, historically determined necessity: *reason* understands it, even if precisely because it understands it, it can no longer adopt it firsthand, it can no longer *believe in it*.

1.5. The experience of history—that is, comprehending oneself as a presence called to overcome the situation through action endowed with secular value—is the founding experience of humankind: indeed, precisely this experience founds consciousness, which is entirely in the operative leeway left by critical moments of existence. But the risk of losing presence also founds humankind, the risk of remaining a prisoner of the situation without operative leeway. Mythical-ritual dehistorification is a technical fiction through which the historicity of human existence—the tension between crisis and operative value—gets concealed, and one is in history as if one were not in it.

1.6. *History*: here is a term that is ambiguous until we distinguish its different meanings. History can simply indicate the immediate experience that humanity has of being the center of secular operativity according to communitarian values: in other words, the experience of a human origin and destination of cultural action as action that overcomes the situation again and again. This experience lies at the root of every form of cultural life; indeed, it is the very possibility of cultural life in general. But "history" can also mean a particular cultural asset in its specificity, that is, the reconstruction of human activity immediately investigating the human reasons and ends that actually promote it above and beyond the subjective limits with which it is immediately experienced by agents and by protagonists. In this sense the word *history* refers to the return of memory in human occurrence, thereby establishing what people have actually done, and because in doing it they claimed to be doing something else from what came of it. While in the first sense *history* only means immediate consciousness of the humanity of action and the worldhood of operating, in the second sense it instead means historiographic knowledge, memory's conscious return to human action and conscious regeneration of it in qualifying thought. Finally, in a third sense history means *historicism*: a particular vision of life and the world for which one states in an explicit and committed way that what is real is perceptible in human cultural valorization; that such valorization entails a wholly human origin and destination of action; and that no human cultural product exists that cannot be fully traced to the humanity of action even if such whole humanity is unconscious for the actors, who on the contrary variously believe to have been moved by gods, superhuman or subhuman forces, by matter or nature, by the unconscious, and by everything else that presents itself as "beyond" real persons living in society.

1.7. The first task of the historian is to ascertain the consciousness that the historical agents contemporary to a period had of a phenomenon (of an institution, the artistic product of a myth, a liturgy, a scientific or philosophical theory of an epoch, etc.). Yet with that the historian's task is anything but finished, because historiographic knowledge does not consist of *repeating* the conscious experience that accompanies a cultural phenomenon but in situating this experience in a network of conditions and results that obviously do not belong to the consciousness of the contemporaries and that nonetheless endow that experience with its reality and truth, its "meaning" and its "importance." Undoubtedly the diametrically opposed danger to a simple "repetition" of the period's consciousness lies in attributing to this very consciousness what in realty belongs to the sphere of unconscious conditions or to perceptible results only in a perspective that developed subsequently: idealist historiography has often been guilty of this arbitrary act. But as long as we see in the historiographic discourse what belongs to the verified consciousness of the time and what belongs to the unconscious conditions that historiographic analysis sheds light on, and what belongs to results that will develop later and that the historiographer identifies with the widest perspective possible, judgment on intentions is the norm in historiographic research. Indeed, the limited consciousness of the "contemporaries" emerges precisely within a dynamic reconstruction that embraces unconscious conditions and results.

A good historiographic work is one that, first, places the reader in a condition of knowing, line by line, what the discourse refers to: whether it is the consciousness of the historical agents, the conditions and motivations they are unconscious of, or the mediated results that made a phenomenon develop beyond the consciousness of its contemporaries.

In a historical monograph the reader should be able to verify, proposition by proposition, when the historiographer's discourse describes the consciousness that historical agents had of the cultural phenomenon in question and when it instead aims to reconstruct the unconscious conditions and motivations of their activity and the mediated results that subsequently had their origin from this action. The affirmation "Men make their own history, but they do not know they are making it" means precisely this, that the consciousness accompanying a certain cultural activity in historical agents is regenerated in a broader consciousness in historiographic reconstruction. The latter is one that—assuming as a point of departure the consciousness of historical agents—inserts itself into a dynamic in which the unconscious, as a condition and result, is continuously put in question. The reduction of a cultural phenomenon to its motivations or to results that are not present to the agents' consciousness, just like its reduction to the simple descriptive repetition of this consciousness, gives rise to serious misunderstandings of the historiographer's task. But precisely because of this the historian's responsibility is called to compose an articulated discourse in which the overall sense of the cultural phenomenon in question arises from unacknowledged conditions of what was claimed to be done in the actuality of consciousness and of what was really done and developed afterward, above and beyond claims and intentions.

The religious life of an epoch lies neither in unconscious motivations nor in the actual consciousness that people had of it, nor by what effectively ensued from it, but from the unitary process that takes place through these different moments. A religious historiography that limits itself to "reliving" and "describing" the limitation of a certain religious consciousness ends up repeating this consciousness, competing with it, with the *mitsingen* that is *verboten*.[12] In other words, it lapses into historiographic irrationalism, so that the historiographer's discourse takes on the tones of an edifying sermon, more or less filled with erudite citations. But when everything is reduced to unconscious "causes" or results that are reached by consciousness only later—that is, when the moment of actual consciousness is overlooked—in the place of a historiographic reconstruction we obtain an abstract rationalistic judgment that *falsifies the documents* no less than the preceding edifying sermon.

Objectivism, neutralism, and technicism are incompatible with historiographic research even if historiography is an objective science that entails an assiduous mental catharsis from the immediate world of passions, and even if it avails itself of different techniques of analysis (ethnographic, archaeological, philological, psychological, psychiatric). The identity of historiography and of the "vision of life and the world" and the actuality of every historiographic study—in the sense that it always arises from a moment of theoretical control and mental elucidation of a problem of *historia condenda*—constitutes two fundamental features of historiographic science's structure. Historians can never claim to place themselves above the fray and to identify themselves with a god, but they are persons among persons, in definite times and places, members of a certain historical society, heirs to a certain culture. What renders them historians is only a wider awareness of the cultural becoming in which they are inserted as persons, which, however, entails a cultural choice that is even more committed than what we usually see with the vast majority of cultural agents in history. There is no history without philosophical options, and those who defend it sooner or later in fact fall to the common law, producing either collections and organizations of materials or histories that include a philosophy that one is not aware of, taking for as "absolute objectivity" this unconscious vision of life and the world that with greater or lesser coherence guides the choice of materials, interpretation, and judgment.

Humankind is in history. But *historicism*[13] is not limited to this affirmation, and still less it means history as the precise "here" and "now" of humanity immersed in time. A great number of misunderstandings about historicism arise from this reduction—and curtailment—of history to temporality, to mere becoming, where for "history" historicism means humanity as a producer of cultural values in the act of transcending the here and now of becoming and raising itself to the ideally immortal permanence of qualified human activity according to certain values. When we say the "good word" to a secular travel companion, or with a heartfelt impulse we give him a hand to keep him from drowning, we transcend the here and now of becoming and establish an action that, because of the very fact of going beyond mere biological individuality, is destined never to perish. Economic activity itself—measured by the criterion of detachment from nature and the material and mental instruments to make a form of life more human—is transcendence of the precise, instantaneous moment of history, thereby inscribing itself in a permanence that defeats time. In a biological sense, individuals undoubtedly die. Their actions can be forgotten in chronologically measurable time, civilizations disappear, and even all of humanity can succumb to a cosmic catastrophe. But the permanence we are speaking of does not belong to the order of measurable time and visible space but is forever conquered in the actuality of action qualified according to value. And even if in the order of measurable time's order and visible spatiality the agent and all humanity were to disappear an instant after the action was carried out, this disastrous material catastrophe could do nothing against the permanence that the action according to value founded in stone. The actuality[14] of action has experienced the inwardly eternal; it has transcended the here and now, and without escaping from the world it has rendered the world immortal beyond any possible cosmic catastrophe. In certain historical conditions, this has needed the protective symbol of individual immortality and mythical metahistory in which all permanences were safe: but this is related to the extreme cultural maturity required for acting according to value, remaining content with the unassailable eternity ushered in with the actuality of the action.

1.8. If we concretely analyze Eliade's stance in *Symbolisme religieux et valorisation de l'angoisse* (in *L'angoisse du temps présent et les devoirs de l'esprit*, Rencontres internationales de Genève [Neuchâtel: Éditions de la Baconnière, 1954]),[15] we clearly see the condition with which his absurd claim maintains a semblance of feasibility. First of all, Eliade does not "decide" the various questions but "describes" the different cultural themes side by side, establishing some external connections. After having indicated the "Western" discovery of the human condition's historicity and having underlined that, for the Indian, the equivalent of this discovery—the veil of Mâyâ[16]—finds its integration in the effort to get free of this illusion, Eliade adds, "It is not for us here to discuss the why and wherefore of this tendency in European thought" (239), and he limits himself to submitting the historicist position of European thought to Indian philosophy. Immediately afterward (241), Eliade tries presenting a possible European objection to the imaginary Indian critique, adding, "It is no part of my purpose to discuss these European philosophical positions." Farther below (243), he indicates the dark foreboding of the end of the world—or more exactly, the foreboding of the end of our world, our civilization—as one of the sources of modern anxiety. But once again he declares, "We will not consider how well-founded this fear may be: enough to recall that it is far from being a modern discovery" [243]. Finally, he relates the story of Rabbi Eisik of Kraków from Martin Buber's *Chassidische Bücher*, and reports Heinrich Zimmer's[17] comment on the "strange and persistent fact, that it is only after a pious journey in a distant region, in a new land, that the meaning of that inner voice guiding us on our search can make itself understood by us" (245). But this is only to say, in concluding his essay, that this road of travels in distant regions, of encounters with humanities different from our own and inner discoveries "might well constitute the point of departure for a new humanism, upon a world scale" (245). Now, one wonders: what does Eliade think? Is it legitimate to treat civilizations like crystals and reduce the task of the scientist to that of the exhibitor of systems of crystallization?

Eliade recognizes the following cultural crystals: (a) the religious belief that before death man recapitulates the story of his life; (b) the modern passion for historiography as revealing the archaic symbolism of death; (c) modern man's anxiety for the historicity of the human condition; (d) "initiation" and its ordeals in ancient civilizations; (e) the valorization of nothingness in the religions and metaphysics of India.

What would a primitive person "say" about Western anxiety in the face of the historicity of the human situation? He "would say" that "the modern world is in the situation of a man swallowed by a monster, struggling in the darkness of its belly," he would say that he is lost in the forest or in a labyrinth, that he thinks he is already dead or on the verge of dying (237).[18] We should note here (a) that this "imaginary" judgment of the primitive person is actually a hidden way Mircea Eliade negatively evaluates Western historicism, and (b) that the misunderstanding lies in the concept of history and historicism, because history creates anxiety in that it has not yet been humanized: the recognition of a becoming molded by man according to human values does not create anxiety but instead cures anxiety.

1.9. Some years ago a European scholar of religious life decided to place himself outside of European civilization and judge that civilization according to a scale of values of a non-European civilization. To justify this intention, the scholar recalled that the present historical moment is characterized by the fact that Europe is no longer alone in making history and that European values are losing their position of cultural privilege. Now, we should note that a claim of this sort is impracticable: the very cultural relativism it is based on is a way of thinking that arose from the so-called crisis of historicism. In other words, it still constitutes a European cultural phenomenon whose period of origin and development might be identified in Germany in the first half of this century. It is not possible to make oneself external to the civilization to which one belongs and by turns judge all human civilizations, one's own included, placing oneself in a perspective that we would call divine if it were not simply a belated surrogate of the mythical orientation of religion. For Europeans, their civilization is their thought itself, and it is something more: an asset to defend, to enrich, and to expand. You can continue to think, choosing you own problems inside of the great alternatives that your own civilization poses, but you cannot pose your own civilization next to others and consider them all as equal perspectives, to choose equally as judging points of view. We cannot defeat cultural "provincialism" this way: we must dialogue with the world, but we need to know our own side well, otherwise we risk falling into tremendous gossip, into ambiguous and foolish chatter, into opportunism that simulates openness and a variety of interests but that is only a mask for a boundless abdication. Moreover, where is this loss of European values? If for Europe we mean not a geographic designation but an orientation to cultural life, what is demanding and decisive in today's world is called Europe. Europe is American culture; the Marxism that stoked the Russian and Chinese Revolutions is European; Christianity is European; the science that has led to the atomic era is European. We are called to decide within this cultural world and to judge according to the parameters it offers us: it is within this fortress that we must choose our battle station.

1.10. What would a primitive person say about Western anxiety in the face of the historicity of the human situation? According to Eliade, he would say "the modern world is in the situation of a man swallowed by a monster, struggling in the darkness of its belly"; he would say that he is lost in the wilderness, or wandering in a labyrinth; he thinks he is already dead or on the point of dying (237[19]). Now, it is undoubtedly true that human history contains an unbounded situation of anxiety precisely because it has never been completely humanizable in the sense of eliminating all of its contradictions and negative aspects. But the point is whether human history's anxiety necessarily entails a metahistorical redemption or whether history—once it has arrived at an awareness of its integral humanity—contains in itself its natural medicine, that is, the consciousness that only the ethos of valorization, of which humankind bears the entire responsibility, can save us not from history but from anxiety. The "primitive" would perhaps say what Eliade imagined him to say, but even the primitive does everything he does relying on the strength of the ethos that supports him, and his religions also arise from this ethos, though not recognized as such. So—this is certain—we cannot reply in good faith like the primitive: all we can do is recognize what the primitive does not recognize and build our history on this recognition.

2. The Apostolic Christian Cultural Apocalypse as Historical Object

2.1. Apostolic Christian cultural apocalypse, as apocalyptic thought operating in history, forms a problem for the historiographer and for the anthropologist in that it is possible to identify in it an internal dynamic that in turn—that is, in various critical moments of historical becoming—contains a horizon of witnessing secular practicability that founds mores, institutions, intersubjective valorizations of life, and concrete modes of communitarian being-in-the-world. There is an apocalypse of the preaching Jesus and the disciples who listened to him, and there is an apocalypse after Jesus's death, that is, of the apostles and disciples who experienced that event and who dramatically, but victoriously, overcame its crisis.

To frame the historiographic-anthropological problem of apostolic Christian apocalypse correctly, it is necessary to reconstruct the incidents to which it was exposed—and especially, the central incident of Jesus's death—as critical moments within the development of the earliest Christian apocalyptic theme from Jesus to Paul to John. It is equally necessary that we interpret such critical moments as psychopathological risks that are incompatible with any cultural resolution whatsoever, and thus as risks recovered and reshaped, time and again, by subsequent modelings of Christian apocalypse.

The symbol of the Kingdom has a conditioning, a genesis, a structural dynamism and a destination that cannot in any way or at any moment exit from human-made history: this is the principle inherent in the craft of the historiographer, a principle that cannot be violated without contradicting the internal logic of that craft.

2.2. [. . .] The symbol is a bridge thrown between the beginning and the end; it is recollecting recovery and prefiguring anticipation that takes away from the dispersive and annihilating risk of the here and now, raising it to tasks of the communitarian valorization of life. Through the symbol, the here and now escapes the inert passing with what passes, the loss of every horizon of practicability that opens to a significant future: through the symbol the mere present instant constitutes itself as presentifying presence, becoming a propitious moment for something, a vibrant reference to cultural practice: "it's time for . . ."

2.3. Methodological questions.

(1) The history of apostolic Christianity, as historiographic research of the generating, structuring, and various operating of a *human* cultural manifestation, necessarily proposes itself the task of analyzing the *human reasons*, conscious or unconscious, that lie at the base, each time and comprehensively, of the temporal dynamic of this cultural manifestation. Such an analysis entails—at least with reference to the general methodological principle—the reabsorption of facts in coherence, conscious or unconscious, of their *entirely human* reasons, without ever—at least with reference to the research

task—making *divine reasons* explicitly intervene; and as much as
possible, without entrusting to them, even only implicitly, the
small and partial function of justification for what occurs. Indeed, it
is part and parcel of historiographic research in the sphere of religious life to completely resolve what to religious actors appeared
to be nonhuman or divine into human becoming and motivation.
At the same time, it is part and parcel of religious-historiographic
research to demonstrate the *historically* necessary and culturally
functional and productive nature of divine appearance—not a
secondary and coincidental nature—in the awareness of historical
actors, in the unconscious human motivations that the historiographer instead arrives at and declares.

(2) The history of apostolic Christianity can only arise as clarification
of "present" operative problems, that is, of the problems of Western people engaged today in the decision of cultural, communitarian living and of their own living as people in a human community:
the being of apostolic Christianity and the duty-to-be of the contemporary West are dialectically joined, and their autonomy is
constituted in this relation.

(3) The fundamental document we have for a history of earliest
Christianity is the New Testament. This means that the history to
be reconstructed through this document is that of the Christian
community, the Church. Jesus never reaches us alone and directly
but through a community that is listening, reacting and witnessing in different ways. Moreover, he reaches us according to a
memory that condenses various moments of reaction in a dynamic
unity, like the memory of speaking Jesus and at the same time the
elaboration and reinterpretation of this memory according to the
communitarian reactions after the violent death their master suffered and under the need to align this death with that memory.
This means that the true subject of apostolic Christian history is
the recollecting community in the dynamic of its recollecting, and
with the caveat that this recollection does not coincide with the
interests of historic reconstruction of what happened but with the
effective construction of that religious occurrence that is called
apostolic Christianity. Therefore, those who face the New Testament with a historiographic interest cannot by definition at any
moment passively certify data from New Testament memory but
submit themselves to the obligation of bringing every moment and
aspect and modality of this memory before the tribunal of effective
memory and historiography.

(4) The history of apostolic Christianity as the history of New Testament memory of Jesus must not forget the following hermeneutic
canons:

    (a) New Testament memory constitutes an organic *unity*, in
    other words, a coherent development that, through various
    moments of construction, forms a significant totality, so that
    the totality resulting from it confirms each moment, and
    each moment refers to the totality.

    (b) New Testament memory constitutes a dynamic unity, which
    the historian can diachronically resolve in its real genesis.

    (c) Although certain historical incidents can be important in this
    dynamic (the violent death of Jesus, the deferral of fulfilling
    the promise of the Kingdom), such incidents do not explain
    its stance and modeling, and they cannot be assumed as
    naturalistic and mechanical causes of its development. In-
    stead, the quality of this memory must result precisely from
    its capacity to transcend and reshape incidents—precisely
    like the death of Jesus and the deferral of the Parousia[20]—that
    could conceivably have dispersed the community. If these
    incidents have instead been elaborated and reshaped into a
    unitary discourse, this means that already from the beginning
    the discourse contained seeds intent on overcoming these
    incidents, and already from the beginning it nurtured forces
    of recovery for which such incidents became the topic and
    confirmation of new cultural-historical vitality.

2.4. Working hypotheses.
The inner movement of the Christian symbol of the end entails

    (a) A progressive extending of the horizon left to the world's practica-
    bility, a progressive extending characterized by the indeterminacy
    of the end's when and where, and by moving this end from immi-
    nence to distance.

    (b) A legitimation and qualification of the practicability thus disclosed,
    a legitimation and qualification obtained through the image of the
    abruptness of the end, its nature as a final and definitive tribunal of
    the actions of individuals, and of the resulting witnessing vigilance
    that it imposes on individuals and on the community of individuals.

    (c) A movement of the accent from the *here* and *now* of operative
    inner-worldly deciding, so that from a *here* and a *now* predomi-
    nantly oriented toward a future hope we pass to an absolute
    guarantee of a past decisive event, at the center of all temporal

becoming, starting from which all heres and all nows of individuals already participate in the eschatological promise. They already begin to look forward to the days of the Lord, they anticipate their certain approach (although indeterminate in the when and where). This is the direction of the passage of Jesus's preaching about the imminence of the Kingdom (which the Christian community before the death of Jesus could experience) to faith in the resurrected who will return (which became established in the community after the death of Christ). This is the same direction of development of the passage from the epoch of Jesus preaching to the disciples to the epoch of the Paracletos[21] disclosed by the Pentecost, which is also the epoch of Church operating in the world and of the sacraments that the Church administers.

(d) A vibrant, operative qualification of the witnessing to be rendered from man to man in order to bring forward and hasten the fulfillment of the promise: love and the missionary preaching of the Gospel.

2.5. Working hypotheses on the Christian cultural apocalypse.

From the beginning of preaching up to the Ascension, this is the arc of the history of redemption narrated in the synoptic Gospels: the Acts begin exactly with Ascension and Pentecost and cover the first steps of the nascent Church up to the imprisonment of St. Paul in Rome.

The narrative of the Acts begins with the apparitions of Jesus to the Apostles for forty days after his death.

This return of the deceased, reshaped into the return of the resurrected, must have given rise to expectations and hopes of the second Parousia. And yet this expectation and hope appear in the Acts reshaped and clarified in the sense of a new epoch of redemptive history beginning with the descent of the Holy Spirit. This dramatic, real process of reshaping and clarification is reflected in 1:3–11,[22] announcing the "baptism in the Holy Spirit"—the second baptism after John's—and it is interpreted by the disciples in an apocalyptic sense: "Lord, is this the time when you will restore the kingdom to Israel?" But Jesus's reply reshapes their expectation, moving the accent from the "date" and "day" of its fulfillment (and thus from the inertia that would risk resulting from it) to the action to be carried out thanks to the Holy Spirit and the *dynamis* of witnessing conferred by its descent. The second baptism is therefore not the millenarian Kingdom of Israel according to a datable when or an immediate proximity, but it is the beginning of the historical era of the apostolate "in all Judea and Samaria, and to the ends of the earth," the beginning of the historical era of the Church, the body of Christ filled with Holy Spirit. We also see in 1:9–11 the reshaping of immediate apocalyptic expectation into a horizon of expectations that open up to witnessing practicability, where through the Ascension an end is put to the mystical, visionary relationship of the forty days of returns and apparitions, and where while Jesus distances himself from the eyes of his disciples, two men dressed in white ask, "Men of Galilee, why do you stand looking up toward heaven?" as if to lead the disciples from the wait for new apparitions—and the hope that one of these marks the second Parousia—to the operative witnessing *through the promise of an indeterminate, but very certain, return of he who, ascended to heaven, will return from heaven in the same way.* The witnessing operative horizon, which in the wait threatens to narrow itself to the point of nullifying itself in an inaction that is incompatible with any cultural life, gets opened up though this reshaping process that defers and makes indeterminate the *when*, and at the same time places the accent on the *already* (Jesus has already come once and guarantees his second and definitive coming; the Kingdom has already begun and will be fulfilled; through the Holy Spirit and the Church the promise will be carried out). But what in this reshaping appears particularly important is the theme of an "already" (Christ dead and resurrected) that orders a development and fulfillment, an "already" that demands witnessing in time to develop and fulfill itself, an "already" that has redemptive value in that it is "not yet"; an "already" that, though paradoxically being a "not yet" necessarily entails the apostolate to the ends of the earth and unfolds the task of the Church in the world. It should be noted in this regard that as the datable *when* of the apocalyptic event contains a risk of inert waiting incompatible with any cultural life, similarly the *already* contains a similar risk when it is experienced as already present *fulfillment*, as a development that has already occurred. This *when* and this *already* both mark the end of worldly operative witnessing, the *when because he will come on such and such datable date* and time and now there is nothing to do but wait for him with a gaze toward heaven, exhausting oneself in an exploration of signs, and this because the fulfillment having taken place, now the only thing left is to enjoy it in the proud and isolating immediate participation of the once and for all development.

But what made Christianity a religion that founded a civilization, what within it disclosed history, was precisely this paradoxical tension between the *already* and *not yet*, this permanent state of vigilant tension between one and the other, this feeling guaranteed by the former and pushed toward the latter, each person's living in the era of the Holy Spirit, of the Church, of the apostolate, of witnessing to the ends of the earth, of the good news to spread among the peoples in a relationship dominated by *agape*. It is precisely this historically defined Christian form of ethos that supports the world. But if this *now* between *already* and *not yet* is the civil greatness of Christianity, it also constitutes its anguish: the *already now* that obscures the *not yet* and the *not yet* that loses the *already* constitute two eccentric forces that manifested the loss of that agape that Paul placed above *pistis* and *elpis*.[23]

The descent of the Holy Spirit (a sound like a wind that blows impetuously, flames that place themselves on each of the apostles, glossolalia) bears the outer signs of a hallucinatory crisis and of tumultuous emergencies of the unconscious in the form of "foreign" languages (2:1–4). But the interpretation of the Acts is that this descent through xenoglossia prefigures and anticipates the proclamation of the Gospel to all peoples (2:5–11), and it prefigures and anticipates the final days as well, when there will be signs of a cosmic catastrophe in heaven and on earth, blood, fire, steam, the darkening of the sun and a moon as red as blood, and the multiplying of prophesies and signs; and all of them will be filled with Holy Spirit (2:17–21) (Joel 3:1–5). This means that the end of the world, the final days, are—through a cultural reshaping of what happened among the apostles on the day of Pentecost on the Mount of Olives—transformed into the prefiguring anticipation of the descent of the Spirit in the final days and of the preaching of the Gospel to all peoples to the ends of the earth. Meanwhile, though, the preaching opens itself up *as a task, as a prospect,* and therefore as a *period of fulfillment and maturation* of the promise inscribed in time through the first Parousia, from the preaching to the passion, death, and resurrection of Christ. Now it lies before the apostles not as the end in an immediate way but precisely this period that must be traversed before the end occurs: and it is this "must" that characterizes and gives a precise cultural sense to Christianity; it identifies it as a historical phenomenon, and it endows it with the foundational power of a "Christian civilization." It is Peter's speech (Acts, 2:16ff.) that illustrates this meaning, otherwise it would have only been a *crisis* without *telos* ("What does this mean?"), one that might even have appeared to be drunkenness. (Peter's speech is connected to the Pauline polemic against the abuse of charisms in the First Letter to the Corinthians: and, in the direction of a structural interpretation of religious experience, we need to establish a comparison between the "telestic mania" Plato spoke of and to which Linforth and Dodds have recently drawn attention with reference to the orgiastic cults of antiquity (in particular the Corybantic cult).[24]

Ascension and Pentecost place an end to the period of crisis of the apostolic Christian community after the death of Jesus. The "return" of Christ in this period seems to take on the characteristic mode of the return of the deceased: Christ's apparitions proliferate; the women at the sepulchre and while they returned, to Peter, to the two of Emmaus, to the

Jerusalemites, to the Sea of Galilee, to Mount Tabor, to dine for the last time. These returns of the deceased can count as evidence of the crisis of mourning for the death of Jesus. But at the same time, in the Gospels they already appear oriented according to two great resolving themes, that is, as a witnessing of the Resurrection and as the presence of the dead and resurrected Christ in his Church until the fulfillment of the temporal plan of redemption with the second Parousia ("syntéleia tou aiónos"[25]), a fulfillment that entails a growth and spread of the Kingdom through the preaching of the gospel to all peoples. The apparitions of Jesus—from the one to the women at the sepulchre to the one at the final meal, and until the Ascension that closes the apostolic Christian cycle of Jesus appearing—mark the times of a great funerary liturgy in the Gospel that provides a model of how to overcome death and the crisis of mourning that accompanies it. After the detachment of the Ascension, the paradigmatic narrative parabola gets completed with the descent of the Holy Spirit, which inaugurates the epoch in which the dead-resurrected will be with his believers every day until the end of the world, and he will give them the missionary *dynamis* that characterizes that epoch.

It is thus possible to interpret the genesis of apostolic Christianity as the exemplification of a historical resolution to the crisis of mourning: this is a resolution that transforms dead Jesus into resurrected Christ, and the deceased-who-returns of the crisis in the resurrected deceased present in the Church and quintessentially in the Eucharistic banquet, until the already occurred of the promise will be carried out through the missionary drive. This suggests a further deepening of the thesis of *Morte e pianto ritual nel mondo antico*[26] and authorizes us to interpret Christianity as a great funerary ritual for a death that exemplarily resolves historical dying and as a pedagogy of detachment and transcendence with regard to what dies. (This could have taken place only because the deceased was the anointed man-God.) This event is also reproduced in the funerary rituals of the ancient world but through a different resolving apparatus, since what was missing in them was precisely what lies at the heart of Christianity: the historical exemplariness of a passage from the crisis of the deceased-who-returns to faith in a resurrected deceased, from the faith in a resurrected deceased to his presence in the community of the faithful, and from his presence in the community of those faithful to the task of ardently witnessing for him in a *Christian life* nestled in the horizon of his promise.

2.6. The *Weltuntergangserlebnis* (the experience of the end of the world) as an anthropological existential risk finds its horizon of reintegration in the mythical-ritual symbol of the Kingdom. This is a horizon that indirectly discloses being-in-the-world through this mythical-ritual consciousness of being-there. By virtue of the Eucharistic symbol the community of the faithful participates in the Eucharist, in a retrospective and perspectival horizon. This horizon is retrospective since the banquet represents the "past" event of Christ at the center of the temporal plan of redemption. It is perspectival in that it anticipates and prefigures the banquet of end-times, when the second, definitive Parousia will take place. But precisely because it is retrospective and perspectival, the Eucharistic symbolic horizon discloses dimensions of the present (and of presence in the world, being-there), inserting it into time and removing it from an isolation that equals losing its possibility, that equals the experience hic et nunc of the catastrophe of the world. The risky appearance of the catastrophe, incompatible with any cultural life—on the contrary, a "symptom" of the catastrophe of the very possibility of human culture—now gets indirectly overcome. With Christ the world has begun to end in the past, in the central point of the divine plan of redemption; with Christ, again in the past, the promise has been made of the future end-times. Finally, with Christ made present in the repetition of the Eucharistic banquet, it is possible to experience in the here and now not the actual, immediate collapse of the world but the past promise and future awaiting an ending, living here and now and not in end-times but the promise of the past and awaiting the future. We thus have the prefiguration, the anticipation, and the pledge of the second Parousia that certainly *will* take place, because it *already* took place with the first. Precisely this *already* and this *not yet* give a horizon to the *Weltuntergangserlebnis*, removing it from the actual, clear, incoherent, catastrophic, uncompensated experience of the world that collapses: the risk is recovered and reshaped by the symbol, which through this reshaping inverts the catastrophe.

Furthermore, the catastrophe of the *Weltuntergangserlebnis* acquires a horizon and inversion not only through the horizon of the Kingdom of God but also through the Eucharistic rite. The Eucharist is a socialized, institutionalized, calendarized celebration of the Last Supper, of the Eucharistic banquet and the feast of end-times: that is, of a past and future that the rite presentifies. Each time the day of the Lord appears in the calendar, the community gathers to celebrate. But already the institution of limiting the celebration of the catastrophe reshaped into recurrent, calendrical moments of time (the days of the Lord) makes the intermediate periods between the subsequent celebrations available for the being-in-the-world. In fact, it frees this time for this being-there, thereby making the varied cultural life possible that is undoubtedly fostered by Sunday liturgical behaviors but which by no means reduces itself to them. The catastrophe of the end undergoes a second inversion: if as a myth of the Kingdom the inversion lies in disclosing the actual and exact tormenting ending to an ending that has already begun and that at the same time will evolve as an end according to a plan of redemption, in the Eucharistic rite the inversion lies in introducing into historical time a periodic, calendrical ritual so that the time between celebrations can be made available for being-in-the-world. This means that in actual fact this time is disclosed to secular agency. If between the "not yet" and the "already" of the Christian mythical-ritual symbol the presence takes a breath and is placed in a condition of unleashing its powers, the periodic calendrical concentration of liturgical behavior frees up time for other cultural behaviors.

Through this dual horizon gained with regard to the incoherent appearance of the *Weltuntergangserlebnis,* finally—precisely in this "anastrophic" horizon—it is possible to free up behaviors of being-in-the-world. Such behaviors are undoubtedly mediated and disclosed through Christian symbolic justification precisely because the appearance of *Weltuntergangserlebnis*—of the world's collapsing here and now—finds its redemption in the disclosed time of the Kingdom that is already and that is not yet and that of the ritual that here and now makes us participate in the divine plan of redemption, restoring extraliturgical agency to the worldly. This also makes possible the great task of love that lies above faith and hope and that is worth more than the gift of languages: agape—the banquet—pours forth like love beyond the liturgical experience; it is love witnessed by people toward all people. Love among people is mediated in the shadow of the Kingdom believed in and hoped for according to Christ's model, a love that in this upside-down perspective makes the Kingdom grow, marking its approach in time and its spread in space. Here the *Weltuntergangserlebnis* undergoes the third inversion: its reopening to that love that in the *Weltuntergangserlebnis* was totally exhausted in the very moment in which an atrocious self-absorption closed the individual in himself and destroyed him as presence.

3. The Limits of Protestant Theology

3.1. Oscar Cullmann, *Christus und die Zeit: Die unchristliche Zeit und Geschichtsaufassung,* 2nd ed. (Zollikon-Zurich: Evangelischer Verlag, 1948), 224.[27]

Until the eighteenth century, two ways of reckoning time mattered: one "after" Christ, founded on the succession of years starting from his birth (AD), and one before his birth, based on the years following the creation of the world. But from the eighteenth century on, the way of reckoning time that takes the birth of Christ as the central event became dominant; starting from this the years "before" and "after" his birth are calculated.

The problem posed by O. Cullmann, whether the center of earliest Christianity is redemptive history redistributed with reference to the historical event of Christ-God, is not a historiographic problem. Even if we ascertain that, for earliest Christianity, this salvific vision of history served as its central nucleus, for the historian it is not enough to identify the essence of earliest Christianity. Instead, it is necessary to identify the human reasons (conscious or unconscious) of this particular consciousness of historical becoming and the human values that (consciously or unconsciously) get mediated by it (e.g., love). It is not a matter of identifying the essence of earliest Christianity, that is, where the emphasis of the conscious sphere lay, but to reconstruct a movement that places a consciousness of redemptive history through Christ at the center of historical becoming.

According to Cullmann (48ff.), *aión* in earliest Christianity has the following distinct meanings:

(a) unlimited time, without a beginning or end, and thus truly infinite, eternal: as the time of God, it tends to lose every concrete temporal meaning;

(b) the limited time between the creation and the end of the world;

(c) unlimited time as beginning and limited as the end: that is, a time "before" creation;

(d) limited time as the beginning but unlimited as the end: that is, a time "after" the end of the world.

This New Testament economy of time is governed by a "divine plan" that determines the *kairói*—the suitable moments—of this rectilinear succession of *aiónes*: Christ lies at the center of the process in the sense that the date of his occurrence and his action manifests to people the entire economy of time, mediating to people—once and for all—the divine plan of redemption.

Cullmann's thesis has the limit of presenting the earliest Christian conception of time as a static totality without development as an essence. The author undoubtedly understands very well the distinction between this conception and that of the Old Testament or the Greek or Iranian ones (and, we could add, Indian). But he does not present the distinct phases or various emphases that within the history of earliest Christianity itself—from its Judaic antecedents to Christ's preaching, from this up to the death of Jesus, from the death of Jesus to Paul and John—experienced the themes of *aión*, *kairós*, the Kingdom, the Parousia, and everything else connected to the end of the world and eschatology, to cosmic becoming and the history of redemption. Earliest Christianity is offered here as a monolithic block, fallen from heaven, and thus without its own history and which Hellenization had to chip away at or even break (Gnosticism). But with regard to time, we should ask whether the end of the world, the wait for the Kingdom, and so forth, were configured with a different emphasis in Jesus and after Jesus's death, in the synoptic Gospels and in Paul, in the fourth Gospel and Revelation. Precisely the history of this different emphasis forms a problem, so it is necessary to break down the *Christus und die Zeit* relationship into others: Jesus and time, the Synoptics and time, Paul and time, the fourth Gospel and time, Revelation and time. The limits of Cullmann's work are fundamentally those of Protestantism: in other words, of research oriented toward an essence of Christianity that was betrayed and that we need to recover.

End-times, Holy Spirit, Church, Eucharist.

[. . .]

Abstractly, the structure of the Kingdom is bristling with contradictions if judged from a modern philosophical point of view. But the problem facing the historian is another: it is a matter of understanding why the contradictions of the Kingdom did not appear to the apostolic Christian consciousness, for example, the incoherence between a redemptive history already entirely planned by God and the merit of saving oneself in a human perspective. Now, precisely when the historian poses this problem, and in order to resolve it appeals to reasons that unconsciously restrained an orientation to gaining awareness of these contradictions, then the incoherences contained in the actual consciousness that the earliest Christian had of the Kingdom show their necessity: the unconscious reasons for the incoherence of the Kingdom reestablish its historically conditioned coherence. Could it not be that a necessary incoherence converts itself into coherence? And an incoherence, indeed, that one manages to establish that the actual consciousness could not and should not recognize for certain reasons: could it not be that this gets reintegrated into rationality, and with this, could it not be historiographically "understood"? The structure of the Kingdom, abstractly considered, is certainly irrational: but the historian is engaged in demonstrating that nothing is left to chance in the various parts of this structure and that given certain existential problems of the period, their coherent solution could only be reached through that organic system of unrecognized incoherences that is exactly the Kingdom.

[. . .] Judaism and Christianity have a different perspective of time: both divide it into the tripartition of time before Creation, time between Creation and the Kingdom, and the time of the Kingdom. But in Judaism secular time—between Creation and the Kingdom—is experienced in the perspective of a future event, the coming of the Messiah. In Christianity, instead, the center is moved back from the future to the past, so after this center "the Kingdom already begins."

The emergence of history within the Christian symbol is carried out through this moving back of the end (the Parousia) to the center (Christ) of the present *aión*, nonetheless maintaining the end as the fulfillment and second Parousia. So from the first to the second Parousia, the Kingdom— which in the Judaic conception is only a promise of the future—begins and grows and is carried out in the here and now, in the liturgical celebration of agape, and in the secular expansion of the very agape stored in the Eucharistic rite. The Eucharist thus takes on the meaning of always re-presenting the "past" center of the history of redemption, that is, the first Parousia, as present time gradually passes: and through this re-presentation of the past center, which is the origin of a new epoch, the present gets reabsorbed in the eschatological plan again and again, entering in participation with the end-times of the second Parousia.

But this Christian symbol in turn has an inner history of development: if Christ for Christians is a past event, the living Jesus obviously could not relive the crucified Christ and resurrected Christ as a "past," but the emphasis on the final end, on the end of the world and on the advent of the Kingdom had to be foregrounded in Him. Jesus was near to the end-times, he touched the margin of a history that had reached its end. For the historian, then, the focus lies on the problem of this continuous movement of emphases in apostolic Christian history, so that the end perspective of Jesus's preaching gets substituted by the perspective of the dead and resurrected Christ as a central past event in redemptive history: the perspective of a Kingdom that has already begun with that death and resurrection and nonetheless still needs to be fulfilled with the second Parousia.

[...]

Here (87–93) it is possible to recognize the typical limit of Cullmann's perspective. In the New Testament the expressions used at times emphasize the "imminence" of the Kingdom, at other times its "future" quality, at other times its "chronological indeterminacy," and at other times the theme of the Kingdom that has "already" begun and grows and expands up to the day of its definitive fulfillment. This fact gets attributed to "psychological causes" that are secondary for theological consideration, for which all of these determinations lie in an organic whole in an essence given once and for all—in other words, the movement of the center from the future to the past, with the resulting change in perspective of redemptive history: Judaism belongs to the epoch in which the Parousia *will be*; Christianity belongs to the epoch between the first and second Parousia, between the beginning of the Kingdom and its completion, between the promise already made and the future fulfillment of this very promise. But from a historical point of view, precisely what Cullmann calls "psychological motivations" takes on great prominence. The Kingdom preached by Jesus, that of the synoptic Gospels written after the death of Jesus, that of Pauline Christology, that of the fourth Gospel and that of the Revelation all participate in a historical movement in which the emphases move around in a certain way and according to a certain coherence and necessity, a movement that historiographic research must reconstruct and understand. For the believer, what in the New Testament appears to be on the same level—that is, as everything given in one time with its various emphases—for the historian displays a succession of moments of development. For the believer, the Kingdom begins with the preaching of Jesus of Nazareth, and it gets modified as a historical product in a change of emphases that is not secondary or merely psychological but primary for understanding. For the believer, the Kingdom appears first as a new perspective of redemption realized in time. For the historian, the apostolic Christian consciousness of time becomes a problem in the sense that this consciousness does not stay abstractly identical but presents levels and moments of development and in the sense that beyond this consciousness extends the sphere of unconscious motivations or results that only later will come to fruition; and in the fundamental sense that, for the historian, the Kingdom can only be an unconscious human cultural creation as such (men make history but do not know they are making it). It is therefore the historian's responsibility to trace human motivations not recognized as such, as well as the historical necessity and function of this not-knowing (or of this mythical knowledge). Cullmann's perspective (the essence of earliest Christianity) is instead animated by an immediate religious concern disguised with the intention of repeating only the apostolic Christian consciousness of time without any reference to its historical moment and its "human" historical motivations.

[. . .]

When we pose the problem of the consciousness that earliest Christianity had of time, we certainly cannot in any way bring into play our consciousness of the distinction between myth and history as if it were present to apostolic Christian consciousness. Indeed, for Christian consciousness Adam as a myth, Jesus of Nazareth as a historical person, and Christ as a myth are not distinguished according to our categories of myth and history. But the historian does not exhaust his task in determining the extent to which his concept of history does not belong to the consciousness of the historical agents he is studying, and in a positive way, how the history of which they are protagonists is reflected in the consciousness of these agents. The task of the historian of apostolic Christianity is to reconstruct the human motivations (conscious or unconscious) and the overall cultural conditions for which the Christian consciousness of history took place—in other words the motivations and conditions for which the Gospel appeared as "good news" and not as a series of biographical facts carefully collected and commented on by the historiographers Matthew, Luke, Mark, and John.

[. . .]

With regard to what Cullmann asserts (97ff.), we should note: that the scriptures are not historiographic books seems all too obvious, but this has nothing to do with the fact that they are not "historical" books, that is, human cultural products. This is necessarily the perspective of the historiographer who approaches them as documents. Since they are not historiographic books—that is, written with the intent of telling the course of human events and recognized as such—they contain affirmations of faith, for example, that Jesus is the son of God, or that his birth was virginal, and so forth and so on; but as historical books that the historiographer approaches, even affirmations of faith belong entirely to human history, and they pose for historiography the problem of how and why in history the consciousness—certainly not historiographic, but mythic—developed that characterizes apostolic Christianity. Thus, if the historiographer has the task of reconstructing the human genesis of cultural products, he cannot halt, claiming incompetence, when faced with cultural products that contain a nonhistoriographic consciousness. Instead, he is called to historically reproduce the mythical consciousness of human history in its motivations, structure, and function. Either a historiography of Christianity is possible—and therefore it is so by taking on the principle inherent in historiographic research that Christianity is a human cultural product that in all of its parts, without exception, can be traced to the human reasons that produced it—or else it is not possible—and so it is entirely impossible, in that the historian looks for humanly motivated human origins, and Christianity instead presents events that fall within a plan of divine actions. We are faced with an either/or here, a choice, and every attempt at compromise gives rise to irreconcilable contradictions. Such contradictions remain concealed when we limit ourselves to describing the Christian consciousness of history: but this concealment is obtained at the price of prohibiting us from narrating how this consciousness was formed and what function it carried out; in other words, it is obtained by eliminating the basic task of the historiographer or limiting it arbitrarily only to certain documents or to certain aspects of these and removing others from historiographic examination as a matter of principle, since they would be under the theologist's exclusive purview.

3.2. *Christus und die Zeit*. Related observations.

As a culturally determined existence, historical existence is always a particular horizon of transcendence of critical moments according to intersubjective values. Indeed, different cultures distinguish themselves according to the number, quality, and frequency of the risks of radical crisis and the nature of the reintegrating apparatus of valorization.

There are three great apparatuses of reintegration with regard to radical crisis. The first apparatus is the following: concealment of the human condition's historicity through the reduction of the critical present and uncertain future to *mystical* models of foundation and resolution. Initiative, choice, and responsible decision cannot yet occur accompanied by the consciousness of a wholly human origin and destination of action, and they protect themselves in a characteristic "as if." One acts, repeating metahistorical models of behavior; the proliferation of becoming is systematically reabsorbed in the hegemonic consciousness of the ritual repetition of always identical mythical origins. The second apparatus is the following: history, which in the preceding model gets continuously absorbed in mythical origins, here instead manifests the dimension of the future to the hegemonic cultural consciousness in the sense of a finite path toward an ultimate end—this too mythical, of an eschatological nature. This is the Judaic perspective, which operates within the horizon of a history between origins and end, between creation, covenant, and waiting for the days of Jehovah; it works by studying signs of divine favor or anger and interpreting all history, from the origins to the eschatological end, as the holy history of a special people. The third apparatus is the Christian one. The eschatological event is not placed at the end of history but at the center, starting from which the end begins [. . .][28]

The eternal return as an image of time is connected to mythical-ritual symbolism of the forms of religious life independent from the Judeo-Christian tradition. Mythical-ritual symbolism of such forms mystifies historical becoming—it conceals it to a possible comprehensive awareness of it—through the articulation of becoming in "critical moments typical of existence," through the reabsorption of these typified critical moments in a metahistorical model of foundation and resolution *in illo tempore*. In this way, by ritually repeating the model of "origins" every critical "now" and "tomorrow" are led to an "already" carried out by the numina once and for all. The model of the center of human history between origins and the end instead belongs to Christianity: a center that, as a decisive event, gives meaning to secular becoming and assigns to single epochs of redemption a univocal place in the "before" and "after" and in the overall "plan" that unfolds from the origins to the end. In this new horizon, repetition no longer concerns the origins (the original foundation) but the central event itself: natural and secular time and astronomical years all get reabsorbed within the same liturgical year, and the liturgical year that is repeated every year in turn repeats the time of the central event with its high point in the Easter of Resurrection. The image of a liturgical year thus contains, as an ideal limit, the complete dehistorification of time: like in a cave dominated by an echo, Christ is repeated indefinitely, even if the sound has different pitches. Every mass repeats the central event, but Christmas Mass and especially Easter Mass refer with greater significance to it: every month, every day, every hour, every instant possesses its repetitive meaning—always as an ideal limit—its calendrical possibility of being reabsorbed and sanctified in the direction of the center. Every day has its own saint, every hour has its prayer, and every month has its festival. Nonetheless, precisely because what gets repeated is not an origin myth but a central event of redemptive history, the Christian paradox of time explodes in all of its seriousness: while the repetition of Christ implies a radical dehistorification, the repetition of the central event that bestows sense on human history gives rise to the consciousness of history within the repetitive mythical-ritual consciousness itself. What appears is the "irreversible process," the deferral of the last days and the Kingdom that has already begun and that expands, the Holy Spirit of Christ to men of the period from the first to the second Parousia, the human witnessing capable of hastening the Kingdom, love above faith and hope, time that must still flow after the central event so that the Gospel can be preached to all peoples and the greatest number of people can be saved. All of these moments imply the responsibility of individual decision in the here and now, a responsibility that in the last instance has nothing repetitive.

Mythical-ritual symbolism reabsorbs the historical proliferation of becoming in the ritual repetition of the mythic foundation. It mystifies it, it conceals it, and with this mystification and concealment it protects the civilized agency of the existential crisis. But when, with Christianity, the consciousness of history began to appear within mythical consciousness itself—when, with Christ, the theme of the repetition of origins was substituted with the repetition of the center of the course of history, and becoming was experienced as epochs of redemption, to which (past, present, and future) that center gave the meaning of a "plan" from an origin to an end—all of the ancient mythical-ritual symbolism embraced a deep paradox.

The need for a symbolic horizon of crisis nonetheless remains: a horizon that embraces a foundational event and a perspectival destination and that gives sense to communitarian life in the unity of an epoch. The years 1–30 were decisive for Christians as years of the birth, preaching, passion, death, and resurrection of Christ, and for nearly two thousand years a civilization has lived in the memory of those years and in the anticipation of the final days, of which those years marked the proclamation and guarantee. But once Christian symbolism freed the sense of history, it was no longer possible in good faith to believe in the decisive character of those years as years of the incarnation of logos in the person of Jesus of Nazareth. It is necessary to recompose our symbolism on an exclusively civil level, participating in a specific epochal horizon, with a beginning and destination that are not absolutes but relative to this epoch, and not entrusted to numina but entirely to people and their institutions. An initial and foundational event anchored in the heart of history, effected entirely by humankind and destined to humankind, a new course in process, a destination in sight: this can only be a revolution, the ten days that shook the world.

(Cullmann, 123). Two thousand years separate us from the days of Christ, and also a spatial distance: the Holy Land. But to the primitive Christian community the scandal and madness of the cross must have appeared much greater than it does to us, since in a well-known village, a man among others proclaimed himself the son of God and was sentenced to death like a criminal.

If the end looms, and if this looming is experienced as a distressing proximity and radicality, or if the end is experienced as already having occurred, so that by now an epoch of decline and collapse has begun that moves rapidly toward catastrophe, then the world and history are no longer practicable, and every margin for cultural life gets restricted and destroyed. But the end that the New Testament speaks of is not this, though it appears as a moment of recovery and redemption. The moment of looming proximity appears in it, especially in the epoch of Jesus's preaching, but it is a proximity that is not concentrated in a when and where. On the contrary, it rejects this when and where to give a horizon to themes of metanoia, witnessing, preparation, vigilance, love, of an extreme tension of communitarian action. After Jesus's death this margin became wider; Christology indicated in the cross an end that belonged to the past and is the guarantee of the second Parousia. The Pentecost discloses the future, that is, the epoch between the two Parousias, and this epoch is not only practicable for those who have received the Holy Spirit but also take the form of a program of Christian life that can hasten and expand the Kingdom. The Church arises, the sacraments are institutionalized, and through the Eucharist the death and resurrection of Christ become the principle of communitarian life, a calendrical moment of the concentration and diffusion of operative energies for everyday life in the perspective of increasingly distant and always deferred final days.

Faith in the event of already-occurred redemption as a surrogate of the still unfulfilled expectation of the Kingdom of God; or, faith in the event of already-occurred redemption as the foundation of the waiting for the second Parousia. We should reject this hermeneutic choice. The "already occurred" as a *psychological surrogate* of the "not yet occurred" is an insufficient interpretative criterion. We should instead speak of a dynamic from the imminence of the future Kingdom to the actuality of the Kingdom that has already begun, from the wait for the final days to the mediating anticipation of the witnessing of works, from the near end to the decisive, already-occurred event and to the present redeemed through this opening.

The eschaton refines itself in this ethical principle: "act as if your decision were the last possible and therefore not correctable with a further decision; as if it were a decision of cosmic and definitive resonance, as if you were at death's door and were dictating your last will." But this is not the apostolic Christian eschaton, even if it can mediate—and indeed has mediated—the sense of a supreme human responsibility in worldly occurrence.

According to Cullmann (218ff.), Christianity's linear conception of time avoids a "mystical" misinterpretation of evangelical contents. This misinterpretation can be avoided only by virtue of the temporality of redemptive history:

> The participation in a timeless myth bears a necessarily mystical character, a fact that we verify in the Hellenistic mystery religions. In a time happening of the *past*, if the past is actually and seriously taken as such, there is only such participation as rests upon faith in the redemptive significance of these facts of the past.[29]

Cullmann thus polemicizes (169) with the interpretation of the "representation" (*Wergegenwartigung*) of the decisive event of the past:

> To be sure, leading Catholic theologians have protested, perhaps not unjustly, against the Protestant misinterpretation according to which the offering of Golgotha is "repeated" in the Mass. In actual fact, the thing in question is not a repetition but a "realization" of the unique happening. But from the basis of the Primitive Christian conception of time, as we have here presented it, this concept of "realization" does not seem to me to do justice to the uniqueness. I too emphasize strongly that the Primitive Christian worship service, with the Eucharist as its indispensable climax, points back to the Crucified and Risen One and forward to Him who comes at the end. But he who now appears in the assembled congregation does not appear as "one being crucified" and rising, any more than he appears as returning for the eschatological Parousia; he appears rather as the one sitting at the right hand of God, who has been crucified and has risen and will return. As such he now offers the forgiveness of

sin, which he has effected and promises the completion, which he will bring. If in Kierkegaard the time from the present to the Christ-event at the mid-point[30] is, so to speak, overleaped in a backward direction, in Catholicism, on the contrary, the leap is made in a forward direction from the Christ-event to the present. If in Kierkegaard the peculiar significance of the present for redemptive history is undervalued, here, on the contrary, in relation to that past central happening, it is overvalued.

According to Cullmann the imminence of the Kingdom, the wait for its coming advent, has its root in the faith that the event of redemption has already taken place, that it has already been produced. We cannot say—again, according to Cullmann—that faith in the Savior who has "already" saved is a surrogate of the disappointed expectation of the coming advent of the Kingdom, but on the contrary, precisely this faith has generated the subsequent wait. The essence of the proclamation "The kingdom is near" certainly concerns chronology but in very close connection with the knowledge of a decision that has already occurred. Therefore, this does not primarily mean delimiting the proximity of the end to a generation, even if we certainly find this delimitation in the Gospel. The theologically important feature in the preaching of the immanence of the Kingdom of God is not this but the implicit affirmation that we, from Christ on, are already in a new temporal epoch and therefore that the end is now near. Apostolic Christianity certainly depicted this proximity at most in decades, not in centuries or millennia: but this error of perspective, which was corrected in the New Testament itself in the Second Epistle of Peter, 3:8, does not affect the theological content of the *ēggiken ē basileía*.[31] This proclamation does not refer primarily to a determination of date or a chronological limitation but to a partition of time: we can explain the error (the proximity of a generation rather than millennia) psychologically in the same way we explain the anticipated predictions of the end of a war when we are convinced that the decisive battle has already taken place.

[...]

Cullmann (149ff.): we should give an affirmative answer to the question of whether Jesus himself believed in an interval between his death and the Parousia. That Jesus, like the primitive Christian community, measured this interval not in centuries and millennia but much more likely in decades is of secondary importance. "For the Primitive Church, at any rate, it is a fixed fact that the present stage of redemptive history is the period of the Church, the earthly body of Christ. [...] The Primitive Church had from its first hour the conviction that it stood in a segment of time [...] between Christ's ascension and his Parousia." The Kingdom of Christ, whose visible body has been inherited by the Church, prepares the Kingdom of

God. "Like the Church, therefore, the Kingdom of Christ has a beginning and an end."

[...]

In the New Testament we see a solidarity between humankind and creation in its entirety.[32] We also find traces of this solidarity in the Old Testament, at least in the sense that sin is considered to be the origin of the curse that weighs on the world and similarly in crossing the Red Sea (Psalm 74:13) and in the apocalypse (new creation and redemption of the people of Israel). But in the Old Testament, this solidarity is not anchored to a timeline whose center is a historical fact. In Matthew 27:51 and Luke 23:45 we read that the moment that Christ was crucified, the sun darkened and the earth shook. The solidarity between man and creation is not limited to the myth of origins and sin but is concentrated in a historical act. In the Epistle to the Colossians 1:19[33] we read that through Christ, God was pleased to reconcile with everything existing in heaven and on earth. In the New Testament we can speak of "Good Friday magic." Now, the whole of creation participates in the particular situation of the present moment with regard to the period between Resurrection and Return. This present moment is already the final moment, although it still belongs to the ancient eon[34]: the Holy Spirit is already in action; death and sin are vanquished but not eliminated. It is the time in which one *still* waits, and at the same time, one waits for the *already*.

Epistle to the Romans 8:19ff.:

> For the creation waits with eager longing for the revealing of the children of God; for the creation was subjected to futility, not of its own will but by the will of the one who subjected it, in hope that the creation itself will be set free from its bondage to decay and will obtain the freedom of the glory of the children of God. We know that the whole creation has been groaning in labour pains until now; and not only the creation, but we ourselves, who have the first fruits of the Spirit, groan inwardly while we wait for adoption, the redemption of our bodies. (Cullmann 101ff.)

Cullmann (157):

> The anti-Christian feature in the apocalyptic evaluation of events in time, as we find this evaluation in later apocalyptic sects down to the present day, is not the fact that such events are in some way interpreted as "preliminary signs," but that from them the time of the end is reckoned. Such a reckoning stands in contradiction to the Primitive Christian belief that the fixing of the *kairoi* belongs solely to the sovereign power of God, and that men, even by their knowledge, have no control over it. Viewed

from this standpoint, it is not a falling away from the Primitive Christian attitude when ever and again, in the course of the centuries, this or that phenomenon is judged to be a manifestation of the Antichrist; but it is such a falling away when such a phenomenon is regarded as his final manifestation and so is used to reckon the date of the end.

Imminence and proximity of the final days as a hegemonic experience is not the sense of the dynamic in earliest Christianity's formation. On the contrary, this sense consists in the progressive widening of the present operative horizon and in the continuous deferral and chronological indeterminacy of the end perspective. Precisely because of this calculability of the "when," the "date" of the end, they do not belong to the main line of Christian cultural life, and if anything they represent a risk for it, a temptation, a "heresy." An end whose date "is known" in fact expresses as a mental representation the "symptom" of the crippling of the future as a horizon for human decision and responsibility: it expresses an annihilation of the sense of the possible and practicable according to human valorizations, a collapse of the ethos of presentification, an incoherent return of the past, the undoing of intersubjective communicability, a retreat into chaos. Those who focus on the calculation of the end's when and on the "knowledge" deriving from it are already lost to any beginning; on the contrary, they manifest the loss of any valorizing initiative, and precisely due to the lethal inertia that grips them they concentrate on the calculation of the end in the distressing wait for that terrible date.

Cullmann (139 ff.; cf. 71–72, 83–84) highlights how the "future" for apostolic Christianity is not, as in Judaism, what gives meaning to redemptive history: the Christian *telos* has already occurred, and the *epháphax* of Christ—and the future—in this perspective of the center, becomes merely the fulfillment of the *telos*. While Judaic eschatology extends from the covenant and day of Jehovah, Christian eschatology assigns to the Christ event the character of a decisive historical beginning of what will be fulfilled with the second Parousia. If Judaism lives waiting for the future *telos*, Christianity instead lives waiting for the fulfillment of the already reached *telos* in the central event of redemptive history.

But this contrast is typological, schematic, of "essences," not genetic or properly historiographic. It reproduces the result of a process that certainly took place in earliest Christianity, but it is as if this result were already completely given from Jesus's preaching on, as if his death had not introduced substantial changes in the process. The passage from the imminence of the Kingdom preached by Jesus to the Christological theme of the meaning of the cross in the economy of redemption does not constitute a problem for Cullmann: the theologist from Basel does not distinguish between the Christian document elaborated after Christ's death and Jesus's preaching before his death, and he repeats the New Testament postmortem perspective without generating it historically from the antemortem perspective of Jesus and his disciples. The displacement of emphasis from the imminence of the final days to the final days that have already begun and are headed toward fulfillment by virtue of Christ's death and resurrection lies outside of Cullman's interpretation. The historian is in fact not a formulator of "essences": the "essence" of a statically conceived earliest Christianity echoes traditional motifs of Protestant theology, but it is extraneous to historical thought.

We need to identify the "crisis" of the end and the cultural redemption carried out by Christianity through the opening of the horizon of practicable history, of a meaningful future. We need to understand the generation of the Victory Day[35] perspective and comprehend how—through the "already" and the "not yet," the first and second Parousias, the beginning and fulfillment—practicable Christian time is disclosed in a characteristic tension that avoids inoperable times of the imminence of the catastrophe as well as the already-occurred catastrophe (again, why take action?). The sense of Christian time goes from the immensity of the catastrophe to the fulfillment of a promise.

O. Cullmann dedicates some pages of *Christus und die Zeit* to the question of the "affirmation" or "denial" of the world in light of the New Testament redemptive history (211–13). The formula "world denial" as an interpretation of the orientation of the first Christians is simplistic.

> Moreover, it is only when Christianity really falls back upon the standpoint of Jewish apocalyptic, where the absolutized hope floats in the air and is not anchored in faith in what has already been fulfilled, that the world is really denied. This has happened in the fanatical apocalyptic movements of all times, and continues to happen. Even in the New Testament period we meet this hope which is sickly because it is separated and isolated from the Christian redemptive history; so, for example, in Thessalonica, where the people, in connection with this false hope, stop working (II Thess. 3:10). This is not the eschatology of redemptive history, but rather eschatological fever. It is possible to make the test in any given case by observing that to a hope that is false, because isolated from the redemptive history, there regularly corresponds a false, that is, an ascetic ethic. But the New Testament ethic likewise runs the risk of being misinterpreted as ascetic wherever the hope is regarded as the center of the Primitive Christian line of salvation and as a result the significance of the present for redemptive history is not recognized. (211–12)

"Praeterit enim figura huius mundi."[36]

Tua res agitur: redemptive history concerns the Christian in a direct way; it involves him in the entirety of his person, pointing its finger at every individual (cf. 217).

The famous passage from 1 Corinthians, 7:30 ff.[37] ("I mean, brothers and sisters, the appointed time has grown short; from now on, let even those who have wives be as though they had none, and those who mourn as though they were not mourning"). We should note how here, in this "as if," the world gets disclosed and at the same time transcended: indeed, it is disclosed, permitted, precisely because it is lived by the Christian in a perspective that transcends it and in an epoch in which this perspective was based on the first Parousia and will be fulfilled with the second. The Apostle thus recommends not to close oneself in the terrestrial, in this or that earthly concern, but to look beyond to the promised Kingdom that has already begun. But his recommendation also means that, precisely by virtue of this promise that now runs through it, the world should not be immediately denied in all respects and conditions. This would justify a Christian society in which virginity is valuable in a hierarchical division of functions and tasks corresponding to the eon in which the decisive battle took place and the final victory will take place in which one meets the bridegroom.

3.3. The following considerations are certainly not interpretative judgments but simple working hypotheses to test and retest in ethnological, religious-historical, and cultural-historical contexts.

The dehistorification of the negative (past, present, possible) through mythical-ritual dehistorification that absorbs the proliferation of human becoming—with its moments of uncertainty and precarity, of unresolving conflict—in the ritual repetition of an identical act of paradigmatic mythical foundation carried out on the metahistorical level. "One is in history as if one weren't" in the sense that the critical moments of a certain regime of existence—that is, the historicity of that regime, its cultural choices, and the initiatives it entails—all get concealed from consciousness, are not recognized, and are led again and again back to the sphere of archetypical behaviors carried out once and for all *in illo tempore*, with all of the exemplary power of mythical agents. In this perspective, a protected regime arises through that bit of initiative, innovation, unrepeatable decision, and choice that all cultural life demands. Again in this perspective, outside of this possibility and this religious obligation to *repeat it* according to its foundational status of mythic origins, the world *collapses*: it loses its practicability in actual fact precisely because historicity loses its protective, dehistorifying disguise, and in losing it, it disintegrates in a chaos of critical moments that are not transcendable.

Sedentary living, agriculture, animal husbandry, handiwork, commerce, social stratification, state bureaucracy, and so forth: to the extent that they expand human civil powers that make the sense of time emerge in cultural consciousness, that indefatigable movement toward the future that characterizes that consciousness. The future thus enters myth in the form of the dehistorification of the future in the eschaton. The present prefiguration of the future endpoint—prophetism, millenarianism, eschatologism—is connected to the reabsorption of the present in the mythical past.

Against the cyclical time of the Greeks and against every metaphysic for which redemption is always available in the "beyond," the time of the New Testament is conceived as the rigorously unilinear development of the Revelation and Salvation. This development gets its sense from a decisive, central historical event, the death and resurrection of Jesus, so that all of the points on the timeline, all of its particular divisions, can be evaluated starting from this decisive central historical event, nonetheless retaining their peculiar temporal meaning. This is what the New Testament designates as *οἰχονομία* (Epistle to the Ephesians 1:10, 3:2; Epistle to the Colossians 1:25; Epistle to the Ephesians 3:9): in other words, the entire divine *plan* of redemption, and *ἐφάπαξ* (Epistle to the Romans 6:10; Epistle to the Hebrews 7:27; 9:12; 10:10); that is, the unrepeatability, the historical uniqueness, the decisive importance of the event of redemption.

Apostolic Christian faith and thought do not start with a spatial opposition of "on this side" and "beyond" but with a temporal distinction of "before," "now," and "after." In the New Testament there undoubtedly also exists a spatial opposition of visible and invisible, of an invisible heaven and visible earth, of invisible forces and powers in action and visible operations carried out by humans through their visible organs. But what is spatially invisible, "beyond," does not entirely underlie the course of time, and the essential thing is not the spatial opposition but the distinction of times according to faith.

The temporal emphasis of all of the expressions of faith connects the New Testament to the Judaic valorization of time (cf. G. Delling, *Das Zeitverständnis des Neuen Testaments*, 1940), which in turn refers to Parsiism.[38] Evidence of this is given by the continual use in the New Testament of temporal expression of decisive value, like *ἡμέρα* (day), *ὥρα* (hour), *χαιρός* (moment), *χρόνος* (time), *αἰών* (epoch of the world), *αἰῶνες* (eternal epochs of the world), *νῦν* (now), and *σήμερον* (today): we can usefully consult Kittel's dictionary[39] for these terms.

In general *kairós* is a particular point of time with reference to content (just as *aión* is instead a limited or unlimited duration of time). In its profane usage, *kairós* indicates a particularly favorable temporal circumstance for an undertaking, the point of time that one already talks a great deal about without knowing the precise date, something like zero hour. The most appropriate moment to carry out certain human actions: this is *kairós* in its profane sense. In the context of redemptive history as understood in the New Testament, *kairós* has the same meaning except that it does not regard human intentions and actions but divine decisions that raise a certain date, this or that date, to a *kairós*, that is, in view of executing a divine plan of redemption.

History is redemptive history, the history of the divine plan of redemption, in that the execution of this plan is connected to certain *kairói*, that is, moments of time chosen by God as the most suitable: and it is precisely the comprehensive order of these *kairói* and not just the mere succession of all moments of time that make up sacred history in a strict sense. From the point of view of human history, the choice of these *kairói* that make up redemptive history is arbitrary: it is to be attributed to the divine almighty—compare Acts 1:7. The time of the second Parousia is precisely a *kairós* whose date cannot be known, that breaks in suddenly like a thief (First Epistle to the Thessalonians 5:1). The Revelation of John (1:3 and 11:18) designates the final event as a *kairós* and says it is "near" in the sense that the Synoptic Gospels say that the Kingdom of God is near.

> Blessed is the one who reads aloud the words of the prophecy, and blessed are those who hear and who keep what is written in it; for the time is near [ὁ γὰρ χαιρός ἐγγύς]. (Revelation 1:3)
>
> And he said, "Beware that you are not led astray; for many will come in my name and say, "I am he!" and, "The time is near!" [ὁ χαιρός ἤγγυχεν] Do not go after them. "When you hear of wars and insurrections, do not be terrified; for these things must take place first, but the end will not follow immediately" [ἀλλ οὐχ εὐδέως τὸ τέλος]. (Luke 21: 8–11)

The Christian liturgical year is a cultural apparatus for the total dehistorification of time: Christ is infinitely repeated like a voice in an echoing cave. And yet, if the calendar of celebrations reabsorbs the historical years of time in a metahistorical year, it rediscloses them one by one in their concrete months, days, hours, and instants, thereby achieving an operative deciding according to values that humans—as long as they are human—cannot avoid in the smallest fraction of time.

3.4. History and eschatology.

The interest in R. Bultmann in Italian culture is a relatively recent development [. . .].[40]

The problem of the relationship between historical becoming and the eschatological moment appears in Bultmann in the circumscribed limits of an operation of identifying and salvaging a nucleus of Christian religious faith that is compatible with modern civilization and in particular with that sense of historicity of the human condition that precisely Christianity contributed to mediating in our current cultural consciousness. Within these limits Bultmann tries to trace a historical outline of the eschatological theme in Western civilization. The earliest Christian community waited for the end of the world and Christ's second Parousia in a climate of expectation that did not give a horizon to history, if not in the sense of the imminent catastrophe of the earthly order. The risks and disappointments to which this wait was necessarily exposed were avoided through the indefinite deferral of the second Parousia and the concentration of Christian experience in the "end" that already occurred with the sacrifice of the God-man (Paul), in the actual belief of dead and resurrected Christ (John), and in the possibility for the Christian to participate presently—through the sacraments administered by the Church—in the supernatural efficacies deriving from the central event of Golgotha, the basic unit of eschatological measure of an absolute before and after in the plan of redemptive history. The secularization of Christianity's eschatological theme took place above all with idealism, materialism, and the positivistic ideology of progress until the very idea of a unitary plan of human history in its entirety entered into crisis with the threat of a relativism without a horizon (consider especially the naturalistic and pessimistic relativism of someone like Spengler). Bultmann intends to exorcise the threat of this relativism, connecting himself to the conception of historicity elaborated by Croce and Collingwood:[41] the sense of humankind's historicity does not lie in the past or even in a future eschaton to which the course of events necessarily leads but is concentrated entirely in the present instant; not in the incoherent and chaotic instant of a simple measuring of time but in that of an actual decision, always renewed, that actively chooses its own past to identify and know and that deliberately assumes its own responsibility toward the future, accepting its risk. In this sense every instant contains an eschatological possibility, threatened by the moral laziness of letting oneself live past history passively and of letting oneself be surprised without preparation by an impending future. Now, according to Bultmann, the eschatological possibility of every instant is realized by Christian faith in an exemplary way, first because the latter recognizes the historicity of the human condition, and second because the eschatological moment of Christianity is not a looming cosmic catastrophe or a mythical metahistory in which the distressing historical proliferation of human becoming gets reabsorbed with ritual and worship but instead is the historical event of Christ. This is an event that, in the decision of faith, proposes itself again and again to the hic et nunc of my historicity, at the same time disclosing freedom to me as a gift of divine grace that, through Christ, belongs to me not as a possession but as the fulfillment of preaching and love. With this it seems to Bultmann to have provided a religious complement and crowning to Heidegger's "being thrown in the world" that cries out to escape its possible note of atheistic desperation. We must say right away that Bultmann's theme of the relations between history and eschatology continuously intersects historiographic interpretations and edifying cues, so that it can be evaluated simultaneously as a religious-historical contribution and a document of religious life in action. This provokes a certain embarrassment in the reader, who risks not ever knowing precisely what it is about, that is, if what is at stake in the work he is reading is a fundamental interest of historical reconstruction inclined to affect the nucleus of faith itself or if in the foreground of the discourse and holding its threads is a concern on the part of the believer who intends to remove precisely a certain nucleus of religious faith from an integral historicization. Moreover, because of the substantial ambiguity of the text, the reader who wants to remain faithful to the coherence of historiographic thought will be dissatisfied by Bultmann's use of interpretative categories like "history" and "myth," and it will seem to him, consequently, that there are numerous limits to his historiographic reconstruction. Instead of being moved by religious concerns, the reader will find that the nucleus of faith saved—freedom as a gift of divine grace through Christ—is still too little, and it will seem to him that, this point being conceded, there is really no reason that all the others are not conceded to his decision, that is, the Trinitarian symbol, the cult of the Madonna and the Saints, the Church and its sacraments, and everything else in Catholic Christianity that speaks to the heart and the imagination. But let us more closely examine the limits of Bultmann's theme, choosing historiographic thought as an evaluative perspective.

It is certainly true that the theme of the historicity of the human condition came into hegemonic cultural consciousness through Christian civilization. But in what sense is this proposition true? In the sense that while non-Christian religious traditions are dominated by mythical-ritual symbolism of reabsorption of the distressing proliferation of becoming in the metahistorical example of the origins (in this regard, see *Le mythe de l'éternel retour* by Mircea Eliade[42]), Christian tradition accepts this proliferation but places a central event—Christ—in the course of time, which bestows becoming with an eschatological meaning. In non-Christian religious traditions, human becoming as unbearable and distressing negativity gets variously rejected by cultural consciousness, which orients its mythical-ritual symbolism to the celebration of exemplary resolving events produced once and for all in the metahistory of origins. In Christian tradition, through the central event of Christ, human history begins to appear in mythical consciousness itself, and it appears there with a positive mark, that is, as a history of redemption. This inaugurated the theme of historicity as transcendence of the situation in intersubjective cultural valorizations and thus the humanistic theme of a historicity that, although tormented by the risk of the negative, contains within it the possibility of a valorizing decision, entirely human in its genesis, destination, and in the quality of value produced. The progressive secularization of the eschaton, the cultural consciousness that the eschatological moment lies not in the return to a paradise of origins or in the imminence of a catastrophe of the earthly order but in the actuality of a decision according to intersubjective values. All this refers to the fact that the humanistic ferment of the positivity of history in its dual aspect of *res gestae* and *historia rerum gestarum* moves within the Christian message: this is a ferment destined to break the protective mythic casing of an eruption of metahistory in history in a privileged moment at the center of universal history (Christ). Now, the limit of Bultmann's position is that, on the one hand, he recognizes the concentration of eschaton in the actuality of valorizing human decision in the transcendence of the situation according to intersubjective values; but then, at the root of this deciding, he maintains the fundamental decision of faith—that is, freedom as a gift of divine grace through Christ and the connected experience of a historicity of the human condition as a "negative" that human forces as such cannot transcend. The ambiguous character of Bultmann's thought derives from this: he unconsciously remains prisoner of the "myth" even if in the attenuated form of a decision for Christ that discloses the task of preaching and love. This is an ambiguity that, among other things, is destined to displease everyone, theists and humanists: the former because they will find too little myth, and the latter because they still find too much.

Another observation regarding Bultmann's theme of the relations between history and eschatology is that Bultmann embraces modern thought's crisis of the "plan of universal history": in other words, of a unilinear process of humanity from an origin to an end. But Bultmann's approval appears as evidence that the "historicity of the human condition," entrusted solely to itself, leads to a horizonless cultural relativism, even in this way displaying its reduction to absurdity and thus the need for the decision of Christian faith, that better than all the others accounts for the "negative" inherent in that historicity and at the same time for the positive of personal decision—continuously renewed with grace through Christ. In reality, between mythical universal history as a more or less divine or secularized "plan" and cultural relativism in the crude form in which we find it—for example, in Benedict's *Patterns of Culture*[43]—there is a third possibility: the recognition of a dispersion of peoples and cultures and at the same time unification as a concrete task.

In particular, the humanist can make a fundamental objection to Bultmann. In my historical position as a modern European, why today should I need the option in favor of the image of the God-man to love people and place myself into question in the face of their pain and suffering? Why do I need a "mediator" to engage myself with the people who live around me and that I encounter in the concreteness of individualized faces recalling hic et nunc personal biographies that must not leave me indifferent? These faces ask of me, here and now, decisions in their name and not in the name of Christ, and already the modern sensibility perceives the beginning of an offense to the other in the need to make a detour, to the *Umweg* of the decision in favor of Christ to identify this other in the crowd, in the neighborhood, in the factory, in the school, in the family, and to reestablish with this other the living circuit of social activity.

[. . .] Today, in the present cultural moment of the West, the recognition that the peoples and cultures of our planet are "dispersed"—not able to be combined in their past histories according to the unity of a divine plan—poses itself as a task of unification according to the lines of development of a critical ethnocentrism that places in question one's own ethnos through a comparison with other ethnic groups. This opens the perspective of a much broader humanism than the traditional one (in which lies the meaning that ethnology has taken on in modern civilization). But Bultmann seems extraneous to this wider humanistic interest: he follows the path of a rigorous dogmatic ethnocentrism, and more precisely, within the limits of a Eurocentrism that, since it appeals to the privilege of an exceptional relationship with the divine, excludes the comparison among humanities and compromises the struggle against the dispersion of peoples and the incoherent multiplicity of their collective histories.

4. From Metahistory to History

4.1. There are three fundamental images of historical becoming: the eternal return of the identical, the unilinearity of development from an *arché*[44] to an *eschaton*, and the disintegration of happening in the relativism of cultures and epochs. The eternal return of the identical was a late speculative heir of the mythical-ritual dehistorification of religions extraneous to the Judeo-Christian tradition. In speculative reflection the periodic reabsorption of becoming's historical proliferation in the exemplariness of a foundational myth in the *illud tempus* of origins corresponds to the theory of periodic destructions and regenerations of the world. The unilinearity of development from an arché to an eschaton began in the Judeo-Christian religious tradition, reshaping specifically in Christianity in a decisive central event for which between the divine founding of the world and its irreversible process of returning to God, a privileged moment of time gets inserted, the incarnation, marking the course of the arché to the eschaton in two phases, in a before and then the after of the promise. This image of history was based on faith in Christ, and outside of this faith it did not have any sense. With the loss of this faith in the central event, two paths were attempted: one of a wholly secular unilinearity of history (the progress of science in the positivistic epoch; the progress of the idea in idealist speculation; the overturning of this progress in the Marxian dialectic), and that of a relativistic fragmentation, now biologizing à la Spengler,[45] now variously connected to the different negative existentialisms, now—under the cover of a new scientism—reshaped into the contemplation of the incoherent multiplicity of human cultures.

Against these images of history, we need to assert today:

(a) The recognition of the current, real dispersion of peoples, cultures, and histories; in other words, the definitive liquidation of the mythical dual legacy of an eternal return of the identical as a unitary plan of universal history.

(b) The recognition of a duty to relate (compare) the actual multiplicity of peoples, cultures, and histories in the perspective of an understanding and operating that *unifies* the dispersed humanity. However, this is a unification that lies before "us" as a task and not as a preestablished plan of God or Matter (which is the same as saying that "we" as people must present ourselves, here and now, as givers of sense of an epoch of human history without ever turning to the lazy assumption that history has this sense independently of us. There is no doubt a set of conditions that delimit the possibility of endowing sense, but history again and again risks losing all sense whatsoever despite all of the conditions for it to have one).

(c) The recognition that "we" as Westerners lie at the center of the comparative, unifying, and planning impulse, in other words, as custodians of the only human culture that, guiding a long historical course, has produced the science of the comparison of self and other cultures: ethnology.

(d) The recognition that the comparison is not a matter of dismissing the West, but putting it in question, to take on an awareness of the limits of its (up to now, corporative) humanism and to restore its compromised hegemonic power: this will be possible if we give an entirely secular and human meaning to Paul's *omnia omnibus factus sum ut omnes facerem salvos* (critical ethnocentrism).[46]

(e) The complement of philosophy in anthropology as the result of humanism promoted by the science of the comparison of ethnic groups, starting from the West and its history as an operative center, comparative and unifying.

Humankind has always lived in history, that is, in the active production of life and communitarian values that make it possible as human life. But aside from Western culture and the Judeo-Christian tradition, humankind has rejected the cultural consciousness of the entirely human genesis and destination of this production, establishing aware hegemonic values in which it articulated the concealment of historicity of human existence in a systematic and organic way. History has undoubtedly defeated this pretense again and again, obliging societies, epochs, and single individuals to shed their dehistorifying disguise; or, once it had adopted one, gradually modify it in time. But whether they shed the disguise or modified the features of the adopted disguise in time, people—again in non-European cultures—never attributed that change or modification to wholly and consciously human operations, but the latter were either not perceived by consciousness or they were attributed to superhuman interventions, to revelations, to the events of demons, heroes, numina operating on a mythical, metahistorical level to "origins," *in illo tempore*. In this way, historicity was doubly exorcised with reference to consciousness: through the disguise that concealed it, and through the concealment of that historical becoming that affected the disguiser itself. The rigid principle inspiring this orientation was to reabsorb the historical proliferation of becoming in the repetition of a same myth of origins of an order; that is, since it was not otherwise possible, to reduce the change to the bursting of the superhuman onto the human scene (dreams, visions, revelations, the power of words and ritual gestures, etc.).

In an area of the world and in an epoch of history, the Judeo-Christian tradition marked the first apparition of history through a dehistorifying consciousness in action itself (i.e., through mythical-ritual symbolism). If only as a history of redemption, a pact between God and the Chosen People, the preaching of Jesus of an approaching Kingdom, Christology and the doctrine of the Paraclete[47] between the two Parousias, history made an opening in mythical-ritual consciousness to an extent unprecedented in all of the other cultures of the ecumene. Subsequently, in the modern world—that is, starting with humanism and the Renaissance—historicity extended itself in cultural consciousness up to the point of claiming consciousness entirely for itself and reshaping itself as an integral humanism or, if you will, as a religion of humankind. But now we need to ask: what does this mean? Where the destiny of humanity was to remain disguised in existence or perish, does this humanism simply mean the defeat of humankind or at least Westerners? And further: given that we cannot even change disguise since now we can only do it as a carnivalesque game—and here it is not a matter of playing carnival but of existing as human beings in society—does this not being able to change disguise perhaps equal a death sentence? The syllogism would be dreadful: humanity can live in history only disguising it, cultural life is this disguise, but on the other hand, humanity that knows this can no longer take on any disguise, and therefore—this is the "syllogism"—humanity (even if it is the humankind that produced Western civilization) is destined to perish in that it demystifies history.

4.2. Humankind has always lived in history, but all human cultures, except Western culture, have spent treasures of creative energy to disguise the historicity of existence. We could say that human cultural history is the history of disguises of the historicity of existence, the history of the ways in which humanity has pretended to be in history as if it were not. But we need to immediately add that these disguises receive their sense in that history has won over and over, requiring either a change in dehistorifying disguise or—as was the case of Judeo-Christian tradition and the culture it fostered—appearing in first person in mythical-ritual consciousness itself to get free of this dramatic and ambiguous consciousness and clamor for it to overlap perfectly with the hegemonic cultural consciousness. What does this paradoxical adventure of humanity as a disguise of its own historicity mean, and what does the defeat of its disguising intent mean? By any chance would it mean the defeat of humankind, were it true that we are disguised in existence or we die? And if this were so, how could we change disguise once we reached the insufferable awareness that it is always a mask and that behind it there is a face? And finally: would this situation not equal a death sentence, seeing that an existence marked by the hypocrisy of the disguise is unbearable since it is not possible to reduce the existential disguise to a carnival party, and moreover the bare historicity of the unmasked face is destined sooner or later to yield the rigidity of a cadaver's face?

Religious culture as a mask for the historicity of existence has performed a positive function and in this epoch of transition in part still performs it. Mythical-ritual symbolism has protected from existential crisis by actually disclosing communitarian practicability of the world. In societies and epochs in which the detachment of culture from nature always ran the risk of failing, it was necessary to dehistorify history in order to allow for it and repress the hegemonic consciousness of historicity in order for human beings to remain in the world as human beings. At the same time, the great alienations connected to critical moments of existence were repressed and inverted on the level of mythical-ritual consciousness that through indirect ways and with appropriate techniques rendered them once again conspiring with worldly living, with deciding and operating in the context of a community of living people. The mythical-ritual symbolism of traditional religions masked the harshness of historicity, and it helped reshape the crisis of alienation according to models of reappropriation of the risk of alienating oneself radically and without compensation. But with the appearance of history within mythical consciousness itself (the God-man, the irreversible divine plan, etc.), the seed was sown for the dissolution of the efficacy of mythical-ritual protection. From that time on, history began to grow, and mythical-ritual symbolism began to decline. At the same time, the awareness of what humankind can do with its own work and own initiative rendered the existential crisis less risky.

4.3. The alternative is clear: either we do or do not accept the reality of the human condition, which is limit and initiative that transcends the limit, situation and value that transcend the situation, death and action that survives death. If we do not accept this condition—because accepting it entails the annihilation of the very civil courage that creates civilization and history—then we have no choice but to negate this condition's reality and conceal and mask it in the great protective themes of religious life, of myth and rite, of theology and metaphysics, of magic and mysticism. In other words, we can only debase the rhythms of everyday action to a world of signs and symbols and carry out the task of establishing, here and now, a new order in the shadow of an already established order *in illo tempore*. The doing will thus be masked in repeating and imitating; staying awake will be encompassed in dreaming; and people will be in history as if they were not in it, because they are already outside it. Meanwhile, though, through this *pia fraus* they will act and create, and they will raise the edifice of civilization. If, instead, they accept the human condition and recognize without outrage that it has a limit that action is ceaselessly called to cross, and beyond the work endowed with value they glimpse the only way of detaching humankind from nature and steering it from the transient to the permanent. If we have the courage and strength to create works of poetry and science, of economics and moral life, without the need for a technical-protective system, works of a true homeland in which everyone has a place and in which we will be reintegrated in the end, then we follow the route of historicist humanism, of modern civilization, of the consciousness that cultural assets have an entirely human origin and destination, are made by humankind for humankind, and they call for judgment and action according to this fundamental criterion. The alternative is clear: but the former will remain standing as long as the mesh of limits in which we are called to act is too thick and sturdy for us to be able to extricate ourselves without appealing to an already made metahistorical world, a divine civilization that reassures Cebes's youth.[48] The latter alternative remains a task to be carried out and a dignity to be protected from the resurging danger of the former option, which pushes in the direction of magic and religion. If we were to define our epoch and ourselves within it, we would have to say that we are currently engaged precisely in this choice, and we are deciding it with suffering and torment. We already have in mind a framework of integral humanism, but in and around us there is the threat of anxiety and the need for a safe haven.

4.4. Why should I need the image of Christ to love people and to put myself into question in the face of their pain and misery? Why need a "mediator" to open myself and commit myself to the people who live around me, whom I encounter in the concreteness of faces that reflect personal biographies and who ask me, here and now, for decisions in their name and not in the name of Christ? Certainly, I might need a stimulus to open myself and place myself into question in front of concrete people, and I can also resort to a good wine to reestablish a relationship that has withered with the world of people. But value does not lie in the stimulus, because it also brings a dark drunkenness that closes instead of opening, submerging in a desperate melancholy that is the negation of love. Value lies in what has been stimulated: that is, in the last instance, in the quality of the witnessing rendered to others, and thus in an intoxication that does not choose us but that we choose lucidly by taking advantage of certain facilitations made to communication when this chalice has been emptied in company. In any case it is a sign of weakness and fragility, an impropriety and a deficiency, to need a mediator—Christ, the chalice of the Eucharistic meal or of the secular meal—to rediscover life in human faces and to reestablish in anonymous crowds, in neighborhoods, in families, the circuit of a communicating social activity. Indeed, the human face as such, without any other stimulus except its very image, contains the strength needed to push us, if we want it, to the great adventure of a transformational encounter. Certainly we might not want this encounter—in fact for the most part we do not want it, and so we turn to the mediator. But if it is true that in this regard we must be indulgent with ourselves and embrace the politics of stimulating symbols, in an extremely rigorous view it is also true that we already begin to offend others when we need a detour, an *Umweg* (as Marx said), in order to reach them.

Today we need the Madonna less and less to offer a cultural model for education and behavior between the sexes in society. Increasingly, in order to know what a woman must do toward a given man, or what a man must do toward a given woman, the memories of faces of men and women in flesh and blood predominate, the model-memories that we each carry within us and that constitute the most precious asset of our symbolic capital.

4.5. Observations on religious freedom. If religious life is a technical system that protects from the risk of not being able to be in any possible civil history and that discloses through a varied human action that a crisis without horizon would compromise, religious freedom proves to be solidly established in the society in which modern civilization is articulated. Who would break a lame person's crutches with the argument that normal walking does not need crutches? What we need is to reduce as much as possible the accidents and illness that make the number of lame people so great as to render the request for or use of crutches inevitable: that is, the problem may be one of substituting the means of crutches with a more effective orthopedic technique. Outside of metaphors, the problem is solely that of a greater power of expansion of modern humanism and a reshaping of society and state that allows for greater existential security and a more solidly based confidence in the power of human action. This means that religious freedom should be safeguarded from the state inasmuch as the state safeguards its own freedom to spread and humanize the *civitas humana* (non *diaboli*!) to whom it is accountable. The use of force against the Church (and we mean the real force that is law) cannot go beyond defense from the usurpations of the *civitas dei* in the sphere of the *civitas humana* presided by the state. But religious persecution as such is an abuse of power with which the state, in place of carrying out its task of rendering a particular existential regime less and less **theogenetic**, claims to directly strike the protective system that—as long as it is required—is giving proof precisely that its task has not been carried out: a dangerous usurpation that either disaggregates society or prepares a more vigorous resurgence of the need for the divine through persecutions and violence. Persecuting a religion that is still in hearts only creates "martyrs," all the more so if the struggle is not carried out in the name of a more elevated religion but in the name of an integral humanism that requires a moral force that is still anachronistic with respect to the real regime of existence.

4

Apocalypse and Decolonization

1. Ethnographic Humanism

1.1. An ethnology suited to the needs of modern humanism must gain awareness that its object is not simply the science of cultures at a low technological level, nonliterate peoples, or "so-called primitives" but instead the science of their relationship to Western culture starting with the ethnographic encounter since it is a thematization of this relationship. [. . .]

The concept of the ethnographic encounter as a thematization of what is ours and what is foreign (*alieno*) in the aforementioned sense entails an inner paradox, and the formulation of an appropriate ethnological methodology depends on the analysis of the latter. Normally it is recommended that the ethnographer *observe* ethnographic facts without preconceptions and *describe them* with exactness. But such a recommendation, precisely because of its obviousness, says very little when one believes to have given the basis of ethnological research with it: in reality, precisely this "foundation" needs to be "founded." When the ethnographer observes foreign cultural phenomena, phenomena that are extraneous to the historical course of development of the culture to which the ethnographer belongs (Western culture, which not coincidentally is the only one to have posed the "scientific" problem of the ethnographic encounter), observation is made possible by particular categories of observation without which the phenomenon is not observable. These categories—which enter into play in the act of surprising a foreign cultural phenomenon *in vivo* and in the ethnographic discourse describing it—are numerous: nature and culture, normal and abnormal, healthy psyche and unhealthy psyche, conscious and unconscious, I and the world, individual and society, evil and good, harmful and useful, ugly and beautiful, true and false, language, economy, technology, rational and irrational, conscious and unconscious,[1] space, time, substance, cause, ends. Now, already just the use of these categories in the ethnographic observation of foreign cultures (and not to use them would be tantamount to not being able to observe or describe any ethnographic fact) unconsciously bears the entire history of Western culture—its decisions and its choices, its polemics and its distinctions—without the ethnographer being in the least protected, as long as this unconsciousness remains, from arbitrarily projecting those decisions and choices, those polemics and distinctions, onto the foreign culture that is extraneous to it or participates in it according to different historical modalities. So, for example, if we use the category "magic" in the observation of ethnographic facts, a whole series of Western historical events comes into play: the Christian polemic against magic as demoniacal usurpation; the polemic of natural magic against low ceremonial magic; the polemic of the new science against ceremonial and natural magic; the various crises of positivistic scientism that have taken place in the modern and contemporary periods; the reassessment of magic on the part of artists and writers; the magic of a child in the perspective of developmental psychology and the magic of the schizophrenic in the perspective of psychopathology; and finally, debates over paranormal aptitudes and in particular over so-called extrasensory perception. In a confused, fragmentary way, more or less unconsciously in relation to their received education and readings, ethnographers make this history return immediately in the very moment they use the category of "magic" as a predicate of ethnographic judgment. But precisely because it is confused, fragmentary, and unconscious, this cultural history risks being transferred in an immediate, acritical and dogmatic way into the observation and interpretation of the foreign cultural phenomenon designated as "magic." (In a note: another example: normal and abnormal, healthy mind and unhealthy mind). The typical paradox of the ethnographic encounter is as follows: either the ethnographer attempts to completely disregard his own cultural history with the presumption of being "naked as a baby" in the face of the cultural phenomena to be observed, and so he becomes blind and mute in front of ethnographic facts and loses, along with the facts to observe and describe, his own specialistic vocation; or else he trusts some "obvious" anthropological categories, taken on in their presumed "average" or "minimal" or "common sense" meaning, and so he exposes himself to the wholesale risk of immediate ethnocentric evaluations, starting with the level of the most elementary observation (in other words, this time his specialistic vocation gets compromised by the impossibility of an "objective" observation). The only way to resolve this paradox is contained within the very concept of the ethnographic encounter as a dual thematization, of "oneself" and the "foreign." The ethnographer is thus called to exercise an ethnographic *epoché*[2] that—stimulated by the encounter with certain culturally foreign behaviors—consists in initiating a systematic and explicit comparison between the history that these behaviors document and the Western cultural history sedimented in the categories that the ethnographer uses to observe, describe, and interpret. This dual thematization of one's own history and foreign history is carried out with the intention of reaching that universally human base in which "one's own" and the "foreign" are exposed as two historical possibilities of being human: therefore, the base starting from which even "we" would have been able to correctly guess the road leading to the foreign humanity facing us in the initial scandal of the ethnographic encounter. In this sense the ethnographic encounter constitutes the opportunity for the most radical examination of consciousness possible to Western man; it is an examination whose outcome mediates a reform of anthropological knowledge and its evaluative categories, a test of human dimensions beyond the awareness that the West has had of being human. Interdisciplinary research. Ethnology as a science that arises out of the comparison of oneself with the foreign (with the most foreign being the ethnographic foreign) thus appears as a recognition of the current dispersion of ethnic groups and their cultures and as a comparative evocation of those incoherent histories that initially lie in a reciprocal scandal within the ethnographic encounter. The unity of mankind is therefore not a speculative presupposition according to the image of a "plan": its ideal and task is the unification of mankind but through the mediating efficacy of an encounter in the field with foreign humanities and of an always renewed thematization of this encounter.

(In an ethnological perspective, the unity of humanity thus appears not as a presupposition but as a task, an ideal of unification, to be realized time and again through research and comparison, starting from the initial recognition of a dispersion and foreignness among living peoples and instituting Western humanity as the center of the heuristic and comparative process since it is "one's own." So neither dogmatic Eurocentrism nor an incoherent cultural relativism forms the basis of ethnological research, rather a critical Eurocentrism, electively inclined toward a real increase in humanistic awareness.)

1.2. [. . .] In this way the distance separating subaltern cultural forms within Western civilization from Indigenous cultures of the colonial period has become shorter. The difference between the two increasingly appears to be one of degree and not kind, and a rigorous distinction between ethnology's object and that of folklore is less and less justifiable, because in both cases they present us with intercultural syncretisms, relations between different levels of culture, and dynamics put into motion by these relations. But there is something more. Not only does ethnology—understood as the science of primitive civilizations—risk losing its object of study, but within European culture the influence of non-Western cultures has contributed to spreading a multifaceted awareness of the importance, for today's West, too, of the archaic, the mythical, the unconscious—not as an obsolete "phase" of an imaginary human history progressing in its unilinear, triumphant march but as a permanent anthropological dimension that the West has clumsily repressed. We see this orientation in a more immediate way in modern art and literature; in psychoanalysis and in the Jungian theory of archetypes; in the resurgence of speculative engagement with myth; in idolizing ideological politics of the *Ur*; in manners and in a certain desperate feeling of protest and escapism.

[. . .] The initial classification dividing humanity in two is truly a "sin": the ethnographer embodies one humanity and the foreign culture provides evidence of another, and they face each other in a scandal of reciprocal incomprehension, in an extreme dearth of common memories. Or else there is a terrible reciprocal judgment whereby the representatives of the most distant foreign cultures mistake the white man for a ghost returning from the world of the dead, and the white man instinctively tends to perceive them as disconcerting specimens of *genus brutorum hominum*.[3] Without the search for the challenge of the culturally foreign, without the intense experience of the scandal formed by the encounter with an enigmatic humanity, and especially without the sense of guilt and remorse in facing a "lost brother" and the dispersion of cultures on our planet, the humanistic ethos of the ethnographic encounter is smitten at its roots. We lose the essential condition that ushers in the most conspicuous task of ethnological research: a meticulous and laborious questioning and self-questioning regarding not only the character and the reasons, but also the origin, structure and function of the foreign human behavior that the ethnographer intends to examine. In a certain sense "ethnographic humanism" is the difficult path of modern humanism, the one that takes as its point of departure what is most humanly distant and that, through an on-the-ground encounter with living peoples, deliberately exposes itself to offending the most cherished cultural memories. Those who cannot bear this offense and who are not capable of turning it into soul-searching are not suited to ethnological research; they would probably do best in the area of philological or classicist humanism, which despite everything is still a dialogue within the same family. We certainly do not need to go very far to experience baffling behavior: our next-door neighbor or even our relatives can manifest it every day, and on each occasion we react to this incomprehensibility with indifference or curiosity, with astonishment, bitterness or rage; or finally, with an effort of reconstruction and comprehension. The ethnographic encounter focuses on this manifold relationship to the other in the most unfavorable circumstances, taking the quintessentially culturally alien as its research topic. This encounter prohibits indifference and systematically exercises an asceticism that re-presses all forms of disdain in order to foster understanding under the worst conditions: when our entire cultural history, the world in which we were born and raised, is called into question.

This ethnological humanism, whose terms were established by the era of geographical discoveries, can come to fruition only now in an era that is experiencing the crisis of colonialism and the society that produced it. It is an era that not only witnesses a proliferation of intercultural relations but that is also engaged more than ever in establishing a new solidarity of human relations on our planet: "the world is scant."

But ethnological research expresses this need and collaborates for the part that regards it not only because it is electively available to focus on "our own" and "the foreign" on an intercultural level but also in another sense:[4] [...]

1.3. Philological-classicist humanism and ethnographic humanism. With the era of geographic discoveries and the foundation of the great colonial empires, the first seed of a possible new humanism was sown, one that only today—in the era of decolonization—is starting to bear fruit. Until the sixteenth century, humanism was humankind's coming to awareness through a diachronic return to classical antiquity: this was the recollection of an illustrious past that expressed the need to widen humanity's aware-ness beyond the limits of Christian-medieval memory. Yet the humanistic memory of the fourteenth and fifteenth centuries constituted all the same an internal expansion of the West's cultural awareness, a pitiful recogni-tion of ancestors that served to reshape the descendants' own biographi-cal awareness through models to imitate or with which to compete. But starting with the age of discovery a new situation came about that con-tained the development of a new humanistic dimension. The discovery of overseas peoples—even if it was in the context of colonial and mis-sionary interests—brought to the fore a new modality of relations with humanity: the modality of the synchronic encounter with peoples that were foreign with respect to Western history and thus also the modality of the scandal and challenge of this foreignness. It was no longer an internal and more extensive recollection of one's own cultural ascendance, to be retraced by making a world that had disappeared forever come back to life in time and through the reading of texts. Instead, it was a discovery of living collateral relatives, humanly enigmatic, faced with whom one could nonetheless only react with an exploratory engagement, since the foundation of the great colonial empires and missionary activity were in any case based on the practices of existing relations—being as it may, too, on practices of domination or conversion. This nascent ethnographic humanism—whether it appealed to the image of the *genus brutorum hominum*, to the proof of original sin, to a comparison with the classical model, or to the myth of the "good savage"—introduced a potential new evaluative dimension: a dimension of comparison between subsequent eras of the West's cultural history that was no longer internal and diachronic but external and synchronic with peoples who were foreign with respect to the entirety of that history and sequence of eras. With this, Western history potentially gained a new humanistic possibility: to place itself in question, to problematize its own course, to emerge from its corporative isolation and dogmatic ethnocentrism, and to obtain a new anthropological horizon through its comparative assessment with other ways of being human in society. This theme, however, could not unfold in all of its breadth and complexity until some conditions had developed: the limit of ethnographic humanism during the era of colonialism and missionary activity was the same limit of colonialism and missionary activity. Undoubtedly there were conditions for the first appearance of ethnographic humanism: the expansion of the European bourgeoisie, the exploitation of transoceanic lands, the protection of new markets, the administrative relationship with "people of color," the dramatic effort connected to the Christianization of the pagans. But only in the period of the second industrial revolution—with the ecumenical spread of technology and the decline of colonialism—could it go beyond the limit inherent to a practical relation founded in the last instance on instrumental reasons of power.

Cultural relativism is the danger facing ethnographic humanism as it unfolds in the era of the second industrial revolution and decolonization. Only the West has generated a true ethnological interest in the broad sense of a need to systematically measure its own culture against others that are synchronic and foreign. However, this comparison can only be carried out from the perspective of a critical ethnocentrism in which Western (or Westernized) ethnologists take the history of their own culture as a unit of measure for foreign cultural histories. At the same time, in the act of measuring, they gain awareness of the historical prison and limits of using their own system of measurement, and they open themselves to the task of reforming the very categories of observation available to them at the beginning of the research. Only by placing Western history at the center of a comparative study in a critical and deliberate way will the ethnologist usher in an anthropological awareness that is wider than the one contained in dogmatic ethnocentrism.

2. Prophetic Movements

2.1. Millenarian movements and psychopathology (from Mühlmann[5]). In analyzing the problem of the relationship between millenarian movements and personality that involve both their initiators (prophets, messiahs) and their followers, Mühlmann (256–60) recognizes the relationship between charismatic personalities and psychopathological features (hysteroids, paranoids, schizoids), the possibility that certain prophets are simply psychotic or endowed with an extremely low level of intelligence, or that they have temporarily experienced psychic disorders of various sorts, and so forth. In particular, he states that there are "distinctive connections" between the eschatological enterprise and the schizophrenic experience of the end of the world (in this, he refers to Jaspers, 294 ff.,[6] where in discussing the patients' specific *Weltanschauungen*, he recalls the schizophrenic's *kosmische Erleben*). At the same time, Mühlmann underlines precisely how psychopathological features can be culturally valorized in a movement's development, so that the millenarianisms present an "amalgam" (*Legierung*) of normality and abnormality of the pathological and the healthy. One must observe, however, that Mühlmann's assessments remain superficial and confused. When, for example, he says that there are "distinctive connections" (*unverkennbare Beziehungen*) between the eschatological experience of the world and the schizophrenic one, the problem is hidden precisely by the adjective *distinctive*. We limit ourselves to noting that there are "distinctive" connections between the charismatic personality and the psychopathological personality, just as one can say that there is a "distinctive difference" between Jesus's eschatological preaching and the behavior of a psychopath. The problem is hiding precisely in this presumed "distinctiveness," which is really nothing of the sort when it is not turned into a "problem," a "subject" that reconsiders all of these presumed "obviousnesses." Nor is it legitimate to believe that we have framed the problem correctly and are headed toward a solution when we say that some prophets present psychotic features, they are undoubtedly psychotic; or when we state that that there can be a cultural use of pathological psychic states, and so forth. In the end, a focus on the relationship between the psychotic and the cultural in religious life more generally, and particularly in the sphere of apocalyptic thought, is ruled out here from systematic reflection. The extreme coarseness of Mühlmann's formulation is apparent in the concept of an "amalgam" (*Legierung*) of psychopathological and healthy features in eschatology. Instead, it is a matter of considering the organic connection of cultural apocalypses with both psychopathological risk and operative reintegration in keeping with communitarian valorizations of human life.

Mühlmann (257, discussing the possible psychopathological features of prophets' individual personalities):

> Unfortunately the reports regarding nativistic movements do not tell us much about the personalities involved, the prophets (or prophetesses), or initiators. The people writing these reports are for the most part missionaries or ethnographers who are lacking a medical perspective. Only in an indirect way and without much certainty can one deduce from these descriptions that in at least some cases we are dealing with deviant personalities. Some cases appear to be of hysteroid *Pseudologia phantastica*,[7] other cases—especially when the discussion is about persecutions in "messianic birth pains"–sound paranoid or schizophrenic, though of course one cannot venture a clinical diagnosis of them. Still others appear substantially watered down, evidently reduced from the normal, average man to that basis of common comprehension that leaves the pathological enough "Fascinans" to effect an attraction but not enough to be repelled. In short, it brings about the aforementioned "amalgam" that the majority of eschatological fantasy images outline: "insane images" for normal sanity but not necessarily "quasi-insane images" in a definably clinical sense. In any case is it striking that the missionaries writing the reports themselves notice that the movements arise from Christianized natives who parade a certain exaggerated piety. In such cases it is obvious that an eye for the pathological is left out altogether. Even a religiously receptive person, perhaps precisely such people, can be appalled in the face of an "excess" of devotion or bigotry, and this is evidently what we see here. Have not precisely religious practitioners often warned of an "exaggeration" in religious things? Yet it is precisely this exaggeration, this excess, that is to be noted in the chiliastic phase of religious productivity: it has a repulsive effect on the rationally tamed observer, even on the Christian missionary.

2.2. Institutionalization and control of psychopathological risks in millenarian movements.

Institutionalization is a fundamental feature of cultural apocalypse in the sense that symptomatic behaviors of the crisis of presence in cultural apocalypse tend to avoid the individual anarchy of their development and are channeled into experiences of communitarian rites of a "sect" or "church." Through such a ritual institutionalization, the various forms of psychomotor excitement and the various ways the characteristic unconscious drives emerge are unified according to socialized models of behavior, receiving a calendarization that disciplines them as to a "when" and a "how long" of their performance (the when and the duration of the ritual) as well as with regard to a how and why of the performance itself (the "how" is moderated in relation to the anarchy of the individual crisis, and the "why" is determined by the overall eschatological meaning of the movement and the myths that form its horizon). In this way, the crisis is *recovered* and *controlled* in a sociocultural sense; it gets aligned within a basically *telestic* framework. Instead of exploding in the anarchy of individual biographies and in the cultural insignificance of a neurotic or psychotic symptom, the crisis receives a date, a duration, a manner, and a meaning (i.e., the ritual's when, an until-when, a how and a why), with the dual result of disclosing the "time off" from the crisis, in order to allow the crisis to be discharged according to a socially and culturally meaningful plan (which represents the cathartic value of the ritual itself). Trance, tremors, glossolalia, echolalia, echomimia, gnashing of the teeth, visions: since they are ritually planned, guided, and so forth, they combat the risk of psychopathology. As Mühlmann states:

> The culturalization of originally (as already mentioned) multiple psychopathological manifestations, the ritualization that is simultaneously institutionalized, at the same time means, however, a certain mitigation of their dangerousness, a neutralizing of the originally individual, spontaneous actions. Everything cultural counts for us as regular, indeed— and everything regular is relatively harmless in comparison with the unpredictability of the demonic Ur-act. Through the mimicry of one's companions one takes up this act, standardizing and typifying it; it gives its approval, detoxifying him and thus delivering him to the harmlessness of the general and ordinary/customary, holistically controlled, collective cultural act, in which it is foreseen that each and every course of events henceforth flows back into the "again normal." (278 ff.)

Compare in this regard H. G. Barnett, *Innovation: The Basis of Cultural Change* (New York: McGraw Hill, 1953), 110ff., and *Indian Shakers: A Messianic Cult of the Pacific Northwest* (Carbondale: Southern Illinois University Press, 1957).

2.3. Apocalyptic thought is teeming with contradictions. The end of the year is proclaimed to be near, nonetheless the wait is never totally passive in desperation or in joy, but in fact it allows and sometimes foments earthly horizons of action that are more or less extensive enough to be to one degree or another compatible with the continuation of communitarian cultural life as a whole. We consider the eschaton to be the elimination of the negative, as the absolute triumph of *value*, but we do not realize that every value gains its status from its existing struggle against the possibility of the corresponding disvalue, satiety against hunger, wealth against poverty, love against hate, peace against war; and further, beauty against ugliness, truth against error, goodness against evil. The end gets predicted as a more or less near and certain when: but each time that the deadlines remain without an outcome, apocalyptic thought defends itself from drawing the logical conclusion of the prediction's failure. Now it looks for reasons to justify this failure, now it turns to postponements and to deferrals, and now it refashions itself, reworking the crisis itself into the new refashioning. These are only some of the most striking contradictions in which apocalyptic thought remains ensnared, in which in fact it necessarily ensnares itself in order to remain as it is. But if such "contradictions" are inevitable, it means that it is the task of the ethnologist and the anthropologist to track down the logic that keeps contradictions hidden, that obliges apocalyptic agents not to take on all of the consequences of the failures of prophesy and millenarianism. It is thus a matter of reestablishing the *cultural-historical coherence* of a certain operative logic implicit in various apocalyptic behaviors, and we can arrive at this logic by including in the analysis everything that does not appear to the consciousness of apocalyptic agents, that is, their unconscious motivations, unconscious risks, and unconscious objectives of reintegration.

2.4. Andreas Lommel, "Modern Culture Influences on the Aborigines," *Oceania* 21 (1950): 14–24, and, by the same author, *Die Unambal* (Hamburg: Museum für Völkerkunde, 1952), 82ff.[8]

Expedition of the Frobenius Institute in Northeast Australia in the year 1938, directed by H. Petri, and whose other members were Agnes Schetz, Gerta Beck-Kleist of Frankfurt am Main and D. C. Fox of New York, Patrick Pentony of Perth (Eastern Australia) and Andreas Lommel. The tribes explored were the Ungarinyin, the Worora, and the Unambal: the first had already been partially studied by Elkin[9] and the second by the missionary Lowe. Petri and Fox dealt above all with the Ungarinyin, and Lommel with the Unambal.

The different groups have differing degrees of relation to Western culture. Lommel distinguishes three fundamental situations:

> (a) Aborigines living in permanent contact with Western culture on farms, at missions, and at government stations. These members have adopted European dress, food, and languages.
>
> (b) Temporary workers at the station, who live half of the year as nomadic hunters, the way their ancestors did.
>
> (c) Small groups, for the most part of the elderly, living in the hinterlands according to traditional mores and avoiding contact with white culture.

The least influenced by contact were the Unambal, whose members were exclusively those of the third group. Demographic decline, disorders in mental balance, the disintegration of social organization as a result of the contact with white culture. Another result: a new cult, Kurrangara, which originated in the south and spread rapidly. To this cult the Ungarinyin and the majority of Worora have been initiated, while other Worora and the majority of Unambal were still waiting to be admitted.[10]

The cult featured wooden boards in the shape of rough *churinga*[11] endowed with power that the initiate appropriated by rubbing smaller boards, otherwise he would succumb to their power. After the initiation, he needed to purify himself carefully to prevent the power radiating from him from killing everyone who did not belong to the group of initiates. Petri had studied the Kurrangara in the territory of the Ungarinyin, where it was already fully developed;[12] Lommel studied it in its initial phase among the Unambal, and therefore in a clearer relationship to the prior cult.

In the old cult, which has fallen into disuse for at least a generation, the boards came from the homeland of a Northern spirit called Nguniai, the civilizing hero of the tribe, inventor of instruments, laws, and circumcision. The hero Nguniai had sculpted the *churinga* and decorated them. Vaybalma stole the boards, and pursued in vain by Nguniai, he gave them to mankind. In the new myth, the boards were prepared by Tjanba, son of Nguniai. He migrated from north to south, and it is believed that today he lives in the desert to the south, from where the Kurrangara boards come. The boards thus follow the same route as that of the old cult, but *in an opposite direction*, from south to north. Proceeding along this route, they will one day reach the region inhabited by Nguniai. The moment that Nguniai sees his son's first board, he will stop producing them himself, and—so the myth concludes—life on Earth *will come to an end*.

The Unambal myth connected to the Kurrangara cult has been most extensively described by Lommel in *Die Unambal* (94ff).[13] The Kurrangara slabs have been crafted by a spirit called Tjanba, son of Nguniai. In mythical time, the son leaves his father and migrates to the south (or southeast) until he arrives in the mythical land of Warmala. From his father the son learned how to create slabs bearing a magical power, and from his father he had received a pointed wand, called *Jinbal*, for carrying out black magic. Tjanba, with other similar spirits, continuously manufactures Kurrangara slabs, and in part he sends them to men using modern means of transportation—steamboats, airplanes, automobiles and trains—and in part the men themselves must go get them, organizing an expedition that concludes with a sudden strike and the theft of the slabs. The thieves, however, are careful to leave wooden female Kurrangara slabs; these, however, despite everything, one day reach the men. When Tjanba sends the men the female slabs, it will be the sign that *the end of the world is not far off*. A new law will enter into effect: women will have all of the power, men will have to carry out women's work, sexual relations will become rare and only at the women's discretion, and they will become risky because of the magical power bestowed on the women by the slabs. Precisely to avoid this, the men do not take female slabs. Tjanba becomes aware of the theft and pursues them unsuccessfully. According to other versions, it is Tjanba himself who sends the slabs and disseminates them among the men. The dissemination takes place from south to north, and thus the slabs will inevitably reach the abode of Tjanba's father, Nguniai. When the first Kurrangara reaches Nguniai's region, Nguniai's closest neighbor finds him going to hunt. The Kurrangara is for Nguniai like a wand message from his son. Nguniai touches the slab and "understands" what its decorations mean: from that moment on, neither the father nor the son will create slabs; the *end of the world and of life* takes place from that moment, everything ceases. We should note, moreover, that Tjanba[14] is depicted with light skin, similar to that of the *whites*; he has horns like a bull on his head; he lives in a house of the type we find in a white people's station. For hunting he uses wooden Kurrangara as weapons: he rests them on his shoulder, aims at his prey, strikes lightening and thunders, the ground trembles, and many kangaroos fall dead to the ground. The Tjanbas enjoy flour, sugar, tea; through their *Jinbal*, they transmit diseases like leprosy and syphilis, which are thought to come from poisonous herbs/grasses that grow around the Tjanbas' houses. The cult requires abundant banquets with tea, sugar, flour, and meat (but not of indigenous animals).

> Modern culture is received by these primitives as something real but as a mythical ghost or a figure. This figure is a personification of all the features of modern culture known to the aborigines. At the same time it retains features of the old mythical ghosts. Thus modern culture is assimilated to a certain extent to the old ideas in imagination. (Lommel 1950, 21)

2.5. Lommel (1952), 98.[15]

A certain dance called *maui* reflects another degree of development of the myth in the context of the myth of Tjanba. "*Maui* is already a first appearance of the legendary supremacy of women that occurs shortly before the end of the world, according to the *Tjanba* myth." The dance, performed by women but in which men also must participate, spreads the "poison" that belongs to Kurrangara even farther among the men. Although the *maui* dance is not yet practiced among the Unambal, it nonetheless has already been narrated, and the Aborigines that have traveled to the south state that they have taken part in it.

Lommel (1950, 24): "Kurrangara and the approaching maui were both regarded as dangerous, and they both made the Aborigines concentrate on the imminent future, which was believed to be *the end* of everything alive. An eschatological myth may have been part of the Aborigines' traditions, but now the approach of modern culture with so many fateful elements accompanying it certainly makes the Aborigines concentrate on the *end of the world*.[16]

Citing again from the *Oceania* article (Lommel 1950, 24): "The Unambal informants, who were deeply impressed by the approaching end of the world, told me that this is going to be announced by the arrival of different Kurrangara slabs sent out by Tjanba's wife" (which would be followed by an overturning of the social order of the two sexes). "My informants used to speak of these inevitable events with serious apprehension and to link with another cult that they expected soon to arrive from north but of which some already claimed to know the essentials."

The following features reveal the sense of the end as a loss of a certain system of valorization of the world due to pressure from the relationship with Western culture:

(1) White men, and their culture, are mythically reshaped into the figure of Tjanba and his band of spirits. Tjanba is modeled on the figure of the traditional civilizing hero, Nguniai, assimilated in the myth as his son. But Tjanba is a Nguniai with a different value, and of a different value appear the corresponding mythical characters:

- Nguniai father-Tjanba son;
- Nguniai north—Tjanba, south, desert areas;
- Magic—destructive magic, the power of death, of which one can nonetheless take possession;
- Nguniai's boards traveling from north to south;
- Tjanba's boards traveling from south to north, and the end of the world when the loop has been completed.

(2) The catastrophe in the Kurrangara myth of the spread of female slabs, avoided until now, approaches with the Maui cult.

2.6. Postponement, deferral, delay of the **Parousia**.
Failures of apocalyptic proclamations.
From Mühlmann (1961, 275 ff.). Failed chiliastic prophesies do not decree the end of a prophetic movement. Ronald Knox, in *Christliches*

Schwärmertum (trans. from English by P. Havelaar and A. Schorn [Cologne: Hegner, 1957], 132),[17] even claims that "All chiliastic movements outlive the non-fulfilment of their prophecies." Mühlmann notes that Knox's statement should be corrected on two counts: in the sense that not all but the majority of movements survive the disappointment that accompanies an unfulfilled prophesy, and also in the sense that such a survival instigates the transformation of the movement into a sect or institutionalized church. This also seems to be proven by American psychologists and sociologists in an experimental study on the Seekers (see the study by Festinger, Riecken and Schacter[18]). The reaction of the *credo quia absurdum*[19] allows the group to survive and consolidate itself or even to expand, but thanks to an institutionalization that tends to crystallize the liveliest aspect of immediate religious life. As an additional confirmation of this theory, Mühlmann recalls, moreover, how the origins of Christianity and Islam were chiliastic, but then both religions turned into solid institutional systems, while the chiliastic element operated again and again as a periodically emerging ferment. And he adds, "The way in which communities still living in the condition of waiting for the end come to terms with the Parousia's delay has not yet been adequately studied in terms of its meaning for an increasing institutionalization. (Mühlmann 1962, 276). Pagan Rome prohibited sibylline writings that prophesied the end of the Roman Empire; Christianity—which in the Second Epistle to the Thessalonians 2:8, and again with Lactantius, considered Rome as a power that held the Parousia back—took precisely Rome as its symbol: papal Rome, which prohibited the writings of Lactantius. As Mühlmann notes, "it is not possible to more clearly indicate the victory of the institution over elementary chiliastic content" (277).

Observations.

In Mühlmann's theory one recognizes the recurrent impropriety of sociological frameworks when they are not aware of the limits to their usefulness. There is a palpable lack of analyses that grasp cultural apocalypses in the act of defending themselves from the risk of psychopathological apocalypses. It nonetheless seems that Mühlmann barely sees the problem (how do communities get over the shock of failed prophesy?), but we must notice that the problem is not framed correctly, because it is always an operative expectation, one that discloses a certain worldly practicable horizon, at least to the extent that psychopathological regression is fought.

2.7. Working hypotheses.

The collapse of the world in the primitive world appears as a threat or punishment for some modification introduced by humankind into the rigorous repetition of an order founded in mythic origins. Where cultural consciousness is oriented toward a reabsorption of the proliferation of becoming in a foundational identity that ritual as well as custom repeat indefinitely, the world collapses as a threat or punishment because this reabsorption did not take place. When the transgression of order affects individuals or groups—as in the case of white colonization or the deportation of slaves from Africa to America—the experience of collapse or the prophesy of an imminent catastrophe makes its appearance. The primitive world preserves itself and is practicable in that it is experienced by cultural consciousness as a world of origins that get repeated ceremonially: the world has been founded "one time," and ritual always leads it back to that founding order and keeps it there. In this way, becoming is concealed: it does not belong to hegemonic cultural consciousness but rather to subaltern consciousness, which in the meantime "is in history" (and thus innovates, decides, adapts itself to changing existential realities) since it cloaks historicity in mythic metahistory.

The inalterability of the "world" order: the world that does not tolerate innovations, initiatives, or human modifications because innovations, initiatives, or modifications of tradition would make the world and its order collapse. This obviously does not mean that innovations, initiatives, and modifications do not take place; it just means that they can only take place if they are disguised in their historicity. Nothing is further from mythical thought than the theorization of historical *Einmaligkeit*:[20] mythic *Einmaligkeit* is a foundational metahistory, exemplary, and historic *Einmaligkeit* can transit in its protective shadow. Only with the rupture of this diving bell in which primitive man is immersed in the ocean of life does the future become a cultural focus, but in order to produce the proclamation of catastrophe and transform the sorcerer into a "prophet" or "messiah."

For some time now religious sciences have placed an emphasis on the *theme of origins* in mythic-ritual consciousness in different ways: the theme of a primordial and inaugural era in which assorted numinous beings (supreme beings, gods, cultural heroes, *Heilbringer*) have founded the current natural, social, and ritual order. This then preserves itself in concrete time since the primordial era of foundation is reactualized again and again by ritual agents who repeat the inaugurating, founding, and ordering acts of the origins' mythical agents. [. . .]

The problem presents itself in the following terms: in traditional societies—in which labor is divided according to sex and age (male/female, young/old) and the autonomy of the natural condition in the production of economic goods does not go beyond the technology of hunting and gathering, nomadic pastoralism and primitive agriculture—the historicity of becoming, individual initiative, change, and innovation must be concealed from consciousness and disclosed through this concealment. One "can" be in history as if one were not in it; in other words, behaviors are learned in the hegemonic cultural consciousness as the ceremonial repetition of a paradigmatic order founded once and for all *in illo tempore*. The future itself is reabsorbed through divination and mythical models of occurrence. In this perspective, the end of the world appears solely as the collapse of this protected regime (ritual negligence, taboo breaking), the impossibility of reactualizing the mythical symbols of origin and foundation in ceremonies again and again.

But with the development of agriculture, settlements, the differentiation of social classes, the birth of cities, and the complexification of state organization, a sense of future appears in the hegemonic cultural consciousness: the horizon of what is going to happen. In agropastoral civilizations we already see a sphere of human planning—conquered through work (e.g., the agricultural year)—that cannot be concealed from consciousness. The reabsorption of becoming in mythical origins is no longer sufficient, and history enters as an "eschaton" in mythical-ritual consciousness itself.

2.8. History without philosophical options.

The fact that Guariglia[21] belongs to his own "school of thought" and that this school reacts differently in its ethnological research—in an explicit or implicit way, tacitly or manifestly—is completely natural: there appears to be no doubt that this school of thought is the Catholic *Weltanschauung*. Moreover, that Lanternari belongs to another school of thought and makes it react, in turn, in his activity as an expert of religious ethnology—this, too, seems to me to be indisputable. Ethnologists, like all social science scholars, do not avoid reactions of this sort, whether they know it or not, admit it or deny it. Now, that said, all polemics of substance are legitimate except one: one that, based on the absurd claim of an ethnology safeguarded from any philosophical, objective, or scientific option, thereby sheltered flaunts the merit of objectivity and scientificness of a given ethnological study because it is lacking philosophical options and denies objectivity and scientificness to another scientific study that embraces such an option. It is extremely easy to demonstrate that in all cases (without exception), those who flaunt their own research as objective and scientific in the aforementioned sense—considering it safe from any philosophical option—and reproach other people's research for being ruined in various ways by philosophy—that is, by the various ways of reacting in the course of the research itself, by a certain conception of life and the world—are actually simply unaware of having made a certain orientation of thought react within their own research, taking the unconscious acceptance of selected philosophical criteria for objectivity and scientificness. In order to say the same thing in simpler words, taking for objectivity and scientificness what is ignorance in the best of cases, and in the worst, an obvious treachery and hypocrisy (indeed, in given cases, it appears very difficult to admit that the person in question "doesn't know how" to use philosophical criteria, and we may legitimately suspect that he is pretending "not to know" due to his own interests).

2.9. Helmut Petri, "Der australische Medizinmann," *Annali Lateranensi* 16 (1952): 159–317.[22]

Prophesies of the end of the world among the Yualayi of New South Wales, nation of the Kamilaroi.

Mrs. Langloh Parker, in discussing Yualayi medicine men (or Euahlayi, according to Langloh Parker's writing)—being one of the tribes of the great nation of the Kamilaroi—refers in her monograph *The Euahlayi Tribe*[23] that among their visions concerning the future there are some that are terrifying. In their magic stones they see their black people[24] become paler and paler as time progresses. Finally, only the whitened faces of the white *wundah* devils appear, and this means that one day on Earth there will no longer be any black people. The reason for this tragic future destiny of their people, according to the old *wirreenun* (medicine man), was that the tribe had distanced itself from its Boorah[25] rites, provoking the wrath of Byamee, the sky god, who rose furiously from his crystal seat located in *Bullimah* (sky). Byamee had once announced that as long as men followed his consecrating norms, he would remain on his crystal throne, and likewise the blacks on the earth and everything would be in order. If, however, it happened that men neglected the Boorah rites, he would leave, and this would mean the end. Humanity would give way to the *wundah*. The result of this prophesy of a looming end of the world was that in Mrs. Parker's time, numerous half-caste[26] newborns were killed because the old *wirreenun* (medicine men prophets) had seen them as an omen of the approaching end (128).

Petri comments on this information, recalling how—independently from the figure of the wizard and his inner illumination—"there was or is among the mythical traditions of numerous Australian tribes the conviction that the world will remain and life will proceed as long as black people obey the sacred laws of primeval times" (129). We find a conviction of this sort, Petri notes, in this or that form throughout the world and in every epoch. But the particular apocalyptic modeling that such a conviction can take on in a case like the one documented by Mrs. Langloh Parker depends on a circumstance that is related to white colonization. As Petri observes, "Because now since the settlement of Australia by the whites the old native cultures have perished for the greater part, and those that have been able to maintain themselves will perish in the shorter or longer term, it is not so very surprising that apocalyptic visions found their way into the black's soul" (129). Petri continues:

> After all, he [the Aborigine] must daily see older and younger clansmen and tribesmen turning aside from the teaching and traditions of the forefathers to tread the paths of the whites. He sees furthermore that western civilization is bringing him no great benefit; that it is unable to compensate him for what he has given up. He sees the mood of hopelessness in his people arising from that, the slow but steady sinking of all courage to face life and of the will to stand one's ground. He finally sees the unavoidable physical extinction of his race, an extinction that is perhaps causally related to the general pessimistic state of mind. Young people to whom the secret, sacred doctrines of the mythical past, guaranteeing continuity in nature and human existence, can be passed on, are becoming fewer and fewer. So in the black's thought the certainty must of necessity grow stronger that the primeval proclamation of doom in the case of renunciation of blackfellow law is now approaching its fulfilment. The pale wundah spirits will people the earth when life is over. We met at the start of this study a similarly gloomy vision of the future from the Kimberley tribes of the northwest: After the disappearance of the old, life-giving Ungud and *Wònd'ina* powers, the strange, skeleton-like *D'anba* spirits from the desert will travel through the dead land taking their restless steps. Similar apocalyptic visions and ones differently constituted could be cited here from different Australian tribes, but we do not want to depart too far from our topic. (129)

> In the northern Kimberleys of Northwest Australia, in the extensive region, still barely developed for white civilization, that is roughly bordered in the west by the Walcott and the King Leopold ranges, in the south by the Mount Anges and Mount Hann tablelands, in the east by the Drysdale River, and in the north by the Timor Sea, live the once very large tribes of the Worora, Ungarinyin and Unambal. (4)

With reference to the Ungarinyin of Walcott River, Petri reports their belief in Ungud (163).

Ungud, a mythical rainbow serpent, has his camp on Earth or in the depths of water holes. Creator of the world, origin of all things that live and grow on Earth, unitary numinous essence that at the beginning of time made the world rise out of the original chaos, drew living beings from the earth or with the rain sent them on the earth. Simultaneously the collective name for rainbow serpents that inhabit the subsoil, the depths of the water caves, and the skies. "We may perhaps *conceive of Ungud as personifications of locally operating forces of generation and fertility*" (5):[27] every single Ungud in the clan territory that brings about the multiplication of animals and plants, creates springs, and every Ungud during the rainy season makes water flow in the riverbeds and creeks. It rises in the sky like a colorful rainbow serpent to devour rains, in other words, to make them stop. The preexisting children-spirits of men and animals originate from Ungud: according to Aboriginal origin theories, they have been found by a dreaming father or in trance and enter into the mother's body to then be born as flesh-and-blood beings.

All Aborigines think of *Ungud* as a beneficent otherworldly power (apart from some local *Ungud* regarded as "evil"), above all they know that what happens in nature, but also the individual's and the community's existences, depends on it. *Ungud* affords life an undisturbed course, however only as long as people live according to its 'laws,' perform the ritual acts of increase annually and observe the taboos. If that does not happen, then *Ungud* sends all-destroying catastrophes of floods and rain. But the opposite can also happen: *Ungud* dies or leaves the land, and the consequence is that the rock pictures fade, the water dries up, animals and people waste away, the plants wither and everything becomes a desert. There comes a world in which only the pale bone-spirits of the dead lead their eternally restless existence. If we consider all these beliefs, we come to the conclusion that in the Aborigens' thought nature and human society on the one and the life- and fertility-promoting power of the mythical rainbow serpent *Ungud* (in its twofold aspect as a being and a multiplicity of beings) on the other, are brought into a relationship of mutual dependence. (6–7)

The ritual multiplication of the species, in one form or the other widespread throughout Australia, among the Ungarinyin and the Worora mainly consists in a regular "touching up" of the rock art "galleries" that are considered true and proper consecrated local totemistic centers. The touch-ups are carried out at the beginning of the rainy season, and they consists in bringing fresh new color to the images of Ungud, Wondjna, and the representations of the local totemic species (plants, animals, natural phenomena, etc.). Sometimes touch-ups are carried out by the *d'òingari* (headman) of a *band'a-òdin* (picture gallery). Among the Unambal, groups of stones (*d'àla-lo*) are prevalent, commonly as totemic and multiplication centers. Among the Ungarinyin we also find Elkin's *Talu-Typus*, widespread throughout all of Northern Australia; however, they play a secondary role in comparison to the "touching up" of rock art galleries (6n9).

"We must regard the close linking of nature, social and intellectual life as a phenomenon common to all Australia and as the actual fundamental principle of Australian totemistic view of the universe" (7n10).

Observations on Petri.

From the way that the end of the world figures in Kamilaroi ideology, it seems that we can advance the following working hypotheses.

The "world" is above all "order": that is, the possible operative horizon of a social group. For a collectivity that lives by hunting and gathering on land where the mode of subsistence largely depends on the rainy season and the rapid reappearance of vegetation after a long period of drought, in an existential regime in which water—whether it is fertilizing rain or comes as a thirst-quenching spring—is at the center of existential possibilities, one can understand how the order is represented by a rainbow serpent, an image that unites in a highly meaningful emotional bond the sky from which rain falls and the earth in the moment in which the rain ceases and vegetation is about to explode. This image excludes—that is, it puts off into disorder—both drought and flooding, and it carries out this exclusion since it is a metahistorical order, founded *in illo tempore* and guaranteed by a force that, at the same time, sits in the crystal [seat] of heaven and divides and diversifies itself in the various clan territories. Undoubtedly the historic order is much more problematic: there can be drought or flooding, plants can dry up and animals can be scarce beyond the bounds of a season. But these real events become bearable and possible to overcome because their historicity is concealed, disguised, and excluded from the dominant cultural consciousness. The rituals uphold the immutable order, they renew the archetypical model, and so forth. If the rites are not celebrated, if Ungud abandons his celestial seat, then the order breaks down. The world is upheld by this exemplarity of behavior, which always leads it back to its archetypical order: this allows possible disorder to be hidden through a ritual action that reabsorbs happening over and over in its mythical model of normative foundation. Ritual is the behavior that leads a historical "this time" over and over to a metahistorical "once upon a time" that is also a "once and for all." Ritual is the form of behavior that is closest to the unchanging order of myth, furthest from the changeability of becoming with its novelty, its unpredictability, its negativity. Indeed, becoming appears reduced to the minimum of repeating what is identical: in each rainy season (the "this time"), the galleries of rock art images are touched up (leading the "this time" to a "once and for all" of the normative foundation). This subject is very important both for understanding the nature of the primitives' supreme being as well as for recognizing the development of depiction of "the end of the world" when the collision with white civilization brings with it the destruction or the decline of traditional mythical-ritual behaviors of the corroborees[28] of the world.

5

The Apocalypse of the West

1. An Apocalypse without Eschaton

1.1. In humanity's religious life the subject of the end of the world appears in different eschatological contexts, either as a periodic cosmic palingenesis or as a definitive redemption from the evils inherent in earthly existence. Consider, for example, the New Year of agrarian civilizations;[1] apocalyptic movements of colonial peoples in the nineteenth and twentieth centuries;[2] redemptive history in the Judeo-Christian tradition; the numerous millenarianisms scattered throughout Western religious history.[3] Against this eschatological perspective, the current cultural climate in the West is familiar with the theme of the end outside of any religious horizon of salvation, that is, as a desperate catastrophe of the worldly, the domestic, the settled, of the signifying and the practicable: a catastrophe that narrates with meticulous, and at times obsessive, accuracy the undoing of what has been formed, the alienation of what is domestic, the unsettling of the settled, the loss of sense of signifiers, the impracticability of the practicable. The West's present cultural climate is not limited to this despairing and desperate subject; even when it lets itself be brushed, touched, or actually hit by stormy gusts, it reacts in various ways to its lethal allure. Nonetheless, the moment of abandoning oneself without compensation to the experience of the end undeniably constitutes an elective orientation of our epoch as attested to by numerous documents taken from custom, literature, the visual arts, music, and finally, from philosophy itself.

Furthermore, the simple fact that atomic catastrophe has been able to take on a concrete significance nowadays—stoking a corresponding terror—demonstrates how, long before becoming the possibility of material self-destruction through the use of human technological power, the risk of the end is rooted in souls. This suggests a much more secret, deep, and invisible catastrophe than what Hiroshima's mushroom cloud offered as a real image on a reduced scale. It would certainly be highly

advisable for someone to decide to offer an overview of this most intimate catastrophe of the modern and contemporary West in a rigorously
cultural-diagnostic perspective, aiming to identify the exact meaning of
symptoms, the extension of the contagion, the conditioning of the illness,
and the powers of healing. A project of this sort could not be carried out
without a continuous comparison between the theme of the end in the
present cultural climate and the theme of the end in an eschatological
perspective; in other words, between an ending experienced as a catastrophe in progress and a culturally redeemed ending as the proclamation
of a palingenesis of existence.

1.2. If we want to illustrate with an example the heuristic value that psychopathological apocalypse bears in the historical and anthropological
study of cultural apocalypses, we must first consider what we have called
the apocalypse without eschaton of the modern and contemporary West.
Just the mere fact that the apocalyptic *Stimmung* is polemically characterized as "without eschaton" indicates how much it appears as bare crisis
and therefore how much it is electively prepared to be illuminated by
the psychopathological document. Precisely because—out of all of the
cultural apocalypses—it appears to be dangerously close to the radical
crisis of the human, the West's apocalypse without eschaton lends itself
in an elective way to illustrate the heuristic value of the psychopathological document.

1.3. The theme of apocalypse has dominated modern literature in various
ways. Now, this theme can be of interest in a critical or scientific perspective from several points of view, but here we are exclusively interested
in it as a *document of custom and symptom of crisis*. Nausea, boredom,
the absurd, incommunicability,[4] or the catastrophe of image or melody:
these interest us only as *cultural clinicians* who intend to participate in a
decisive consultation. This is definitely not a question of the objectivist
conception of illness, which places the healthy doctor on one side and the
patient on the other. Here, the doctor fighting the illness must first and
foremost defeat it in himself, and the patient is also someone who must
heal and receive ongoing healing powers.

   The world as a familiar, domestic, settled, obvious, normal, habitual
backdrop serves as an indicator of possible practicable paths in which the
human activity of millennia lives; the **handy** formations that have developed in ages of traditions; and finally, individual biographies up to the
present situation: through this multifaceted and choral resounding of traditionalized and transmitted communitarian efforts, the world takes on an
initial, fundamental sense of practicability. The familiar, the domestic, and

so forth, only mean this: go ahead, you're not alone, you're not the first, you're not the only one; but you are in an immense, marching legion that only in an infinitesimally small part is currently made up of living people.

1.4. The "crisis" in Western visual arts, music, narrative, poetry, theater, philosophy, and the ethical-political life is a crisis in that the break with a theological plan of history and the sense deriving from it (the plan of providence, the plan of evolution, the dialectical plan of ideas) does not become a stimulus for a new effort of descent into chaos and anabasis toward order but a fall into hell with no return, an idolization of the contingent, the senseless, the merely possible, the relative, the incoherent, the thoughtless, the immediately experienced, the incommunicable, the solipsistic, and so forth. That the West feels a deep need for a bath in life, and that this need bears witness to its attempt to reembrace a vitality that escapes it, is understandable in an epoch of crisis, senility, and confusion. But one cannot abstractly prescribe what the orderly world needs to lose to be brought back to order; what is important is that the recovery takes place, whatever may be the level to which one must descend for that recovery—a recovery taking place toward form and values, toward an intersubjective, communicable and human order. In the present cultural climate the danger nonetheless remains of having many catabases without anabasis: and this is certainly illness.

1.5. [We refer] "to things themselves," to the immediacy of life, to Zen moments, to myokinetic activities, and so forth and so on, but what does this desperate nostalgia of *things themselves* express if not *that malady of objects*,[5] indeed, of the very objectivization that is the end of the world? And it is about this illness that we must first of all speak.

   Art is a way of recovering events threatened by hardening and chaos, and it is thus the way of curing and healing the always possible malady of objects. But this recovery is achieved on various levels according to various historical circumstances and various cultural climates. If there is always a moment of descent into hell in art—to the level in which the object is in crisis—it is not possible to establish once and for all how many steps one can acceptably move down in order to carry out the anabasis. What is important is that the level is reached and that the anabasis is carried out (that it is communicable, intersubjective, reintegrating) so that the individual action allows us to read this incident. What is important is that the moment of descent is not mistaken for liberation and that the ruthless pursuit of the "malady of objects" is not exhibited as healing or idealized precisely as an illness. In this perspective it is possible to judge so-called contemporary art, which should not be condemned because it has left behind naturalism and perpetrated the figure's catastrophe. These are extremely crude judgments: in reality, Renaissance visual art did not need to descend very far in order to recuperate objects and events and to carry out the anabasis toward form, while contemporary art must reach much deeper levels in order to attempt a catharsis. Furthermore, this aspect of contemporary art constitutes a document of how deep the roots of the illness are, of how serious the danger is of the *end of the world*.

Disorder, indeterminacy, complementarity, probability, randomness, cultural relativism: all this and more marks the end of a certain concept of order borrowed from theology and from this past to idealism and positivist scientism (also being reflected in Marxism, especially as mediated by Engels). But culture is an ethos of order; disorder, indeterminacy, and so forth, do not pose an ideal but rather an internal limit and irony of every cultural project of world unification, a limit and irony that guarantee history, the inexhaustibility of ordering **projection**.

Neugier, unsatisfied and insatiable longing for the new; gossipy and consuming curiosity; delusional search for a "convenience" that defeats the state of discomfort once and for all; the roaring time of fetishized technology followed by the immense emptiness of free time and "pastimes"; continuous generation and destruction of the small artificial paradises of fashion; the spasm of success and prestige; the stolid sense of being-thrown-into-the-world; mystery novels, sporting crowds, "modern" art: *"Verse-nous ton poison pour qu'il nous reconforte / nous voulons, tant ce feu nous brûle le cerveau, / plonger au fond du giuffre, Ciel, Enfer qu'importe, / au fond de l'inconnu pour trouver de nouveau!"*[6]

The struggle against the "normal," the "domestic," the "familiar," and the "habitual" prominently characterizes the modern and contemporary cultural climate manifesting itself in art, poetry, philosophy, and custom. The abnormal, the unsettling, the extraneous, the monstrous, the gratuitous without actual sense, the conventional and the mechanical: these are culture's central themes in all of its manifestations. But it is necessary to recall that everydayness is not necessarily vulgar but becomes so only if norms, domestic and familiar atmospheres, and habits lose their secret affective charge of loyalty to concrete valorizations of the world, as a communitarian achievement transmitted in the course of generations and ages.

1.6. Two contradictory terrors dominate the epoch in which we live: that of "losing the world" and that of "being lost in the world." In one respect we fear losing—not so much through death, but in the course of existence itself—the splendor and joy of earthly life, the energy that drives toward communitarian projects of civil life, toward technology and science, moral solidarity and social justice, poetry and philosophy. In another respect, we consider the world to be a danger that threatens the most authentic human destiny and thus a temptation from which to be saved. On the one hand, the world appears to be a lost paradise of lived participations, and we curse technology and science that have given us astronomy's stupid sun in exchange for Helios. On the other hand, the catastrophe appears precisely in the will to close oneself in the worldly horizon without an intuition of, a hope or faith in, "another" world; this is a closure and restriction for which even the world of earthly existence is destined to collapse, exhausting its foolhardy Promethean drive in nothingness. And furthermore, the "end of the world" is at times connected to the Judeo-Christian tradition of the end of *this* world and the advent of the Kingdom, at times it is presented in lay, secular terms of the end of *a certain* specific historical world (the end of bourgeois civilization), and finally, at times it is oriented toward a more or less desperate nihilism that, in its extreme form, almost always touches the limits of psychopathology.

1.7. Hiroshima, two hundred thousand dead in an instant through the action of a single man, Eatherly. Six million Jews assassinated according to an administrative plan, of which Eichmann was the bookkeeper. Günther Anders says that such events are unimaginable and therefore do not permit repentance, moral reparation.[7] Indeed, Eichmann continues his tasks, as before, even if now it is to defend himself in court; and Eatherly came out of it with a devastated mind. It was once possible in history to imagine the pain not of two hundred thousand or six million people but of all the people of the past, present, and future, and this image was called Christ: he suffered for everyone on the cross, enabling their regeneration, but as a man-God, not just as a man. Now we should ask if precisely this image of the God-man is necessary in order to be able to adequately imagine the human condition and the subhuman temptations that torment it, or whether we have reached an epoch in which a real image of a single, suffering human face is enough, rather than two hundred thousand or six million human faces, to shed light on the precise sense of our simple duty and stop the finger from pressing the button.

When you are seized with the temptation to push that button—and we fall into that temptation just by admitting that one day someone will have to push it "if necessary"—when you are the victim of this temptation, do not remember the two hundred thousand of Hiroshima or the six million Jews but a single human face in pain, some concrete face of a person you have loved and have seen suffer, some ragged, crying little girl you have encountered in the street, once, on a certain day in a certain month of your life. Remember—do not "imagine"—this insignificant, unremarkable episode that at other times seemed "sentimental" to you, for which you perhaps were "ashamed" as if it were a "weakness." And if you do not see all faces—and your own—in that face, if you still need Christ for this memory, or indeed, if you do not remember anything; if you say that it is a sign of virility not to remember in this moment, then today or tomorrow someone—perhaps you yourselves—will push the button.

"Nuclear war" is a brief chain of truly perfect crimes that no one will even discover for the simple reason that no one will remain to discover them, and no one will be able to be their judge, casting the first stone.

"I am no man, I am dynamite."[8]

Nuclear war is not the end of the world as a risk or a mythical-ritual symbol of reintegration but as a technological gesture of a hand, lucidly prepared by the mobilization of all the resources of science in the context of a politics that coincides with the death drive.

1.8. Cultural homelands. Nature in itself.

The modern world has become particularly sensitive to the problems raised by different cultural homelands and their relations precisely because we live in an epoch of migrations, encounters, and exchanges, and therefore also of cultural homelands suddenly exposed to the ordeal referred to in Aranda myth and that Bambara groups have experienced in the suburbs of Accra.[9] Among the poems that Albino Pierro, a Lucanian poet from Tursi, has recently published in Rome, where for some years he has led the unsettled life of an emigrant, there is one that goes more or less like this translated into Italian from his native dialect:

The fire burning within
Shows plainly in my eyes.
What am I going to do, Mother of God,
what am I going to do?
I've left the town
that gave me the wide breathing of the sky,
and in this city now
the walls alone crash hard against my face;
the things of the world, the endless shouts
plague me like nests of worms.
If I turn my head
I feel almost afraid:
people's eyes
seem to be casting stones,
and at the break of dawn
my feet become entangled in a rope
that grips even more tightly than a hand.

What am I going to do, Mother of God,
what am I going to do?
This poor frightened heart
Is gasping for breath now
And the mask I wear
So I won't seem a wreckage
Is heavier than the world itself to bear.[10]

But is the crisis of cultural homelands a phenomenon that only regards non-Westerners or the insufficiently Westernized, the primitives, the emigrants coming from underdeveloped areas—in short, always the *others* and never *us*? It would suffice to consider certain recurring themes in the various writings of existentialist literature—for example Sartre's "nausea" or the "malady of objects" that Moravia speaks of in *Boredom*—to realize how the world's unsettling and impracticability are risks that threaten our cultural homeland too. Similarly, the task of remodeling our cultural homeland in a way that renders the world meaningful and inhabitable is also ours to a degree never perceived before as much as today. Without being a southern immigrant in Turin, Cesare Pavese was haunted by his childhood in Santo Stefano Belbo, and precisely because of this uninterrupted and resurgent memory, at a certain point he turned to reading ethnological books; and as long as he withstood, he drew on it as a subject for poetry.[11] The central point nonetheless remains this: to withstand, to reshape the domesticity of the world again and again with valorizing action.

It seems to us here that the scientific ideal of considering men as ants gets transformed into the prophetic message of a humanity that will inevitably reduce itself to a sort of anthill; in other words, into the mirage of a humanity that moves fatally forward toward an apocalypse without eschaton, an apocalypse of the worldly and the human. From a discourse that seemed to have become exclusively methodological, we are thus unexpectedly led back to the subject of apocalypse, but this time a nonreligious apocalypse in which no small part of Western culture finds itself insidiously involved. The problem of Third World prophetisms and eschatologisms therefore takes us far if we are truly ready for research that calls us into question as Western researchers. So it will not be enough to compare Third World prophetic and eschatological movements with the great Judeo-Christian apocalyptic tradition because what also comes into play is the comparison with that insidious Western apocalypse characterized by the loss of domesticity and sense of the world, the failure of intersubjective relations, and the ominous shrinking of any horizon of a communitarian, practicable future according to human freedom and dignity.

1.9. The bell tower of Marcellinara.[12]

I remember a sunset when driving along some solitary road in Calabria. We weren't sure that our route was right, and we were relieved to come across an old shepherd. We stopped our car and asked him the information we wanted, but his indications were so confusing we asked him to get in the car and take us to the right turnoff, a few kilometers away: we would pay him for his trouble. He accepted our request with some mistrust, as if he feared an obscure threat, a trap laid for him: it may be that distant memories of episodes of banditry cropped up in his imagination. Along the brief route his mistrust increased and became an outright anxiety, because now, from the window from which he kept looking out, he had lost the familiar view of the bell tower of Marcellinara, the reference point of his minuscule existential space. Because of that missing bell tower, the poor old man felt completely unsettled: he got agitated, showing signs of desperation and terror to such an extent that we decided to take him back to the point where we had met him. On the way back, he kept his head out the window the whole time, anxiously scanning the horizon to see the domestic bell tower reappear. When he finally saw it, his face relaxed, his old heart was placated as if he had reconquered a lost homeland. When we arrived at our meeting point, he asked us to hurry up and open his door. He dashed out the car before it came to a complete stop, wildly disappearing into the brush without replying to our goodbye, almost as if he were escaping from an unbearable nightmare, from a sinister adventure that had threatened to tear him away from his *Lebensraum*, from his only possible *Umwelt*, precipitating into chaos. From what people say, even astronauts can suffer from anxiety when they travel in the silence and solitude of the cosmos, so very far from that "bell tower of Marcellinara" that is the planet Earth. They speak and speak continuously with the earthlings not only to inform them of their journey but also as a way of not losing "their land" (*terra*).[13] This means that presence is endangered when it touches the boundaries of its existential homeland, when it no longer sees its "bell tower of Marcellinara," when it loses the culturalized horizon beyond which it cannot go and within which it carries out its operative "beyond": that is, when it looks out onto nothingness.

1.10. Mounier.

Mounier's[14] fundamental thesis is that the modern apocalypse, unlike the Christian one of the apostolic period and the year 1000, is "torturous," lacking a horizon, pathological—a full-fledged *mal du siècle*. It is the downside of prodigious contemporary technicism, whose constructions are found to be resting on the abyss and perceived to be extremely fragile. The modern apocalypse was "not born of a profoundly hopeful prophecy, but of a general disorder of structure and belief" (14). The modern apocalypse arises out of the fall "of the two great religions of the modern world; Christianity and Rationalism" (14).

> I do not wish to prejudge the quality and the duration of this breakdown. I observe its sociological extent. Where, only a century ago, out of a hundred men, a majority would be professing Christians and most of the others stoutly convinced of the unlimited infallibility of Reason supported by Science, to-day we could only count about 10% of convinced Christians and I doubt whether the percentage of convinced Rationalists would be much higher. In addition, our economic structures and our sociological framework reveal every day their anachronism, their impotence, the absurdity of their survival. Without orientation, without support in this sphere, twentieth-century man feels *lost*, in both senses of the word, in a universe growing simultaneously more overpowering and more insignificant, before his eyes. Hence come those descriptions, shaped by philosophers, using formulae for this new terror which seem less elucidation than a cry for help—man is alone, thrown about, for nothing, in an absurd world, *sans rime ni raison*.[15] He is superfluous, everything is superfluous with a nauseating superfluity. (14–15)

"He has, it is true, the vocation to become a god, but he is irrevocably doomed to fail in this vocation. This transforms his aspirations into a new source of grotesque disgust" (14–15). Modern man arose from the breakdown of the circular, closed universe: but the image of the modern universe "opening out on to an irresistible adventure, is the gift of Christianity" (19–20). "Our panic is the panic of coastal craft that suddenly find themselves on the high seas. Our artifices have developed a rhythm which proves much more rapid than our rhythm of assimilation" (20). "What we can no longer control with our hands, we are also beginning to fail to contain in our minds" (21). Humanity today is not condemned to its future; it has to choose it: the meaning of the atom bomb is in this real possibility of choice between life and suicide. "One might say that humanity has now become adult" (22).

The Christian apocalypse is not closing ourselves off in the actual experience of the end or in the anticipation of a datable end in a more or less near future. Nor is it the terror of an indeterminate end that weighs on all moments of time, suffocating each of them. The Christian apocalypse is a historical movement that rises up from the experience of an already finished world or from the expectation of a datable ending or from the nihilism of an indeterminate end that is always looming; it discloses a laborious witnessing, a worldly witnessing for the end of the world, preparation for the day of the Lord, a progressive establishment of the Christian world. The Christian apocalypse is movement that founds a world, creates a civilization. It reshapes the ending as a crisis—and the terror of every worldly beginning—into a protective, justifying horizon for the unfolding of Christian virtues. The end as a crisis is recovered through this cultural reshaping; it is overcome in the ending as an eschaton, unleashing the margin of a Christian world in expansion between the two. Even in the course of Jesus's preaching the proximity of the Kingdom is never stifling but is illuminated with the Sermon on the Mount and with a project of life in common that it founds. In the movement of the apostolic era's history, the emphasis moved increasingly from the proclamation of the Kingdom and from the *metanoia* that it entails to the Kingdom that has already begun with the death and resurrection of Christ. But "it has already begun" in the sense that its already-occurred beginning is experienced sacramentally—in the Eucharist—and its fulfillment is expected in the Church and its teaching, so that because of this initial deferral, the Christian feels called to witness in the world, day by day, with civic actions.

2. The Ruptures of Aesthetic Modernity

2.1. Hans Sedlmayr, *Verlust der Mitte* (1948; Salzburg: O. Mueller, 1955).[16]

Hans Sedlmayr was born on 18 January 1896 in Hohenstein in Burgenland, on the Austrian-Hungarian border. He attended high school in Vienna-Döhling from 1907 to 1913. He fought in World War I, and he was in Austria's eastern army. After the war, in 1918 he was at Vienna's Technische Hochschule; under the influence of the lessons and personality of Max Dvořák, in 1920 he switched from architecture to art history. In 1933 he was a lecturer at the Technische Hochschule and in 1934 at the University of Vienna. From 1936 he succeeded Schlosser in the Viennese chair. From 1951 he was at the University of Munich. From 1941 he was a full member of the Wiener Akademie der Wissenschaften, and in the same year he became a member of the Erfurt Scientific Academy and in 1955 a full member of the Bayerische Akademie der Wissenschaften.

Sedlmayr proposes to analyze the symptoms of the crisis of our times in modern art,[17] attempting the diagnosis and prognosis of an illness that torments modern civilization. Just as psychotherapy helps the individual resolve unconscious conflicts by coming to a lived awareness of them, so too in a collective perspective the coming to awareness of what modern art unconsciously expresses can contribute to some degree to the resolution of the crisis. The choice of art rather than other products of cultural life is based on the principle that for the history of human societies, art is what the individual's dream represents for the psychiatrist (René Huyghe, 1939[18]): in this sphere it therefore reveals itself more easily than other products of cultural life in that it draws on the sphere of immediate sensation, lived *Stimmungen* and possession. In this respect, what is most nonsensical, absurd, and outlandish in modern art is of interest because nonsensical, absurd, and outlandish does not at all mean that it is lacking sense in the diagnostic framework adopted here; rather, precisely this non-sense makes up a problem of "clinical" investigation and stimulates finding the "reasons" for the non-sense.

"Ce sont les abus qui caractérisent le mieux les tendances,"[19] the French historian of architecture Auguste Choisy once wrote, and an *abus* in the sphere of dwellings reveals certain symptoms of the crisis better than no less outlandish architectural pretentions.

> Here we are beginning to deal with the zone of the unconscious, for the actual meaning of such forms is hidden from their creators, and when these are asked to explain them, the purpose they declare themselves to have had in mind provides a completely inadequate explanation for their actual product. (4)

A critique of the spirit of the modern world starting from art, in the perspective of art, according to what the artistic document expresses: this is the task that Sedlmayr proposes. This is thus no longer a *history of modern art*, of *works of art*, but rather of the dangers expressed in the epoch and evidenced in artistic products, be they successes or failures.

[...]

2.2. Modern poetry.

Comments on Hugo Friedrich, *Die Struktur der modernen Lyrik* (Hamburg: Rowohlt-Taschenbuch, 1956).[20]

Modern poetry's relationship to reality: it is not one of *description* or *familiar warmth* but one of *deformation, alienation*, the *nonfamiliar*. Aggressiveness toward sentiment as a world of communitarian, domestic, settled emotions. The reader of this poetry is shocked and feels introduced into a world lacking security, alarming, and nonetheless beguiling. Surprise, amazement, and "abnormal" make this poetry impossible to absorb for a broad public.

This poetry fights the reader's *habits*, and in this regard it is a parade of "abnormality." Eluding oppressive reality dominated by technology, "clock time," and so forth. "Thus linguistic magic, in the service of enchantment, is allowed to smash the world into fragments"; "I would almost say that chaos must glimmer through any poem," said Novalis (14).

The "ordinary" world suffers from "hyperclarity": "An impassive inwardness in lieu of feelings, imagination instead of reality, universal ruin

rather than unity, an amalgam of heterogeneous things, chaos, the fascination of obscurity and verbal magic, as well as an impersonal manipulating,
conceived of as analogous to mathematics and making the familiar alien"
(14): this is the poetic theory of Baudelaire, the poetry of Rimbaud, Mallarmé, and their contemporaries.

"Bitterness, a taste of ashes," melancholy and *Weltschmerz*, "unmotivated melancholy," fascination for "destructiveness, morbidity and crime"
(15–16).

"Elevation and downfall": the attempt to escape the world of the me-
tropolis; the attempt to escape into the paradise of art; and finally, the
"fascination of the destructive" and the "scornful rebellion against God";
"peace in death." Schema of *Les fleurs du mal* [cf. 23].

"Poverty, decay, evil, the nocturnal, and the artificial" as the stimulating material for poetry [cf. 25].

"[I]rritation at the banal and conventional"; the banal "deformed into
something bizarre" in the " 'union of the terrifying with the foolish'" [cf. 26].

The absurd as grotesque in which ideality clashes with the devil and in
which the chaotic appears as irony within the ideal [cf. 26–27].

Flight from the ordinary world; the new as undefinable, as emptiness
contrasted to the desolation of the real. Empty transcendence.

Dream as productive power, endowed with its own rigorous coherence, "fueled by narcotics or result from a psychopathic state" [34].

"[T]he beginning of the artistic act" as "decomposition," "a destructive
process," "deformation" of confining reality, "deliberate distancing" from
it, "derealization" [cf. 36].

But what do we mean here, in the climate of decadence, by "reality" to
be "derealized"? The "reality" we are speaking of is the universe of science
and technology in the context of bourgeois society, and—always in this
context—the everydayness of the bureaucrat, the office worker, or even
someone who benefits from an affluent society and who is merely inserted
into its spiral of needs, conveniences, fashions, publicity, goods. The reality
we are speaking of is still one of habits, norms, etiquettes, and even emotions in which we no longer participate in an authentically communitarian
way, and this is because the social institutions embodying them have entered into crisis. The reality we are speaking of here is the world of things at
hand, the horizon of handy practicability, of which nowadays we only perceive the resulting subjection, its substantial alienation from humankind.

2.3. Rimbaud.

Jean-Arthur Rimbaud (1854–91), *Oeuvres, vers et proses* (Paris: Mercure
de France, 1912).[21] His poetic period was limited to the years 1870–1875;
then he completely abandoned literature for the most diverse affairs and

adventures in the most diverse parts of the world. For the history of "the end of the world" in the crisis of Western civilization, his theory of the seer is particularly interesting (letter to G. Izambard, 7 May 1871, and letter to P. Demeny, 15 May 1871), subsequently applied in his work *Illuminations*.

The poet must make himself a seer "by a long, gigantic and rational derangement of all the senses." But after having abandoned vision, Rimbaud recognizes its futility and impossibility, and he returns to that "rough" reality that he thought he had overcome and that now embraces him, desolating and brutal. *Une saison en enfer* is evidence of this painful refutation: the poet abandoned literature for everyday life. Just before his death, he converted to Catholicism.[22]

J. Rivière, *Rimbaud* (Paris 1930), cited in H. Friedrich, *Die Struktur der modernen Lyrik* (Hamburg: Rowohlt-Taschenbuch, 1956; It. trans., p. 108),[23] writes with regard to Rimbaud: "The help he brings us consists in his making our stay on Earth impossible . . . The world sinks back into its primal chaos; things emerge with the terrible freedom that was theirs when they served no purpose." And Friedrich adds, on his part, that "foundering before the 'unknown' [Rimbaud] evoked chaos in order to replace it." He sought a language suited to expressing this movement toward chaos. Then, when he reached a point in which chaos drowned his poetic language itself, he "had enough character to put down his pen" and transformed poetry into freedom, turning to the rough reality of adventures in the outside world, travels and affairs, in a boredom that practical agitation was unable to blunt.

With regard to things attained in the "terrible freedom" that "was theirs when they served no purpose," we should observe that the claim to this attainment is absurd because things, if they are such—that is, if they belong to a world—always belong to a cultural history, and therefore, first and foremost, to the sphere of handiness, to the communitarian project of things at hand. The very claim of attaining them "before anyone found any use for them" is culturally conditioned; in Rimbaud's case it reflects the crisis of bourgeois handiness of the world, the unsettling of all relations up to that inaugural relation that is handy valorization. In Rimbaud the very ethos of transcendence of life in distinct communitarian valorizations, the *very duty-to-be-in-the-world*, retreats in the face of the risk of not being there; it is overturned, disarticulated and isolated in the idolization of the risk itself. He contradictorily tries to establish a language that narrates the nonhistory of an ever-lower fall, to the point of silence. In the context of a history of European custom in the last hundred years, this bookkeeper of profligacy is highly significant: but he remains generally extraneous to poetry because poetry is a foretelling that transcends certain historical spheres of handiness, but it can never propose destroying handiness as such.

Rimbaud: the rebellion against scientism as a presumption of the complete scientific explainability of the universe and humankind; unreal chaos as redemption of oppressive reality; the "explosion" of the worldly order. Empty transcendence, contrasted to the habitual and the real, alterity as such, lacking content. Reality intentionally shattered. The emphasis on passivity, the subconscious, and so forth. "I am thought," "I is another," being-acted-upon. The coercive power of the prepersonal, oppression from below. The chaos of the unconscious and the new experiences it dictates. "To work" means to plan this dissoluteness, appropriating it in a deliberated way: long, gigantic and rational derangement of all the senses. Self-destructive behavior, an intentional uglifying of the soul. Abnormality as an intentional exile. The worker of obliteration, he who works toward the explosion of the world. The destruction of the Musée du Louvre, a fire at the Bibliothèque nationale. Total detachment from the past. The shattering of what is given. Leave the continent, get away from the Western swamps. Escape from Europe, embrace rough reality, blunt himself with practical activities. From damnation to chaos, from chaos to silence. He remained silent before the world he shattered. Unsettlement, hate for common impulses, for the heart, dehumanization.

[...]

The rebellion rebels against itself. Only the conclusion draws all this to an end in the farewell to every spiritual existence. Movement from lightness to darkness: *Le dormeur du val*.[24] A storm opens cracks in the walls ... breaks up the boundaries between apartments. The action that dissolves boundaries through the irruption of stormy distances. (Universe in tension: the spread of the destructive contagion starting from an epidemic center of the real: *Larme*[25]). The destructive freedom of a lonesome, shipwrecked man in *Le bateau ivre*:[26] repulsion and revolt, escape in the oversized, sinking in the stillness of obliteration. At the end of the chain is Nothingness. No longer filled by faith, philosophy, or myth, the unknown becomes empty transcendence. The passion for empty transcendence becomes a pointless destruction of reality. Water and wind expand into flooding forces. The superobjective tensions of objects; the ugly; magical beauty = obliteration. Things removed from the real. Shatter the ordinary, the comfortable, the habitual, the natural, and so forth. The inorganic, the mineral, as a sign of unreality. Crush the world. The fusion of different things: the erasure of their respective distinctions [...]

"The Poet makes himself a *seer* by a long, gigantic and rational *derangement* of *all the senses*" (letter to Paul Demeny, 15 May 1871[27]).

Work now?—never, never, I am on strike. Now, I am degrading myself as much as possible. Why? I want to be a poet, and I am working to make myself a Seer: you will not understand this, and I don't know how to explain it to you. It is a question of reaching the unknown by the derangement of *all the senses*. (Letter to Georges Izambard, 13 May 1871)[28]

"What does it matter for us, my heart [...]," *Oeuvres* (215).[29] In this poem, the week of the Commune's blood became the celebration of the obliteration of any order. The moment of the reduction to zero, destruction, is isolated without recovery or prospect, involving not only the bourgeois order but all of history ("power, justice, history, down with you!"), the cosmic order itself, and the very protagonists of the Communard apocalypse ("Europe, Asia, America, disappear / Our avenging march has occupied every place, / City and country!—We will be overcome! / Volcanoes will explode! and the ocean struck ... / [...] the earth melts ..."). In this dizziness of destruction, the "seer" associates himself with the romantic friends of the Commune, but he associates them in delusion, and thus with a bit of ironic skepticism on those whom he *imagines* brothers ("Who would stir up the whirlwinds of furious fire, / Except ourselves and those we imagine brothers?"): but he does reward these "dark strangers" as certain brothers if they join the seer in the act of destruction. An "awakening" follows in the last verse, he is as desperate in his existential solitude as the unrealistically choral, communitarian, destructive orgy is empty: "It is nothing! I am here! I am still here." In the letter to P. Demeny the destruction involves all Western poetry, from the Greeks to the Romantics: "From Greece to the romantic movement—Middle Ages—there are writers and versifiers ... Racine is pure, strong and great."

The poet as "the great patient, the great criminal, the one accursed," and nonetheless as a systematic anarchist that introduces the spirit of system, rigorous method, thought-out planning into sickness, crime, accursedness, and the derangement of all the senses. The drugs that abolish the categories of space and time and lead to artificial paradises ("We assert you, method! I believe in that poison"[30]); fasting, nighttime work, the abuse of sexual life and pederasty; the great dream of escaping from reality, the search for magical powers, secrets to transform life, the adamant engagement with "gnarled reality to embrace,"[31] the abandonment of the anarchic revolt for a life of adventures and "affairs" abroad against the backdrop of a tremendous boredom, and finally, on his deathbed, the so-called return—in any case ambiguous—to religion (but we don't even know exactly to which, since during his agony he prayed to Allah!)

2.4. Thomas Mann, *Death in Venice*.[32]

The appearance of the world-traveling foreigner and the sudden desire for exotic, primitive experiences.

It was a desire to flee, he had to admit to himself, this yearning for the distant and the novel, this desire for liberty, for being free of burden, for being able to forget—the desire to escape his work, the commonplace location of a rigorous, frigid, and ardent duty. [. . .] He was afraid of the summer in the countryside, alone in that little house with the maidservant who prepared the food for him and the manservant who served it; he feared the familiar sight of the mountains and steep cliffs that would surround his listless dullness. And so there was a need for something different, some living without a set plan, some fresh air from remote places, an infusion of fresh blood to make the summer more tolerable and productive. So travel it would be—he was content with himself. Not that far, certainly not to the tigers. (5)

Typical representative of bourgeois order, conscientiousness, and control, of form and equilibrium, of a relentless and heroic resistance against life's negativity:

Gustav Aschenbach was the poet of all those who were laboring on the brink of exhaustion, the overburdened and worn out, who still tried to keep upright, those moralists of performance, who, being lanky and of limited means, through willpower and clever management can conjure the effect of greatness at least for a time. They are numerous, they are the heroes of our age. And they all recognized themselves in his work, they found themselves vindicated, elevated, celebrated in it, thanked him generously and spread his name. (8)

Nonetheless Aschenbach chooses Venice as his destination, and this choice is already telling. A city that is simultaneously alive and dead, the lagoon, the putrid canals, the architecture recalling a historical glory that has long been buried, and especially the gondolas:

Who would not have had to fight a slight unease, a secret resentment and trepidation when one, for the first or after a long time, had to get into a Venetian gondola? That strange vehicle, which seems unchanged from more fanciful times and which is so strangely black like normally only coffins are, reminds one of silent and criminal adventures in the lapping night, furthermore it is reminiscent of death itself, the bier, the drab funeral and the final, wordless ride. And has one noticed that the coffin-black-varnished, black-upholstered chair in such a barge is the softest, most luxurious, most deeply relaxing seat in the whole world? [. . .] The trip will be short, he thought; oh would it last forever! (15)

He loved the ocean for important reasons: out of the desire for tranquility harbored by the hard-working artist, who seeks to conceal himself from the multitude of possibilities by embracing the simple and immense; out of a forbidden proclivity for the unordered, the immeasurable, the eternal, the void that was made even more attractive by running counter to his work. To find peace in the presence of the faultless is the desire of the one who seeks excellence; and is not nothingness a form of perfection? While he was dreaming into the deepness of space, he suddenly became aware of a human figure close to the shoreline and when he collected his glance from the unlimited, it turned out to be the beautiful boy, who, coming from the left, was crossing the sand before him. (22–23)

The city's atmosphere, "the putrid smell of the lagoon." But the city cloaked in soft suggestions of death is also objectively threatened by disease: the threat of a cholera epidemic weighs on it. The authorities keep the threat secret to prevent hurting tourism. Even Aschenbach, who fears Tadzio's departure, becomes an accomplice to the silence:

"One should keep silent!" Aschenbach thought excitedly and threw the journals back onto their table. "One should keep silent about this!" But at the same time his heart filled with satisfaction about what the outside world was about to go through. Because passion, like crime, does not like everyday order and well-being and every slight undoing of the bourgeois system, every confusion and infestation of the world is welcome to it, because it can unconditionally expect to find its advantage in it. So Aschenbach felt a somber content about the cover-up of the terrible happenings in the grimy streets of the city that merged with his own innermost secret, happenings in the covertness of which he also had an interest. (39)

The city was diseased and kept it hidden because of its thirst for profit. "One should keep silent," he whispered impetuously. And: "'I will keep silent!' The knowledge of his complicity intoxicated him, like a small amount of liquor intoxicates an old and faded brain. [. . .] What was art and virtue to him compared to the advantages of disorder?" This sinister complicity of passion and death prevented Aschenbach from carrying out the "cathartic and decent deed" of warning Tadzio's family of the truth the everyone's selfishness kept concealed: "There is cholera in Venice." That step "would lead him back, give his soul back to himself; but when one is frantic, the last thing one desires is to be oneself again." "One should keep silent," he whispered impetuously. And: "I will keep silent!" (47–48).

Aschenbach's nightmare, in a wooded Alpine landscape, the terrible eruption of the alien god's ravaging bacchanalia. "His abhorrence and his fear were big, his will was honorable, to defend what was his against that stranger, the enemy of the sober and dignified mind." Nonetheless "[h] is heart was booming with the drumbeats, his brain was gyrating, anger gripped him, blindness, deadening sexual lust and his soul desired to join the god's dance." And finally, "his soul tasted fornication and the fury of downfall." "Following the handsome lad, Aschenbach had ventured deeply into the labyrinth of the afflicted city" (48–50).

The story ends with the scene of Aschenbach dying, in the act of embracing a hint of ethereal promise on the part of the handsome boy, while all around him we grasp the anxiety of the diseased city and the escape of vacationers and tourists stirred by the mortal truth now made public. Gustav von Aschenbach, whose very name embraces the image of flowing liquid and extinguished fire ("ashen brook") fulfills his destiny: the evasion from form and value, the escape from the action of firm and dignified spirit, the desperate love for the image of the handsome boy, the devastating struggle against time and old age, the danger of the alien god and the temptation of chaos, and finally, death before the final image of the handsome boy, in the background of the diseased city that has become aware of the mortal danger that it harbored in its breast.

3. We Have Lost the Sun

David Herbert Lawrence, 1883[33]–1930. Born in Eastwood, Nottinghamshire, 11 September 1885. His works date from 1912 to 1930. Frazer, Frobenius,[34] and Freud were authors from whom he drew some themes that recur in his literary ethnologism. "Our science is a science of a dead world." Lawrence's themes: polemic against scientism, against the reduction of knowledge—true knowledge—to science; the human epoch of cosmic participation, symbolic life, esoteric knowledge extending to the Egyptians and Greeks, then lost in the Judeo-Christian tradition negating the world, flesh; magic, divinatory degeneration of this ancient esoteric wisdom; polemic against the *Urdummheit*, the devaluation of the pagan world, devaluation of Western civilization that led to mechanism, technicism, antihistoricism, antievolutionism, the eternal return; theme of the end of the world.

We find many important and indicative themes in Lawrence: nostalgia for paganism, mistrust toward the intellectualistic tradition that broke ties with the cosmos, Western civilization's escape, ethnologism, the sense of the "end" of our world through the end of communion with the cosmos and the death of participation.

[. . .]

[W]e have lost the sun and the planets, and the Lord with the seven stars of the Bear in his right hand. Poor, paltry, creeping little world we live in, even the keys of death and Hades are lost. How shut in we are! All we can do, with our brotherly love, is to shut one another in. We are so afraid somebody else might be lordly and splendid, when we can't. Petty little bolshevists, every one of us today, we are determined that *no* man shall shine like the sun in full strength, for he would certainly outshine us.[35]

Suddenly we see some of the old pagan splendour, that delighted in the might and the magnificence of the cosmos, and man who was as a star in the cosmos. Suddenly we feel again the nostalgia for the old pagan world, long before John's day, we feel an immense yearning to be freed from this petty personal entanglement of weak life, to be back in the far-off world before men became "afraid." We want to be freed from our tight little automatic "universe" to go back to the great living cosmos of the "unenlightened" pagans.

Perhaps the greatest difference between us and the pagans lies in our different relation to the cosmos. With us, all is personal. Landscape and sky, these are to us the delicious background of our personal life, and no more. Even the universe of the scientist is little more than an extension of our personality, to us. To the pagan, landscape and personal background were on the whole indifferent. But the cosmos was a very real thing. A man *lived* with the cosmos, and know it greater than himself. (40–41)

Don't let us imagine we see the sun as the old civilizations saw it. All we see is a scientific little luminary, dwindled to a ball of blazing gas. In the centuries before Ezekiel and John, the sun was still a magnificent reality, men drew forth from him strength and splendour, and gave him back homage and lustre and thanks. But in us, the connection is broken, the responsive centres are dead. Our sun is a quite different thing from the cosmic sun of the ancient, so much more trivial. We may see what we call the sun, but we have lost Helios forever, and the great orb of the Chaldeans still more. We have lost the cosmos, by coming out of responsive connection with it, and this is our chief tragedy. What is our petty little love of nature—Nature!!—compared to the ancient magnificent living with the cosmos, and being honoured by the cosmos! (41–2)

[. . .]

By the time of John of Patmos, men, especially educated men, had already almost lost the cosmos. The sun, the moon, the planets, instead of being the communers, the comminglers, the life-givers, the splendid ones, the awful ones, had already fallen into a sort of deadness; they were the arbitrary, almost mechanical engineers of fate and destiny. By the time of Jesus, men had turned the heavens into a mechanism of fate and destiny, a prison. The Christians escaped this prison by denying the body altogether. But alas, these little escapes! especially the escapes by denial!—they are the most fatal of evasions. Christianity and our ideal civilization have been one long evasion. It has caused endless lying and misery, misery such as people know today, not of physical want but of far more deadly vital want. Better lack bread than lack life. The long evasion, whose only fruit is the machine!

We have lost the cosmos. The sun strengths us no more, neither does the moon. In mystic language, the moon is black to us, and the sun is as sackcloth.

Now we have to get back the cosmos, and it can't be done by a trick. The great range of responses that have fallen dead in us have to come to life again. It has taken two thousand years to kill them. Who knows how long it will take to bring them to life?

When I hear modern people complain of being lonely then I know what has happened. They have lost the cosmos.—It is nothing human and personal that we are short of. What we lack is cosmic life, the sun in us and the moon in us. We can't get the sun in us by lying naked like pigs on a beach. The very sun that is bronzing us is inwardly disintegrating us—as we know later. Process of katabolism. We can only get the sun by a sort of worship: and the same with the moon. By *going forth* to worship the sun, worship that is felt in the blood. Tricks and postures only make matters worse.[36]

Karl Kerényi, *Töchter der Sonne* (Zurick: Rascher, 1944), 17–18:[37] "Besides describing the situation today these words contain a theory that merits attention because it emanates from the spontaneity of a great poet. [...] [It is the theory] of the 'little blazing consciousness' that intertwines us in the sun's 'great blazing consciousness.'" Our "solar intimacy." The "nervous and personal consciousness" in us "as something secondary": feelings and personal ideas.

The literary roots of cultural relativism:

The instinctive policy of Christianity toward all true pagan evidence has been and is still—suppress it, destroy it, deny it. This dishonesty has vitiated Christian thought from the start. It has, even more curiously, vitiated ethnological scientific thought the same. Curiously enough, we do not look on the Greeks and the Romans, after about 600 BC, as real pagans:

not like Hindus or Persians, Babylonians or Egyptians, or even Cretans, for example. We accept the Greeks and Romans as the initiators of our intellectual and political civilization, the Jews as the fathers of our moral-religious civilization. So these are "our sort." All the rest are mere nothing, almost idiots. All that can be attributed to the "barbarian" beyond the Greek pale: that is, to Minoans, Etruscans, Egyptians, Chaldeans, Persians, and Hindus, Is, in the famous phrase of a famous German professor: Urdummheit. Urdummheit, or primal stupidity. Is the state of all mankind before precious Homer, and of all races, all, except Greek, Jew, Roman, and—ourselves! (67–68)

Culture and civilisation are tested by vital consciousness. Are we more vitally conscious than an Egyptian 3000 years BC was? Are we? Probably we are less. Our conscious range is wide, but shallow as a sheet of paper. We have no depth to our consciousness. (74)

Our bald processes of thought no longer are life to us. For the sphinx-riddle of man is as terrifying today as it was before Oedipus, and more so. For now it is the riddle of the dead-alive man, which it never was before. (79)

[…]

With the coming of Socrates and "the spirit," the cosmos died. For two thousand years man has been living in a dead or dying cosmos, hoping for a heaven hereafter. And all the religions have been religions of the dead body and the postponed reward: eschatological, to use a pet word of the philosophers. (85)

Gone is the great Mother of the cosmos, crowned with a diadem of the twelve great stars of the zodiac. She is driven to the desert and the dragon of the watery chaos spues floods upon her. But kind Earth swallows the floods, and the great woman, winged for flight like an eagle, must remain lost in the desert for a time, and times, and half a time. Which is like the three and a half days, or years, of other parts of the Apocalypse, and means half of a time period.

That is the last we have seen of her. She has been in the desert ever since, the great cosmic Mother crowned with all the signs of the zodiac. Since she fled, we have had nothing but virgins and harlots, half-women: the half-women of the Christian era. For the great woman of the pagan cosmos was driven into the wilderness at the end of the old epoch, and she has never been called back. (139–40)

The catastrophe of women in the ancient world is discerned here with a telling sensitivity. Today we certainly do not need the Madonna to reveal respect for women to us. We only need some concrete female figure whom we have loved and to whom we owe a debt we think we will never be able to pay back: a real figure whose memory accompanies us and serves as a rule every time we are called to decide what we should or should not do with a woman. But Lawrence's sensitivity does not pass from the Christian woman to the real woman: it returns to the pagan Great Mother and attempts to revive its mystique in an immediate way, as if (note: "as if") this were authentically possible today. Lawrence's outburst only displays hatred for the Christian order, a hatred that becomes vulgarity and profanity. He does not want to pass from the Madonna to women but wants a mystification of women that is better suited to the mental debauchery in which he takes pleasure. Saint Teresa was half a woman, indeed! In the human world, sex-nature is always culturally remodeled, and if the Christian remodeling today no longer corresponds to society's forms, a "pagan" remodeling does so even less (granting that the category of "paganism" is valid).

[...]

[...] [T]he power of the old cosmos, superseded, becomes demonic and harmful to the new creation. [...] Therefore the whole cosmos has its malefic aspect. The sun, the great sun, in so far as he is the old sun of a superseded cosmic day, is hateful and malevolent to the newborn, tender thing I am. He does me harm, in my struggling self, for he still has power over my old self and he is hostile.

Likewise the waters of the cosmos, in their oldness and their superseded or abysmal nature, are malevolent to life, especially to the life of man. The great Moon and mother of my inner water-streams, in so far as she is the old, dead moon, is hostile, hurtful, and hateful to my flesh, for she still has a power over my old flesh. (114–15).

[...]

When Moses set up the brazen serpent in the wilderness, an act that dominated the imagination of the Jews for many centuries, he was substituting the potency of the good dragon for the sting of the bad dragon, or serpents. [...] The great problem, in the past, was the conquest of the inimical serpent and the liberation within the self of the gleaming bright serpent of gold, golden fluid life within the body, the rousing of the splendid divine dragon within a man, or within a woman.

What ails men today is that thousands of little serpents sting and envenom them all the time, and the great divine dragon is inert. We cannot wake him to life, in modern days. He wakes on the lower planes of life: for a while in an airman like Lindbergh or in a boxer like Dempsey. It is the little serpent of gold that lifts these two men for a brief time into a certain level of heroism. But on the higher planes, there is no glimpse or gleam of the great dragon. (144–45)

And today, in the day of the dirty-white dragon of the Logos and the Steel Age, the socialists have taken up the oldest of life colors, and the whole world trembles at a suggestion of vermilion. [. . .] [T]he red and gold dragons of the Gold Age and the Silver Age, the green dragon of the Bronze Age, the white dragon of the Iron Age, the dirty-white dragon, or gray dragon of the Steel Age: and then a return once more to the first brilliant red dragon. (In the Apocalypse red and purple are anathema: every heroic epoch instinctively turns to red or gold.) (156)

[. . .]

Lawrence's preface to Frederick Carter's *Dragon of the Apocalypse*.[38]
    The theme of myth as experience that is never exhausted and will never be. Symbols are complexes of emotional experience: symbols arouse these complexes.

Many ages of accumulated experience still throb within a symbol. [. . .] No man can invent symbols. It takes centuries to create a really significant symbol . . . [. . .]. Some images, in the course of many generations of men, become symbols, embedded in the soul and ready to start alive when touched, carried on in the human consciousness for centuries. And again, when men become unresponsive and half dead, symbols die. (49)

I would like to know the stars again as the Chaldeans knew them, two thousand years before Christ. I would like to be able to put my ego in the sun, and my personality in the moon, and my character into the planets and live the life of the heavens, as the early Chaldeans did. [. . .] [S]omewhere within us the old experience of the Euphrates, Mesopotamia between the rivers, lives still. (51)

Do you think you can put the universe apart, a dead lump here, a ball of gas there, a bit of fume somewhere else? How puerile it is, as if the universe were the back yard of some human chemical works! How gibbering man becomes, when he is really clever, and thinks he is giving the ultimate and final description of the universe! Can't he see that he is merely describing himself, and that the self he is describing is merely one of the more dead and dreary states that man can exist in? (53)

Is our description true? Not for a single moment, once you change your state of mind: or your state of soul. *It is true for our present deadened state of mind.*[39] Our state of mind is becoming unbearable. We shall have to change it. And when we have changed it, we shall change our description of the universe entirely. We shall not call the moon Artemis, but the new name will be nearer to Artemis than to a dead lump or an extinct globe. We shall not get back the Chaldean vision of the living heavens. But the heavens will come to life again for us, and the vision will express also the new men that we are.

    And so the value of these studies in the Apocalypse. They wake the imagination and give us at moments a new universe to live in. We may think it is the old cosmos of the Babylonians, but it isn't. We can never recover an old vision, once it has been supplanted. But what we can do is to discover a new vision in harmony with the memories of old, far-off, far, far-off experience that lie within us. So long as we are not deadened or drossy, memories of Chaldean experience still live within us, at great depths . . . (54)

Lawrence's work, like other voices of the literature on crisis, is a document for evaluating the nature of the crisis itself, to measure its breadth and motivations, and to clarify the prognosis and therapy within the limits of a cultural-historical analysis. Lawrence contains a vibrant protest against the naturalism that is given as a vision of life and the world, but the limits of awareness in which his protest moves demonstrate how he is fully struggling in the crisis. No doubt when the consciousness that reason has of itself coincides with the consciousness of the intellect and the operations that belong to it, a truncation of humanity begins that leads to that world of the near-dead that Lawrence refers to so many times. The ethos of transcendence, going beyond the situation, coincides with this broader reason that beyond the coherence of consciousness discovers the coherence of the unconscious, and beyond the operative power of the intellect discovers the other powers of cultural life, each endowed with its own coherence. What cannot be transcended is precisely this ethos of transcendence, this articulating and legitimating rationality of cultural coherences: and it cannot be transcended precisely because it is the inner rule, the supreme guardian of transcendence, of the modes of presentification and order that it assembles in various epochs and different cultures. The ethos of transcendence—reason unfolding in the distinction of operative powers and that promotes, watches over, controls this unfolding—is really the ultimate Thule, the roof of the world, the Atlas that holds it up. This entirely human strength can only have a foundation in itself: every one of our evaluations, every one of our actions, every one of our cultural institutions, every one of our symbols is inside this primordial human energy, and the highest possible effort conceded it is that of explicitly recognizing itself, enhancing and purifying itself through this recognition. Now, the "naturalism" of sciences is *one* positive power freed up by reason: the crisis begins when, driven by the successes of this power, reason limits consciousness of itself to this power alone, as happens in present-day positivistic scientism and technicism, mortifying any horizon *beyond* intellect (but not reason!).

4. The World Is Indigestible

Sartre.[40]

[...]

Sartre's nausea is an *indigestible world*, and vomit is the symbol of this world that *sits on the stomach* because of an impossible digestion. ("Existence is not something which lets itself be thought of from a distance: it must invade you suddenly, master you, weigh heavily on your heart like a great motionless beast—or else there is nothing more at all" (132). The pebble, the glass of beer at the Café Mably, Adolphe's suspenders, the roots of a chestnut tree in a public park are, as bare existence, indigestible: they sit on the stomach, unleashing nausea. But what exactly does it mean that the world becomes indigestible? Simply that the world is no longer included in transcendence, that is, in that historical hierarchy of valorizing presentifications that is consumed in the history of the human society we belong to and that places individual historical persons that make it up— and myself among them—in a "settled," domestic, familiar world in which I can still decide something without suffering from the zero experience of fallenness (*deiezione*).[41] The world is, first and foremost, the horizon of the signs of human activity, of others' decisions taken on and recognized: it is familiar because the human cultural family left a trace of itself there, documenting its history. The world is the living history of others in us, and it does not matter whether this life now moves in us as habit, as a continuous evocation of mechanically executed technical gestures, as an obvious employing and using this or that, as an anonymous "one does it so" operating on the margins of awareness. In this system of opaque allegiances an appropriation of the human still takes place, if only in the form of the readaptation to the individual's situation, that is certainly always new and to some degree without a "model." Furthermore, being-there in a familiar world in a habitual, obvious, anonymous way frees up availability for more individual initiatives, for the most personal decisions, for the most engaging transcendences. But even here we are never totally alone, and the world still appears in its history in that our choice still and above all chooses a world of operative cultural memories that are not only ours to be transferred into our action. Humanity is always in transcendence: but it is precisely for this reason that it never transcends a zero but a choral cultural worlding that conditions us in transcendence. When people really experience the limit of their world and look out onto nothingness, it is because they no longer know how transcend it (the bell tower of Marcellinara[42]); when the order of their cultural memories dissipates, it is the world that collapses. And this experience is hardly to be celebrated as freedom since it is an extreme subjugation, a catastrophe of existence and the existing: bare existence—that is, barren of human history—is total absence, the annihilation of the self and the world, radical disloyalty to the true *human condition*. Certainly, Sartre's nausea circumscribes a real risk: but this nausea must be concealed, and precisely this *necessary concealment* founds human civilizations, concrete cultural worlds in which to live and execute, if historically necessary, the most radical changes. It is not "disguising" the nausea, but on the contrary, "exposing it," removing it from the religious prestige that still adorns it with tragic splendors: we can gain an indication of exactly what it is in psychopathology, beyond the mystifications of the crisis, through an analysis of nausea, anxiety, depersonalization, and the end of the world.

Nausea is the risk of a bare existence, one stripped of valorizing human presentification, of all operative memories of culture, of all the names evoking these memories, of all the habits that make the world familiar. It is thus the risk of nothingness, the end of the world, the annihilation of any margin with regard to the world. Actually, existence cannot be bare, and it cannot because it must not, and it must not because it must be the intersubjective ethos of transcendence.

Nausea is an indigestible world, and vomit is the somatic element of this indigestion, the "symptom" of the world that abruptly intrudes and "weighs heavily on your heart." The pebble, the glass of beer at Café Mably, Adophe's suspenders, the roots of a chestnut tree in a public park are all minute existential events, futile pretexts for unleashing the nausea. Indeed, a world that is, after all, already intimately collapsing can signal its collapse into nothingness through the most minute event and the most futile pretext: it is sufficient to have a pebble, a glass of beer, a pair of suspenders, a chestnut root to set off the cosmic contagion of annihilation. Why exactly a pebble? And on the other hand, why something else? The choice of the thing is irrelevant when its collapse is the collapse of the world. But the lesson we draw from Sartre's motif of nausea is important:

if the world is formed, maintained, and renewed through a continuous transcendence of nothingness in the being of values, if this transcendence is the primordial ethos of culture and history, the inversion of this ethos appears as the gaping of nothingness and the somatic degradation of *transcending* into *vomiting*. One *vomits* the world as undigested food; through the collapse of valorizing transcendence it gets deworlded and obliterated. Because of this collapse the world cannot convert itself into nourishment, and thus is no longer "world." The experience of "nausea" is a symptom of transcendence's failure.

I feel like "something has changed."

Loss of the familiar, the habitual, being-acted-upon:

> Something has happened to me. I can't doubt it any more. It came as an illness does, not like an ordinary certainty, not like anything evident. It came cunningly, little by little; I felt a little strange, a little put out, that's all. Once established it never moved, it stayed quiet, and I was able to persuade myself that nothing was the matter with me, that it was a false alarm. And now, it's blossoming. (4)

Antoine Roquentin perceives that there is something new in his most habitual actions: for example, picking up his pipe or a fork. The doorknob he holds attracts his attention, exposing itself as a cold object in his hand, as an object endowed with a personality. The custodian of Bouville's library, a familiar figure, becomes recognizable only after some delay, even if it was only ten seconds.[43]. In the usual handshake greeting his hand appears alien, detached with respect to the familiar unity into which it is integrated, and through this strangeness and through this detachment his whole arm takes on a suspect, deformed character: "a fat white worm." In the streets, there are creeping, suspicious noises. Where did the change take place? Is it he, Antoine Roquentin, who has changed, or is it the world surrounding him? He has to choose.

"It is an abstract change without object." The glass of beer, among other things. But even in this glass of beer there is something else. "Almost nothing." Fear. He tries unsuccessfully to pick up a paper lying on the ground, he gets the obsessive idea that he is not free.

"Objects should not *touch* because they are not alive. You use them, put them back in place, you live among them: they are useful, nothing more. But they touch me, it is unbearable. I am afraid of being in contact with them as though they were living beasts" (10).

The world of things at hand, manageable, instrumental, is the cultural horizon immune from "being touched" in that its handiness, manipulation, and instrumentalization is decided. This materializing decision not only has its own heroism but also represents the inaugural value of presentification, the first witnessing of detachment and transcendence. To be there, indeed, it is necessary to ceaselessly circumscribe presence with respect to a resistant, inert world of body instruments—starting with one's own body—and with respect to an order of social collaborations conditioning use. If we are not loyal to a certain sphere of the inert, of what can be treated as a "thing" or what is usable as "material," and if this loyalty does not consider the whole order of "treatments" and "uses" of a given society, we also lose every other possibility of transcendence and presentification.

The image of a "primitive" entirely immersed in touching participations, the *Sehnsucht* (yearning) of highly creative epochs that have not yet been ruined by the phase of handiness, and which would have lived wholly in a contented koinonia with the stars, plants, animals, and the entire cosmos, certainly have their motivation and reasons: but these are basically expressions of the literature of the crisis, whether ethnological, philosophical, nonfiction, fiction, or poetry.

[...]

When the ethos of transcendence "undergoes an inversion"—that is, on the whole it lets its drive fall, giving way to the radical risk of not being able to be in any possible cultural world—precisely the world of things at hand (of the "familiar") is struck by the crisis, because it constitutes the fundamental evidence of being-in-the-world. And so the pipe, the fork, the doorknob, or the glass of beer becomes a problem: they lose their meaning as cultural solutions of things at hand and gape, so to speak, onto "nothingness." The instrumentality of one's own body gets problematized in that it is stripped of its instrumental character, so that we continuously appropriate our limbs and organs according to a mimical-operative cultural tradition that continuously gets redecided, *never starting from zero, and always adding something beyond zero* (every mimical-operative decision has some fringe of novelty, as habitual as it may be). And so, bending over to pick up a piece of paper without succeeding is an act that lets go of the continuous process of bodily appropriation. It is perceived as a subservient being-acted-upon: a small operative failure gives rise to an experience of dispossession that gets translated into the obsessive thought of no longer being free. In short, even in the mimical-operative sphere one is no longer capable of appropriation or resistance: one gets stripped of appropriation. As for the "others"—to the extent that the "others" are included in the world of things at hand (the custodian at hand of the Bouville library, whose face is familiar for Roquentin solely in the perspective of that handiness)—they also lose their memorability, their being notoriously projectable for our use, their coefficient of social recognizability:

so during the handshake the custodian's hand and arm appear not to be participating in the unity of use in which they were "normally" integrated, just as his face was simply "a" face.

The "being touched" that Roquentin speaks of is thus an "unbearable" experience; it is the experience of "nothingness." This is not a healthy sense of nonbeing that stimulates every being-for-value, every concrete effort of presentification, but rather the nonbeing of value that gets transformed into a blind impulse and strikes the inaugural sphere of valorization, in other worlds the world—culturally determined and determinable—of handiness and that at the very least does not leave any leeway for a world at hand of being-there. The gaping onto nothingness on the part of projectable objects and on the part of projecting actions is the obliteration of presentification. Bodies are what can be done with them according to practicable cultural memories each time evoked, tested, re-adapted, and modified according to levels of awareness that range from good everyday habits to ingenious technological inventions: the total collapse of presentification loses the historicity of these memories and along with this experiences the obliteration of being-in-the-world and dreads the zero experience that advances. But since the zero experience is the obliteration of the ethos of presentification, this obliteration is not per se a zero even if it makes zero advance: it is an obliteration in which *suspicion* and *monstrosity* take shape ("There are a great number of suspicious noises in the streets"; the custodian's arm that becomes "a fat white worm"), and in general an *overturned intentionality* loaded with destructive unfamiliarity, the loss of intentional presentification under a form of being-acted-upon, of secret intrigue, of suspect allusiveness, and finally representational monstrosity.

> I ruminate heavily near the gas stove; I know in advance the day is lost. I shall do nothing good, except, perhaps, after nightfall. It is because of the sun; it ephemerally touches the dirty-white wisps of fog, which float in the air above the construction-yards, it flows into my room, all gold, all pale, it spreads four dull, false reflections on my table. [. . .] My pipe is daubed with a golden varnish which first catches the eye by its bright appearance; *you look at it and the varnish melts*, nothing is left but a great dull streak on a piece of wood. [. . .] (14)[44]

> I move through this pale light; I see it change beneath my hands and on the sleeves of my coat: I cannot describe how much it disgusts me. I yawn. I light the lamp on the table: perhaps its light will be able to combat the light of day. But no: the lamp makes nothing more than a pitiful pond around its base. I turn it out; I get up. There is a white hole in the wall, a

mirror. It is a trap. I know I am going to let myself be caught in it. I have. The grey thing appears in the mirror. I go over and look at it, I can no longer get away. It is the reflection of my face. Often in these lost days I study it. I can understand nothing of this face. The faces of others have some sense, some direction. Not mine. [. . .] When I was little, my Aunt Bigeois told me "If you look at yourself too long in the mirror, you'll see a monkey." I must have looked at myself even longer than that: what I see is well below the monkey, on the fringe of the vegetable world, at the level of jellyfish. (16–17)

Perhaps it is impossible to understand one's own face. Or perhaps it is because I am a single man? People who live in society have learned how to see themselves in mirrors as they appear to their friends. I have no friends. Is that why *my flesh is so naked*? You might say—yes you might say, nature without humanity. (18)

When the patronne goes shopping her cousin replaces her at the bar. His name is Adolphe. I began looking at him as I sat down and I have kept on *because I cannot turn my head*. (19)

Recall the glass of beer that Roquentin could not look at because he was tormented by nothingness: "there is something else. Almost nothing." (Here, instead, he cannot look at Adolphe).

He is in shirtsleeves, with purple suspenders; he has rolled the sleeves of his shirt above the elbows. The suspenders can hardly be seen against the blue shirt, they are all obliterated, buried in the blue, but it is false humility; in fact, they will not let themselves be forgotten, they annoy me by their sheep-like stubbornness, as if, starting to become purple, they stopped somewhere along the way without giving up their pretentions. You feel like saying "All right, *become* purple and let's hear no more about it." But now, *they stay in suspense, stubborn in their defeat*. Sometimes the blue which surrounds them slips over and covers them completely: I stay an instant without seeing them. But it is merely a passing wave, soon the blue pales in places and I see the small island of hesitant purple reappear, grow larger, rejoin and reconstitute the suspenders. (19)

The cardplayers at the Café Mably:

What an odd occupation: it doesn't look like a game or a rite, or a habit. I think they do it to pass the time, nothing more. But time is too large, it can't be filled up. Everything you plunge into it is stretched and disintegrates. That gesture, for instance, the red hand picking up the cards and fumbling: it is all flabby. It would have to be ripped apart and tailored inside. (20–21)

At the Café Mably. The sudden though of the death of M. Fasquelle. A stuffed egg whose yellow mayonnaise becomes blood. The vision: "At heart, I didn't believe he was dead and this was precisely what irritated me: it was a floating idea which I could neither persuade myself to believe or disbelieve" (76).

The inconsistency of objects.

The *library* with its stove, its shelves, and so forth. "As long as you stay between these walls, whatever happens must happen on the right or the left of the stove." The "powerful and squat" books, with the stove, and so forth. "Usually . . . they dam up the future." The fixed "the limits of probability" (76).

> Today they fixed nothing at all: it seems that their very existence was subject to doubt, that they had the greatest difficulty in passing from one instant to the next. I held the book I was reading tightly in my hands: but the most violent sensations went dead. Nothing seemed true; *I felt surrounded by cardboard scenery* which could quickly be removed. *The world was waiting, holding its breath, making itself small—it was waiting for its convulsion, its Nausea* . . . [. . .]
>
> I got up. I could not longer keep my place in the midst of these unnatural objects. I went to the window and glanced out at the skull of Impétraz. I murmured: *Anything* can happen, *anything.* [. . .]
>
> Frightened, I looked at these unstable beings which, in an hour, in a minute, were perhaps *going to crumble*: yes, I was there, living in the midst of these books full of knowledge describing the immutable forms of the animals species, explaining that the right quantity of energy is kept integral in the universe; I was there, standing in front of a window whose panes had a definite refraction index. But what *feeble barriers*! I suppose it is out of laziness that the world is the same day after day. Today it seemed to want to *change*. And then, *anything, anything* could happen. (76–77)[45]

Roquentin feels that the root of his uneasiness was the Café Mably affair, the thought that Fasquelle was dead. Panic. He runs along the docks.

> I repeated with anguish: Where shall I go? where shall I go? *Anything* can happen. Sometimes, my heart pounding, I made a sudden right-about-turn: what was happening behind my back? Maybe it would *start* behind me and when I would turn around, suddenly, it would be too late. As

long as I could *stare at things* nothing would happen: I looked at them as
much as I could, pavements, houses, gaslights; my eyes went rapidly from
one to the other, to *catch them unawares, stop them in the midst of their
metamorphosis.* They didn't look too *natural*, but I told myself forcibly:
this is a gaslight, this is a drinking fountain, and I *tried to reduce them
to their everyday aspect* by the power of my gaze. Several times I came
across barriers in my path: the Café des Bretons, the Bar de la Marine. I
stopped, hesitated in front of their pink net curtains: perhaps these snug
places had been spared, perhaps they still held *a bit of yesterday's world,*
isolated, forgotten. (78).[46]

The crisis of presentification that affects the worldly in its familiar, domestic horizon of handiness can translate into various experiences that
are not simply enumerable in their randomness but are solely understandable as variations of a single fundamental experience, as limited ways
in which this fundamental experience—the risk of not being able to be
in any cultural world—can emerge into consciousness. These ways are
(a) the experience of alteration; (b) radical unfamiliarity; (c) dispossession, being-acted-upon; (d) too much or too little semanticity, of semantic "weakness" or "strength"; (e) the fixedness, artificiality, or chaotic
all-allusiveness (anything can happen); suspicion, plot, the representa-
tionally monstrous, overturned intentionality, cosmic catastrophe; and
still others.

The experience of semantic deficit. The inconsistency of objects. "Unstable" objects. Unreal objects. Artificial objects, cardboard, scenery, theatrical. Collapsed objects. All of these experiences are to be interpreted
as a lack of the objects' "beyond," a loss of their operative projectability:
a lack and loss that reflects the crisis of transcendence, the drop in presentification's energy, the disappearance of the possible "going beyond"
of handiness with the corresponding cultural memories accumulated in
habit, education, and technical notions.

The experience of semantic excess is diametrically opposed to that of
deficit, according to an antinomic passage from too little to too much.
Objects refer obscurely beyond their limits, they are strong, all allusive,
but in vain we seek their empty beyond in what is deformed, in monstrous fluidity loaded with overturned intentionality. The other becomes
a wholly other that nonetheless regards us in a way that is closest, most
immediate, peremptory, intimate, direct; and yet in a sense that is hostile,
evil, an attacker, dispossessing, conspiring, and destructive. And this experience of semantic excess, just as with semantic deficiency, reflects the
crisis of transcendence's energy: precisely because the beyond of valorization retreats, the world of things at hand is struck by semantic eccentricity,

expressing a power that subjugates and destroys, that is, the very power of the beyond's wandering ceaselessly without a destination.

The antinomy between semantic deficit and excess of things at hand remains unresolved until the ethos of presentification regains its positivity. There is no reason whatsoever to *choose* excess or deficit as such: one references the other, one bears the fringe of the other even if concretely we can *be chosen* by one of the two constraints, that is, by one way or the other to be predominantly ill. Likewise we can say about the antinomy "the world has changed"—"I am changed," and for all the other unresolvable questions in which the crisis is trapped. Indeed, all of these antinomies of the crisis arise because of the decline in the power to decide according to values. They are the sign of this decline and of the corresponding establishment of a realm of antinomy without solution, of the ambivalent without value, of the ambiguous without the norm of ethos or logos.

5. The World Is Absurd

5.1. Sartre, "A Commentary on *The Stranger*" (1947).[47]

Humankind's relationship to the world is absurd: "the schism between man's aspirations for unity and the insurmountable dualism of mind and nature, between man's drive to attain the eternal and the *finite* nature of existence, between the 'concern' that constitutes his very essence and the vanity of his efforts" (74). The absurd is the human condition itself, being-in-the-world.

> "Get up, take subway, work four hours, eat, sleep—Monday-Tuesday-Wednesday-Thursday-Friday-Saturday—always the same routine . . . ," and then suddenly, "the stage set collapses" and we are immersed in hopeless lucidity. So if we manage to reject the misleading promises of religion or existential philosophies, we come into possession of certain basic truths: the world is chaos, a "divine equivalence born of anarchy"; and tomorrow does not exist, since we all die. "In a universe suddenly deprived of illusions and enlightenment, man feels like a stranger. This exile is irrevocable, since he has no memories of a lost homeland, nor any hope of a promised land." (77)

If I were a tree, sky, stars, and everything in the world! But no: my consciousness makes me oppose the world: " 'It is this preposterous reason that sets me against all of creation' " (77). From these passages in *The Myth of Sisyphus* we understand the subject of *The Stranger*: as Sartre says, "the 'stranger' is man confronting the world" (77). But "the stranger" is also a person among persons (in the dual sense of estrangement of others to me and of me to others, and me in relation to myself; " 'The stranger who, at certain moments, confronts us in the mirror' " (78). The absurd man does not commit suicide; he wants to live without hope, without illusions, without resignation, in rebellion. Sentenced to death, without a tomorrow, without God, all experiences are the same to him, and all deserve to be experienced in their atomistic instantaneousness. " 'For the absurd man, the ideal is the present and the succession of present moments before an ever-conscious spirit' " (78). All values collapse in this quantitative ethic to accumulate the greatest quantity of experiences.

The absurd person "thrown into the world," in a state of rebellion, irresponsible, innocent, to whom everything is permitted, an "idiot," someone who lives in a perpetual present " 'tinged with smiles and indifference' " like Prince Mishkin[48] (78).

The Stranger intentionally opens with a shocking scene:

> Maman died today. Or yesterday maybe, I don't know. I got a telegram from the home: "Mother deceased. Funeral tomorrow. Faithfully yours." That doesn't mean anything. Maybe it was yesterday. [. . .] It occurred to me anyway one more Sunday was over, that Maman was buried now, that I was going back to work, and that, really, nothing had changed. (3, 24)

Not resignation, but recognition in revolt of the limits of human thought. This is the gratuitousness of the "novel." The sense of contingency involves the very work that describes the contingent: it becomes the theme to the point that, intentionally, *The Stranger* is stylistically constructed in such a way as to give the reader the sense that it could also not have been written. This creates a communion between the author and reader, "beyond reason—in the realm of the absurd" (81).

> I am not constantly thinking about the people I love, yet I claim to love them even when I am not thinking about them—and I would be capable of compromising my well-being in the name of an abstract feeling, in the absence of any real and immediate emotion. Meursault thinks and acts in a different way: he has no desire to know those noble, continuous, and identical feelings. For him, neither love nor even romantic relationships exist. All that counts is the present—the concrete. He goes to see his mother when he feels like it, and that's that. (83)

The Stranger aims to inspire the "feeling" of the absurd: it is a novel of *décalage*, divorce, the unsettling, *Unheimlichkeit*: the absurdity of "too little" (strangeness, alienation, absurdity, ironic description, theatrics, artificiality, facticity, contingency, mechanicalness, mechanical disorder, insignificance), just as in Kafka the absurdity of "too much" dominates, of "signs," of "allusions" with which the universe is filled without us being able to understand them and that are ambiguous, cryptic, disturbing. The stranger is peaceful in the heart of disorder (cf. 88–89).

"'Men also secrete the inhuman . . . Sometimes, in moments of lucidity, the mechanical aspect of their gestures and their senseless pantomime make everything around them seem stupid'" (*The Myth of Sisyphus*, cited in Sartre, 90). "'A man is talking on the telephone behind a glass partition. We cannot hear him, but we can see his senseless mimicry. We wonder why he is alive.'" Camus places a glass cabin between the characters he speaks of and the reader: the result is a transparency of things and an opacity of meaning (cf. 91). This yields a humorous descriptivism: something similar, except of course the intention, to the descriptivism of ethnologists of the positivist era who described in detail the facts of primitive customs, and they created from that an involuntarily ridiculous image, like the technical gestures of swimming repeated by someone who is out of water. The humor arises from the fact that we are not dealing with primitive peoples but us Europeans, our world, our bodies, and so forth, and that it is not a casual description but guided precisely to this end thanks to the lived experience of the absurd and a literary eagerness to represent it.

Our life without tomorrow, a mere succession of present days, of instants, so that in the literary context every phrase forms an island, and the archipelago of semantic islands arises from the ocean of nothingness, only to then sink back down. "The world is destroyed and reborn from one sentence to the next" in a time without duration (93–94).

"The hen is laying an egg?" "There is the hen and she is laying an egg." Sartre comments (96), "Camus and many other contemporary writers . . . like things for their own sake, and do not want to dilute them in the flux of duration."

"There is water": in this we hold a small piece of eternity—passive, impenetrable, incommunicable, and gleaming. What a sensual delight—if we could only touch it! To the absurd man, this is the only good thing in this world. That is why the novelist prefers this transient twinkling of tiny sparkles, each bringing us a moment of pleasure, to an organized narrative. (96)

The monotonous melopoeia unwinding like the nasal chanting of an Arab.

"*The Stranger* is a classical work, a clearly orchestrated work, composed about, and against, the absurd" (97): at least this is the impression it makes on the reader.

5.2. Albert Camus, *Le mythe de Sisyphe* (1942; Paris: Gallimard, 1962).[49]

The argument of this essay is the *absurd sensitivity* that is widespread in our century: this sensitivity is taken as a starting point, and the essay only gives a description of it *in the pure state*, as an "intellectual malady." "No metaphysic, no belief is involved in it for the moment" (2). In what, descriptively, does this absurd sensitivity consist?

It is first and foremost the crisis of the familiar, habitual world, and the experience of a universe "divested of illusions and lights" (6), in which one feels alien. It is feeling exiled in the most radical way, without "memory of a lost home or the hope of a promised land"; it is a longing for death (6). It is the feeling of "the impossibility of constituting the world as a unity . . .", "waterless deserts where thought reaches its confines" (9). This feeling of the absurd, that suddenly surprises ("At any streetcorner the feeling of absurdity can strike any man in the face": "As it is, in its distressing nudity, in its light without effulgence, it is elusive" (10–11). It has a "ridiculous" beginning (12); it is a "void" experienced that forms the first sign of the absurdity: it is an "odd state of soul in which the void becomes eloquent, in which the chain of daily gestures is broken, in which the heart vainly seeks the link that will connect it again . . ." (12).

> It happens that the stage sets collapse. Rising, streetcar, four hours in the office or the factory, meal, streetcar, four hours of work, meal, sleep and Monday Tuesday Wednesday Thursday Friday and Saturday according to the same rhythm—this path is easily followed most of the time. But one day the "why" arises and everything begins in that weariness tinged with amazement. "Begins"—this is important. Weariness comes at the end of the acts of a mechanical life, but at the same time it inaugurates the impulse of consciousness. (12–13)

The feeling of the absurd is *strangeness*. We realize that the world is "dense," ". . . sensing to what a degree a stone is foreign and irreducible to us" (compare with Roquentin's pebble in *Nausea*!), "with what intensity nature or a landscape can negate us" (14):

> At the heart of all beauty lies something inhuman, and these hills, the softness of the sky, the outline of these trees at this very minute lose the illusory meaning with which we had clothed them, henceforth more remote than a lost paradise. The primitive hostility of the world rises up to face us across millennia. For a second we cease to understand it because for centuries we have understood in it solely the images and designs that we had attributed to it beforehand, because henceforth we lack the power to make use of that artifice. The world evades us because it

becomes itself again. That stage scenery masked by habit becomes again what it is. It withdraws at a distance from us. [. . .] . . . [T]hat denseness and that strangeness of the world is the absurd.

Men, too, secrete the inhuman. [. . .] [T]he mechanical aspects of their gestures, their meaningless pantomime makes silly everything that surrounds them. A man is talking on the telephone behind a glass partition; you cannot hear him, but you see his incomprehensible dumb show: you wonder why he is alive. This discomfort in the face of man's own inhumanity, this incalculable tumble before the image of what we are, this "nausea" as a writer of today calls it, is also the *absurd*.[50] (14–15)

And finally, the absurd, the feeling of the absurd can strike us with regard to ourselves: "Likewise the stranger who at certain seconds comes to meet us in a mirror, the familiar and yet alarming brother we encounter in our own photographs is also the absurd" (15).

The feeling of the absurd also grips us before a corpse:

This elementary and definitive aspect of the adventure constitutes the absurd feeling. Under the fatal lighting of that destiny, its uselessness becomes evident. No code of ethics and no effort are justifiable a priori in the face of the cruel mathematics that command our condition. (15–16)

But what is absurd is the confrontation of this irrational and the wild longing for clarity whose call echoes in the human heart. (21)

From the moment absurdity is recognized, it becomes a passion, the most harrowing of all. (22)

From Jaspers to Heidegger, from Kierkegaard to Chestov, from the phenomenologists to Scheler,[51] on the logical plane and on the moral plane, a whole family of minds related by their nostalgia but opposed by their methods or their aims, have persisted in blocking the royal road of reason and in recovering the direct paths of truth. [. . .] Whatever may be or have been their ambitions, all started out from that indescribable universe where contradiction, antinomy, anguish or impotence reigns. (23)

All of these are bound by a common relationship; they are grouped "around a privileged and bitter moment in which hope has no further place"; they proclaim that "nothing is clear, all is chaos, that all man has is his lucidity and his definite knowledge of the walls surrounding him" (27). "The feeling of the absurd is not [. . .] the notion of the absurd. It lays the foundations for it [. . . manifesting itself] in the brief moment when it passes judgment on the universe" (28). "[T]he Absurd is not in man [. . .] nor in the world, but in their presence together" (30).

The absurd that (existential philosophers) have recognized, the "absurd climate" of human existence: "all of them without exception suggest escape" (32): "[T]hey deify what crushes them and find reason to hope in what impoverishes them. That forced hope is religious in all of them. It deserves attention" (32). "Thus the absurd becomes god [. . .] and that inability to understand becomes the existence that illuminates everything" (33). A leap is carried out here that recalls mysticism (33). Chestov says, "We turn toward God only to obtain the impossible. As for the possible, men suffice" (34). Instead of saying "this is absurd," he says, "this is God": perhaps a jealous and hateful God, incomprehensible and contradictory, but precisely for this reason "powerful" (34). Man integrates the absurd into religion. When Kierkegaard makes antinomy and paradox the criteria of the religious, "[h]e makes of the absurd the criterion of the other world, whereas it is simply a residue of the experience of this world (37–38).

The "passion for the absurd" in Camus consists of the intention of hanging in the balance in the polarity of the human condition, on the one hand the desire for unity, the hunger for a solution, the need for clarity and coherence, and on the other hand the irreducible chaos of worldhood, the sovereign contingency of situations, the "divine equivalence which springs from anarchy" (51). But this hanging in the balance, this "dizzying crest" described as "integrity" in the face of various unbalancing subterfuges, is an intellectualistic construction arising from a morbid sensibility. It is an "honesty" that is wholly literary, wholly unrealistic, wholly rhetorical, and wholly hypocritical, since—fortunately—humanity's real situation is that of being "dishonest," that is, of "never being able to hang in the balance," at the zero point of a paradoxical tension in existence, but to lean either toward the concrete choice of a certain clarity, of an operative project full of sense, or toward a fall into chaos and "pure" experiences of madness.

The pure feeling of the absurd in Camus—like Sartre's nausea or Moravia's boredom—is actually not pure. It is necessary to look for its purity, in other words, understanding it for what it signifies, in the great Janet's descriptions in *Les obsessions et la psychasthénie*[52] and in psychiatric works more generally.

6. The World Bores Me

6.1. Alberto Moravia, born in Rome in 1907.[53]

Gli indifferenti (the figure of Michele): the crisis of moral values; the destruction of the means and reasons for action; desperation; bare, premoral existence. The risk of solitude. Indifference. The risk of conformism.

Sex as a mediator for making contact with reality.

None of the dwellings in Moravia give the impression of being truly habit-able places; the rooms always seem too big, too empty, filled with spaces that are too bare and discouraging, at times cluttered with antique and outlandish furniture. The impossibility of a relationship with the world is expressed in an admirable manner by this fundamental inadequacy of the inhabitant's dwelling. Man remains a stranger in the midst of things that surround him. The only objects that have a useful role are the clothes.

Especially underwear. Dominique Fernandez, *Il romanzo italiano e la crisi della coscienza moderna* (Milan: Lerici, 1960), 51. On nature cf. 50.

Moravia's investigation into the possibilities of the human heart and the opportunities to find a coherent and harmonic world had to lead him to the unique and unreserved recognition of the sexual fact. The sexual fact has this priceless advantage in a world in decomposition in which moral values have fallen clamorously into hate, rage, and scorn, or slowly into indifference and conformism: to be itself an undecomposable truth, the pure and uncorrupted residue of a thorough analysis . . . Sex is the dis-covery of the incontestable, simultaneously passionate and patient, that gives to the spirt the certainty it was lacking. (52)

The general sexualization of the universe. That objects have the same intense presence as sexual objects. Regeneration through sex (55). Instru-ment of relation with the world, it is what allows people to enter into contact with others and with things, and to discover, beyond moral and intellectual solitude, a possible fraternity, a common participation in a goodness and a beauty that redeem (56ff.). Exaltation of the prostitute: one enters into relation with the world, a way of escaping from the relation between isolated beings (the betrothed of chaste traditional love) (57ff.).

The transformation of the familiar into the hostile in Luca's delusion, a radical refusal of the world, transformed by the nurse in sweet acceptance (63) in *Disobedience*.[54] Sex as "nature" is obviously incapable of disclos-ing the "world." Sexual maturation has such great importance in human existence because it is always included in the beyond of socialization and culturalization and because social and cultural rules relative to sex form, in the history of individuals, the first access to a world of values, the first chance to choose according to patterns (and thus the chosen field for conflicts and crises). Human behaviors begin as behaviors with regard to family members; family behaviors shaping sexual maturation depend on the cultural choices of adults; the cultural choices of adults are closely connected to their socioeconomic choices; and furthermore, the socio-economic and cultural choices of adults must reckon with the conflicts and crises of their sexual maturation in the family according to an inter-action that cannot be settled with the absolute primacy of libido (indi-vidualistic materialism), of society (historical materialism), or of abstract values (idealism). The sole primacy lies with the ethos of transcendence, to overcome situations in categorial cultural values.

6.2. Alberto Moravia, *La noia* (Milan: Bompiani, 1960).[55]

Boredom to me consists in a kind of insufficiency, or inadequacy, or lack of reality. Reality, when I am bored, has always had the same disconcert-ing effect upon me as (to use a metaphor) a too-short blanket has upon a sleeping man on a winter night: he pulls it down over his feet and his chests gets cold, then he pulls it up on to his chest and his feet get cold, and so he never succeeds in falling properly asleep. Or again (to make use of a different comparison) my boredom resembles a repeated and mysterious interruption of the electric current inside a house: at one mo-ment everything is clear and obvious—here are armchairs, over there are sofas, beyond are cupboards, side tables, pictures, curtains, carpets, win-dows, doors; a moment later there is nothing but darkness and an empty void. Yet again (a third comparison) my boredom might be described as a malady affecting external objects and consisting of a withering process; an almost instantaneous loss of vitality—just as though one saw a flower change in a few seconds from a bud to decay and dust.

The feeling of boredom originates for me in a sense of the absurdity of a reality which is insufficient, or anyhow unable, to convince me of its own effective existence. For example, I may be looking with some degree of attentiveness at a tumbler. As long as I say to myself that this tumbler is a glass or metal vessel made for the purpose of putting liquid into it and carrying it to one's lips without upsetting it—as long as I am able to represent the tumbler to myself in a convincing manner—so long shall I feel that I have some sort of relationship with it, a relationship close enough to make me believe in its existence and also, on a subordinate level, in my own. But once the tumbler withers away and loses its vitality in the manner I have described, or, in other words, reveals itself to me as something foreign, something with which I have no relationship, once it appears to me as an absurd object—then from that very absurdity springs boredom, which when all is said and done is simply a kind of incommu-nicability and the incapacity to disengage oneself from it. But this bore-dom, in turn, would not cause me to suffer so much if I did not know that, although I myself have no relationship with the tumbler, such a tumbler exists in some unknown paradise in which objects do not for one moment cease to be objects. For me, therefore, boredom is not only the inability to escape from myself but is also the consciousness that theoretically I might be able to disengage myself from it, thanks to a miracle of some sort. (5–6)

When he was a child, he often suffered from this:

During those years, I would suddenly stop playing and remain motionless for hours on end, as though in astonishment, in reality overcome by the uneasiness inspired in me by what I have called the withering of objects, the obscure consciousness that between myself and external things there was no relationship. If at such times my mother came into the room, and seeing me dumb and inert and pale with distress, asked what was wrong with me, I answered invariably, "I'm bored," thus explaining a vague and indefinite state of mind in a single word of clear, narrow significance. (6–7)

His mother would kiss him and promise to take him to the movies, but "Neither with her lips, nor with her arms, nor yet with the pictures had I any sort of relationship at that moment" (7).

What struck me above all was that I did not want to do simply anything, although I desired eagerly to do something. Anything I might wish to do presented itself to me like a Siamese twin joined inseparably to some opposite thing which I equally did not wish to do. Thus I felt that I did not want to see people nor yet to be alone; that I did not want to stay at home nor yet to go out; that I did not want to travel nor yet to go on living in Rome; that I did not want to travel nor yet to paint; that I did not want to stay awake nor yet to go to sleep; that I did not want to make love nor yet not do so; and so on. When I say "I felt" I ought rather to say that I was filled with repugnance, with disgust, with horror.

I used to ask myself, between these frenzied bouts of boredom, whether perhaps I did not want to die; it was a reasonable question, seeing that I disliked living so much. But then, to my surprise, I realized that although I did not like living, I yet did not want to die. Thus the inseparable alternatives which filed through my mind like a sinister ballet did not halt even in face of the extreme choice between life and death. The truth of the matter, I sometimes thought, was not so much that I wanted to die as that I wanted not to go on living in my present manner. (18–19)

Just before this, Moravia mentions aggressive and destructive drives that break these unresolving, antinomic alternatives:

> I would take down a book [. . .] but very soon I would let it drop [. . .] or perhaps in an impulse of rage fling it into a corner and turn to music. Who was it who said that music always acts in some kind of way, that is, makes itself listened to forcibly, so to speak, by even the most distracted person? (18)

> Boredom, for me, was like a kind of fog in which my thought was constantly losing its way, catching glimpses only at intervals of some detail of reality: like a person in a thick mist who catches a glimpse now of the corner of a house, now of the figures of a passer-by, now of some other object, but only for an instant, before they vanish. (63–64)

Alberto Moravia, *La disubbidienza* (Milan: Bompiani, 1948).[56]
[. . .]
Luca's decisive crisis began like this, that is, that dedication to dying that was so full that he no longer even desired death, being entirely incorporated in dying. This is a crisis that Moravia represents as a bodily fever without establishing the nature of the disease, and he is right to be silent about it from a literary perspective because it is only a matter of using the fever to justify a delusion of the end of the world, a catastrophe of objects tied to the death of adolescence and the detachment from the "parents' world." Objects get destroyed in sinister representations, and the bedroom gets filled with monstrous presences:

> But all the time, even as he lay helpless beneath the nightmares of delirium, he had the sensation that he was making some progress amongst his hallucinations, like a traveller amongst the tree-trunks and shadows of a forest, towards an opening that he could not fail to find. (126)

The outcome is represented by a real female figure, the nurse, whom Luca sees one day next to his bed in the act of holding his forehead with one hand and with the other feeding him: and through this female figure contact with reality gets reestablished, chaos in the cosmos gets reordered.

> The nurse, in spite of being middle-aged and having lost her looks, the room, which he had once hated, every single object, in fact, appeared to him in a new light—serene, clean, familiar, lovable, and, so to speak, appetizing. He noted with surprise that he did not so much look at things as cast his eyes greedily upon them, just as a hungry animal throws itself

upon a piece of food after a long fast. There beside him, for instance, was a little table covered with phials and bottles amongst which, during his delirium, he had seemed to see those filthy little dwarfs chasing each other. Now he saw honest, simple bottles of different-coloured or clear glass, with corks or metal screw-tops, and adorned with labels upon which even the flowing, hurried handwriting of the chemists who had written out the instructions had a reassuring and affectionate look. (128)

He turned his eyes to the coatstand which, during his delirium, he had seen changed into a snail running up and down the walls, and saw now that it was just an ordinary coatstand with three arms; and he was pleased to see that a petticoat and a chemise belonging to the nurse were hanging on it, and was also pleased to notice that they were unpretentious garments, like those of a poor person. Everything, in fact, to these new eyes of his, seemed to have a significance—a very humble and homely significance, it is true, but a positive one. To the benevolence that coloured all reality with fellow-feeling there was added, besides, the sense of an established order, modest but necessary, in which nothing now appeared, as formerly, absurd and devoid of usefulness. Those bottles were just bottles, that coatstand was just a coatstand; nor was there any danger now of seeing the dwarfs' heads sticking out of the former, or of seeing the latter run up the wall. (129–30)

7. The World Is Empty

Samuel Beckett, *En attendant Godot*,[57] first performed in Paris in 1953, characters Estragon, Vladimir, Lucky, Pozzo, a boy.

What "presence" (being-there) means in Beckett's theater is illustrated by *Waiting for Godot*. One waits for Godot, who never comes; one waits without being able to leave the scene, without hope, without anxiety, and without desperation: he is awaited in a situation structured by nothingness, uselessness, rumor, forgetfulness and repetition. The refrain is: "Let's go. We can't. Why not? We're waiting for Godot."

The wait for Godot is the wait for the Kingdom but lived in the clear-headed consciousness that the human condition is presence to nothingness, rumor, insignificance, the instant: it is a wait without witnessing, without decision, without passion for life, the wait of someone who is already culturally dead or dying. It is a wait whose time must be filled by a thousand trivialities, by clown-like gestures, by a continuous restlessness, by a myriad of misunderstandings of verbal communication, the spirit of gossip and chatter, without the projectability of value ever intervening, the creation of a work, the horizon of human coexistence, the impetus toward the universalization of private feeling. On the contrary, everything recedes, gets restricted, becomes endlessly elusive, from bad to worse. It is a continuous falling, going asleep, losing the power of the senses: the characters cannot stay standing, they fight against sleep, they lose their sight and hearing, from bad to worse in the wait for Godot who never arrives. This is what the great Christian theological theme becomes:

> Given the existence as uttered forth in the public works of Puncher and Wattmann of a personal God quaquaquaqua with a white beard quaquaquaqua outside time without extension who from the heights of divine apathia divine athambia divine aphasia loves us dearly with some exceptions for reasons unknown but time will tell and suffers like the divine Miranda with those who for reasons unknown but time will tell are plunged in torment plunged in fire . . . (28)

In act 2, Pozzo asks for help from Gogo and Didi, which leads to the following comment from Didi:

> Let us not waste our time in idle discourse! Let us do something, while we have the chance! It is not every day that we are needed. Not indeed that we personally are needed. Others would meet the case equally well, if not better. To all mankind they were addressed, those cries for help still ringing in our ears! But at this place, at this moment of time, all mankind is us, whether we like it or not. Let us make the most of it, before it is too late! Let us represent worthily for once the foul brood to which a cruel fate consigned us! What do you say? (51)

These are the only sanely human, *normal* words in the whole play, but Estragon replies immediately: "I didn't hear,"[58] and moreover Vladimir himself recognized the very fact of weighing the pros and cons with arms crossed is "a credit" to the human condition, revealing something abnormal in the very appearance of normality. Choice is suffocated by the "problem" of existence, by the human condition. "Yes, in this immense confusion one thing alone is clear. We are waiting for Godot to come." "Or for night to fall." A line before this he says, "What are we doing here, that is the question. And we are blessed in this, that we happen to know the answer." Anyway, the attempt at help fails, and all four end up on the ground (Pozzo: Help. Vladimir: We've arrived. Pozzo: Who are you? Vladimir: We are men) (51–53).

> VLADIMIR. All I know is that the hours are long, under these conditions, and constrain us to beguile them with proceedings which—how shall

I say—which may at first sight seem reasonable, until they become a habit. You may say it is to prevent our reason from foundering. No doubt. But has it not long been straying in the night without end of the abyssal depths? That's what I sometimes wonder. You follow my reasoning?

ESTRAGON. We are all born mad. Some remain so. (51)

"They give birth astride of a grave, the light gleams an instant, then it's night once more" (57).

The instantaneous presence, without time, forgetful, dreaming excitedly of gossipy life; a life of chatter and individual, solitary movement, for which the other is always one whose breath stinks or who, when he decides to help someone, at most manages to be dragged into his ruin: all this, waiting for Godot who never comes. This is the human condition as existentialism understands it.

Alain Robbe-Grillet, "Samuel Beckett, or Presence on the Stage,", in *Una via per il romanzo futuro* [For a new novel] (Milan: Rusconi e Paolazzi, 1961), 111ff.[59]

The human condition as being-there, the theatrical character is on stage, "is there." Already in his narratives, man in Beckett gradually deteriorates: Murphy, Molloy, Malone, Mahood, Worm. But it is *Waiting for Godot* and *Endgame* that are spectacles deliberately made out of emptiness, with characters who do nothing, "who have no other quality than to be present," following a sequence that has neither beginning nor end. We watch "a kind of regression *beyond* nothing," a regression in which that little charge of zero that is offered at the beginning turns, from degradation to degradation, to zero. Pozzo returns without sight, the carrot of the first act becomes a radish. Repetition and degradation are the sole two forms of happening permitted, with a forced march toward the insignificant, as through a sort of reverse *itinerarium mentis ad deum*,[60] we are given to understand the continuous "not enough." We are waiting for Godot, who never arrives; this is the theme and, at the same time, the "refrain": one waits without being able to leave the stage, without hope, without anxiety, without desperation. The culminating point of this "general dilapidation" is the precipitation of the three characters with the secret ("We are men!").

"[A]lone on stage, standing there, futile, without past or future, irremediably present": if this is the sinister message of *Waiting for Godot*, in *Endgame* ("old endgame lost of old"), even men disintegrate.

A paralyzed, blind man in an armchair is helped by a half-impotent attendant who carries out his work dragging the armchair along the high, bare walls that imprison the stage. The paralyzed, blind prisoner follows the parabola toward solitude and absolute immobility, accompanied by a bloody handkerchief that covers his mouth after having given up speaking.

> Without past, without place elsewhere, without any future but death, the universe thus defined is necessarily deprived of sense in the two acceptations of the term in French: it excludes any idea of *direction* as well as any *signification*. [. . .] The stage, privileged site of *presence*, has not resisted the contagion for long. [. . .] "I was never there," Hamm says, and in the face of this admission nothing else counts, for it is impossible to understand it other than in its most general form: *No one was ever there.* (123–25[61])

The possibility of "touching the world" in its "being in itself," in its being "in flesh and blood," the possibility of "presentifying oneself," of "participating," is obtained by "suspending" the world only in the sense of "calling it into question" through comparison, stimulated by the concrete situation of a relationship with the Other.[62] More precisely, what gets called into question, deliberately assumed and retraced, redecided and reformed, is not the world in general but the history of Western civilization, from the Greeks to today. This assumption, retracing, redecision, and reform are mediated by an ethnological humanism, by the comparison with all other ethnic groups, in view of a cultural unification of our historically determined planet, the fundamental task of our epoch.

6

Anthropology and Marxism

1. Croce's Legacy

1.1. In all of his work Croce led an ongoing polemic against what is morbid, against the breakdown of "spiritual life," against the collapse of the ethos that supports human existence. His criticism targeted decadentism, militancy, and existentialism precisely because, in various ways, they were evidence of this. His "philosophy of the spirit" is, after all, a project of harmonious, healthy, balanced human life in which themes of lucidity, tranquility, and a tenacious loyalty to what "counts" predominate. But now, after him, it is necessary to descend once more to the underworld, certainly not to make it our abode but to understand better than he could the risks and temptations that threaten humanity and to make the project he held so dearly of a "healthy life" more successful. Croce was familiar with the dramatic experience of "breakdown," as when in his youth he nurtured ideas about suicide, or as an adult he suffered to the limit of madness from the loss of a dearly beloved child. But what was most "private" in this experience remains hidden from us, and we almost always have only indirect traces of it mixed in with the publicity of a problem, as when he wrote the passage on the "departed."[1] Today we are grateful to him for this discretion, which alone could make us understand the impulse of valorization, the ethos of transcendence that, as a true Atlas, holds up the world. But precisely in order not to lose this understanding, it is necessary for someone to testify to the worst, in the face of which the philosopher—due to a sort of compassion concealed as insensitivity—preferred to remain silent or for his chosen tasks utilized the weapon of irony, banter, or rigorous, ruthless criticism. It is our task to descend anew to the underworld if at present we want to consolidate the power of the upper world.

1.2. Autobiographical accounts.
    Fausto Nicolini, *Benedetto Croce* (Turin: Unione tipografico-editrice torinese, 1962).

Young Croce, in the years immediately following the disaster of 1881, when he lost his parents and sister in the Casamicciola earthquake:

> The unhealthy state of my body that was not suffering from any illness and yet seemed to suffer from all illnesses, the loss of lucidity in myself and on the path I should take, uncertain ideas about the aims and meaning of living, and other connected anxieties of youth: this took away all glad hope, and I was inclined to consider myself withered before blossoming, old before being young. Those years were the gloomiest and most pain-ful: the only years in which very often at night, laying my head on the pillow, I strongly desired to not awaken in the morning, and thoughts of suicide arose. (71)

"In the first stage, pain is madness or nearly, etc." (Croce who loses the woman he loves).

Croce to Renato Serra (1913):

> Please allow me, dear Serra, to recommend to you, you who have such a good heart, to recommend you the seriousness of life, in this hour in which pain is tormenting and overwhelming me. We cannot live on feel-ings for things or persons: we must love and bind ourselves, but we must do so ready to detach ourselves without falling. And, to not fall, there is no other way but to carry out in oneself the sense of duty to life. Other-wise, what is left? Filthy suicide and a filthy madhouse.

General Gandolfi to Croce, narrating the impressions of his first com-bat: "In that whistling of cannonballs, in that confusion, I felt no other need but to move, that I should also do something; and, doing so, I re-gained myself and overcame my disorientation." And Croce, in relating the anecdote in 1939, commented,

> Gandolfi certainly did not think that he was providing me with support, and nonetheless that evening he provided me with it. I don't know how many times I have thought about, and continue to think about what he said, and I gained strength and continue to gain strength from it. In my greatest anguish, in the most disheartening blows I have suffered and continue to suffer, a voice sounds inside of me: Do something. And then I return stubbornly to doing what I have to do, what my aptitudes and education have prepared me to do; and I take comfort in that action, calming myself down. And "do something" is the advice that I give, or rather, transmit, because acting this way we live and rekindle life in our world that, in our moments of depression and lacking faith, seems to us

to have gone to ruin; and that does not want to go to ruin and cannot do so, and, to keep itself steadfast, requires and commands us to "do something," our work. (474ff.)

[...]

1.3. Croce and the apocalypse (review chapter on Spengler; Mounier chapter).

From 1946 to 1948 Croce wrote some notes with a common inspiration: "La fine della civiltà," "L'Anticristo che è in noi," "Il progresso come stato d'animo e il progresso come concetto filosofico," "Esperienze storiche attuali e conclusioni per la storiografia," collected under the general title "Verità ed errore delle previsioni pessimistiche" in *Filosofia e storiografia*, 302ff.[2]

The immediate stimulus for writing these pages appears to be the disorientation of spirits in the postwar period, made deeper by the reemergence of age-old declines in the moral energy of European civilization, by the practice of totalitarian regimes and wartime barbarization. But even more, the stimulus for these writings appears to have been the specter of communism and the state of alert that Italy experienced until April 18.[3] But above and beyond this immediate polemical motivation, which in Croce's writings should always be properly noted—the ones from this period, like for example his piece on "Humanity and nature" (247ff.),[4] with the de facto distinction between "men who are actors (in history) and men who are in history passively, etc.," there are some lines of thought that should be kept because they may in turn serve as a stimulus for us nearly twenty years later.

Croce observed the budding concern about an end to civilization or European civilization that left its mark after World War I; now, after World War II, it had become a "widespread sentiment." And he noted that "in this form and scope" it was a sentiment "new in the centuries of European history because medieval apocalypse was enlivened by Christian hope, and the subsequent eras of Humanism, the Renaissance, the Enlightenment, and the Liberal period each in its own way had a confident certainty in the life of culture. "But now," says Croce, "spirits are imbued with sadness, minds with predictions of the worst, and the trusting impulse that good work requires is missing" (304). He complained that "the end of civilization that people are talking about, of civilization in the universal sense, [was] not an elevation of tradition but its breakdown, the introduction of barbarisms." Certainly, he argued, "the fate of moral life is always in danger" (308), and the treasure of European cultural tradition could get lost (307); but to want to understand this with the mind and to want to face the dangers with will, it was necessary to turn to the dialectic of vitality and morality, of fortune and virtue, precluding horror and the gloomy melancholy that enfeeble action, at the same time educating it with the vigil sense of what can get lost (308ff.). In "The Antichrist within us" he explains what properly makes up the danger:

> The Antichrist we are discussing is not simply the human sinfulness, the abandoning of oneself to evil with the interfering consciousness that this is evil, with the clarity of moral concepts that has been observed many times with astonishment even in those criminal men who treat moral virtues with reverence, all the while knowing that they lie above them like an unattainable heaven for them, and therefore they give up attempting to put them into practice. The true Antichrist lies in the repudiation, the negation, the violation, the derision of the values themselves, declared to be empty words, humbug, or still worse, hypocritical trickery to hide and pass the only reality more easily before the blinded eyes of the ingenuous and foolish: personal desire and avarice, wholly directed to pleasure and leisure. This is the true Antichrist opposed to Christ: the Antichrist who destroys the world, delighting in its destruction, heedless of being unable to construct anything but a more and more dramatic process of this very destruction, the negative that wants to appear positive and as such is no longer a creation but, if we may put it so, discreation. (314ff.)

"It appears certain that the threat of the Antichrist against Christ has been raised" (316). In the same condemnation, (Croce) includes the so-called opponents of the Antichrist themselves, as if the Evil One had won them over to his ranks. Nonetheless he had in mind above all Marxism and the rapid conversions of intellectuals to it, which seemed to him to weaken the front of resistance: but in our perspective this casual or secondary element, as much as it might be important in Croce's political decision-making, is not what interests us.

[. . .] Returning to the subject in "Current historical experiences and conclusions for historiography," Croce clarifies where his thinking aimed regarding the Antichrist within us:

> The theory formulated in historical materialism would never have had the reception and diffusion that it has had and continues to have had it not encountered a condition of spirit that developed in today's world and which would be very long to describe: born from a second-rate and sensuous romanticism, in which the sentiment of freedom and human dignity lapsed and was dulled, as well as the elevation of thought and its religiosity, of which today's literature and pseudo-poetry are a

mirror, along with fashionable decadent and dim-witted philosophies. From this we have not only indifference to time-honored human values, [. . .] but also a sort of merriment of destruction that contains something diabolical. (332)

Nor did he hesitate to confess that

The men of the old generation who lived in the first decades following the Italian Risorgimento and in a Liberal Europe wonder in astonishment where all these new people have come from (some have even misinterpreted their appearance as a sign of God's condemnation), and they wonder from whence they draw the strength and taste for living in the desert they have created in themselves and into which they seek to lead all men. (332ff.)

In every age there has undoubtedly been a struggle between a higher and lower form of humanity, like the struggle between secularism and ecclesiastic oppression, between freedom and absolute monarchies, between concretely historical freedom and Enlightenment fanaticism. But in their own way these lower forms against which the higher forms battle contain "old and abstract moral ideals" that in turn had a positive effect in history. In the current epoch, instead, a full-fledged "negation of the very roots of humanity" (333) is taking place, characterizing it in comparison with all the others. At least in the Middle Ages "there was a light of Romanity that was not entirely extinguished and the warmth of the new Christian faith": but for our epoch the danger remains, if not of the end of humanity, of too long a period of barbaric and semibarbaric decadence in the course of which "the tradition of European history will be weakened as never before" (333); it will be weakened not by primitive and generous barbarity but by a "barbarity of reflection" (334).

On apocalypses, see also "The character of modern philosophy" (199ff.)[5] which, however, refers to other concerns around 1940 and in which Marxism again and Mazzinianism[6] were considered secular apocalypses inspired just like others by the "substance of things hoped for," imaginative depictions and the hypostasis of the human soul's aspirations for purity, justice, and goodness.

2. Presence, Vitality, Historicity

2.1. Human vitality is not vitality that is "raw and green, savage and untouched by any further education."[7] That is the vitality of plants or animals, not humans. Human vitality is presence, that is, life that makes itself present to itself and that makes itself the center of synthetic energy according to distinct operative powers. It is the unity that conditions the distinction of cultural forms and at the same time the trigger of opposition within each of these forms. It is the technical domination of nature, the manufacture of instruments, the regime of production of economic goods; the social, legal and political organization of human groups; the struggle for power and hegemony on the part of individuals and groups. And it is this same dialectical unity that, in order to be the power of all forms, goes beyond the **useful** and the economic, extending itself in complete cultural becoming, in an ethos, art, and logos.

Or else it is the vitality of humans, but as natural beings, as bodily organisms, and thus not as *humans*. But human vitality already presents this "additional education": that is, vitality that makes itself present to itself, that contrasts itself to the merely biological vital per se, undivided and indiscriminate. Human vitality is thus presence as a center of synthetic energy according to distinct operative forms.

Nature is incapable of culture precisely because there is no presence that bursts forth with the works and days of human civilization. Moreover, presence does not coincide with economic form because this form is a distinct power of doing that entails the technical domination of nature, while presence is, as already stated, the synthetic power that conditions all single forms of cultural life, so that every single form is conditioned, in order to be able to express itself, by the integrity of the synthetic power of presence. The technical domination of nature does not take place in the heart of nature itself but only through the economic form of cultural life. Nature knows nothing of economic regimes or material and mental work instruments, of society and state and juridical norms, and everything else that presupposes a synthetic construction of presence, a specific initiative according to the particular coherence of the useful and utilitarian calculation: everything else is made possible only by presence.

2.2. The "most elementary" form of praxis is for Croce the utilitarian or economic, hedonistic vital, and it is marked by the dialectic of pleasure and pain. Now to me it seems that the dialectic of pleasure and pain certainly belongs to biological vitality (and to our bodily vitality), but economic life cannot also be reduced to this dialectic. The economically useful is not only pleasure but a calculation of pleasure, a choice and an institutional creation of practical instruments (material and mental) to control nature technologically and bend it to human ends. Out of the economically useful come forth regimes of the production of goods, society and state, the natural sciences and mathematics: all of these things cannot be derived from the pleasure and pain that we have in common with the animal world (and indeed, in the animal world they do not exist). In order to express itself the useful already contains a principle of autonomous synthesis; pleasure and pain, drive and instinct, satisfaction and satiation are all outside of the autonomous synthesis and utilitarian cultural creation (cf. *Ultimi saggi*, 1935 [written in 1933], 190, note).

[. . .]

It is necessary to try to think of the economic as the *value of securitas* and thus as the inaugural value in which the ethos of the transcendence of life must be realized. The economic is the horizon of the domestic, of *at hand givenness*, of a world of "things" and "names" related according to a communitarian project of possible or actual handiness. Something useful can be made of this world precisely because it is given, and its givenness, indeed, indicates its character of practicable resistance. Through this horizon of the domestic, being-there first of all finds itself as the center of utilitarian agency, as a center of loyalty to past sureties (*sicurezze*) converted into effortless habits, and as a center of initiative for establishing, here and now, the preeminent security (*sicurezza*) that it needs.[8] And through this finding itself and placing itself, and again finding itself and placing itself "in a safe place," being-there emerges ushered in by life: first and foremost it generates and regenerates itself, laying the initial basis of its cultural life. Being-there for value has its first test in this functioning dialectic of being safe and securing itself again and again, in this inaugural socioeconomic being-there, in this history of things at hand as a nexus of intersubjective loyalty blurring into the anonymous and habituality and of liberal initiative that readapt and increase the common heritage of "things at hand." Being-there has it precisely in that domain of the vital that would seem to be the sovereign realm of the most solitary, closed individuality of pleasure and pain, of need and satisfaction. Only on the basis of this intersubjective domain of "security"—increasingly put into question and expanded in history, always "given" and always "givable"—can other horizons of the world's valorization be constructed. The economic cannot be the only value because the ethos of transcendence does not exhaust itself in a particular value: on the contrary, it carries out its valorizing function only when it does not suffocate all of the other valorizations, when it does not substitute itself for them and does not claim to exhaust being-there (the duty to be there).

2.3. What is the origin of the dialectic?

[. . .]

The nonbeing of presence—that is, the collapse of the possibility to go beyond the biologically vital and open the self to the distinction of the useful, morality, art, and logos[9]—is itself a relative, not absolute nonbeing.

Nothingness is so insignificant that it is biological vitality, in itself indiscriminate and indistinct—"raw and green vitality," without further education, "nature," instincts, the unconscious, or however we want to call it—but always positive. If it is experienced as nothingness, if indeed it appears as nothingness par excellence, if the spasm of anxiety proclaims it to us as an extreme risk, this always happens because the cultural polemic here is radicalized in extreme positions in that the very possibility of any cultural life enters into crisis. If the nothingness of a single cultural form is another cultural form that gets confused with it, the annihilation of presence is the loss of culture; it is a submersion in nature in a total wreckage of the human. Or: it is no longer being in human history, it is madness.

Presence, being-in-the-world, and being-there in history are equivalent expressions for designating human vitality in the act of distinguishing itself from the biological vital and opening itself to the distinction of the distinct operative forces creating culture and history: the useful, moral life, art, and logos.

The concept of presence as the synthesizing unity of the single operative possibilities and as a dynamic condition for their expression poses the problem of the relationship between presence, vitality, and utility. How are these concepts connected to one another? It is evident that presence cannot be identified with mere biological vitality, per se indiscriminate and undivided, incapable of autonomously antagonizing itself and deciding with a deliberate choice. Biological or, if one prefers, natural vitality is "raw and green, without further education," indeed incapable of entering into the process of "education," and only through a play of imagination can we attribute to nature the aptitude of making itself present to itself, of choosing to deliberate according to distinct cultural forms. Such a play of imagination leads to animism and panpsychism or to a fantasy of "nature's spirituality" that would be capable in its own way of memory and judgment, of passion and accounting, of moral sacrifice and economic calculation: except that we need to add, because of a sort of modesty, that nature realizes all this in *its own way*, implying that it would be indiscrete to know more.

2.4. Value. The detachment from natural vitality as culture.

Detachment from the mere naturalness of living in order to open toward the world of values constitutes culture. This detachment can be narrated, but the fundamental need that promotes it is its underivable presupposition. The historiography of cultural life can never be narrated as starting from a natural without the human, passing to the human and the cultural, but only as the human that rises up from naturalness.

Human worldhood is the order of meaningful agency that produces values, overcoming the situations and negativity that harms them, through the historically conditioned permanence of values. Detachment from the naturalness of living is carried out by interspersing the order of material instruments and the regimes of production of economic goods; the order of mental instruments for bending nature to the needs of individuals and groups; the order of social rules for disciplining the division of labor and relations between persons and groups; the order of moral rules to educate the individual to go beyond the "libido" and to give a horizon to feelings that imply gratitude and love; the order of aesthetic catharsis and the self-consciousness of human operating and producing and rising above nature. Culture is this moral energy of detachment from nature to establish a human world. The roughest man knows that he is not called to live like a beast, just as the poet knows "you were not made to live as brutes."[10] How does religious life fit into this system of worldly values and coherences of action? What does its coherence consist of—that is, its genesis, structure, and function? And above all, can we speak of a religious life that is a value on par with other secular and profane values or even above them? A simple observation warns us that we cannot present the same discourse for religious life as we do for secular values. The aspirations included in these values are in fact executable: they take place in history in the form of human works, monuments and documents of human action; the hunter-gatherer economy, primitive agriculture, cereal agriculture, pastoralism, and industrial civilization all constitute just as many economic "works" that lie before us, full of reality. Classificatory systems of kinship, matrilineal or patrilineal descent, and the monogamous family are also social works full of reality. The aspiration to elaborate systems of mental instruments for the control of nature has its validation in the discoveries and inventions that fill our cities with noise and lights but already appears in the arrowhead or trap of hunter-gatherer peoples. The aspiration to free oneself through artistic and poetic creation is realized in images, melodies, fables, sculptures and architectures, dances, epic poems, dramas, lyrics, (more recently) some films, and so forth. But the religious aspiration to enter into a relationship with metahistory cannot as such boast of a single work because action is possible only in history and through secular values, and the attempt to exit from the world remains an attempt within the world. Religious aspiration, unlike worldly values, has not left a single document for the historian: in our ethnographic museums, we can see demons, numina, and sacred objects; we learn about myths and rites of so-called primitives from reports or from our direct observation. We can get informed about the great religions that are living or have vanished, read religious and mystical texts, and in our own civilization glimpse infinite evidence of this sort in churches, in the rites celebrated in them, in the solemn unfolding of the liturgical cycle of the year. But this is all proof that refers not to the realization of the religious aspiration but only to the inexecutable attempt it contains for those involved: the attempt to enter into relations with metahistory. In this sense, the history of religions is in the very strange condition of being a history of an attempt that, by definition, never places an end to a work, and of an aspiration that never leaves the smallest proof of its own executability.

2.5. The human condition is characterized by the dissolution of what is becoming into the permanence of what counts, into the dialectic quality of the relation between becoming and value, between passing and making things pass according to a rule. The human condition is nature that, through the ethos of presence, rises to culture. This dissolution, this dialectic quality, this making things pass and this rising are all the human condition, which can be lost as a wreckage of presence (psychosis and neurosis) but never transcended, as magic and religion claim. The aspiration to transcend the human condition as such—that is, historicity—is so little feasible that the historiographer connects it to history and does not find any document here in favor of a successful escape for the simple reason that a document of this sort cannot exist. As long as mystics speak or in any case document themselves, in effect they bear witness either to the loss of presence or to its reintegration: if this reintegrating passes by way of the technical horizon of mythical-ritual metahistory, then that metahistorical horizon, as a protective technique, is a part of history and culture. When mystics are silent, everything ineffable about them is on the threshold of nothingness.

As energy that transcends the situation in value, the human condition can be lost but never "transcended." The magical-religious aspiration to transcend not merely situations in secular values but the human condition itself in mythical-ritual metahistory is a technical horizon of alienating the presence as an operative center for society and history. This self-alienating is self-annihilation, a wreckage: the mythical-ritual horizon stops, configures and recovers the alienation, disclosing it to secular values compromised by the crisis. It therefore participates in human history as a technical horizon of signaling and reintegration, not as an impossible pretense of escaping from history.

The articulation of becoming in a system of certain critical moments (hunting, war, the phases of agricultural labor, birth, marriage, death . . .) in which historicity protrudes—that is, the passage from one situation to another gets manifested and at the same time, the limit of a human rule of passing. The dissolution of the chaotic all-allusiveness of beginning in a socialized and traditionalized system of symbols: the "everything can allude to everything" is substituted by "this is the symbol of that," yielding a host of symbolic spheres, of separate ("sacred") realities and particular negative or positive behaviors.

What risks losing presence is the manifesting of the historicity of human condition, the protruding of this historicity in critical moments of existence. To say the least, every experience of a "new" situation is critical, and in a given society it is every new situation that brings about an awareness of the distance between happening in a natural sense (which is or can be against humankind) and making things happen in a cultural sense (which tends to decide situations according to human values, according to initiatives inserted in traditions of acting). When a situation occurs where a culture lacks a tradition of realistically efficacious behavior (as in great natural catastrophes, fatal diseases, and death), it is the presence itself that gets lost, remains without leeway for action, and disappears.

Presence is realistically efficacious cultural behavior, detachment from the natural condition through work endowed with human value: for example the manufacture of instruments, the establishment of socio-economic regimes; moral, juridical, and political relations; poetic works; the natural and human sciences—these are all secular, lay values that are realistically oriented in the sense that through them the detachment from naturalness is actually carried out and culture gets established. Religious life is the technical mediation of this detachment: it protects the presence from the risk of "passing with what passes" in historical conditions in which this risk is great and the cultural powers of worldly action are in various ways restricted and not yet developed for a self-awareness of their human origin and destination. Through this technical mediation of worldly values compromised by the crisis, and due to the particular nature of this mediation (i.e., the mythical-ritual nexus), magic and religion enter into cultural life and form a moment of it that acquires more or less importance according to the civilization, epoch, and social environment.

2.6. Animal vitality.

The risk of losing presence occurs in critical moments of existence when the naturalness of what passes without and against us protrudes. Religion is a technique (a) of dehistorification of the critical passage, (b) of recovery of the alienated psychic situations, and (c) of a return to the historicity of existing.

[...]

Dehistorification—that is, the concealment of the historicity of the critical passage—is obtained through the ritualism of acting: we pass ritually, in other words, repeating what the numen already did in metahistory. What is historical is resolved as something identical to the metahistorical that gets repeated. The historicity of the passage is concealed.

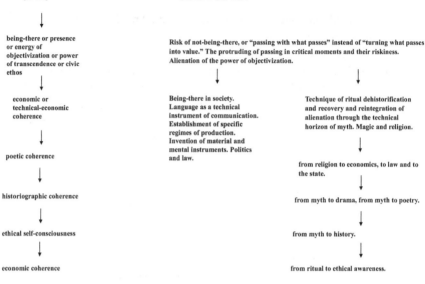

The alienation of presence.

(a) Presence that gets "alienated" into the **wholly other** is recovered in the representation of the wholly other as a numen with which one must enter into relation. Religion offers cultural models of these representations in which the recovery is carried out.

(b) Presence that runs the risk of crisis during the critical passage conceals that risk, resolving it in repetition.

(c) Ritual dehistorification as technical cultural models, as the attenuation of passing's historicity, and as the institution of a presence operating in a reduced mode—in other words as the repeater of rigid models of behavior.

(d) Ritual dehistorification as recovery from the alienation of presence.

3. Marxism and Religion

3.1. Marxist apocalypse. The continuation of the apocalyptic theme in new forms (Mühlmann 418 ff.).[11]

The error of continuing to pursue once-important phenomena according to lines that have become outdated has been committed, too, by the first historian of millenarianism, the Swiss Corrodi, in his *Kritische Geschichte des Chiliasmus*, 4 vols. (Zurich, 1781–83). He very usefully distinguishes a Judaic epoch from a Judeo-Christian one, whether we are dealing with

Anabaptists, Quakers, or other enthusiasts, to then—as he moves closer to his own period—get lost in unimportant minutiae regarding obscure local prophets, apocalyptic interpreters, and founders of the minuscule sects. We clearly see how the phenomenon in its real quality and dimension escapes him, and how he desperately struggles with case examples while only managing to accumulate trifles that—where sources permit it—could still offer some usefulness from a social and psychological point of view but hardly have any historical significance. In reality the important lines do not run in the history of sects but in political utopias, and in Corrodi's time (or shortly thereafter) activist millenarianism should be sought first and foremost among the Jacobins, whose substantially "religious fanatism" fits Corrodi's definition better than the obscure founders of eighteenth-century sects.

The same phenomenon repeats for utopias. It is possible to trace them as a literary genre from Plato's Republic up to present-day science fiction; one can also analyze their realizations, for example, in the foundation of colonies by pietistic sects or (with a more anarchic character) by a John Ruskin or other dreamers. The problem is, though, whether or not here, too, the historically important lines of development follow their course in a certain underground way in places that are totally different only to emerge again suddenly in a decidedly new key, as in the Zionist establishment of the state of Israel or—with completely different features—in the "dictatorships of saviors" of a Lenin or a Hitler or—with still other features—in the welfare state. [...] "Secularized" religion does not mean a crippling of religious energies but can also mean that these energies present themselves today under other symbolic keys. For example, the eagerly debated question of whether the Orthodox Church is still alive in the Soviet Union, whether it can have an impact, whether its services are more or less attended—in our view all of these questions have a secondary value with respect to the establishment of the fact that Soviet Communism is itself a new religion, one that is professed by millions of men. [...] When, some ten years ago, the author treated communism as a "new religion" at a congress on religious history, this was perceived as an interesting analogy, but it was not understand that the presentation should be taken seriously. In our textbooks of comparative religious history, modern Communism obviously does not appear, precisely because there is not a sense for the transformation of symbolic keys. (419–20)

Mühlmann notes that Communism certainly denies being a religion among others: but no religion has ever arisen actually recognizing this, instead asserting to be "the truth." Moreover, from the time of the *Aufklärung* (Enlightenment) on, truth has presented itself clothed in

"science," transforming belief into knowledge that claims to be scientific
knowledge. The Communist religion thus presents itself as "scientific
socialism" or "dialectical materialism." "As Löwith says, 'Historical materialism is redemptive history in the language of national economy.' "[12]
In dialectical materialism, the modern reshaping of a gnostic dualism
takes place: it is the dualism of the Manicheans and the Bogomils,[13] but
reversed (420).

> One has characterized old believers in Russia by the following assertion:
> striving for the realization of the Christian absolute on historical Earth is
> "a characteristic temptation for the Russian soul." Yet we would prefer to
> say: this effort toward the absolute and perfection is one of the character-
> istics of chiliastic thought, and it is a Russian characteristic only insofar as
> a certain inclination to millenarianism is visible in the Russian spirit. How-
> ever, this, in turn, is not the result of any mysterious, "mystical" disposition
> of that people, but because the spiritual structure of the Russian people
> has preserved some "medieval" dispositions that among us in Central and
> Western Europe were pushed to the background through the Renaissance
> and the Baroque periods, in which Russia did not take part. (322)

With regard to the "Slavic line of eschatology": influences of anti-
institutionalism "on Protestant pietism, on Leibniz, Herder, Schelling
and the Romantics, on Hegel, through Schelling again on Russia, through
Hegel and Marx, and through Marx in turn on Russian bolshevism." And
that for example the Marxian idea of the state's dying in the final period
clearly goes back to the eschatological root of anti-institutionalism. "The
militant version of this doctrine is the trade unionists' doctrine of the
necessary destruction of the state." Weitling's anti-institutionalism arose
in a sectarian context of East Saxony, and it bore Hussite-Taborite and
Anabaptist influences.[14]

3.2. As already stated in its subtitle, Norman Cohn's book *The Pursuit of
the Millennium: Revolutionary Messianism in Medieval and Reformation
Europe and Its Bearing on Modern Totalitarian Movements* (London: Mercury Books, 1962; first published 1957 by Seeker and Warburg [London])
aims to be an overview of revolutionary messianism from the end of
the eleventh century to the first half of the sixteenth century. This is an
overview traced in view of the relationship between this messianism
and modern totalitarian movements such as German Nazism and Soviet
Communism. The author's perspective clarifies its own sense above all in
the conclusion (307–19). In revolutionary messianism, we find motifs of
terrestrial and collective salvation, from the advent of a celestial city on

Earth, of a chosen people that declares and hastens the coming of the Antichrist and the final cataclysmic and decisive battle, after which the world would emerge totally transformed and redeemed, without the negativity, the conflicts, and the tensions that characterize the present world. But the two most significant totalitarian movements of our time—Communism and Nazism—kept these fundamental motifs, if in another form: the history of revolutionary messianism from the end of the twelfth century to the first half of the sixteenth century can thus be considered "as a prologue to the vast revolutionary upheavals of the present century" (309). The proof that Cohn gives of this connection is limited to some essential indications. As regards Nazism, Rosenberg (2011) dedicates a chapter of his *The Myth of the Twentieth Century* to an enthusiastic and imaginative presentation of German heterodox mysticism of the fourteenth century, and a historian of the regime dedicated an entire volume to interpreting the message of upper-Rhine revolutionaries. For their part, in one volume after another the Communists have continued to elaborate the cult of Thomas Müntzer initiated by Engels.[15] According to Cohn, these references to revolutionary messianism by Nazis and Communists—whatever may be the evaluation that Nazis and Communists give of such movements—have a precise meaning: Communism and Nazism were inspired by archaic fantasies of a revolutionary-chiliastic type. It is true that traditional messianisms are religious, while the new social eschatologism declared itself "scientific" and substituted the "will of God" with the "purposes of History." But even with this secularization the apocalyptic theme has remained a perspective on a world to be purged of corrupt agents, tensions and conflicts. The social identification of such agents ("the great ones," the Jews, the clergy, the bourgeoisie) can vary, but the fundamental orientation remains. And similarly, the final framework remains of a society rendered unanimous in its beliefs and free of conflicts (309 ff.).

Who does not recall how the idea of an international Jewish conspiracy is a relic of medieval demonology and recall in this regard Rosenberg's inspiring language in his comment on the *Protocols of the Elders of Zion* and Hitler's in *Mein Kampf* (where the chosen people, freeing humanity from the Jewish octopus that sucks blood and money from the nations takes on a universal mission of liberation, whose failure would mark the end of the world)?

Cohn's ([1957] 1962) attitude toward Marxism and Communism is declared in the following passage:

> Communists and Nazis have been at one in their murderous hatred of Liberals and Socialists and reformers of every kind—and the reason for this is that Communists no less than Nazis have been obsessed by the

vision of a prodigious "final, decisive struggle" in which a "chosen people" will destroy a world tyranny and thereby inaugurate a new epoch in
world history. As in the Nazi apocalypse the "Aryan race" was to purify
the earth by annihilating the "Jewish race," so in the Communist apocalypse the "bourgeoisie" is to be exterminated by the "proletariat." And
here too we are faced with a secularized version of a phantasy that is
many centuries old.

For what Marx passed on to present-day Communism was not the
fruit of his long years of study in the fields of economics and sociology
but a quasi-apocalyptic phantasy which as a young man, unquestion-
ingly and almost unconsciously, he had assimilated from a crowd of obscure writers and journalists. Capitalism as a perfect hell in which an
ever smaller number of enormously wealthy men ruthlessly exploit and
tyrannise over an ever larger mass of pauperized workers—capitalism
as a monstrous realm whose masters have both the cruelty and the hypocrisy of Antichrist—capitalism as Babylon, now about to go under in
a sea of blood and fire so that the way shall be cleared for the egalitarian
Millennium—this vision was very familiar to the radical intelligentsia of
France and Germany around 1840 . . . (Lamenais, Weitling). (311–12)[16]

According to Cohn, Marx secularized the apocalypse, inserting motifs
of an all-encompassing philosophy of history into it: he thereby guaranteed its survival into the current century, although in different circumstances from those he foresaw. Indeed, it was not the workers in countries
of more advanced industrial capitalism but more economically underdeveloped regions like Russia and China who translated the theme into
effective revolution (312). "However modern their terminology, however
realistic their tactics, in their basic attitudes Communism and Nazism follow an ancient tradition—and are baffling to the rest of us because of those
very features that would have seemed so familiar to a chiliastic *propheta* of
the Middle Ages" (313).

Overpopulation, wars, epidemics, famines, and so forth favor millenarianisms, and so forth.

3.3. Marxist religious historiography is undeniably childish. First of all
we need to explain the historical reasons of this childishness, since an
understanding of these reasons also constitutes the best means for helping
the child to become an adolescent and finally—after a crisis of puberty—to
become an adult. First, we should not forget that historical materialism
developed in a sharp polemic not only with Hegel but also with the idealism of the young Hegelians and especially that of Bauer, Strauss, and
Stirner:[17] in this polemic, religion—and in particular the idealist history

of religion—played a significant part, so that the birth of historical materialism and the polemic against a religious vision of the world (explicit in the historical religions and disguised in idealism) end up getting mixed together and confused. Second, Marxism's positivistic barbarization was certainly not fortunate for its development, the primary responsibility of this lying with Friedrich Engels: the most fertile seeds contained in the works of the young Marx thus gradually got suffocated wholly in favor of vulgar materialism. Moreover, it was precisely Engels who had the task of orienting the first studies of religious historiography in a Marxist sense so that the Marxists from then on had those studies as a model and were inspired by them, all the more easily in that—besides being the only ones suffused with the authority of the two founders of historical materialism—also due to their crude simplification of problems, they were the most accessible for an average scientific intellect and the most promising for allowing one to discuss the religious life of humanity with little effort. And so it happens that Engels's interpretation of Marxism and the bit of actual historiographic work that connects it to religion passed for the Marxist theory of religion and the Marxist methodology of the historiography of religious life, operating an inverse selection between historical intellects in that the best among these realized that they could not work with these instruments, and only the most indolent and superficial of them found their key to open all locks and do a cheap religious historiography. Third, we should note that Marxism as a revolutionary theory destined to transform social reality, as a weapon in mass struggle, and as an ideology of workers' parties found itself fighting the alliance between the churches and the bourgeoisie in a period in which religion effectively was exhausting its historical functions and was increasingly appearing to be reactionary and conservative "opium." What happened in Russia following the Revolution certainly did not create a propitious environment for the progress of religious-historical studies. Between the thesis of the "eternal value" of traditional religious life and the opposing one of religion as a "factor of backwardness" of social reality, as "illusion," "stupidity," "extravagance," "reflex," and so forth, there is the thesis of religion as a historical institution, which in certain conditions of social and economic development carries out a positive function of reintegration and mediation of cultural values. (While today, in the current phase of the history of the West, it has had a crisis if not as religion *sic et simpliciter*, certainly as traditionally religious content of something beyond the human and the historical. Beyond the human and the historical as religious content, is it possible to substitute an awareness of the human and the historical as a continuous "valorizing transcendence" of material life?)

3.4. "Criticism has plucked the imaginary flowers on the chain not in order that man shall continue to bear that chain without fantasy or consolation, but so that he shall throw off the chain and pluck the living flower."[18]

In the context of the 1844 essay, this quote underlines in an exemplary way the limits of every critique of religious life that is not also a revolutionary theory of the juridical, political, economic—and social—reality that generates religions: critique that is not also a critique of **hierogonic** societies, in other words, ones in which the contradictions of their human and secular horizon necessarily need a metahistorical compensatory and reintegrating complement. But this quote is also interesting, because it implicitly indicates the danger of mere irreligious critique—and of the skeptical outcome resulting from it—when the hierogonic features of social existence are left intact. In this case, the "chains" remain, but without fantasy or "hope," and this exasperates the existential crisis, unleashes horizonless anxieties, and pushes the need for religion toward an unresolving nostalgia or toward miserable surrogates: that is, it prepares more or less inauthentic restorations. We should note, moreover, how in this quote (and the ones preceding it) the need for a religious "reflex" in hierogonic societies is not sufficiently expressed: the analysis focuses on hierogonic features to be eliminated and not on the positive reintegrating function of the metahistorical horizon (of mythical-ritual symbolism) in hierogonic societies. For this direction of analysis, a historiographic reconstruction of the *coherence* and the *rationality* of religious life in the context of a given hierogonic society risks remaining outside any possible perspective of scientific research: religion tends to appear as something negative—as an element of backwardness, and so forth—in any historic society or human epoch. And since it cannot be reduced to socioeconomic reality it passes for stupidity, gratuitous proliferation of the imagination—indeed, a sort of cancer of imagination itself. It is no longer a matter of polemicizing against the theological idea and the confessional origin of an *autonomous* religious historiography in which religious ideas arise from other ideas and produce still other ideas without ever placing these ideas in relation to concrete social existence and to people in the world and society as they transcend the immediacy of living according to certain specific ways. The danger arises of a complete disinterest for the historically circumscribed function of such ideas, now belittled to groundless imaginings, illusions, and so forth. Instead of identifying how in each case in hierogonic societies the road toward the partial recognition of humanity runs through religion, and instead of highlighting—together with the limit of that recognition—the need and the coherence of the extended road of religious alienation and the reintegrating function, in certain conditions, of that "long" road, we run the risk of ending up in a sort of short circuit of historiographic judgment. Having correctly identified the process by which in bourgeois society in crisis and in the socialist society that is its heir, religion comes to lose its function, its cultural-historical necessity, its relationship with corresponding hierogonic particularities of existence, and so forth, we risk uncritically projecting this judgment as well on civilizations and historical epochs in which religious life effectively served as a *bridge* between the horizonless, culturally sterile existential crisis and the operative reintegration into a world of people for a world of people. But there is a final observation. A socialist or communist society eliminates neither the negativity of existence nor history: it does not eliminate death, physical pain, or struggle but amputates them of their hierogonic aspect by embracing the individual in a society entirely dedicated to individuals and mobilized for the individualization of individuals without group privileges. But, first of all, it is necessary to ask over and over whether the socialist edifice entails—if only temporarily—new hierogonic features (personality cult, bureaucracy, etc.), and in the second place whether the elimination of bourgeois society's hierogonic features ever means elimination of the existential crisis, and therefore the need for a symbolic reintegration, if now oriented toward a secular, humanistic, historical, civil symbolism.

3.5. Marxism and religion (second draft).[19] "Die Religion ist [. . .] die Anerkennung des Menchen auf einem Umweg, durch einen Mittler."[20] Marx, "Zur Judenfrage," in *Historisch-kritische Gesamtausgabe* (Frankfurt am Main, 1927), 1 Abteilung, Band 1, vol. 1, 383.

Religion as an "indirect and extended road" for the recognition of humanity contains a profound truth and at the same time the possibility of a serious misinterpretation. Indeed, the image of an "indirect and extended road" suggests another one of a "waste of time that could be avoided" and therefore confirms the hasty judgment of religion as a "factor of backwardness" in civilization's development in any epoch or social condition. Now, we should note that traditional religion—that is, based on mythical-ritual symbols—constitutes a *historically necessary mediation* in preclassist societies and classist ones, and it so little represents an "extended and indirect" road (in the sense of a "waste of time" and a "factor of backwardness") that in that given historical and social conditioning it constitutes the only road possible for protecting human groups from existential crisis and for disclosing a certain consciousness of humanity and a certain practicability according to worldly values. If in modern civilization the alternative has effectively been opened for a recognition of humanity that does without the mythical-religious detour, this only means that for modern civilization the mythical-religious is becoming a detour that is impossible without "wasting time," and this is precisely so because a peremptory antinomy has arisen in modern civilization between the consciousness of humanity that reabsorbs the divine within it and traditional religious consciousness closed within the divine horizon of humanity. But the historian must be prepared to render justice to civilizations and epochs in which what for us appears a "route that lengthens the road" instead constitutes the necessary route for being-in-the-world, and it is antihistorical to judge those civilizations and epochs by bringing immediately to bear the perspective of a *shortcut* toward humanity that we are only just reaching in our own time and with so much difficulty.

This perspective certainly does not remain inactive in the historiographic task but must bring itself to bear indirectly in carrying out this task: in other words, the historian must in each case reconstruct the concrete dynamic that leads from critical moments of existence to mythical-religious dehistorification and thus to the disclosure of a certain awareness of humanity and the worldly through the religious road. In this, the religious road appears as a route and not an *Umweg* (detour) to reach, within certain limits, this awareness.

3.6. In Engels's letter to Conrad Schmidt of 27 October 1890[21] with regard to natural religions—that is, ones before society's class division—we find mention of the "pedantry" of wanting to look for "economic causes" of primitive "stupidity." This basically means that each time we do not manage to trace the "false representations" of so-called natural religions to economic causes, we are dealing with "primitive stupidity." This is an extremely dangerous criterion, because the stupid proliferation of imaginations risks, precisely because it is stupid, being left to its own devices as irrelevant for the historian and not deserving the effort of an explanation other than stupidity. This is an excellent system for getting rid of something that embarrasses interpretative theory, to always make it "square" and to prevent it from renewing and modifying itself in concrete interpretative exercise. Now, it happens that precisely this sphere of primitive "stupidity" contains institutions of notable anthropological importance for which weak economic development, the false representations of nature, and imaginings caused by ignorance assist very little toward understanding. These are institutions that, *in those specific conditions of economic development*, carry out a positive function of protection and reintegration of humanity, operating as apparatuses endowed with their own internal coherence with the aim of making a given intersubjective activity possible in an economic, social, juridical, artistic, elementarily cognitive, and so forth, way. Religion is certainly the recognition of humanity *auf einem Umweg*: but if it allows for even an extremely limited recognition of humanity, this *Umweg* obliges the historian to seek understanding in what conditions, and through what "coherences," the religious *Umweg*—mythical-ritual symbolism—operates. This means that from a methodological point of view, it is necessary to appeal as little as possible to "human stupidity" as an explanation. People often appear "stupid" when the data and instruments of analysis at one's disposal are insufficient for evaluating their behavior, and their stupidity always poses the question of the limits of our wisdom as interpreters.

3.7. In his discourse on Marx's tomb, Engles summarizes Marx's thought in this way:

> Just as Darwin discovered the law of development or organic nature, so Marx discovered the law of development of human history: the simple fact, hitherto concealed by an overgrowth of ideology, that mankind must first of all eat, drink, have shelter and clothing, before it can pursue politics, science, art, religion, etc.; that therefore the production of the immediate material means, and consequently the degree of economic development attained by a given people or during a given epoch, form the foundation upon which the state institutions, the legal conceptions, art, and even the ideas on religion, of the people concerned have been evolved, and in the light of which they must, therefore, be explained, instead of vice versa, as had hitherto been the case.[22]

And nonetheless, "eat, drink, have shelter and clothing" are in turn evidence of a primordial ethos of making the self present to the world of humanity, that is, of the ethos of presence as an energy of presentification according to intersubjective values. Indeed, a certain economic regime entails a socialized choice, a will to emerge from natural conditions through a division of productive tasks, a loyalty to a chosen regime that obliges respect for certain objective conditionings in economic operations, and at the same time, a margin of initiative expressed in technological inventions, in reshapings and redistributions of the economic and social order itself. Now, all this is already ethos that goes beyond mere natural individuality, and if this ethos is lost, the stone tools of the Paleolithic, the division of labor between hunting (assigned to men) and gathering (assigned to women and their digging tools) would have been impossible. Economy is already an intersubjective value, although we are speaking of the material subsistence of human groups. And since it is intersubjective, it presupposes a will to history, a transcending of mere individuality to be with others in the world, and thus an energy of transcendence and presentification that in the last instance does not derive from the socioeconomic order but conditions it at its root. Society can offer better conditions of existence, work without exploitation, the security of tomorrow, paid vacations, the possibility of choosing the most suitable employment, free medicine and doctors. But if the primordial ethos of presence is lost, no one will benefit from all these possibilities; on the contrary, they will lose the very will to "eat, drink, have shelter and clothing" in a world that is losing every human prospect for being worthy to be lived in.

We see an internal limit of Marxism in the idea that the religion of nature disappears in the face of the science of nature, and that religion is a reflex of the contradictions of a society divided into classes that will disappear when society becomes classless. The socialist transformation of society is undoubtedly a fundamental condition for the deterioration, agony, and, finally, the death of the sacred as mythical-ritual symbolism, but this transformation is not possible without the moral energy of socialistically transforming the world, an energy of which Marxism is itself a product, whether we consider it as Marxist theory or as a particular phase of the workers' movement. The moral energy of socialist transformation of the world certainly does not fall from heaven, but it is in turn possible in the concreteness of capitalistic society ensnared in its contradictions and destined to be increasingly lacerated because of the intrinsic logic of its development. Nonetheless, what lies at the basis of all economic regimes is precisely this noneconomic energy that produces them, just as it produces all other forms of cultural coherence. It is the limit of Marxism to have neglected this fundamental ethos, the reason of all of its analytical inadequacies, such as the scant attention to the positive function of mythical-ritual symbolism and, in class-divided societies, the lack of understanding of the permanent function of symbolic life (even in socialist society), and finally, the belief that a science of nature and a science of society as such can "substitute" for religion once classless society has been achieved.

3.8. Historiography, as a critical science of human cultural activity, is measurement of operative human *pretentions*, the passage from what people think they are doing to what they actually do, therefore the analysis of the unconscious motivations and results of a given action. But what people believe they are doing is not random in relation to what they really do, and it is a bad historiography that limits itself to reducing all human pretentions to their effective reality, since in this way the other important moment of historiographic research remains in the dark: that is, the reconstruction of the historical necessity of a world of pretentions and the function, certainly in part positive—even if in relation to an epoch, a civilization, and so forth—of a coming to awareness according to pretention. The sacred and mythical-ritual symbolism entail, for example, a series of pretentions. But where one believes to have carried out one's historiographic task, limiting oneself to reducing that symbolism "to what people really do," a host of problems of fundamental historiographic importance would get lost, that is, the genesis, structure, and function of mythical-ritual symbolism and its various connections to the entirety of cultural life. It is not enough to read a mythical-ritual symbol as a reversed image of conditions of existence; it is necessary to establish the dynamic of that "reversal" and its mediation of a form of historically conditioned cultural reintegration in the face of extreme risks of not being able to be in any possible world.

The history of nature is a moment of the history of culture in the sense that the concepts of nature and history are both historically conditioned cultural products achieved by the West, especially from the beginning of the modern age on, and so forth.

(Putting mythical-ritual consciousness back on its feet, reversing the mythical-ritual reversal, already means "walking upright" and prevent us from "walking upside-down.")

3.9. That religion as myth is becoming an *Umweg* that is no longer authentically feasible for humanity does not mean that it has always been so. Marxist religious historiography is weighed down by the danger of a continuous exchange between the *revolutionary coming to awareness* of the agony of the divine in our civilization and the criterion for interpreting religious life in human civilization, between the present struggle against religion that has become an *Umweg* and the understanding of religious *Wege* in civilizations lacking all of the conditions for our current awareness of religion as a detour. Within certain limits an effective comparison is useful here: in the context of an industrial transformation of agriculture, the old animal-drawn plow is backward compared to the mechanized plow, but for the historian of agricultural civilizations that used the animal-drawn plow, it makes no sense to bring to bear in an immediate way judgments that are appropriate only in the perspective of someone who today manages a farm in the Po Valley (or of a politician of the Italian Republic who poses the problem of Southern Italy's industrialization).

3.10. For the *Critique of Hegel's Philosophy of Right*, introduction, in *Annales franco-allemandes* (Paris, 1844).

[...]

Marx's predictions about German emancipation, about the union of philosophy with the proletariat, about the already complete development of "German philosophy" as the critique of religion, and about the proletariat as a class held by radical chains, the dissolution of all groups, the victim per se of an injustice, the total loss of man that, regaining himself, regains humanity as a whole, and so forth: the failure of these predictions.

One wonders whether Marx only apparently attempts an analysis of the conditions through which the German proletariat would have played an initial part in the emancipation of humanity as a whole and whether he does not instead make recourse to ethical themes such as class, which expresses the radical wretchedness of humankind in a cultural world in which thinking has reached the highest peaks, and the impulse deriving precisely from the conditions of this immense distance between the abstract idea of humanity in consciousness and the real wretchedness of humanity in a particular force of concrete society.

The conditions are necessary but not sufficient: they are required, but not enough. What makes them sufficient, adequate? The ethos of transcendence of the situation in intersubjective valorization.

3.11. That theistic religious consciousness is an alienated consciousness of a world turned upside-down, in which humanity has *lost* or no longer found itself, is a very important Marxian theme that needs to be explored. To the degree that the individual is abstracted from society—and this abstraction is inevitable to the extent that society is not made for the individual—for various reasons the individual feels "miserable," "limited," "destined to end," "exposed to critical moments in which there is nothing one can do." "Overcoming" the situation itself is struck at the root, and it becomes the risk of becoming another, losing oneself as the active center of decision and choice according to practicable communitarian values. This radical losing of oneself constitutes the radical risk of alienation, the total annihilation of the human; against this risk, religious alienation forms an institutional level of arrest, configuration, and recovery from self-alienation as mere crisis. In this way, religious "transcendence" forms a plan of cultural defense from the crisis of transcending the situation in intersubjective valorization: the other that is radically other in which one risks losing oneself gets inverted, becoming the mythical other open to ritual reappropriation, variously called to conspiring with the human and finally opening up the process of valorization threatened by the crisis.

4. Limits of Historical Materialism

4.1. With regard to Marx.
[. . .]
The chief defect of all hitherto existing materialism [. . .] is that the thing, reality, sensuousness, is conceived only in the form of *the object*

or of contemplation but not as *sensuous human activity, practice,* not subjectively.[23]

The inaugural ethos of handiness makes the world possible. It is only within a **communitarian project of things at hand** that a "world" gains significance, an order of entities within-the-world with their comprehensive horizon gets articulated and spreads. "Resistant, external nature" is not an independent thing in itself in which human work is inserted, but on the contrary, exteriority and resistance are possible only inasmuch as a task of intersubjective utilizing valorization emerges and inasmuch as life *must* first of all manifest itself in the perspective and limits of this "utilizing knowledge." What people produce with their work, the sphere of control that they encompass in their work, constitute the center of relation and reference for the domestication of the world: and even the "sun" or the "moon" or the "sky" are "normal," settled, domesticated in that they have been "worked" by humanity, and they present themselves with all of the traces of settlement that this work has inserted. It is human work that "makes the world," and it grounds exteriority and resistance as experiences inside of working: naive realism and vulgar materialism are only the absolutization of a perspective that belongs solely to the "duty" to work for use (similarly, in the idea idealism absolutizes—and overturns—the real, inexhaustible process of transcendence).

The possibility of a world, and therefore of the entities within-the-world, is contained in the inaugural transcendence that the transcendental ethos of the transcendence of life in value carries out, thanks to that particular valorization of life that is the communitarian project of things at hand. The entities within-the-world are above all the sign of what we can do for the utilization of life, resistances, and the limits of our handy ability to act. They substantially delimit our possible needs and the possibility of satisfying our needs in certain ways and the conditionings to which the indefinite proliferation of needing and new handinesses, of new handy techniques, must subject itself.

4.2. The sensible world and the material production of life, the inaugural nature of material production and the utilizing detachment from nature, nature and culture, sociality of the perceptible world, the sensuous world and social production of material life

[...]

The sensible world—as we would say today, the world of everyday perception—is understood by Marx as the whole of living, sensuous activity of the people that shape it. In the succession of generations the given world, the world in which we come to find ourselves, is the settlement resulting from sensuous activity in its history, the indicator of possible behaviors that refer to concrete practicable items and at the same time the domestic background on which the very particular practicable matter stands out that requires, here and now, to be continued through our initiative. But it is also a world of "limits," paths in exteriority and resistant bodies that dictate the conditions of being able or not being able to act (*utilizzare*)—here, too, according to a linkage that, through our personal biography, our received education and acquired abilities, reconnects us to living society, to the chain of generations, and finally to the entire history of humanity and the universe.

This sensuous activity, sedimented in handy "objects," this living hodology[24] of handiness contained in the world of external bodies and their properties, does not only concern objects manufactured by humankind, the products of human industry, since even so-called virgin nature and the stars in heaven, and in general everything perceivable—whether "natural" or "artificial"—lives within a social relationship, getting sedimented in the chain of generations. This is a connection interwoven with the efforts of different handy adaptations, with memories of what can be feared or obtained from it, and with appropriate behaviors. Moreover, not only is the boundary between the natural and the artificial mobile in relation to sensuous activity and the "material production of life" in different civilizations, epochs, or even social classes, occupations, professions, skills, and so forth, but in general the extension of the "material production of life" also reshapes and configures what appears most distant from this shaping or polemically marks its limit (which in reality, however, is never without some shaping). But Marx seems to say something more: that this science of nature itself is conditioned by a certain degree of development of the "material production of life," and therefore we can obtain no argument in favor of "nature per se," "before humankind and without it," from physics, chemistry, or astronomy, and so on, since "nature" is included in sensuous activity in such a way that by removing the history of the material production of life from nature, even nature dissolves into human society.

It is nonetheless necessary to highlight that in the Marxian framework we find a certain oscillation of concepts so that the dissolution of nature into sensuous activity and the material production of life is still accompanied at least by the shadow of "nature per se": see *The German Ideology*[25]: "the nature that preceded human history . . . today no longer exists anywhere (except perhaps on a few Australian coral-islands of recent origin) [. . .]" Compare "[. . .] the restricted relation of men to nature determines their restricted relation to one another, and their restricted relation to one another determines men's restricted relation to nature [. . .] just because nature is as yet hardly modified historically."

Nature that "precedes" human history, or has not yet been modified by humankind, reappears here in all of its metaphysical magnitude. Herein lie the seeds of the positivistic and scientistic motifs that subsequently tormented Marxism, giving rise to the current of "dialectical materialism," the "dialectic of nature," and so forth.

4.3. Marxist materialism as an ethos of transcendence that is ashamed of itself.

"Die Menschen haben Geschichte, weil sie ihr Leben *produzieren* müssen, und zwar müssen auf *bestimmte* Weise: dies müssen durch ihre physische Organisation gegeben; ebenso wie ihr Bewusstsein" (*Deutsche Ideologie, Gesamtausgabe*, sec. 1, vol. 5, p. 19, Marx's note).[26]

The principle that makes the detachment of culture from nature intelligible, first and foremost in the inaugural transcendence of the production of material life and in the concrete historical modes of this transcendence and then in the transcendence of the communitarian project of things at hand through other cultural transcendences (law, politics, ethics, art, religion, philosophy, science . . .), remains here in Marx's hidden and lost note. *Produzieren* is emphasized: the *must* is understood as an obvious obligation by virtue of physical organization. But in reality, the *müssen* is a transcendental *sollen*, and without this transcendental ethos of transcendence, without this principle of intelligibility, the detachment of "culture" from "nature"—and thus from history—in general remains a mystery and in particular the inaugural production itself of life in a specific mode. Marx can so little do without the activity of this *sollen* that Marxism itself becomes comprehensible, in the last instance, as a *sollen* disguised from itself and not recognized: disguised for polemical reasons toward idealisms, theologisms, utopianisms, moralisms, and the abstract "must be's" of his time.

4.4. "Deutsche Ideologie," "Gesamtausgabe."

The production of material life, both of one's own through work and others' through procreation, never repeats the natural condition in human history but is inserted into the latter as a cultural choice of a certain regime of production and procreation, a cultural choice that shapes the range and modes of life's handiness as well as the society's form of handy cooperation and articulation. But this nonrepeating, this transcending of mere vitality, this modeling that transcends the physiological order in handiness itself, becomes unintelligible precisely in its more specifically human history without the presupposition of an ethical, transcendental activity that founds and regulates the valorizing transcendences.

[The Marxian conception of history] shows that history does not end by being resolved into "self-consciousness" as "spirit of the spirit" but that each stage contains a material result, a sum of productive forces, a historically created relation to nature and of individuals to one another, which is handed down to each generation from its predecessor; a mass of productive forces, capital funds and circumstances, which on the one hand is indeed modified by the new generation, but on the other also prescribes for it its conditions of life and gives it a definite development, a special character (80).[27]

This sum of productive forces, capital funds, and social forms of intercourse, which every individual and every generation finds in existence as something given, is the real basis of what the philosophers [. . .] have deified and attacked: a real basis that is not in the least disturbed in its effect and influence on the development of men by the fact that these philosophers revolt against it as "self-consciousness" and the "unique." [. . .] In the whole conception of history up to the present, this real basis of history has either been totally disregarded or else considered as a minor matter quite irrelevant to the course of history. History must, therefore, always be written according to an extraneous standard; the real production of life appears as nonhistorical, while the historical appears as something separated from ordinary life, something extrasuperterrestrial. With this the relation of man to nature is excluded from history, and hence the antithesis of nature and history is created. The exponents of this conception of history have consequently only been able to see in history the spectacular political events and religious and other theoretical struggles, and in particular with regard to each historical epoch they were compelled to *share the illusion of that epoch* (81–82).

While the French and the English at least stick to the political illusion, which is after all closer to reality, the Germans move in the realm of the "pure spirit" and make religious illusion the driving force of history (82).

Critical observations on 81ff.:

These passages bring together the great motif of truth of Marxian philosophy and at the same time its limits. Further below (p. 89), again in polemic with the "German ideology," Marx observes that "Whilst in ordinary life every shopkeeper is very well able to distinguish between what somebody professes to be and what he really is, our historiography has not yet won this trivial insight. It takes every epoch at its word and believes that everything it says and imagines about itself is true." We should fully endorse this, even if historiography from Marx's time on and due to his influence has taken on a necessary "cunning" in the analysis of cultural products of this or that epoch. Specifically regarding "religion," the historiographic guilelessness that Marx critiqued still appears very tenacious, and the problem of putting religions back "on their feet" is still completely current when we consider the influence of a Rudolf Otto, a Mircea Eliade, a Walter Otto, a Jung, or a Kerényi in the field of "religious sciences." Having said this, however, let us turn to reservations. A religious symbol like "the realm of God" is, for Marx, a whimsy (83), and the task of historiography lies in explaining this whimsy of theoretical bubble blowing, demonstrating how it arose from a real, worldly situation: an explanation that does not even seem of great moment (Marx calls it a "learned pastime" and adds, "for it is nothing more"). With respect to the only real base—the material production of life—spiritual reflections, ideas, and so forth are arranged in a series of increasing distance from reality: and if in "politics" the reflection is closer to reality, in religion it reaches the greatest distance and therefore also the greatest "arbitrariness" (whimsy, etc.). Following this route dispels not only a religious historiography that shares the image that religious man has of himself and the world and the reasons for his belief but also any historical understanding of religious life. Religion is a "whimsy," a "chimera": the historian can, within certain limits, explain this whimsy by demonstrating its connection to the real base, reducing it to this real base; but this does not change the fact that in the final instance it remains stupidity, an *Umweg*, a detour, a waste of time, a factor in backwardness, a negative element, frivolousness, and inaccuracy.

4.5. "Theses on Feuerbach," 1845.[28]

What is real, sensuous, an object is *sensuous human activity*, and objectivity gets decided practically through effective worldly action (1st thesis, 2nd thesis): but the *man* he speaks of is not an abstract, isolated individual, nor is it *the human species* naturalistically conceived of as the mere multiplicity of individuals, but *concrete, historical man, that is, inserted into a specific set of social relations* in motion (6th thesis). Moreover the *practical activity* referred to here is first and foremost *economic activity*, the inaugural detachment of "nature" thanks to a particular mode of the social production of material goods.

With regard to the precise sense to attribute to this sensuous activity, the following passage of the *Deutsche Ideologie* is particularly important:

> So much is this activity, this unceasing sensuous labour and creation, this production, the basis of the whole sensuous world as it now exists, that, were it interrupted only for a year, Feuerbach would not only find an enormous change in the natural world, but would very soon find that the whole world of men and his own perceptive faculty, nay his own existence, were missing.[29]

In the same polemical context, Marx reprimands Feuerbach for not conceiving the sensuous world "as the total living sensuous activity of the individuals composing it":

[Feuerbach] does not see that the sensuous world around him is not a thing given direct from all eternity, remaining ever the same, but the product of industry and of the state of society; and, indeed [a product] in the sense that it is an historical product, the result of the activity of a whole succession of generations, each standing on the shoulders of the preceding one, developing its industry and its intercourse, and modifying its social system according to the changed needs.[30]

Man always has before him "a historical nature and a natural history" without ever chancing on a *nature per se* or a human history that does not include nature; and the science of nature itself is conditioned by commerce and industry: "Even this 'pure' natural science is provided with an aim, as with its material, only through trade and industry, through the sensuous activity of men."[31]

The "total living sensuous activity" of man in society as the inaugural foundation of the "world" is the projecting communitarian handiness of life: but this energy of detachment of the human from the natural, again and again founding the distinction between the detached and the detaching, is neither mere vital energy nor handiness of life but the transcendental ethos of the transcendence of life in distinct human valorizations, that is, in distinct intersubjective projections, an ethos capable of the inaugural transcendence of things at hand as well as the transcendence of what is handy in other valorizations. Precisely because it is an ethos, that is, a conditioning principle and task ceaselessly renewing itself, its *in-der-Welt-sein-sollen* is exposed to an extreme risk, to the possibility of a "drop" in its tension, to the point of involving the handy world itself. The individual risks becoming "really" abstract, getting separated from the "total sensuous activity" of generations and thus losing the world that ensues from it, the sensuousness of this world, the experiencing of one's own corporality, the mastery of one's own thoughts and actions, in a progressive destructuring.

It is necessary to rethink and examine this Marxian theme of the world as "total sensuous activity" of concrete and living humankind, comparing it with studies in modern psychology (psychoanalysis, gestalt, developmental), with the most recent ethnological knowledge, and finally with phenomenological and existential themes.

In commenting on the "Theses on Feuerbach," Auguste Cornu[32] (*K. Marx*, It. trans. [Milan, 1946], 357ff.) places particular emphasis on the polemic with traditional materialism, which does not go beyond the interpretation of the "sensible world" and reality as objects of human knowledge and the polemic against idealism, which instead conceives the Spirit as nonsensuous activity in which the world is reduced to thought. By focusing on sensuous practical activity, Marx objectivizes and does justice to the abstract object, the "isolated" individual, and speaks of the concrete man, that is, *integrated into society*, in social life, which is precisely a practical union of the natural and the human realizing itself "in human activity and especially in economic activity" (359). Now, we should observe— regarding the "Theses on Feuerbach" as presented by Cornu—that the difficulty of historical materialism lies entirely in that "especially" and its possible interpretations. There is human activity in a transcendental sense, in other words, as a principle that renders intelligible any worldly and concrete activity, whether it is aimed at the utilization of nature or oriented toward other valorizations: but this activity in a transcendental sense, as a principle of intelligibility, is the ethos of valorizing transcendence. That the realization of this principle begins necessarily with a communitarian project of the things at hand, that this project lies at the basis of further transcendences, and that it constitutes an indispensable document for measuring in every cultural field the distance between what men think they are doing and what they are really doing, all this does not mean that the "superstructures" are to be reduced to "structures" and that all cultural values are "disguises" of the economic (as the positivistic degeneration of Marxism—dialectical materialism—has mistakenly theorized).

The ethos of transcendence of life—or of "nature"—in value is transcendental in a dual sense as the principle of intelligibility of human, historical, cultural reality and as a regulative ideal of the inexhaustibility of the process of transcendence and valorization. As a transcendental principle and regulative ideal, this ethos operates even if it is not recognized, even if it bears a contradictory, limited, and confused consciousness of its own nature, and finally, even if it is polemically negated in religions, theologies, and philosophies. Through various human valorizing actions a civilization, an epoch, a historical world generally reach a specific consciousness of this ethos. They reach it, giving proof of it first with the socioeconomic order and then with the political and juridical forms of life, the arts, poetry, and science, with the various symbolisms that take the existential crisis and disclose it to the task of valorizing practicability. And if revolutions are conditioned by the maturity of social and economic forces called to carry them out, the effective change of the socioeconomic "base" is not produced automatically; it is not written in any heaven or on any earth but remains only a concrete possibility from which the ethos, if it has matured, will benefit (but it can also not benefit).

The ethos of transcendence is activity in a dual sense: in its own principle it contains the impulse toward actualization (as well as the risk of its own fall), and on the other hand it is not illusory, moralistic preaching, utopia because it gets actualized according to concrete evidence according to a Calvary that does not spare any of its painful stations. The ethos of transcendence is measured by the conditions that it was able to create in being performed and by the momentum with which it carries out the next step ahead: conditions without momentum and momentum without conditions only give proof of its fall, its indolence, its lethargy.

4.6. Loss of object and of sensuous activity.
   Alienation.

The ancient ideology of alienation is basically mythical-religious: it narrates the detachment of humankind from absolute being and the subsequent human reintegration into it. In the Judeo-Christian tradition this narration is articulated in the times of creation, the fall, incarnation, and the second coming; in Hegel it takes on an idealistic and immanentistic[33] form of the idea, of alienation of the idea in nature, and of the progressive realization of the idea in the course of human history. Feuerbach instead assigns an inverse meaning to alienation: God alienates himself in the world or the idea that alienates itself in nature become here man that, for practical reasons of protection and consolation alienates his own essence in God, imagining himself as a being in which to project his highest qualities and to whom he attributes, reversing the real terms, the creation of nature and man. Marx, through the mediation of Hess,[34] assigns the root of religious alienation to socioeconomic alienation. The loss of essence that is manifested in religious alienation depends in the last instance on the loss of human activity that takes place in the alienated work of class-divided societies and especially in capitalist society, which leads the contradiction of alienated work to the point of definitive solution. Indeed, because of its internal dialectic, this society entails the development of the proletariat, that is, of a class whose alienation is exasperated to the point of revolutionary consciousness and in which the contradiction between the "universal" character of *production* and the "individual" one of "appropriation" acquires, through the proletariat and its ideologues, the resolving movement toward communist society.

For Marx, alienation has two distinct or connected meanings: it is the *loss of the product* of work, which becomes extraneous to the worker and hostile to him, and it is the *loss of work*, of work activity, which does not belong to the worker but to another; so that man, manifesting himself in his essence—that is, as work activity—does not belong to himself but to another. Alienation thus contains a double *loss* in the sense of a double *dispossession* (or a double expropriation). Moreover the loss of the product of work and its spontaneous activity of producing not only alienates man from himself but also man with respect to other men: that man is alienated in his essence because of the aforementioned double dispossession means that men are alienated with respect to one another, and concretely this means that a class of men is dispossessed of its work activity by another class of men who exploit this activity and reap its benefits.

This Marxian theory of alienation is based on a concept of human essence as *sensuous, objective activity*: that is, as an *active going beyond nature* and nature's immediate life. In the *Manuscripts of 1844*[35] we read, "Man *lives* on nature—means that nature is his *body*, with which he must remain in continuous interchange if he is not to die" (31). Through this *progress* (detachment, transcendence), man "duplicates himself [. . .] actively, in reality, and therefore he sees himself in a world that he has created" (32). So when in a regime of *alienated work* the object of production is taken from man, his fundamental, constitutive principle is taken from him, his essence, his objective, world-making spontaneity, and the active duplication of work is followed by the servile duplication of dispossessing alienation, of *working for an owner*.

We can certainly trace the truth of Marxian theory of the essence of man and alienation of this essence first and foremost to the concept of the essence of man as activity, as "going beyond." But this going beyond that founds all possible transcendences is not identical to handiness because handiness as a communitarian project of things at hand entails loyalty and initiative, discipline and courage, a will for relations and coherence that go beyond the simple satisfaction of a need, mere "vitality," and because beyond the operative coherence of handiness other communitarian projects of value open up, other valorizations of life.

There is thus a transcendental principle that makes handiness and other valorizations intelligible, and this principle is the transcendental ethos of transcendence of life in value: activity, but also *ethos*, duty-to-be-in-the-world for value, for the valorizing activity that makes the world a world, that founds and supports it. The *reduction* of man's essential activity to economic subjectivity forms the limit of historical materialism, while we should say that Marxian doctrine itself would not have been possible without the ethos that traverses it and supports it even if it is an ethos that is ashamed of itself and does not recognize itself as the transcendental foundation of the very revolutionary coming to awareness and the very praxis that transforms the "bourgeois" world into a "better" world.

The second kernel of Marxian theory's truth is contained in the privileged position that economic activity has in it, the communitarian project of things at hand. In effect the inaugural testimony with which the duty-to-be-in-the-world is manifested (concrete demonstration belongs to the same transcendental ethos of the transcendence of life in value) is constituted by the mode of production of material goods and by the form of society. The communitarian project of things at hand, as an inaugural detachment of the human from the natural, marks the limit within which the other valorizing transcendences will be able to take place and the influences that these other transcendences exercise on the regime of production of material goods and on the form of society. This has a particular meaning for the historiographic interpretation of epochs and civilizations and for the current transformation of the world in which we live. For historiographic interpretation, this means a precise methodological caution: never to forget to compare what people think they are doing with what they really do and to read what they really do keeping in mind their real economic and social relations. For the current transformation of the world this means that every revolutionary transformation must begin by demonstrating itself through the transformation of the socioeconomic base and that this transformation is not possible if the real productive forces for promoting it have not come to maturity.

4.7. What can "historical materialism" mean today, for people today? In the context of historiographic methodology it means the historicization of economic and social forms and particularly the economic and social form based on private property, the division of society in classes, and the people's exploitation of other people. In a bourgeois perspective this economic and social form tends to take on the character of a subject removed from history, of an essential nature of humankind, of an unalterable category of communitarian life. In the context of a political ideal, it means a coming to awareness on the part of certain productive forces that the economic and social order must be a communitarian project of things at hand in which humanity forms a utilizing center and not a mere utilized instrument, an object, a thing, a natural entity, a machine. And finally, in the context of scientific knowledge and practice—that is, of a vision of life and the world—it means the cognitive and practicable stance that the forms of society in which we live today, in the present cultural moment, must be analyzed and transformed on the basis of the fundamental criterion of an ethos that transcends life to valorize it according to certain intersubjective values, starting with the intersubjective valorization of economic and social life itself.

4.8. The strike (on the occasion of the French miners' strike against De Gaulle[36]). The strike is a great human force, a total demystification of Judgment Day; a concrete, intimate, solemn, and collective assessment of humanity's power to transform its society and shape it according to justice. The strike is not "violence": the more it is itself, responsible, disciplined, and extended to hundreds of thousands of workers, the less it needs picketing, episodes of violence and rebellion against the police; and the more it takes place in a formidable calm that does not react to provocations, confident of itself and its own unlimited power, and tranquil in its awareness of not abusing the power at its disposal. This atmosphere, this ethos is the ideal end to which a strike tends: if anything the strike is pure, irresistible moral and material force that arouses waves of growing solidarity and against which force and violence can do nothing. A tank is sufficient to defeat tens of thousands of workers bent on material violence, but all of the nuclear strength available to modern states is not enough to make a single worker capitulate. The "strike" is the weapon of a new world, the weapon that opens a passage to it.

4.9. In *Ludwig Feuerbach and the End of Classical German Philosophy*,[37] Engels, narrating the formation of the Hegelian Left around the end of the decade 1830–40, mentions the decisive importance of the destruction of traditional religion and the existing state (i.e., the struggle against orthodox bigotry and the feudal reaction of Friedrich Wilhelm IV) and specifies that "At that time [...] politics was a very thorny field, and hence the main fight came to be directed against religion." Strauss, Bauer, and Stirner all follow this line. In this struggle against religion, most of the young, more determined Hegelians were led to Anglo-Franco materialism out of the struggle's practical necessities, thereby entering into conflict with the Hegelian system, idealism. In this way the essence of Feuerbach's Christianity appeared, breaking the "system" and overturning it. "Enthusiasm was general; we all became at once Feuerbachians," says Engels, who also cites "The Holy Family"[38] to show the influence of this book on Marx. True socialism was connected to Feuerbachism, for example, that of Karl Grün,[39] as was Marx's scientific socialism through his "Theses."

We should investigate this genesis of Marxism—or more precisely, the importance of this current in the genesis of Marxism. Meanwhile, however, the fact that Marxism arose in an atmosphere filled with religious and religious-historical polemics can never be emphasized enough, nor that it fundamentally always remained at the level of these polemics, which were not updated: they did not keep in contact with their historical development, losing the drive of the historical climate that produced them and getting reduced to formulas to apply.

4.10. Antonio Gramsci, *Il materialismo storico e la filosofia di B. Croce* (Turin: Einaudi, 1948).[40]

Clearly, for the philosophy of praxis, "matter" should be understood neither in the meaning that it has acquired in the natural sciences (physics, chemistry, mechanics, etc.—meanings to be noted and studied in the terms of their historical development), nor in any of the meanings that one finds in the various materialistic metaphysics. The various physical (chemical, mechanical, etc.) properties of matter which together constitute matter itself (unless one is to fall back on a conception of the Kantian noumenon) should be considered, but only to the extent that they become a *productive "economic element."* Matter as such therefore is not our subject but how it is socially and historically organised for production, and natural science should be seen correspondingly as essentially an historical category, a human relation.

Electricity is historically active, not merely however as a natural force (e.g. an electrical discharge which causes a fire) but as a productive element dominated by man and incorporated into the ensemble of the material forces of production, an object of private property. As an abstract natural force electricity existed even before its reduction to a productive force, but it was not historically operative and was just a subject of hypothetical discourse in natural history (earlier still it was historical "nothingness," since no one was interested in it or indeed knew anything about it). (465–67)

Objective means humanly and socially being projected for things at hand.

In science, too, to seek reality outside of humanity, understood in a religious or metaphorical sense, seems nothing other than paradoxical. Without humanity what would the reality of the universe mean? The whole of science is bound to needs, to life, to the activity of humanity. Without humanity's activity, which creates all, even scientific, values, what would "objectivity" be? A chaos, i.e. nothing, a void. If one can indeed say that, because in reality, if one imagines that humanity does not exist, one cannot imagine language and thought. For the philosophy of praxis, being cannot be separated from thinking, humanity from nature, activity from matter, subject from object; if one carries out this separation, one falls into one of the many forms of religion or into senseless abstraction.[41]

There exists therefore a struggle for objectivity (to free oneself from partial and fallacious ideologies) and this struggle is the same as the struggle for the cultural unification of the human race. What the idealists call "spirit" is not a point of departure but a point of arrival, it is the ensemble of the superstructures moving toward concrete and objectively universal unification and it is not a unitary presupposition. (445–46)

We know reality only in relation to man, and since man is historical becoming, knowledge and reality are also a becoming and so is objectivity, etc. (446)

[T]his process of historical unification takes place through the disappearance of the internal contradictions which tear apart human society ... (445)

Thus "matter," but organized, historicized, anthropologized through
sensuous human activity: connection with the *Economic and Philosophical
Manuscripts of 1844* and the "Theses on Feuerbach."

Gramsci's taking back up of these themes in young Marx is very important, with the triple stimulus of the positivistic barbarization of Marxism (Engels), its mythologization as concretely operating revolutionary
energy in a particular country among the masses in movement and in a
particular cultural environment (Lenin, Stalin), and the renewed idealistic exorcism that in Italy goes by the name of Croce. Gramsci effectively
begins a further exploration and development of Marxism, and his "time-
liness" is destined to be greater and greater, even if for the moment his
influence in Italian culture (and even more so worldwide) is relatively
modest or not what it merits. Against the positivistic barbarization of
Marxism, Gramsci restored "matter" with its historical meaning as a
result—continuously in progress—of the sensuous activity of humankind
in society; so this activity, conditioned and modified over and over, is on
the one hand "objectivation," "perception of objects," and on the other
hand "objectivation" as the transformation of situations (but the actual
"perception of objects" is always a taking possession of prior historical
"transformations," and the current transformation is an institution of new
perceptive and operative conditions for the future) without it ever being
possible to encounter the object per se, nature per se, and so forth, or
absolute Spirit. But this historical "practice" in Gramsci lacks a transcendental principle of intelligibility. That is, without further qualification of
the internal force of dialectical organization that detaches the human from
the natural over and over according to a practice that gets inaugurated
with sensuous activity, with the material production of life, but which
never exhausts this activity (like the myth of a nature entirely subjugated
by humans). Nor is it exhausted as sensuous activity and the material production of life since a host of valorizations that are not reducible to the
communitarian project of things at hand get inserted in this valorizing
activity and in turn react variously on it. Gramsci's "practice" (like sensuous activity in the young Marx, moreover) is a simple presupposition
(that it is like this because it is like this) without reaching the intelligible
internal principle of its dialectical movement beyond nature into the economic and "beyond" the economic in other valorizations. This principle,
which is the transcendental ethos of transcendence of life in valorizing,
intersubjective (social) activities has no place in Gramsci (the historical
reasons for this are transparent: as already in the young Marx, in Gramsci

we find the polemical reasons against the idealistic "Spirit" still operating in an immediate way, and these reasons conceal to him, as they did to Marx, not the abstraction of the spirit but the power that conditions every abstraction and every return to the concrete—in other words, precisely the ethos of transcendence). Gramsci's missing recognition of the ethos of transcendence is responsible for some mythologizing shadows that still weigh on his reformed Marxism: when Gramsci speaks of a process of unifying humanity that leads to the "disappearance of the internal contradictions that lacerate society," or of a "struggle for objectivity" as a point of arrival that, once reached, will allow us to speak again about Spirit, the theme—of a religious, theological, idealistic-Hegelian derivation—crops back up of a short-term process and the historical exhaustibility of the struggle for objectivity. That "bourgeois society" contains contradictions, that these contradictions ripen for the emergence of socialist society, that among these conditions there are new historical forces that can realize this emergence, that everyone today must work as best they know and can to suppress the contradictions of bourgeois society: all this does not mean that socialist (and communist) society will once and for all eliminate "all" possible social contradictions, that new ones never experienced in human history will not be generated, and that we will not have to become aware of being and fighting for their elimination. Nor does this mean, moreover, that the detachment of humanity from nature will cease to be a problem through socialist planning of the technical domination of nature, that nature will be entirely "subjugated" to humanity, and "spirit" will be liberated once and for all (all phrases that can also, in the emotion of revolutionary action, have a compelling significance, but in which in the last instance we do not think at all about what they are saying, because what they say is nothing, and in reality we only think something very historically determined; that is, we think that the contradictions of bourgeois society "must" be eliminated and that the debate should be moved to a more human level, more homogeneous with the real development reached by humanity).

4.11. Marx and Merleau-Ponty.
   [...]
   In the first thesis on Feuerbach we read, "The chief defect of all hitherto existing materialism [...] is that the thing, reality, sensuousness, is conceived only in the form of the *object or of contemplation*, but not as *sensuous human activity, practice*, not subjectively."[42] This discloses a conception of *praxis* that no longer has its support in a process that necessarily leads to a final synthesis (as in Judeo-Christian tradition or in Hegel himself) but which has its sole resource in a coming to awareness that decides about

humanity and the world: a coming to awareness exposed concretely to infinite vicissitudes and perils, which "can" also dim and annihilate itself, not producing a "revolution" but chaos. When Merleau-Ponty says that Marxism charges man with an immense responsibility (*Sense et non-sense* [Paris: Nagel, 1948][43]), he is certainly in the right. It is precisely because of the terror of this responsibility—that is, the extreme effort that Marxism asks of praxis and its *ethos*—that the ancient metaphysic of necessity and vulgar materialism troubles the history of Marxism itself and that, in another sense, such a large part of humanity clasps desperately to its old God with an agony that seems like it will not raise humankind but destroy the world.

[. . .]

"Religion is more than a hollow appearance; it is a phenomenon based on interpersonal relationships" (128). Correct: but religion does not have reality only as "the realization in fantasy of the human essence" (127) according to what we read in the "Introduction" A Contribution to the Critique of Hegel's Philosophy of Right," or as "symbolic expression of the social and human drama" (127), but as a horizon of reintegration of the human with respect to the risk of alienation in civilizations and epochs in which the religious detour was the only *road* possible. Only with modern civilization, that is, with the coming to awareness that religious life is a detour, is this *road* becoming authentically impracticable precisely because it has entered into conflict with the awareness of a detour for reaching the human, of a "long road" as opposed to a "short road." Mystification arises through persisting with the "long road" when the exploring consciousness of life has discovered a "short road" and cannot authentically follow both. The tracks of human steps begin to get erased along the harsh and torturous mountain path, with grass covering it, and it crosses the most impassable mountain chains in tunnels: but when this road was not yet constructed, the path abandoned today was the only line of communication. Moreover, there is hardly a comparison because we are still constructing the valley road and many still follow the old path; and even because once we have constructed it, we will still need to protect it from the wear of time, and we will be able to abandon it for an easier and better route. Indeed, the accessibility of human communication has no definitive solutions.

[. . .]

7

Anthropology and Philosophy

1. The Communitarian Project of Things at Hand

1.1. [...] The world of things at hand, which in Heidegger coincides with inauthentic existence, is correctly redeemed in Abbagnano.[1] But we need to keep in mind that the world of things at hand is already valorized; indeed, it receives its first, initial valorization, the concrete base of all the others. Second, the world is at hand through the productive social coexistence of practicable, instrumental, and technical memories of economic needs and of goods aiming to satisfy them and in particular the fundamental means of interpersonal communication that is language. Third, handiness forms the basis of the human world, its first inaugural "project," but the other valorizations modify the world, making it domestic, culturally meaningful, and practicable. [...]

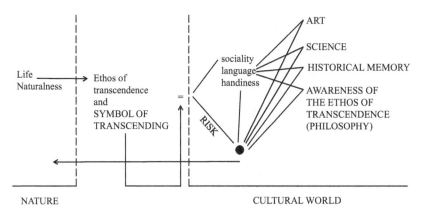

1.2. The initial valorization of the transcendence of life in value is communitarian being-with[2] in a domestic world of things at hand. This being-with, which entails loyalties and initiatives, encompasses within its own sphere of valorization the instincts of communitarian life; control of the human body with corresponding instruments of human communication with things (senses) and of people among themselves (language); the economic regime of the production of goods and the shaping of needs; technological procedures for controlling nature ("material instruments" and "mental instruments"). With this, life has already transcended in a cultural sense: the fundamental historical condition of a "world" gets shaped in which the valorizing presentification of the *ethos* can move forth—that is, the distinction of other autonomous intersubjective valorizations such as the natural sciences, art, historiographic consciousness, philosophy, and finally, the awareness the *ethos* achieves of itself in moral doctrines and theories of manners.

1.3. Paci.[3] The *ethos* of transcendence in the value of valorization. Is the *ethos* of transcendence a value among values? What is its relationship to other values? Is it form? What is its relationship to other forms and how do we justify the movement from one form to another and the negative of each of them? And above all: what is the relationship of this *ethos* with existence? This unavoidable problematic must return to central consideration if we want to remove Italian historicism from the impasse in which it seems to me to be stuck from the time of the Croce-Paci polemic.[4]

Paci's solution—that is, that the useful is the existential matter from which spiritual forms raise themselves—is unacceptable for two reasons. The first reason is that the useful, the vital, and the economic appear in the Crocean formulation to be enveloped by a certain confusion, since in a same categorical denomination one puts together "raw and green" vitality,[5] lacking any further education whatsoever, and the socioeconomic shaping that instead constitutes an intersubjective value, a certain historically determined communitarian project of satisfying needs in a coherent way.[6] Now, this socioeconomic shaping is hardly comparable to vitality, hardly "raw and green" and "lacking any further education," since any socioeconomic regime is an extremely complex organism of production technologies, of the distribution of labor, of coordinated and interacting individual skills, of social groupings and relations among them. The quality and quantity of individual needs, the means of satisfying or renouncing them, and in general the very possibility of an economic projection of the life of individuals cannot disregard the socioeconomic system in which individuals live, that is, the cultural form that the economic and social have shaped with an "education" that broadly conditions everyone who participates in the system. Moreover, technological innovations, changes in productive regimes, the formation of new social strata, and political-economic revolutions are not ascribable to the vitality-matter that troubles single individuals as such but to a formal coherence that transcends it in every sense, to a value that models the very world of "needs," that educates and regulates their rhythm in a communitarian way.

The second reason that makes Paci's theorization unacceptable is that conceiving the useful as the essential matter of spiritual forms[7] in no way facilitates an understanding of the passage to these forms, since precisely what induces existential matter to pass to spiritual forms remains unclear. In the last instance, it lacks the justification of this passage, that is, the power that transcends the sphere of needs, just as it transcends all of the other categorial values without however ever being able to transcend itself, being the rule of all transcendences.

In Paci's solution the movement is oratorically asserted, not justified. Indeed, we do not understand why the natural moment of humanity—humankind that is hungry, thirsty, sleepy, and sexual in the same way as every other beast—does not stay in the opaque beastliness of its need but carries out a double transcendence in the sense of choosing a particular socioeconomic regime and being able to live only within this formal horizon, and in the other sense, of going beyond material needs that are in any case satisfied. One will say that existence encompasses all the other forms embryonically, and—besides matter—*also* these spiritual forms. But who or what will awaken them from their slumber? Who or what will take them from potential to action? Who or what transforms the animal into culturally determined humans? The *also* that Paci speaks of is gratuitous; it is a sermon superimposed on the real, not the reason for the real.

But Paci's theorization of existential matter and spiritual forms obscures the very dynamic of socioeconomic life. Existential matter is certainly not lacking in history: the great merit of historical materialism is its having given great significance to the historicity of economic matter. But if it were really "matter" in Paci's sense, what actually forms the reason of its internal movement, its passing from one economic regime to another, from one form of society to another? The laws of development of a certain socioeconomic order, the contradictions in which it gets wrapped up, per se already represent a mystery in the sphere of the raw and green "vitality" Croce speaks of. But in the sphere of "existential matter" that Paci speaks of, what actually prevents a society from perishing because of its contradictions (a possibility that in fact should not be ruled out)? And what, instead, makes it transform into another society? Where does that "better, more just world" come from that in the consciousness of certain rising new classes guarantees the transformation? Is that "better" or more just reducible to the more economically advanced, or is the possibility of this economically "more advanced" not enough to make the more advanced become reality? Does not that revolutionary consciousness of the most just suggest a force that we would try in vain to reduce to laws of the development of society even if it requires certain economic-historical and social-historical conditions?

We should thus by no means consider existential matter incapable of carrying out the dynamic functions that Paci assigns it, or that the *transcending force* is Croce's "vitality" or Paci's "existential matter," but an *ethical force*, the *ethos* of transcendence. How should we understand this force? First of all, we should rule out that it is a categorial value that can be confused with the moral awareness that a given person, civilization, or epoch has of itself—when we say, for example, "in coming generously to the aid of this person in need, that person did a good deed," or "this mother sacrificed herself for her children," or "the ruling class of this country has a strong sense of its public duties," or "the first Christian communities based moral relations on love for one's neighbor." The *ethos* of transcendence is a force operating much more deeply, a force that conditions the unfolding of all categorial values, starting with the socioeconomic one. The *ethos* of transcendence is a unique drive to transcend natural vitality in categorial values, and the totality of these valorizing transcendences conditions existence as individual life that the *ethos* makes pass into the socioeconomic universalization and the others.

1.4. Through the horizon of handiness, life receives its initial shaping for humanity as a "world of domestic things" subdivided according to spheres of utilitarian practicability. This domesticity of the world, the result of a culturally conditioned education and personal attitudes, in part forms the opaque background of daily life (things at hand not actually used but that can always be used if needed). In part it appears in actual decisions that are so simple they do not require a particular effort on the part of consciousness (the daily deployment of minute operative skills, the habitual use of useful things, etc.); in part it emerges in handiness behaviors that require great exertion for their success, a vigilant sense of responsibility, or even the inventive effort of a new technique or skill. In the domesticity of the world—of a certain culturally conditioned world—lives a host of actual or possible memories, of effective behaviors and operative limits to these behaviors; the skills achieved by past generations live in it, the results of the work of innumerable contemporaries, the outcome of our being educated from our earliest infancy to act in such and such a way with the things of the world and our bodies. And at various levels of awareness, in this tradition of things at hand it is called to produce itself, thereby bringing its manifold contribution. Things are traces of what a culture usually makes of them for the useful and of what we can do with them here and now: multifaceted echoes of utilizing decisions and of our own education with reference to things at hand, they exist through these echoes, they are supported and receive their first sense from them. And our being-there is first and foremost founded by this duty to be in the world of handiness, by this uninterrupted transcending of life through the intersubjective order of appropriate skills, by this shaping of needs and ways to satisfy them according to the intersubjective value of the economic [. . .].

1.5. These subjects in Paci's (and Abbagnano's) positive existentialism are largely in line with the perspective I have chosen for my monograph on the "end of the world." The transcendental *ethos* of the transcendence of life in value is in line with the interpretation of Kant's transcendental proposed by Paci[8] and is contained in Abbagnano's concept of "structure of existence." Similarly, the collapse of the *ethos* of valorizing transcendence along the entire possible front of valorization (i.e., the collapse of the transcendental value of valorization itself, of being's duty-to-be) is connected to Abbagnano's (and Paci's) theme of a foundation of existing that can be lost, undone, and therefore of a world that "can" or "cannot" have its foundation. It is necessary to point out, however, that in my perspective the world *must* be founded precisely because it can lose its foundation; that founding the world means valorizing life not according to being but according to distinct values of the duty-to-be; that the initial evidence of this valorization is given by the communitarian project of an at-hand world, and that further transcendences are disclosed by this initial valorization; that the risk of the *ethos* of transcendence's collapse entails the risk of being-in-the-world's collapse; and that this possibility gives rise to the radical nothingness of the collapse of valorization along the whole gamut of the valorizable as well as the dialectic of negative and positive in the sphere of specific individual valorizations; and finally, that if being is a duty-to-be, being-there gets founded as duty-to-be [*doverci essere*] for value, and existing is not "nothingness" but always constitutes itself anew as the passage from the nothingness of nonvalorized life to the duty-to-be of valorization (i.e., it constitutes itself through transcendence and first and foremost through socioeconomic transcendence). Two problems therefore arise: that of the nexus of valorizations in the progress of the *ethos* of transcendence's self-consciousness, and that of mythical-ritual symbolism as a means of recovery from the risk *ethos* of transcendence's total collapse.

1.6. Enzo Paci, *Il nulla e il problema dell'uomo* (Turin: Taylor, 1950) (with regard to *Il mondo magico*[9]). "The risk of a personality getting lost in anxiety represents the utilitarian moment" (125).[10] This is where Paci and I disagree. The risk of losing presence, as I theorized it in *Mondo magico*, should not be traced to the economic, because the economic is the

economic order, and the economic order is anything but the risk of losing presence; on the contrary, it is the initial value with which the *ethos*
of transcendence overcomes that risk. An economic order based on the
division of labor between males and females—in which the males devote
themselves to big game hunting, the females to small game hunting and
the gathering of edible roots—already contains a certain project for the
shaping and satisfaction of communitarian needs in relation to the need
for nourishment. To the extent that this project is carried out, presentification takes place, and an economic and instrumental domesticity of the
world gets established, if only an extremely circumscribed and precarious
one. The risk of losing presence threatens the entire, vast sphere of life that
falls outside the control of the economic coherence of a hunter-gatherer
society and that does not find answers in the available technologies and
instruments. Even in the sphere of hunting and gathering itself there is a
wide margin for the irrational, for what escapes civil control: the encounter with an edible animal has risks, and moreover edible species may be
lacking; gathering may not give the desired results, and so forth. Like
Croce, Paci confuses economicity—which is the value of a certain specialized order of needs and the means for satisfying them—with vitality as a
generic need in order to live. Paci does not realize that a sphere of the irrational arises only in relation to the perspective, even a restricted one, of
a world that people control with their "work." "The barbarism that is always threatening, Vico's Lernean Hydra, is the loss of the categories that
make up man in his historicity" (126). Agreed, but with the caveat that
among the categories we lose is the initial one of the communitarian handiness of the vital, the projecting being-with for needing a certain food and
for feeding ourselves, the constructive dialogue among these needy people, so that it is forbidden for people to isolate themselves in the sphere itself of nourishment. In this relationship, people are animals in which even
eating becomes a "problem" and in which organic "hunger" is reshaped
into regimes of "appetites" and "tastes" corresponding to the search for
and production of foods according to rules, in an asking and a receiving
of produced food—again, according to rules—in a shaping of organic ap-
petite itself according to socialized and familiar foods, and above all in being able to call into question rules and models of communitarian feeding,
establishing new coherences. [. . .]

2. Nature Is in Culture

2.1. [. . .] Naturalism,[11] aestheticism, and so forth. Fetishizing absolutization.
    The struggle against naturalism is not the struggle against the science
of nature in the name of philosophy but the struggle against the absoluti-

zation of a particular valorization in the name of being's duty-to-be. Similarly, in the name of the same need we must fight against the absolutization
of art (aestheticism), of politics (the perfect and definitive society, the
state that prescribes culture's mandatory *itinera*; legislation that claims
to exhaust justice and as such is unreformable; legalism that suffocates
every other possible evaluation of humankind, etc.), of the philosophical solution that extinguishes philosophizing in a closed system of being
and that establishes once and for all the necessary plan of human history
up to its conclusion. We find a response to the same need in the struggle
against moralism that presumes to absolutize a particular historical form of
awareness of the ethos of transcendence, forgetting that that ethos is an
inexhaustible beyond, carried out in every particular form of valorization—
even in the "duty-to-be for the handiness of life." The struggle against
these different modes of absolutization, which is carried out every day by
ordinary people and which is the eminent task of philosophizing, simply
means this: that if the value of valorization is the nontranscendable that
presides over all valorizing transcendences, and if, owing to its duty-to-be,
it is never exhaustible in and of itself or in any of its particular valorizations, no work according to value exhausts the value whose work it is, and
no value according to the ethos of transcendence exhausts this ethos. So
if life must be transcended in work that has value, the work that has value
must be transcended not only in another work according to the same value
but also according to work that realizes another value, and so forth, again
and again, perpetually. [. . .]

2.2. Nature per se.

Nature per se, before and independently of any human intervention,
can have a practical meaning in the sense that it is of *practical use* in the
operations that humankind carries out to exercise its effective domination
over nature, behaving *as if* there were a nature before and independent of
any human intervention. But this fundamental methodological principle
of the natural sciences, this "nature" that is not controlled if not by "obey-
ing it," this operative "as if" that postulates a "per se" on which it operates
is an abstraction carried out *within* the cultural history of man and that,
in its ways as in its outcomes and effective practices, is entirely conditioned by that history. In other words it is always included in a practical
activity of detachment from the immediacy of living in the concreteness
of a specific society. In this perspective humankind is always detaching
itself from nature and can never skip this cultural-historical detaching
to definitively reach "nature per se." And the cultural-historical detaching itself from nature, and always being inside this movement of detachment, founds natural "things"—that is, a certain background of possible

handinesses[12] in which each current handiness stands out. This is a "domestic" background, a "world" that is domestic, a world in that it contains human projects that were once carried out and therefore became projectable or aimed to become a stimulus and support for new handinesses and projections.

Nature is the horizon that signals the inexhaustibility of the valorization of life according to a communitarian project of things at hand. In this sense it always lies "beyond" at-hand projection, manifesting itself as resistance, as substance, as exteriority that in and of itself conspires with humanity. But at the same time, nature is what lies "inside" at-hand projection, as a horizon of the possible handinesses accumulated in a whole society's own cultural history. It is therefore implicit and expressible memory of a certain order of skills and practicable technologies that I can avail myself of and of which I am in fact availing myself of now in the modality of habit, as obvious behavior that serves as a background to everyday life; now in the routine of a trade and profession; and finally, now as the invention of a new technology, in the elaboration of new material and mental instruments for handiness. This "beyond" and this "inside" are correlative and inseparable in that the beyond takes shape within a particular projection that one has available and that can be concretely implemented, and it never appears "per se." Similarly, as the available projectability always entails a specific limit, a circumscribed sphere of possible operations—and therefore a beyond that resists—it escapes, opposing itself to the project, rebelling against handiness as a never-tamed "per se," and indicating an unlimited series of new efforts to tame it.

Nature always appears *in* culture, at least if culture is led back to the overall ethos that encompasses its valorizing transcendences and to the consciousness of that ethos without being fetishized in one of its dimensions, as, for example, the naturalistic valorization of the sciences (where nature is effectively assumed as if it were prior and independent of any human cultural molding).

2.3. Life and handiness.

The horizon of "world" remains inexplicable without life and handiness as a particular valorization of life. The sun, the moon, the stars, heaven, clouds, mountains, plants, animals, people, dwellings, material instruments, our body itself as the nearest instrument: all of these form the "world" horizon in its initial valorization, which is the actual or possible handiness. The "things" surrounding us, present or absent with regard to our actual purposeful effort, are "things" in that they refer to our possible behavior to them according to the value of handiness, that is, according to a project that inseparably includes a resistance to usability (*adoperabilità*), as well as usability in a certain way and within certain limits. The sun is what we can do with it: it indicates a limited sphere of usability, and precisely this sphere with its limits (and with its *resistance* to an unlimited usability) constitutes it as a "thing" of the world. The sun is what heats, but it can burn; it is what illuminates the human workday and what, when we wake up in the morning and perceive its light, shapes the time of that work; it is what is connected to the seasons and therefore to the time of doing this or that for our benefit; and so forth. The sun, as a thing, is a center of practicable possibilities within certain limits: possibilities and limits that make it domestic, familiar, worldly. But precisely because of its inseparable relation with practicable, usable possibility, the sun is a "culturally conditioned object," since every civilization differently constructs the extension and quality of handiness with reference to it: it is always the same sun life, but the intention in which it is embraced is different in a civilization of hunter-gatherers, nomadic pastoralists, farmers, or a great industrial city. In any case, in one way or another the sun is "domesticated," and to the extent that it is domesticated, that is, transcended in handiness, it can become obvious, and as obviousness excluded from actual perception and relegated to the background, leaving presentification free and available for other perceptions of at-hand things. As something at-hand the sun is fortunately not an always-presentified entity: every day we live in solar light "thinking of something else." But this happens to the extent that the sun, which through cultural effort has become *obviously useful*, can become *unconsciously used* in our daily activities. In this unconsciousness, however, the human history of cultural handinesses of the sun lives in an implicit way, with its alternatives and its decisions: it lives in a hut or in a house that protects us from the sun's burning rays, or in a warming fire that substitutes for its heat; it lives in all of the technologies produced by humankind to defend itself from the sun or harness its power for civilized uses. The "obviousness" of the sun, the disidentification of its cultural history, the ability to forget it in order to deal with other things, relegating it to the sphere of the unconscious as-if, do not constitute "losing the sun" or "losing oneself in the habitual with regard to the sun"[13] but on the contrary, *our liberation from the sun as actual handy* (utilizzante) *perception*, a conserving of it in the world of things already transcended in handiness, so that it is possible to direct intentionality elsewhere, to what lies in our daily life as much less *obvious*. Moreover the sun is *obvious* only in a relative way, that is, in relation to the limits in which its handy acculturation has been successful and in which it circumscribes a sphere of useful behaviors that are so obvious as to be able to be carried out without significant or problematic effort: we open our windows to the morning light in the freedom of being able to concentrate our attention elsewhere.

But as little we touch of the limits of the sun's cultural practicability (and every civilization and regime of existence poses these limits differently), the star returns and emerges in purposeful presentification; its cultural history must be regained within the limits it has reached in order to adapt it to the critical situation, to decide and overcome this situation with an initiative that is "original" to varying degrees.

2.4. The "world" is always *given* in its communitarian totality in order to be *regained* in the specificity and peculiarity of a valorization, and it is always *removed* in the habitual in order to trace the intimate, personal, emerging figure of one's own personal valorizing initiative in this more or less anonymous and socialized experience. But the givenness, the habitualness and the obviousness of the world are possible as immediate loyalty to the initiatives of past generations, or to our past and everything that connects us to it through our cultural biography: if they make a ground and homeland on which my personal task of the moment rises up, it is because only through this anonymous domesticity of the world it is possible to make oneself available to perform it in the continually renewing recovery of "my" original and individualized choices. The individual can "restart" some aspect of the world—and one always restarts it as if one were the first person to begin being a person for the first time—only if all other aspects momentarily serve as a background, and moreover if this background implicitly includes a human meaning, a work of humanization developed in the obvious domesticity of the environment, a fundamental proof of nonsolitude, of a subdued, practicable chorus spreading out in space and time. Givenness and recovery thus lie in a dialectic nexus whose disarticulation signals the collapse of the world and presentification to it. So, for example, when the world's subdued, practicable chorus loses its quality as a "foundation" in which my valorizing initiative is inaugurated, when the background becomes a problem and everything is called into question without leaving leeway for transcendence and without making itself the "launching point" for the "initial leap," the world loses its moment of "domesticity," as a "homeland of action," a solid "ground" on which to place skilled practicable roots, and it becomes something that dispossesses, that steals every private sphere (see the passage by Minkowski cited in note a, p. 331, of Merleau-Ponty's *Phénomenologie* . . .[14]).
   [. . .]

2.5. It is a world of adults that founds civilization and its values and that shapes and orients the childhood and puberty of new generations through education. The family, the economic and social order, the system of prohibitions and obligations, the norms of interpersonal relations, the variety of cultural institutions, mythical-ritual symbols, the arts and more or less advanced mental and technological instruments for controlling nature: all these constitute the adult world's choices, initiatives that had their origin in adults' decisions and that have acquired the strength of traditions to be transmitted to children and youths. There are civilizations that differ greatly with regard to the "position" of males and females, fathers and mothers, or other "relatives" of this or that social group, but there has never been and there can never be a civilization in which children and the very young have a culturally hegemonic function. Once they become adults (according to norms and "passages" that vary from civilization to civilization), the new generations undoubtedly enter in varying degrees into the hegemonic sphere of civilization in motion, of the power of control and initiative: but until they become adults, they do not possess *pleno iure* this human right. Infants find the fundamental norm itself of interpersonal communication, language, already forged by adults: they learn it gradually, up to the moment they become adults, and in turn they will participate more or less actively in the "history of the language." Now the limit and, basically, the misunderstanding of psychoanalysis lies in its claim to want to deduce the adult cultural world from the history of childhood; or—in other words—to reduce the cultural values of the adult world, part of a given civilization or historical epoch, to a superego that is the "product" of that history. The arbitrary and unilateral "as if" of that deduction and reduction is concealed in the concept of "displacement," the true knot of contradictions in the psychoanalytic approach. What gets repressed and pushed into the unconscious is the product of the pressure exercised by the system of choices decided by the adult world: how can this system of choices in turn be considered exclusively the product of childhood repressions (projections, sublimations, etc.)? The truth is that it is necessary to start from the concreteness of a specific adult cultural life and subsequently ask how an adult world shapes new generations, grafting a specific cultural order onto a merely biological order: from this, a particular way of "becoming adults" surely develops that in turn conditions the system of choices. But in the last instance, primacy lies with mature humanity.

3. Lived World, Lived Body

3.1. Proust.

The world as a familiar, settled, and normal backdrop for our valorizing emergence is the hidden and always available indicator of possible practicable paths. However, these paths are obvious and habitual in that they conserve the human action of settlement carried out across millennia

to reach the here and now of the present emergence[15] through our biography. The present beyond of valorization runs through them all suddenly in order to be gathered in the valorizing transcendence in question
here and now. Suddenly transcending to be gathered in presentification
founds the relative security of the world, its being able to be lived as a
backdrop and support for ongoing initiative and as a welcoming homeland
for being-there.

Suddenly transcending means "entrusting oneself to others who have
transcended," accepting the multifaceted, choral resonance of the human
work of settlement, relying on this settling diligence with an act of humility and devoted loyalty, to remain available for the task of valorization that
awaits us here and now. The familiarity, settlement, and normality of the
world—this homeland backdrop of our emergence—contain a message
whose warmth gets confused with the obvious feeling of being a living
body: "Come on, you're not alone," this message says, "but along the path
you are accompanied by the work of an infinite multitude of people, a
multitude that includes the dead and the living, and even if it reaches you
through your most direct educators, in reality it makes you a part of by-
gone ages and vanished civilizations."

Compare the theme of reawakening in Proust's *Recherche*.

3.2. The world as a practicable backdrop. The world as skilled emergence.
The theme of reawakening in *La recherche du temps perdu*.[16]

Proust's analysis illustrates very well how being-in-the-world—finding
oneself in it as in a familiar, settled, obvious backdrop from which the
various dominant actualities presentifying being-in-the-world emerge
in a continuous flow—in reality contains an immense human history
lived through personal biography and joined with the entire history of
humanity through education.[17] The distinction between the world as a
domestic backdrop of practicability and the world as a flow of hegemonic
emergences in which being-there gathers again and again in its valorizing transcendence indicates the degree to which individual being-there
is chorally, collectively conditioned. Without a backdrop of domesticity,
of anonymous and settled givenness, it is not possible to establish the
here and now of presentification; but that domestic, settled horizon is
such inasmuch as we instantly climb the slope of a very strenuous human
history in it without a memory of names, dates, and events, giving proof
of itself solely in the domesticity and settlement of the backdrop. This
history is certainly indistinct, buried in the unconscious, squeezed within
the obvious and habitual, but nonetheless existing if the domesticity and
settlement of its backdrop conditions and supports our emergence, and

if its dismantling marks the closure of any possible practicable horizon and proclaims the radical catastrophe of being-in-the-world.

[...]

> A sleeping man holds in a circle around him the sequence of the hours, the order of the years and worlds. He consults them instinctively as he wakes and reads in a second the point on the earth he occupies, the time that has elapsed before his waking; but their ranks can be mixed up, broken. (5)

Proust gives a fine analysis of the disorientation that can follow reawakening. He describes how he sometimes woke up in the middle of the night, not knowing where he was and who he was, experiencing existence with the primordial elementariness that an animal feels throbbing in its gut: it is a disorientation in which he was "more destitute than a cave dweller."[18] A series of evocations for a few moments helped him to regain his where and when and his relationship to the world:

> [T]hen the memory—not yet of the place where I was, but of several of those where I had lived and where I might have been—would come to me like help from on high to pull me out of the void from which I could not have got out on my own; I crossed centuries of civilization in one second, and the image confusedly glimpsed of oil lamps, then of wing-collar shirts, gradually recomposed my self's original features. (5–6)

When he reawakened in this "historic" disorientation, while he fretted unsuccessfully in order to find where he was, everything spun around him in the darkness: "things, countries, years." But his reconquest takes place through his body; indeed, it is the conquest of his own body in relation to the external world:

> My body, too benumbed to move, would try to locate, according to the form of its fatigue, the position of its limbs so as to deduce from this the direction of the wall, the placement of the furniture, so as to reconstruct and name the dwelling in which it found itself. Its memory, the memory of its ribs, its knees, its shoulders, offered in succession several of the rooms where it had slept, while around it the invisible walls, changing place according to the shape of the imagined room, spun through the shadows. And even before my mind, hesitating on the thresholds of times and shapes, had identified the house by reassembling the circumstances, it—my body—would recall the kind of bed in each one, the location of

the doors, the angle at which the light came in through the windows, the existence of a hallway, along with the thought I had had as I fell asleep and that I had recovered upon waking. [...] [A]nd my body, the side on which I was resting, faithful guardians of a past my mind ought never to have forgotten, recalled to me the flame of the night-light of Bohemian glass, in the shape of an urn, which hung from the ceiling by little chains, the mantlepiece of Siena marble, in my bedroom at Combray, at my grand-parents' house, in faraway days which at this moment I imagined were present without picturing them to myself exactly and which I would see more clearly in a little while when I was fully awake. (6; cf. Sartre and Merleau-Ponty on the body)

Habit! That skillful but very slow housekeeper who begins by letting our mind suffer for weeks in a temporary arrangement; but whom we are nevertheless truly happy to discover, for without habit our mind, reduced to no more than its own resources, would be powerless to make a lodging habitable. (8)

On the *memories* and *recollections* buried in things and that suddenly and involuntarily rise again by chance, and so forth:

I find the Celtic belief very reasonable, that the souls of those we have lost are held captive in some inferior creature, in an animal, in a plant, in some inanimate object, effectively lost to us until the day, which for many never comes, when we happen to pass close to the tree, come into possession of the object that is their prison. Then they quiver, they call out to us, and as soon as we have recognized them, the spell is broken. Delivered by us, they have overcome death and they return to live with us.

It is the same with our past. It is a waste of effort for us to try to sum-mon it, all the exertions of our intelligence are useless. The past is hid-den outside the realm of our intelligence and beyond its reach, in some material object (in the sensation that this material object would give us) which we do not suspect. It depends on chance whether we encounter this object before we die, or do not encounter it. (44)

[...]

All of Combray unfolded, emerged, from that cup of tea: through the smell and flavor, the taste of that piece of madeleine dipped in the lime-blossom tea that Aunt Léonie used to give him in Combray, from the knowledge of that smell and that flavor, even if only much later he would discover the reasons (47ff.).

Even the very simple act that we call "seeing a person we know" is in part an intellectual one. We fill the physical appearance of the individual we see with all the notions we have about him, and of the total picture that we form for ourselves, these notions certainly occupy the greater part. In the end they swell his cheeks so perfectly, follow the line of his nose in an adherence so exact, they do so well at nuancing the sonority of his voice as though the latter were only a transparent envelope that each time we see this face and hear this voice, it is these notions that we encounter again, that we hear. (19)

Compare Sarte, in *Nausea*, the library employee's face,[19] and so forth.

What does the Proustian search for lost time express? Not the free unfolding of poetic memory, the lyrical effusion of recollection in the recreating and transforming energy of poetry, but instead the problematization of that very power of recalling the past in a valorizing, practicable horizon that is at the root of any cultural life and any being-in-the-world according to intersubjective values. Proust experiences the crisis of an I-world relationship; he descends to a level in which things, persons, and one's own body become anonymous tombs—indeed, mass graves—of the past. What surprises is the emergence of a primordial remembering from which the world gains sense and for which it can be constituted and maintained as an obvious, domestic, at-hand world—the initial form of our freedom. Combray that rises up from a cup of tea means that on a gloomy winter day and with the prospect of a sad tomorrow, when it seems that the world is crumbling, a turnaround can begin even with a cup of tea. In the mystery of a murky affectivity the recovery reconnects the tie with days in Combray and, through this very concrete fragment of experienced cosmogony, reconquers the beyond of a world that until then was suffered as worn out, transient, and collapsing.

As soon as I had recognized the taste of the piece of madeleine dipped in lime-blossom tea that my aunt used to give me (though I did not yet know and had to put off to much later discovering why this memory made me so happy), immediately the old gray house on the street, where her bedroom was, came like a stage set to attach itself to the little wing opening onto the garden that had been built for my parents behind it [. . .] and with the house the town, from morning to night and in all weathers, the Square, where they sent me before lunch, the streets where I went on errands, the paths we took if the weather was fine. And as in that game enjoyed by the Japanese in which they fill a porcelain bowl with water and steeping in it little pieces of paper until then indistinct which, the

moment they are immersed, stretch and twist, assume colors and distinctive shapes, become flowers, houses, human figures, firm and recognizable, so now all the flowers in our garden and in M. Swann's park, and
the water lilies on the Vivonne, and the good people of the village and
their little dwellings and the church and all of Combray and its surroundings, all of this which is acquiring form and solidity, emerged, town and
gardens alike, from my cup of tea. (47–48)

All this has come out of my teacup: that is, the affective transformation
contained in a savored sip of tea in turn contained these implicit memories, only later made explicit by a memory and reflection that were no
longer strictly immediate, improvised, and random.

The Proustian search for lost time does not so much express the free
unfolding of poetry's recreating and transfiguring energy (though at
times this poetry shows up in the current of remembrance) as it does
the problematization of a primordial power at the root of all cultural life
and all being-in-the-world according to intersubjective values: the power
to recall the past again and again, at various levels of effort and awareness, and the power to recover this past again and again in a valorizing,
practicable horizon. Proust is the literary expert—at times the poet—of
the crisis of the I-world relationship: he descends to the level in which
things, persons, his own body become anonymous tombs, indeed, mass
graves of the past; but he descends in order to capture the emergence of
a primordial remembrance that gives sense to the world and guarantees
the initial freedom of a domestic, communitarian backdrop of agency. The
famous teacup resurrection of Combray means that on a gloomy winter
day and in view of a sad tomorrow, when this connection of remembrance
appears to break and the world fades and time withers, even a teacup
can be the start of a turnaround, a warm affective wave that contains the
cosmogonic days of Combray and that through the aroma of those days,
expanding out, reweaves the weft of a practicable world. In the "awak-
enings" with which the *Recherche* opens, Proust surprises with a very
fine analysis of the paths pursued to being-there starting from a radical
risk of nothingness. Keeping in a circle around him while he sleeps, that
"sequence of the hours, the order of the years and worlds"; the possible
breaking of that sequence upon reawakening so that one feels totally unsettled; finding himself "more destitute than a cave dweller" and crossing
"centuries of civilization" in a second; rediscovering in the confusedly
glimpsed image of a lamp or a wing-collar shirt a first anchoring of re-
orienting cultural memories and a virtual entrance card to the historical
domesticity of the world; recomposing the historicity of the moment by
retracing the course "of things, towns, years"; and reliving—through the

evocation of memories stored in his own body—the other rooms he has slept in—the bedrooms of Combray, Tansonville, Balbec: all this illuminates the secret folds of an entire cosmogony that plays out in us at every moment even if it is concealed by the obviousness and domesticity of the practicable backdrop that make our freedom available. Indeed, it should be said that the obviousness and domesticity of this backdrop are possible in that these latent memories are there, reconnecting us implicitly to the sequence of hours, the order of years and worlds, back to the caveman, memories preserving not only our family history but also—for generations and eras—the communitarian projects that have made the world the cultural homeland of humanity. Only in the destabilization of this course, in the risk of an upheaval, does the rock of domesticity begin to crumble.

3.3. J.-P. Sartre, *L'être et le néant* (1943; Paris: Gallimard, 1950), 320ff.[20]
Sartre defines the body, one's own body, as "the total center of reference which things indicate," "the instrument and end of our actions" (320).

Objects are revealed to us at the heart of a complex instrumentality in which they occupy a determined place. This place is not defined by pure spatial co-ordinates but in relation to the axes of practical reference. "*The glass is on the coffee table*," this means that we must be careful not to upset the glass if we move the table. *The package of tobacco is on the mantle piece*, this means that we must clear a distance of three yards if we want to go from the pipe to the tobacco while avoiding certain obstacles—end tables, footstools, etc.—which are placed between the mantle piece and the table. In this sense *perception is in no way to be distinguished from the practical organization of existents into a world*. Each instrument refers to other instruments, to those which are its keys and to those for which it is the key. But these references could not be grasped by a purely contemplative consciousness. For such a consciousness the hammer would not refer to the nails but would be alongside them; furthermore the expression "alongside" [*à côté*] loses all meaning if it does not outline a path which goes from the hammer to the nail and which must be cleared. The space which is originally revealed to me is *hodological* space;[21] it is furrowed with paths and highways; it is instrumental and it is the location of tools. Thus the world from the moment of the upsurge of my For-itself is revealed as the indication of acts to be performed; these acts refer to other acts, and those to others, and so on. It is to be noted however that if from this point of view perception and action are indistinguishable, action is nevertheless presented as a future efficacy which surpasses and transcends the pure and simple perceived ... [The perceived thing refers to others, each referral having the meaning of future commitment.]

Thus I am in the presence of things which are only promises beyond an ineffable presence which I can not possess and which is the pure "being-there" of things; that is, the "mine," my facticity, my body. [. . .] Thus the world as the correlate of the possibilities which I am appears from the moment of my upsurge as the enormous skeletal outline of all my possible actions. Perception is naturally surpassed toward action; *better yet, it can be revealed only in and through projects of action.* (321–22)[22]

The instrumental-things indicate other instruments or objective ways of making use of them: the nail is "to be pounded in" this way or that, the hammer is "to be held by the handle," the cup is "to be picked up by its handle," etc. All these properties of things are immediately revealed, and the Latin gerundives perfectly translate them. [. . .] Thus the world [. . .] [as a structure of potentialities, absences, instrumentalities] never refers to a creative subjectivity, but to an infiniteness of instrumental complexes. (322–23)

But the entirety of these "references" of handiness within a horizon of things at hand is a perspectival and differentiated whole, a whole that is not equivalent in its single possibilities in that it refers to a key instrument, to a necessary center of reference, to the body as stopping point for the references and their result:

The first term is present everywhere, but it is only indicated: I do not apprehend my hand in the act of writing, but only the pen which is writing; this means that I use my pen in order to form letters, but not *my* hand in order to hold the pen. I am not in relation to my hand in the same utilizing attitude as I am in relation to the pen: *I am* my hand. That is, my hand is the arresting of references and their ultimate end. The hand [. . .] is at once the unknowable and non-utilizable which the last instrument of the series indicates ("book to be read—characters to be formed on the paper—pen"), and at the same time the orientation of the entire series (the printed book itself refers back to the hand). But I can apprehend it—at least in so far as it is acting—only as the perpetual, evanescent reference of the whole series. . . . [While I write the hand] is lost in the complex system of instrumentality in order that this system may exist. It is simply the meaning and the orientation of the system. (323)

The world as a horizon of things at-hand revealing themselves through practicable projects—hammering nails, sowing wheat—and as a system of references that receive sense and orientation from the extreme instrument, from the center instrument, from the handy instrument, and from the instrument that we do not use but that we are: the *body*. The body "is given to us in no other way than by the instrumental order of the world, by hodological space, by the univocal or reciprocal relations of machines, but it can not be given to my action" (324).

Lived and not known body (324).

The resistance of things:

> What I perceive when I want to lift this glass to my mouth is not my effort but the *heaviness of the glass*—that is, its resistance to entering into an instrumental complex which I have made appear in the world. [. . .] [I]t is in relation to an original instrumental complex that things reveal their resistance and their adversity. [. . .] [E]very means is simultaneously favorable and adverse but within the limits of the fundamental project realized by the upsurge of the For-itself in the world. [. . .] My body is everywhere [. . .] it is at the end of the cane on which I lean and against the earth; it is at the end of the telescope which shows me the starts; it is on the chair, in the whole house; for it is my adaptation to these tools. (324–25)

Sensations, action, perception, their unity (325).

The body as the "permanent condition of possibility for my consciousness as consciousness of the world and as a transcendent project toward my future" (328). My body is birth, race, class, physiological structure, character: it is "all this in so far as I surpass it in the synthetic unity of my being-in-the-world" (328).

> [T]he body is the contingent form which is taken up by the necessity of my contingency. [. . .] Even this disability from which I suffer I have assumed by the very fact that I live; I surpass it toward my own projects, I make of it the necessary obstacle for my being, and I can not be crippled without choosing myself as crippled. This means that I choose the way in which I constitute my disability (as "unbearable," "humiliating," "to be hidden," "to be revealed to all," "an object of pride," "the justification for my failures," etc.). But this inapprehensible body is precisely the necessity that there be a choice, that I do not exist all at once. In this sense my finitude is the condition of my freedom. (328)

Since it is inapprehensible, my body does not belong to the world of objects: but what is my body for me?

(1) "[T]he body is what is indicated by all the instruments I grasp, and I apprehend the body without knowing it in the very indications that I perceive on the instruments" (329).

(2) "[T]he point of view on which I can no longer take a point of view" (329).
(3) Consciousness of bodily pain as a project toward a further consciousness without pain (333).
(4) Coenesthetic affectivity as pure apprehension of self as a factual existence:

This perpetual apprehension on the part of my for-itself of an insipid taste which I cannot place, which accompanies me even in my efforts to get away from it, and which is my taste—this is what we have described elsewhere under the name of Nausea. A dull and inescapable nausea perpetually reveals my body to my consciousness. Sometimes we look for the pleasant or for physical pain to free ourselves from this nausea; but as soon as the pain and the pleasure are existed by consciousness, they in turn manifest its facticity and its contingency; and it is on the ground of this nausea that they are revealed. We must not take the term nausea as a metaphor derived from our physiological disgust. On the contrary, we must realize that it is on the foundation of this nausea that all concrete and empirical nauseas (nausea caused by spoiled meat, fresh blood, excrement, etc.) are produced and make us vomit. (338–39)

3.4. J.-P. Sartre, *L'être et le néant* (Paris: Gallimard, 1943), 307.[23]

Thus by the mere fact that *there is* a world, this world can not exist without a univocal orientation in relation to me. Idealism has rightly insisted on the fact that relation makes the world. But since idealism took its position on the ground of Newtonian science, it conceived this relation as a relation of reciprocity. Thus it attained only abstract concepts of pure exteriority, of action and reaction, etc., and due to this very fact it missed the world and succeeded only in making explicit the limiting concept of absolute objectivity. This concept in short amounted to that of a "desert world" or of "a world without men"; that is, to a contradiction, since it is through human reality that there is a world. Thus the concept of objectivity, which aimed at replacing the in-itself of dogmatic truth by a pure relation of reciprocal agreement between representations, is self-destructive if pushed to the limit.

Moreover the progress of science has led to rejecting this notion of absolute objectivity. What Broglie is led to call "experience" is a system of univocal relations from which the observer is not excluded. If microphysics can reintegrate the observer into the heart of the scientific system, this is not by virtue of pure subjectivity—this notion would have no more meaning than that of pure objectivity—but as an original relation to the world, as a place, as that toward which all envisaged relations are oriented. Thus, for example, Heisenberg's principle of indeterminacy can not be considered either an invalidation or a validation of the determinist postulate. Instead of being a pure connection between things, it includes within itself the original relation of man to things and his place in the world. (307)

The concept of the world is thus a "cultural" concept, that is, intelligible in the human effort of valorizing life, of transcending it in value: more precisely, of transcending it in the intersubjective value of life's handiness, so that entities within-the-world are made possible in the horizon of "world." What the world is "per se," a "desert world," a "world without people" is not a philosophical problem: its tenacious appearance arises from the absolutization of handy valorization, that in its immediacy finds an external and resistant "world" to use for "human needs" and that certainly cannot do without the "as if" of the exteriority and resistance of the world. The realism of natural science and common sense depends on the absolutization of this "as if" inherent in the structure of handy work: moreover, given the character of "initial evidence" that the ethos of transcendence gives of itself through the handy valorization [...][24]

3.5. Sartre, in *Esquisse d'une théorie des émotions* (Paris: Hermann, 1939),[25] contrasts the hodological *Umwelt* to the magical world. The hodological *Umwelt* is furrowed on all sides by "strict and narrow paths" (57) through which our needs and desires can be satisfied. It is a world of *itinera*, of practicable projects, actual or possible technological actions. This world of *itinera* is a world of objects as instruments. It appears to consciousness

as a complex of instruments so organized that, if one wished to produce a determined effect, it would be necessary to act upon the determined elements of the complex. In this case, each instrument refers to other instruments and the totality of utensils; there is no absolute action and radical change that one can immediately introduce into this world. It is necessary to modify a particular instrument and this by means of another instrument which refers to other instruments and so on to infinity. (89–90)

Sartre writes,

When the paths traced out become too difficult, or when we see no path, we can no longer live in so urgent and difficult a world. All the ways are barred. However, we must act. So we try to change the world, that is, to live as if the connection between things and their potentialities were not ruled by deterministic processes, but by magic. (58–59)

The magical world is a world apprehended as "a non-instrumental totality" (90), as an immediate presence in the face of consciousness.

For example, the face which appeared behind the window ten yards from me must be lived as immediately present to me in its menacing. But this is possible only in an act of consciousness which *destroys all the structures of the world which might reject the magical and reduce the event to its proper proportions.* (87)[26]

Finally, Sartre notes that the horrible "*is not possible* in the deterministic world of instruments" (88–89) and "can appear only in the kind of world whose existants are magical by nature and whose possible recourse against the existants are magical" (89). Thus, there are two different ways for the consciousness to *verstehen* (understand) its own *in-der-Welt-sein*: being in a world of instruments and being in the magical world: the latter way marks the return of consciousness to one of the great attitudes essential to it, the magical-emotional attitude, with the appearance of a corresponding world, the magical world (89–91). The magical-emotional understands the object as "something which exceeds it beyond measure" (79), "an overwhelming and definitive quality of the thing" (80–81), and in particular,

The horrible is not only the present state of the thing; it is threatened for the future; it spreads itself over the whole future and darkens it; it is a revelation of the meaning of the world. "The horrible" means precisely that the horrible is a substantial quality; it means that there is the horrible in the world. [. . .] We live emotively a quality which penetrates us, which we suffer, and which exceeds us on every side." (81)

These considerations by Sartre demonstrate that the "world" is first and foremost possible as a certain order of things at hand; that is, it constitutes itself within that particular intersubjective valorization of life that is precisely handiness. To all appearances the world is given "before," and people "find themselves" in a "world of objects," so that only "after," through this finding themselves, they use it variously or fashion these "instruments" anew. In reality this appearance is part of handiness itself: it is conditioned by use (*l'utilizzare*), in the sense that an "external world" of "resistant objects" appears external and resistant precisely because the act of use signals exteriority and resistance again and again, manifesting them in handy labor and through this labor. The communitarian project of things at hand—always generating and regenerating itself anew and consisting in transmissible and further expanding tradition—constitute the "world" as a horizon of within-the-world entities and the order itself of the within-the-world entities as related indexes of handinesses and resistances, of practicable *itinera* and the limits to the *itinera*'s feasibility. In the "world" we never encounter "things per se," removed from any domestication and coming, so to speak, from the hands of the creator: the fact that this encounter takes place is due to the whole coherence of handy labor, not to the transcendental perspective that refers to the ethos itself of transcendence of life in value.

The "world" as conditioned by a certain communitarian project of things at hand undoubtedly presents limits of worlding or cosmicization inherent in this culturally conditioned project. And since the utilitarian valorization, like every other intersubjective valorization, never gets exhausted (if it got exhausted, this would mark the death of the ethos of transcendence), the world is never entirely at hand but only at hand within the historical limits of a certain projecting. This means that beyond these limits, things or another world do not exist per se but the nonworld, the a-cosmic, chaos, nothingness. The "world" therefore includes the possibility of its "ending," and every "cultural world" is profoundly tormented by this, just as it rests entirely on the ethos of valorization and on the initial impulse of handy valorization. This collapse of the world as a collapse of things at hand can best be analyzed in madness and especially in the experiences of depersonalization and derealization, in the delusion of negation and in experiences of the end of the world. When this is announced in the various modes that analysis must clarify, we have a reversal of purposeful transcendence that strikes and disarticulates the initial order itself of a "possible world": this is a collapse that converts the other into wholly other and appears as a quintessential existential risk. On the level of recovery from this risk, and as an anastrophe reintegrating in value, the cultural institutions participating in the symbolic horizon become available (the mythical-ritual symbol, magic and religion, civil symbolism).

The use that Sartre makes of the term *magic* thus confuses the moment of the crisis with that of the symbolic, cultural recovery: Sartre theorizes the magical world as a mode of being-in-the-world, whereas it is necessary to distinguish the risk of not being able to be in any possible world from the cultural defense that magical institutions represent, disclosing the at-hand world through mythical-ritual dehistorification.

3.6. I must never be alone: this is the fundamental ethical imperative that founds my personhood, and at the same time founds the intersubjectivity of my distinct valorizations of life, of my continuous transcending in value.[27] I must never be alone: still less am I and should I be alone in that initial act of my duty-to-be-in-the-world that gets expressed in handiness, that is, in the incessant participation in a communitarian project of things at hand. This is not merely physical being together, since one can be alone in a crowd, and one can live a multifaceted life of impetuous communication in the silence of a study, a prison, or a monastery cell. The truth is that this imperative accompanies us and supports us from the cradle to the grave, and it is so deeply rooted in our being-there that it accompanies and supports us even when we do not have theoretical awareness of it and even when we formulate individualistic or even solipsistic ideologies (with which we are not in fact consistent in life, unless we want to pay the price of that consistency with madness).

Moreover this communion with others that inhabits our past—and that in memory reaches only a few faces of people close to us—is continuously renewed in the actuality of a need, even physical, to maintain old relations and to build new ones: amiable conversations, the joy of a good dinner in an outing with friends, the assorted forms of associational life, the feeling of a festival experienced together, all not only give proof of us to ourselves, and they habituate us to the humility of a continuous comparison of our ideas and our emotions, but they also form our personhood, pulling it back again and again from that abyss that is *le moi haïssable* and pushing it again and again, with renewed courage and self-confidence, toward the green fields of life.

In the *Recherche* Proust narrates how once, during a stroll, he felt the desire to look at the landscape in the company of a certain girl, and how through this imagining the landscape was filled with "a new quality": the girl started to live "in the color of the tiles on the farms, etc." J. H. van den Berg, in *The Phenomenological Approach to Psychiatry* (1955), relating this and other similar illustrations, writes:

> the word, the look or the gesture of a fellow man can brighten or darken my world. The fellow man is not an isolated entity, standing beside me, pouring words into my ear; who, just as myself, would remain foreign to the things of the world. He is primarily one who is or is not "together" with me and the degree of this being together with me or not is no metaphysical abstraction, but a reality, visible in the things which he and I observe. Our being together or not appears in the physiognomy of the world. The physiognomy may be familiar or unfamiliar, near or far. (50–51)

The truth is that even when we do not feel the need to be with others, even when we think we are alone, others live in our habits, in the techniques of our body, in the world as a horizon of things at hand, in the hodological space whose practicable *itinera* bear the mark of a collective domestication that harkens back to society and its history and that is constituted for each of us through this mark as a worldly space, living and practicable. In Proust nonetheless—and this is the limit of his *Recherche*—this connection is dissolved in a memory that disperses, disaggregates, and subjugates, since it starts from a present emptiness, from a wavering of the ethos of the transcendence of life in value: so Croce was not incorrect when he spoke of "a true unburdening of the nerves by means of the imagination."[28]

3.7. The individual and individuals in the community of individuals.

The transcendental principle of the ethos of transcendence of life in value, through the *duty-to-be* that it entails, can only be realized in the finiteness of the individual: indeed, only in this finiteness can it carry out its inexhaustible task of valorization, its inexhaustible duty-to-be for value. If the principle were being and not a duty-to-be, the finiteness of the individual would be a mystery: the question of "the reason for individual finiteness" could only have a religious answer, for example, through the Christian myth of sin, fall, and redemption. But the subsequent question, "Why this sin and fall and the need for redemption?" reproposes a query that—as long as we start from it already being exhausted in itself, that it is already everything that it must be—can only be suspended or evaded through faith, by the practical need for protection of our createdness and finiteness, and so forth. If instead the principle is a duty-to-be—a transcendental principle—the finiteness of the individual partakes of the same reason as its principle: an individual can never exhaust the duty-to-be, the duty-to-be that founds it, because if he ever exhausted it, he would deny it and not draw from being but from nothingness (since life that does not surpass itself in valorization is nothingness, as is the valorization that it claims to fully actualize and has nothing more to valorize). Moreover, if in this perspective the individual can only be finite, since only this finiteness assures the inexhaustibility of its principle (of the duty to be), that principle, precisely because it is inexhaustible, cannot be exhausted in a single individual or in an incoherent multiplicity of individuals but unfolds as a society of individuals operating and communicating and relating their works and is taken to the limit as an "idea of humanity." The duty-to-be is not compatible with an individual who incarnates it in such a way that all being is actualized, nor is it compatible with a chaotic clash of individuals, each of whom would try to actualize it in an incoherent way. The duty-to-be presents itself first and foremost as *society*, as a communitarian project of the things at hand, of communicating and relating needs and satisfactions, of producing goods and instruments. Danger lies only in the possibility that a society gets closed, fetishizes itself, and ends up suffocating individuals in this lack of relationality with itself and other societies (but then the danger does not lie in the society as such but in the group of individuals who hold economic and political power and who limit or arrest the development of the society itself).

3.8. The lived heart of one's own body (third draft).

The lived heart of one's own body marks in the most visceral way our internal calendar of existing. Much earlier than the celestial rhythms, our heartbeat participates in time and reveals it, marking the epochs of creational joy and desperation, of anxious awaiting and melancholy, of pleasure and fury, sensitive to such a degree that it reacts to the stimuli of the unconscious. Nonetheless, precisely because of this immediate participation in the rhythm of existing, because of this subjection of its rhythm to changes in lived experience, the heartbeat cannot measure time the way the solar or lunar cycle can, and humanity has entrusted itself to the regular cycle of the sun and the moon in order to protect the too labile, interior calendar of hearts, inscribing its precarious order in that broad and stable one of heaven. If the time of heaven was learned, it was because the lived heart of one's body already contained the request for permanence and a return. And, moreover, so that this request kept an order that was not only biological, celestial regularity's cultural assistance intervened as the measure of human practicability in time. "The starry sky outside me" and "the moral law within me": between these two regularities, the lived heart of our body beats.

Being-there is an agile gathering of being in the here and now of a continuously renewing decision-making and an agile opening of the here and how to the task of intersubjective valorization. The beating heart of being-there lies in these systole and diastole that concentrate and distribute according to loyalty and initiative. And we can well understand how the lived heart of one's own body was able to transform itself into a symbol.

3.9. Techniques of the body.[29]

[. . .] The two hands appear differently valued in human cultural life. The right hand is the hegemonic hand—the strong and effective master— that promotes, preserves, and increases the technical order of skills, the legal and moral order, the liturgical order of the relationship with the divine. The left hand is the vicarious one—subordinated, servile, and weak—that must be forced to collaborate with the right's social activity and that per se, as a left hand, tends to subversion and disorder in all spheres of human activity; in the sphere of the sacred itself, it is connected to the obscure world of demons or to the antisocial practices of black magic. In other words, the right hand is the hand of projecting communitarian life according to values, while the left hand marks the limit of this projecting, the resistance that it is necessary to steer as much as possible toward the aims of the hegemonic operative directions, the constant temptation of subverting that order, the sphere of the negative and the unresolved that again and again fosters this temptation and that can even appear as a vicarious horizon of assorted antisocial activities (i.e., against a certain order of the society) within the group itself. This means that we should basically connect the different valorization of the two to the limit of communitarian projecting of things at hand and to the economically nonprojectable and impracticable that lies as an inexhaustible residue of every communitarian projection and practicability of things at hand. Precisely through this existential experience connected to all human manual labor and through the necessity of protecting the horizon of being-there that coincides with the horizon of the manually practicable, this horizon was included in the other one of the polarity of sacred splendor (*fasto*) and sacred perniciousness (*nefasto*), the sacred and the profane, the right hand and the left hand. Therefore, although the projectable-nonprojectable opposition is inherent in all "manual" labor, the religiously valorized right-left opposition forms a protective horizon for the sphere of the projectable (and therefore for being-in-the-world).

3.10. "I'm putting salt in my soup, my hand is your hand, you're not dead."

Navel, the author of *Travaux* and *Parcours*, surprises himself in the habitual gesture, every evening upon returning home from work, of opening the door to the cupboard to take the saltcellar and salt his soup.[30] And while his fingers hold the pinch of salt and get ready to perform the gesture of salting, he recalls the gesture that he had seen his mother do so many times, and he speaks to her in the rapidity of a dream: "I'm putting salt in my soup, my hand is your hand, you're not dead." And through his mother Navel perceives all of the dead, he reconnects to all those who have shaped his hand just as it is, with its skills and practicable limits, with its being and nonbeing, in the continuous duty-to-be where it acts as his operating hand. First, in his habitual gesture, in the skill wielded in a twilight state of consciousness, all this was there, but dormant. And precisely because it was there, even if dormant, his hand became his with such obvious skills that they could be performed in the ease of a habit that freed up other skills to be learned and invented. But if his hand was his and if it was part of him, an articulated possession in the horizon of his body, if it was his as a *habit freeing up technical gestures* in the twilight of consciousness, or even in its nighttime, so that he could turn to other things in the midday fullness of consciousness itself, this was all possible because *he was never alone*, thrown into the world, but accompanied, supported, guided by a personal and collective history, unfolding in the time of human generations, in the flow of their valorizations of the world.

A person who withdraws into himself discovers his own solipsistic solitude; in reality he only discovers his own moral wretchedness, the interrupted thread of his own historic loyalties, the satanic pride of the unique, and in the last instance, the will to "isolate oneself" that is an immoral nostalgia of nothingness.

3.11. (fifth draft). Our cosmogonic experience began through the warmth of the maternal body, when the initial horizon of a homeland dimly began to be experienced, based on a boundary of warm skin. In the affective background of that warmth (and in its memory we speak of a quintessential "warmth of affection") we conquered our mouth by sucking milk, and as a mouth we wallowed in the greedy pleasure of feeding. Under the caress of a maternal hand, the surfaces of our body got described and defined, just as through the image of a maternal face we trained our capacity to concentrate our gaze and reveal the first wavering figure from the world's fog: "incipe, parve puer, risu cognoscere matrem."[31] The first space to be moved through was disclosed to us with what a mother, rocking us, offered us and took away in equal measure, sweetening it with the hushed repetitions of a lullaby: a model space of safety whose initiative was spared us and whose movement in two directions was followed by a return that undid it again and again, while the first domestic voice helped us with its melopoeia to make this economical becoming acceptable to us. Through this space and this safe movement analogous to the orbit of a planet, we achieved our first cultural possibility—and not only biological—of human sleep precisely because the sweet rocking likened us to the dominant cosmic rhythms of the eternal return (cf. *Timaeus*, . . .).[32] Finally, through our mother we also achieved crying and pain for her desired, contested, or lost breast, and especially for her disappearing figure, when the tough pedagogy of detachments began and we started to experience the harsh norm of human initiative that renders time irreversible.

3.12. [. . .] But let us better analyze the horizon of the body's handiness as a *duty* to walk erect. As a "skill" so obvious as not to require the concentration of conscious attention, this horizon includes a complete personal and human *history* (the effort we make as infants when we learn to walk and the slow achievement of erect posture in hominids). In this sense we never walk "alone" but with the entire personal and human history of the particular technique of the body that is knowing how to walk. In walking we are accompanied and supported by this history and by the efforts, studies, inventions, and learning that this entails. Certainly, in order to walk the adult human has no need to learn this history in detail: one walks and that's that. But in an implicit way, inchoate, summarized in an extreme manner, and resolved in an "obvious" practicable skill, this history is *recovered* every time a person walks, so that if he had really totally forgotten it, he could not even walk: he would have simply unlearned this technique. This "not knowing extensively," this "relative" forgetting, this easy unfolding of deambulatory skill in a "relative" unawareness (i.e., "relative" to other valorizing presentifications that eminently require our effort and remain available) is part and parcel of an always renewed liberation from givenness that makes up the emergence of being-there, the continuous renewal of its margin of availability for value. Walking thus takes its place alongside a host of simple and relatively unaware transcendences—that is, less aware and simpler—and cultural and personal shaping that can yield highly characterized walking, used for a very special occasion in life in which a gait becomes highly expressive. If walking were not an easy transcendence, we would not be able to transcend walking while we walk, for example in walking while we talk with a friend!

As already noted, it is not a matter of totally forgetting our walking, nor of a walking that does not entail, even to a minimal and extremely easy degree, a readaptation, a shaping, a calling into question of the corresponding operative memories. We must not walk in general, but here and now, in a certain situation, on a certain ground, slowly or hurriedly, avoiding certain obstacles, and so forth (not to mention other technical modes of moving the body in space: e.g., running, stepping down, stepping up, climbing, jumping, swimming).

Limiting ourselves here to walking, the easiest walking always involves a readaptation of the technique to the concrete situation, an avoidance of obstacles, a measuring of distances, a hurrying up or a slowing down, a calculation of dangers, and so forth. Despite the ease of the reprise operating in a sort of limbo of presentification, this extremely easy reprise is still a reprise. The moment of the reprise and presentification in walking has varying degrees in relation to the difficulty of the task: from this point of view, we should note that we are "always alone" walking, in the sense that in this matter of walking there is always a margin entrusted to our responsibility, our invention, our initiative. It is not a margin that is totally absorbed by the "past" and its technical models. When we want to "pay attention to where we are placing our feet," walk across the street in heavy traffic, walk in the darkness of a room, in all of the situations in which we do not have full use of our legs or when we are simply exhausted from a long walk, walking's moment of reprise becomes more

and more hegemonic and imperative: the intensification of presentification increases since we experience the limits of practicability in walking
as a technique of the body moving in space in an erect posture. In such
extreme situations the margin of availability for other transcendences increasingly shrinks, and the entire technical effort tends to concentrate on
the "problem" of walking.

Walking as reprise and as transcendence is manifested in the clearest
way in what makes up the shaping of a gait, in a social and cultural sense,
as a personal style, and as the expression of mood, of particular *Stimmungen*, of the temporary assumption of particular social roles, and so forth.

Shepherds, peasants, horsemen, and soldiers have their characteristic
gaits that make them immediately recognizable, all the more so if this
blends with other signs of bearing and role. Maori girls learned *anioi* from
their mothers, a particular style of wiggling gait greatly admired by men,
and they were scolded by their mothers when they did not perform it
properly. Anyone who has been forced for a length of time to comply with
the prison routine of daily walks in a line in the prison courtyard subsequently maintains a rather stiff gait, with the swing of the arms reduced to
a minimum; while people who have not undergone this experience of an
unnatural and submissive walk, and having a frivolous and conceited character, always want to exhibit their self-assuredness and nonchalance: they
move with rapid steps, putting forward alternately the right and left parts
of the torso and shoulders, balancing the agile rhythm with a corresponding alternation, in front of themselves and their shoulders, of vigorously
bent arms: practiced in ordinary life and outside of any sport, this certainly moves us to laughter and commiseration. Among the personal styles
of walking, we all remember old Croce, with his slow and solemn gait,
slightly dragging the leg he fractured in the Casamicciola earthquake [...].

4. Readings of Martin Heidegger: The Everydayness of Being-There, Being-towards-Death[33]

4.1. In *Being and Time*, Martin Heidegger theorizes the everyday mode
of being-there as "the they" (*das Man*).[34]

[...]

Now, there is much to be said with regard to the dictatorship of the
"they," of the "inconspicuous domination of Others," of the being-there
whose being is "taken away" by others" (*die Anderen haben ihm das Sein
abgenommen*),[35] and that it is in the mode of "inconstancy" and "inauthenticity," losing and concealing itself in the natural anonymity of everydayness, and so forth: indeed, in Heidegger's *das Man* a dialectic is
destroyed that instead takes on great significance in the perspective of

the transcendental ethos of the transcendence of life in value. In this perspective, being-in-the-world becomes a duty-to-be for valorization, and
the communitarian project of things at hand becomes the initial value of
the authenticity of being-there, so that for being-in-the-world—to emerge
as existence, to be there concretely—the duty-to-be-there is *above all*
necessary: as loyalty, as an initiative, on various levels of awareness, in a
certain communitarian project of life's handiness. Consider the handiness
of one's own body, the relative techniques, and the uninterrupted transcendences only through which we are present as corporeality. Very often
these are extremely effortless because of acquired skills performed in the
twilight of consciousness or are a *hexis* that we do not habitually need but
when necessary can always be conjured up, forming the body's indistinct
background of normal and immediate feeling. Now, in these techniques
of the body, the *das Man* plays a great role, the socially and culturally
conditioned "one does it this way," the received education and thus the
immense debt that *we must* pay to the anonymous others, making our own
selves anonymous in them, since our body can only be ours within this
debt that constitutes it as a body supported by infinite decisions of others, by the joint effort of "society" and "history." In a talk presented at the
Société de Psychologie on 17 May 1934 (*Journal de Psychologie* 32, no. 3/4
[1936]), and republished in *Sociologie et Anthropologie* ([1950; 2nd ed.,
Paris: Presses universitaires de France, 1960], 335–86),[36] Marcel Mauss
highlighted the problem of techniques of the body. In the preface to the
second edition in *Sociologie et Anthropologie*, Claude Lévi-Strauss writes,

> In stating the crucial value, for the sciences of man, of a study of the man-
> ner in which each society imposes a rigorously determined use of the
> body upon the individual, Mauss was announcing the most up-to-date
> concerns of the American Anthropological Society today, as expressed in
> the work of Ruth Benedict, Margaret Mead and the majority of the young
> generation of American anthropologists. The social structure leaves its
> imprint on individuals through the training of the child's bodily needs
> and activities. (4)[37]

And further,

> Every technique, every mode of behaviour, learned and transmitted by
> tradition, is founded on certain nervous and muscular synergies which
> constitute veritable systems, bound up with a whole sociological con-
> text. That is true of the humblest techniques, like lighting fires by fric-
> tion or fashioning stone tools by knapping; and it is much more true of
> those grand constructs, simultaneously social and physical, which are the

different kinds of gymnastics (including Chinese gymnastics, so different from our own, and the internal gymnastics of the ancient Maori, about which we know next to nothing); or the Chinese and Hindu breathing techniques; or the circus acts which are a very old patrimony of our own culture, and which we leave to the chance effects of personal callings and family traditions to preserve from extinction. (7)

It would be very welcome if an international organisation such as UNESCO would commit itself to carrying into effect the programme which Mauss mapped out in that paper. The publication of *International Archives of Body Techniques* would be of truly international benefit, providing an inventory of all the possibilities of the human body and of the methods of apprenticeship and training employed to build up each technique, for there is not one human group in the world which could not make an original contribution to such an enterprise. What is more, it is a common patrimony, one which is immediately accessible to all of humanity, with roots that go right back through the millennia, and with a practical value that remains and will always remain relevant; putting it at the disposition of one and all would do more than anything else could (because it takes the form of lived experiences) to make each of us aware of our mental and physical connections with the whole of humanity. It would also be a project eminently well fitted for countering racial prejudices, since it would contradict the racialist conceptions which try to make out that man is a product of his body [. . .]. It would produce an unexpected wealth of information about migrations, cultural contacts and borrowings made in the distant past. (8–9)

4.2. [. . .] Comments.

In-der-Welt-sein as an essential foundation of being-there can give rise to two interpretations. The first is that being-there, including being-in-the-world in its structure, can nonetheless exist in different modes, one of which is the psychopathological modality: from this we get the analysis of the modification of *in-der-Welt-sein* of Dasein in incipient schizophrenia, and so forth. This is the route that Binswanger follows, as does existential psychopathology more generally. It is a route that refers, for example, to Storch's famous monograph on the "world of incipient schizophrenia" as compared to the world of so-called primitive civilizations.[38] In this view, there is a "world" of the schizophrenic, one of the "primitive," one of the "child," and so forth (cf. Heinz Werner[39]), and all these worlds are modes of *in-der-Welt-sein* as a transcendental structure of Dasein, as an a priori condition that a world is generally possible. The second interpretation considers *in-der-Welt-sein* as a *sein-sollen*, a primordial duty-to-be of pre-sentification and thus of being-there in a cultural world, in one way or another giving evidence of and for it. This *in-der-Welt-sein-sollen* is the relational obligation par excellence, that is, the ethos Croce spoke of in a page of *Storia come pensiero e azione*[40] that makes any specific cultural *Welt* possible, starting with the socioeconomic one. But precisely because the Dasein is essentially founded by this *in-der-Welt-sein-sollen*, the radical threat of not being in any possible cultural world harms it: this is a threat that is tantamount to not-being-there, the loss of presence, modes of depresentification and deworlding. This threat is generally the most "concealed" structural moment of being-there precisely because culture as a whole moves in the direction of this concealment, and only the development of certain historical circumstances—like those of the modern world—permit reflection to grasp this moment of extreme risk that accompanies the *sein-sollen* of Dasein and bestows its *Sein* with the significance of *Sollen*. From this we see the great heuristic importance of the contributions of existential psychopathology, where the experiences of not-being-there (depersonalization, etc.) and the end of the world tend to get isolated and the presence "loses itself" and "disperses."

4.3. The average everydayness of being-there in Heidegger's discussion confuses different interpretative concepts: (a) the risk of not-being-in-the-world, the loss of presence; (b) degrees of the ethos of transcendence, the greater or lesser energy with which it asserts itself: whereby it happens that in daily life we are not always heroes, and besides, we live beneficially out of habit, passively embraced customs, common opinions, ceremonial phrases or gestures, anonymity or even stereotypes. Precisely the different energy with which the ethos of transcendence makes humankind human—as a being who works but also gets tired and takes refuge in restful dwellings where, along with restorative sleep, there are habits, passively embraced customs, and so forth; (c) the relative depreciation of those forms of transcendence of things at hand, involvement,[41] and especially the socioeconomic relation in all of its complexity: it is as if this form of transcendence could not manifest its own heroism, its will to culture and history, and on the contrary, as if humanity did not need to orient its ethos in this direction first and foremost, detaching itself from "nature" through the initial invention of a mode of being in society, of producing and distributing goods according to "rules" (certainly here, too, there is courage and indolence, anonymity and passivity in a given system, as well as personal contribution, discovery innovation, revolution: even here we see the hierarchy of degrees of the ethos of transcendence discussed in b).

4.4. Being-in-the-world has its basis in the *duty* (*dover*) to transcend situations again and again, deciding them according to intersubjective values.

Precisely this *imperative beyond* (*doveroso oltre*), this *ethos of transcendence*, grounds and conditions the situation one is emerging from and the valorization contained in the duty to emerge. Precisely this desire for a leeway that counts establishes the distance between situation and value, the distance that is crossed again and again, the perspective that is always renewing itself, that in continuous intentional presentification makes the "there" of being-there-in-the-world appear and preserves it in its characteristic tension of this or that world one has the duty-to-be in, this or that modality of being-there. This desire for leeway called to act ceaselessly is nontranscendable precisely because it is the condition of all transcendences. It can withdraw, in other words, give in to the risk of not being able to be in any possible world, of not being able to open itself to any sphere of cultural valorization, of not being able to give itself leeway or distance or perspective, thereby losing presentification itself, together with the world and "situations," and dissipating toward absence. Reflection can gain awareness of this risk, too, drawing on the mature thought of the ethos of transcendence, in other words a fundamental ethical principle that in itself combats the radical risk of not being implemented, against the risk of the *fatal illness* of nonpresentification and nonintentionality. This is an illness worse than any particular moral error, because moral error is open to remorse, atonement, forgiveness, and everything else that carries out the function of recovery and reintegration, while the risk of not being able to be in any possible cultural world—in any intersubjective valorization—is marked by an impossibility to recover and reintegrate, a passing with what passes instead of transcending it, the inversion of being-in-the-world, a being defined by deworlding and depresentification instead of worlding presentification.

The duty-to-be-in-the-world—the transcendence through which the presentifying and presentified get constituted—is always a duty-to-be, it is always a duty-to-be hic et nunc according to particular loyalties and initiatives. Moreover, this duty-to-be always follows a hierarchical relation of specific valorizations in which the cultural world as a whole is articulated so that each time "a" valorization rises as a hegemonic task, the others operate quietly, so to speak, at times reduced to the relative obscurity of conventions, habits, and technical automatisms, but all, in this diversified energy of presentification, form the living, dynamic context of presence in action.

4.5. Anxiety (*L'angoscia*).

Anxiety as experiencing the risk of not being able to be in any possible cultural world. It is therefore anxiety in the face of *nothingness*, but "nothingness" here means the possibility that the ethos of worlding pre-sentification "gets obliterated." [...] Accordingly, we do not have anxiety because of an entity within-the-world, some phenomenon that threatens us, some bad thought, but because of the pure and simple experience of the inexorable shrinking of the leeway beyond which the world is generally possible. The end of the world in its various connotations—for example, the world of adolescence, the world of our loved ones, an epoch or civilization—does not necessarily produce anxiety, at least to the extent that we are able to overcome the respective situations, opening ourselves to the world of maturity, to loving memories, to a new epoch or civilization. Furthermore anxiety can take its cue from episodes that are entirely insignificant or explode without any apparent situation. Precisely this means that it is not "this" or "that" we are facing with anxiety but the restriction of any perspective in which a this or that can be located.

In Heidegger's anxiety, we have anxiety over worldhood as such, of pure being-in-the-world. But this appraisal of anxiety arises from having already exhausted possible worlds in *in-der-Welt-sein*, having lost that *sein-sollen* that formally guarantees the passage to concrete cultural-historical worlds in which being-there *must* always be there. Hollowed out in this way, being-in-the-world is interpreted ontologically as thrownness, where it is always projecting according to value (initial projecting of a world at hand), and being thrown is always in relation to no longer being able to project.

Being-in-the-world as a formal determination is insufficient in that it makes the duty-to-be-in-the-world through intersubjective valorization disappear and not being able to be in any world possible as a radical risk. Worldness as a mere possibility of worlding, as a simple *potentiality of being* (*poter essere*) does not guarantee or ground the passage to concrete cultural worlds, which do not appeal to a *potentiality* but to a *must* (*dovere*). Anxiety is interpreted as bare experience of worldliness, in the *versinken* of within-the-world things at hand and the Dasein-with (*con-esserci*) with others, while in reality it is a fall in transcending energy, the loss of presentification as a transcendental duty conditioning all other tasks.

[...]

We are not "unsettled" because we experience pure worldness as a possibility but because we lose the ethos of worlding and we experience the impossibility of being able to be there in a cultural world, starting from its base of things at hand, the instrumental, the social. An "unsettled" person is one who no longer manages to feel in a "homeland" (*paese*), in a culturally coherent and meaningful "domestic" order, in one's own home, in the land of one's forebears or homeland (*Unheimlich, nicht-zu-Hause*, etc.). It is no coincidence that the terms used to symbolically express this experience refer to the family (familiarity), home, and homeland.

4.6. [...] After having demonstrated anxiety's "feeling unsettled" as proof of the most proper being-towards-death, in paragraph 51,[42] Heidegger demonstrates the concealment that this feeling receives in the everydayness of being-there, that is, in the average everydayness of public interpretative states, in the everydayness of "one dies," conceived of as a positive relation being there with itself but in itself "concealed" in *das Man*. In such states we speak of "cases of death"—always of "others" and always already actual—concealing death as a possibility. The *They* is based on the temptation to conceal its own being-towards-death. The features of the concealment of death in everydayness:

a. calming the dying person, consoling him, etc.;
b. calming those doing the consoling;
c. death as a social disturbance (the death of Ivan Illyich in Tolstoy), for which public life must take measures.

In this perspective the rules for behaving in the face of death, and therefore also institutionalized funerary customs, get interpreted as manifestations of the existential modality for which "the 'they' does not permit us the courage for anxiety in the face of death" (298). Anxiety is, on the contrary, considered by the they as a weakness of being-there, a flight before the world, or more exactly, anxiety gets ambiguously trivialized as fear, and this fear gets considered cowardliness. The "they" thus preaches an alienation (*Entfremdung*) of being-there as well as its ownmost and unconditioned potentiality of being. In conclusion, even in average everydayness being-there moves in this ownmost, unconditioned and unsurpassable potentiality of being, even "when its concern is merely in the mode of an *'untroubled' indifference*" (*unbehelligte Gleichgültigkeit*) toward the uttermost possibility of its own existence" (299[43]).

Everydayness "covers up" dying to alleviate being thrown toward death (300). Its truth about death is "an inappropriate way of holding-for-true" (301). The inauthenticity of the everyday understanding of death "characterizes a kind of Being in which Dasein can divert itself and has for the most part always diverted itself; but Dasein does not necessarily and constantly have to divert itself into this kind of Being" (303).

4.7. If on the one hand Heidegger's being-there suffers from the lack of *Sein-sollen* (*in-der-Welt-sein-sollen*), on the other hand it also suffers from the lack of transcendence as valorizing.

For Heidegger, anxiety is "the state of mind which can hold open the utter and constant threat to itself arising from Dasein's ownmost individualized Being" (310). Anxiety reveals "the lostness [of Dasein] in the they-self [. . .], primarily unsupported by concernful solicitude," bringing being-there "face to face with the possibility of being itself . . . in an impassioned *freedom towards death*—a freedom which has been released from the Illusions of the 'they,' and which is factical,[44] certain of itself, and anxious" (311).

For me, instead, anxiety opens up the risk of not being able to be in any possible cultural world, and thus of not being there at all, of losing oneself in an "isolated," private, and incommunicable intimacy, of being unsettled with respect to every possible "home," to lose the beyond that conditions the "world" since presentification is valorizing worlding. In Heidegger "average everydayness" is an inauthentic mode of existing, a cover, a source of illusions, loss in anonymity, alienation, and so forth. Now, the world of things at hand and the social is actually the initial witnessing of the ethos of transcendence in that it founds a world of intersubjective "loyalty" that goes well "beyond" "individual" pleasure and pain, at the same time founding a horizon of possible initiatives. Within a society— that is, within the social transcendence of being-there as being-there-in-society—authenticity and inauthenticity lie in continuous conflict, and the danger always exists that the form of society suffocates the real productive forces, thereby becoming inauthentic, alienating, anonymizing, and so forth. But if the contradictions within a society are felt to the point of a revolution leading to a new form of society, this is due to the possibility of going beyond a certain socioeconomic world and founding a "more just" one: in other words, the possibility disclosed by the ethos of transcendence, therefore a certain "world" of things at hand and the socialized (the contradictions of a certain social regime as such are necessary but not sufficient conditions for a revolution). This "can" gets transformed into action only through a "must" that belongs to presentification. Furthermore, the world of things at hand and the socialized contains the inaugural commitment of the beyond, the one that conditions all the others: and we document the *Weltanschaaung* of an epoch or civilization principally by measuring the socioeconomic "world" that it has created.

But Heidegger's misunderstanding of the world of things at hand and the socialized is manifested in his analysis of death, where the inauthentic interpretation of dying is precisely that of "average everydayness."

Anxiety is hardly an unveiling of the most authentic being of being-there as being-towards-death. In reality the authentic lies precisely in the social covering of anxiety, not in the sense of an inert acceptance of the anonymous "one dies" but in the sense that precisely this "one dies," distractedness from one's own death, rescue with traditionalized behaviors in mourning, and finally, educating to overcome bereavement all disclose the ethos of transcendence combating the risk of anxiety. When Heidegger says that "the 'they' does not permit us the courage for anxiety in the face of death," he is forgetting that it is not a matter of a lack of courage but, on the contrary, of the institutionalization of the courageous overcoming of death in place of risking to pass along with those who die. Funeral rituals are a work of wisdom, not cowardliness; they do not express being-there in the inauthenticity of the "they" but in the intersubjective loyalty summoned in the moment that we are most tempted to fall into the disloyalty of tormented intimacy, of feeling unsettled by another's death that threatens to involve our own as well.

In anxiety the world is revealed as pure possibility, a mere potentiality of being. But this empty worldhood, this formal potentiality of being is not-being-there, nonworld, the collapse of the ethos of transcendence. In other words, it is the most inauthentic being-there possible, a being-there that loses the ethos that founds and supports it and, through this ethos, renews victory—valorizing and worlding—over its always-looming death. Through this ethos we are always *on this side* of death, in *cultural life*, being-towards-the-end is concealed because it *must* be, in that being-there is being for value in a continuous struggle against being-towards-the-end. Being-towards-death is thus not the ownmost being of being-there, unconditioned and unsurpassable. Being-there always works to overcome death, not only that of every moment but also that of the supreme instant, and it works at this through the "There" (*Ci*) as a power of the beyond, and across the beyond that can transcend the "There" in only one possible way: entrusting it, finally, to other beings-there in the intersubjective communicability of its beyond (i.e., in works that "are worthy"). [. . .]

4.8. The individual as finiteness that transcends itself again and again in intersubjective valorization.

What is the individual? A finiteness that *must* universalize itself, a nothingness that must be there for intersubjective values, a communitarian project of things at hand, poetry, science, philosophical, and moral awareness. It is through this continuous transcending the immediacy of bodily life that being-there constitutes and maintains itself, and it is through this universalizing that its singularization emerges: this means that the transcendental principle that grounds individuality is the transcendence of life in value and being as the duty-to-be for valorization. Furthermore, through this very transcendental principle of the resolution of being in the duty-to-be of valorization, the valorizing task of being-there is inexhaustible, both with regard to the horizon of single valorizations and with regard to the absolute value of valorizing. No being-there can ever realize all of the possible duty-to-be of being, all of the valorizable of a particular valorization (i.e., all poetry or science, etc.). And finally, through this very transcendental principle, the individual as finite life—as need and negativity that is always needing—must die for the same ethical reason that is called again and again to transcend death. But since in this transcending it produces action—great and small alike, but always to some degree with values—it is through this deindividualized realm of actions that the positive of each person continues to live and act in the universal circuit of history and culture, even if it does not bear the memory of a "name" and even if devout visits to a grave get less frequent over time.

4.9. *Geworfenheit* and the loss of valorization.

Geworfenheit, thrownness, total responsibility for decision, the absence of a "table of values" or other truths written in heaven, humanity as a project, anxiety as consciousness of possibility: these are all existentialist themes that characterize the epoch in which the symbols of Judeo-Christian tradition have fallen, the ideal of a universal human nature, the plan of universal history, the horizon of progress, and so forth. But if the downside of atheism is this solitude of humankind, we should ask up to what point this solitude is fundamentally still a reflection of that bourgeois world against which, at least in Sartre, so much derision has been profusely aimed.

Impossibility of "starting from scratch," from zero experience.

The aberration of existentialism is precisely this decision to start from zero, the great solitude and this immense silence from which choice is supposed to emerge. In reality people are never thrown into the world, because the world is always a historical world, in other words, *culturally constructed*, and the culturally constructed world is always interwoven with memories, customs, and values transmitted by upbringing; with specifically modeled alternatives; with conditions incorporating the voices, conflicts, toils, hopes, techniques, and ideas of innumerable human beings. The initiative to which each individual is called arises within a certain loyalty to a being that is not solely mine, even if the initiative can only be mine: in any case, what is missing is zero experience, an absolute beginning from the start. Because of its insertion in a specific social world, the individual's decision is never experiencing freedom as pure possibility but as a choice of a particular loyalty to what has already been decided by others—by innumerable others, some others, or a single other—and as a continuation of their deciding in the new, unrepeatable, individual situation. When zero experience emerges, when anxiety explodes, when no historical or social model comes to the rescue, when the wisdom of any tradition is dismissed (and not only, in a polemical way, a specific tradition), then we have anxiety, but as the collapse of the ethos of transcendence, as the impossibility of choice, as not being able to be in any possible world, and not—as Sartre would have it—the anxiety of freedom.

5. For a Reformed Ethnology

5.1. Presentification.

Presence is presentification: it is always in a situation, and at the same time, always in decision,[45] that is, always in the process of *going beyond*—of transcending—the situation, of emerging from it as the moral energy of intersubjective valorization, of universalizing communication. Presence is being-in-the-world, and its norm of existence is entirely contained in that *there* that enacts being and opens itself to being, that regains the past and discloses itself to the future. The world in which presence is *there* in a detachment that always renews itself is the world of nature and history, of society and historically determined culture. But precisely because presence has its norm in this, it contains the "no" of its "yes": the risk of remaining a prisoner of the situation, of *not* deciding, *not* going beyond it, *not* transcending it, *not* emerging from it as moral energy of intersubjective valorization and universalizing communication. It is the risk of not-being-in-the-world, not passing with the situation instead of transcending in value, repeating it instead of deciding it, not regaining the past, remaining exposed to its incoherent return in the cipher of closed symptoms, returning to the beginning, losing a prospect for the future by retreating aghast before the possible, refusing to become a field of the projectable and acting like a projecting power. It is the risk of remaining without leeway in the face of nature to be humanly controlled and of progressively isolating oneself from society, history and culture, reversing the movement from the private to the public to an indefinite privatization that cuts all ties with life in society. And, finally, it is the risk of absence, of presence that disperses and disappears, a risk against which presentification is called to combat. A person's death marks the end of a personal effort of presentification, but even this very end, imbued with all the powers of the negative, poses the problem of detachment, the beyond, in two senses: with regard to the survivors as a detachment from the situation of bereavement through the continuation of the actions left by the deceased, through the latter's tradition or memory; and with regard to the prospect of our death as a detachment from it through the exercise of our valorizing presentification and the intersubjectivity that continuously ensues from it.

5.2. Negative of a particular valorization and nothingness of the valorization along the whole gamut of the valorizable.

Being is valorizing presentification; nothingness is the obliteration of valorization. It is impossible to separate being from human valorizing and nothingness from devaluing. Precisely because being is always manifested as being that is worth something, nonbeing is always manifested through the disappointed expectation of something that is worthy. Now, valorizing presentification is a primal stance that lies at the root of all particular categorial valorizations; it is a primordial duty-to-be that opens itself again and again to the valorization of being and seeks the being of each value again and again. Obliteration can concern the primordial duty-to-be, the ethos of presentification, and thus we run the risk of not being-able-to-be-in-any-possible-cultural-world: it is absolute obliteration that advances. But it can concern this or that particular valorization and therefore take on the relative form of *not this* but *is* that of a particular disappointed expectation (e.g., it is not poetry but political propaganda; it is not politics but utopic wishful thinking; it is not science but imagination and fantasy, etc., or there is the haunt with all of its regulars but *not* the friend that I am looking for. There is a house, a door, a bell that I ring; the housekeeper who opens the door for me, but not the person whom I came to visit; there is a road, a crowd, the agreed corner for an appointment, the wristwatch I look at continuously, but the friend I am waiting for does *not* appear). Both in absolute and relative obliteration, nothingness is a matter of a *disappointed expectation*; while in relative obliteration the disappointed expectation concerns a particular emergent valorization from the ground of being, in absolute obliteration the very possibility of a ground of being is called into question, a ground from which this or that valorization can emerge. In other words, what is called into question is the valorizing ethos of presentification itself and not this or that particular value whose absence is noted.

5.3. Values.

When we speak of "values of existence," we are using an expression that can give rise to a serious misunderstanding, almost as if there were on the one hand existence, in itself significant, and then on the other, its values: participation in a certain socioeconomic life; political, legal and moral ideals; poetry and science; an entire vision of life and the world. In reality human existence lies precisely in the movement toward intersubjective and communicable values: one exists, one defeats the risk of not emerging as presence through this always self-renewing opening to valorization, through this uninterrupted transcending the situation in communicative value. This opening and transcending is a will to existence and history, culturally conditioned energy of choice, and thus the "value of values" as a primordial ethos that conditions and supports the operation of all the others, combating the radical risk of the negative that is not being able to be in any possible intersubjective world (as happens, e.g., in *Weltuntergangs-erlebnis*). Language, intersubjective communication, the expression and publicizing of the private; continuous listening and interiorization of the public, valorizing choice that always transcends situations: all this does not add to presence but grounds and supports and develops it, forming the very "norm" that makes it "normal." When, as in existential anxiety, speech is lost and communication is impossible, the private becomes ineffable, the relationship with the historical world is jeopardized at its root, and deciding according to intersubjective values is spent in a sort of moral exhaustion, then one experiences the loss of presence's "norm," the inversion of presentification, and one therefore loses presence itself. One lives in the terror of nothingness where nothingness has, however, the fundamental sense of the ethically negative par excellence: in other words, the feeling of an experienced retreat and obliteration of the primordial ethos of presentification and transcendence.

5.4. One of the most fruitful highpoints of Italian positive existentialism in its polemic with Heidegger's and Jaspers's negative existentialism has certainly been the awareness achieved that the basis of human existence is not being but the *duty-to-be*: in other words a valorizing, intersubjective impulse of life, a continuously renewing communitarian projecting of the practicable, an emerging from the situation through the manifold effort of deciding on it according to value. In one respect all this establishes the finiteness of each person and the inexhaustibility of their operative task, and in another respect it guarantees the opening of the person to being, their possibility to be secure—through the intersubjectivity of worthy action—a redemption from simple positive existentialism, so that existing is always in this valorizing transcendence that detaches itself from a situation, transcending it in a valorizing, practicable project. This ethos of transcendence is thus the true principle that makes a world become possible in which we are present. It is a principle that, while being the internal rule of all transcendences, cannot in turn be transcended but is only achievable in the highest striving of existence's self-consciousness.

The recognition that the fundamental base of being-there is not being-in-the-world but the duty-to-be-in-the-world entails a series of analytic orientations that are of decisive importance for a correct approach to studying cultural apocalypses. First, as a principle the duty-to-be-in-the-world entails the radical risk of not being able to be in any possible world, the possibility of a collapse of the ethos of transcendence that supports the world precisely because it sustains and nurtures, making oneself present to it with the engagement and energy of transcending its situations. The ethos of valorizing transcendence, precisely because of its quality as primordial evidence of *humanitas*, is threatened by a drop in its impulse along the whole gamut of possible valorization. It appears threatened precisely in its character as a principle, by an inversion that involves the *ending of the world and presentification to the world*. This is the meaning of the recognition that "what can be lost, what can in any case be nullified, is the very metaphysical foundation of being." Undoubtedly the ethos of transcendence is called again and again to combat the extreme threat of losing or nullifying oneself. What we call *culture* in its positivity is precisely humanity's victorious struggle to keep the possibility always open of a possible cultural world—a solemn exorcism that, against the risk of "ending," doggedly brings to bear the various powers of worthy action and the *mores* that it generates and sustains. But, at the same time, culture's drama takes on its fullest human value precisely because "the duty-to-be in a culturally meaningful world" is exposed to the risk of "not being able to be in any cultural world possible," and can thus at most dissipate in the symptoms of a fatal illness, heading without hope of recovery to its catastrophic outcome. In this sense "the end of the world" is a permanent anthropological possibility that torments all human cultures. Here we already see a first, profound divergence separating the orientation of our analysis from what might derive from Heideggerian existentialism. In the latter perspective, being-there necessarily contains being-in-the-world in its transcendental structure: the analysis of being-there is thus necessarily resolved in a review of the various modalities of being-in-the-world. In the perspective adopted here, instead, the transcendental structure of being-there is the duty-to-be-in-the-world in the process of asserting itself against the risk of not being able to be in any possible cultural world. The catastrophe of the worldly therefore does not appear in the analysis as a mode of being-in-the-world but as a permanent threat, at times mastered and resolved, at times triumphant, to which the duty-to-be-in-the-world is exposed in a coessential way to its very quality as the supreme operative principle that lies at the root of human presentifying to the world[46] and [...].

5.5. Progress.

If by "progress" we mean the ethos of intersubjective valorization of life, every civilization—as long as it lasts in history—is progress, that is, valorizing emergence from natural conditions, whatever consciousness it has of this emerging, and even if it denies it in religious behaviors based on the ritual repetition of mythical origins or on mystical pretentions of escaping the "world" once and for all or mystical expectations of a definitive eschaton of human history. In order for a civilization to exist, a society to function, a language to communicate, and values to circulate, it is it necessary to *progress* beyond naturalness, transcending life: and it is precisely this ethos of progress or an active force of cultural life whose decline marks the end of both individuals and groups.

The plan of a universal history from an *a quo* of the beginning to an *ad quem* of eschaton should be rejected as a vestige of the theological vision of history that developed within the Judeo-Christian tradition. But the negation of a plan inscribed in the order of divine providence or the Spirit of the World or the history of productive forces of material life does not mean the negation of projects for unifying human dispersion and the multiplicity of traditions and cultures: a projecting of this sort poses unity as a task that can even be unfulfilled and assign to unification the character of a choice that may not take place even if all of the conditions are favorable for it. Progress has a margin of indeterminacy and a temptation for death, and this margin and this temptation make up precisely[47] [. . .]

5.6. The ethos of transcendence is quintessential human experience, since it is energy transcending situations—that is, valorizing action and, simultaneously, operative valorization. In order for there to be a world and one's situation in it, it is necessary to emerge from it, create for oneself margin or a horizon of qualification and behavior with regard to it, not coinciding immediately with the situation but detaching itself from it again and again, and again and again measuring the established distance in each case according to certain parameters (values). This beyond, this emerging, this margin, this horizon, this power of detachment and measuring specifically make up a primordial ethos that grounds all transcendences and does not entail any legitimate beyond in the sense of "pure matter" or "pure spirit." As an ethos, a primal will to culture and history, it is exposed to an extreme risk, to the collapse of the power of valorization on the whole gamut of the valorizable; and inversion of its impulse is experienced as catastrophe that strikes presentification and the world that it makes itself present to. Human cultures are indeed evidence of this struggle against the temptation of nothingness that harms the duty-to-be for value, that is, as attested to by weapons used, setbacks endured, epochs of health, health threatened, and illness. History is the search for this ethos in consciousness, placing its meaning in this search for those acting in it as well as for those who judge its cultures, epochs, and the geniuses in which it is manifested.

5.7. Being-there and the ethos of transcendence.

Being-there in society, in a world of things at hand that is always so-cialized, contains in an inaugural way the fundamental recourse to inter-subjectivity in human life, to an allegiance to others even in the sphere of material needs. Precisely because humankind is in society and publicly oriented, the commitment to other intersubjective allegiances that lie beyond things at hand in a strict sense is justified: the commitment to render one's own activity public, to come out of one's own incommuni-cable "intimacy," to dedicate oneself to being a controller who is, simulta-neously, open to being controlled and confirmed. To the extent that they are not "ill," the alienated, the rootless, rebels and recluses also participate in being-there-in-society, and mystics too. Furthermore, being-there in society cannot exhaust all being-there without leaving any "beyond": oth-erwise one lapses into the flattest totalitarian conformity, into technicism, and so forth.

The ethos of transcendence is a *precategorial value*,[48] not in the sense of pure and simple *life* but in the sense of a *life captured in the process of opening itself to categorial values*, that is, to forms of cultural coherence. This ethos of transcendence, this *dutiful going beyond according to cat-egorial values*, is the supreme value, the condition for their unfolding: a primordial going beyond that can never be transcended because every transcendence according to categorial values is carried out in it and for it. The ethos of transcendence can nonetheless *pass*, establishing the extreme risk of all values that thereby prove to be struck at the very root: this is the closing of cultural life's array, the not being able to be in any possible cul-tural world. It can pass into itself, giving rise to psychopathological modes of existence; but it can also pass in the sense of not being-there faithfully in a distinct categorial value (a lack of allegiance to be understood as a confusion of several categorial values as well as the tendency to fetishize myself: poetry-propaganda, aestheticism).

The ethos of transcendence can pass in various senses: (1) in an exis-tential sense, giving rise to psychopathological states; (2) in a categorial sense, that is, within each form of valorization, giving rise to its "negative"; (3) in a natural sense, with a person's death.

5.8. The ethos of transcendence of life in value founds individual valoriz-ing transcendences. As a norm of potentiality and regulating endpoint of all valorizing transcendences, per se it cannot be transcended in the sense that neither life nor value can be drawn on once and for all. The primordial "duty-to-be" of this ethos lies wholly in the beyond of its movement, pass-ing from life to the intersubjective valorization of life, and in reposing this passage again and again. The risk of this beyond lies in its fall, but its fall leads neither to the immediacy of life nor to the absoluteness of value; instead, it leads to nothingness, to death, to madness.

The living, true, full "world" is not the fetishized one in which "one gets lost" but the one that we resolve to lose or regain, to call into question or recover in the enactment of a ceaseless presentification. It is a world that must stubbornly die and be reborn, one we must continue to build after our sleep, one that even in our sleep and dreams we continue to build and is certainly not interrupted by death. As a risk the end of the world is the collapse of the ethos of transcendence along the whole gamut of the valorizable: and this risk striking individuals can menace entire societies, even humanity as a whole. But the heart of the matter is always the person who possesses it.

The "no man's land" between existence and being, between the temporal and the eternal, emerges from a decline in the ethos of transcendence and therefore from no longer recognizing (or from not yet realizing) that the presumed no man's land is not only always occupied but also the only land in which a person is sovereign. More precisely, "to exist" means to always open oneself to being, and this "worthy" being is never separable from the "duty-to-be" that strives toward it.

No individual, no value that a person opens to, no epoch, no society, no civilization can claim to have "exhausted being." Such a claim is the risk that threatens the ethos of transcendence, because "to exhaust being" simply means "the being that exhausts itself as being and becomes nothingness."

5.9. The subjects forming a philosophy of valorizing presentification are

(a) The assertion of a transcendental ethos of transcendence of life in intersubjective valorization

(b) The inaugural nature of the communitarian project of things at hand, within which the following take on significance: (1) the multiplicity of individuals; (2) the social relationality of individuals; (3) the order of external material bodies; (4) the order of the instruments of material and mental control (natural science and technology); (5) individuals' embodiment; (6) regimes of production and distribution of economic goods

(c) The other communitarian projects besides handiness (art, philosophy, self-aware ethos or moral life)

(d) The crisis of the ethos of transcendence along the whole gamut of the valorizable

(e) The symbolic order (mythical-ritual or civil) intent on recovering the crisis or reversing it, disclosing valorization

In this perspective no individual, historically existing society, epoch, action performed within a value, or particular form of valorization can exhaust the transcendental ethos of transcendence, which is the condition and telos that on the one hand impose incessant going beyond and on the other hand, pose the "finiteness" (and thus the limit) of every individual, historically existing society, epoch, action according to value, and finally, form of valorization.

5.10. The principle of the ethos of transcendence of life in intersubjective valorization justifies and founds the particular valorization of a science of biological conditioning of psychic phenomena. What it certainly refuses is the absolutization of this perspective as with any materialist metaphysic. This principle simply expresses the coming to awareness that all specific valorizations of life—and thus also of the natural sciences—become intelligible *within* it and that we can never get outside of it in order to reach life or nature per se, independent from every possible human transcendence, or a valorization closed in on itself and exhausted, with no possible beyond. The ethos of transcendence can recognize its foundational and never-transcendable primariness: and in this awareness it becomes an explicit rule of life that makes itself into culture, while before it was an implicit rule, unaware and nonetheless operative. This is the absolute as a *duty-to-be for the intersubjective valorization of life*: but it is an "absolute" that as an inexhaustible "duty-to-be" intervenes again and again to call into question the presumptions of absolutization of the single specific valorizations of actions and assigns them the limits within which they are valid.

The principle of the ethos of transcendence contains a concept—and an image—of human culture in the act of shaping ever anew its effort to raise itself from life as immediate finiteness and need. Human culture is this ethos that we are seeking, and being sought it tries various paths, as many as there are human cultures that have seen the light of day on our planet. But on one of these paths, the one followed by Western civilization, the ethos is achieving consciousness of itself with great difficulty, hence it is so engrossed, confirmed, and defended in consciousness to be able to move forward to a new reshaping of all humanity, to an exchange, a dialogue and a unification of the divided peoples and the multitudinous cultural origins. This is therefore not an image of progress as unilineal development in phases through which all of humanity has supposedly solidly passed: it is instead an ethos of the valorization of life that has proceeded up to now in various directions to find itself, and only now, because of the eminent effort of a single culture—Western culture—it begins to recognize itself in its true nature; that is, not as a divine product, not as "subject," "spirit," "matter," "nature," "handiness," "technology," or "classes," but precisely as an ethos that moves beyond the immediacy and finiteness of mute and solitary living, needy and avaricious, clogged with individuality and doomed to death, proud of and tormented by its own flesh. And it moves beyond toward the communitarian and the intersubjective, the communicable and the expressive, to the point that it recognizes itself in this task and takes it on deliberately as a transforming mission of humanity, society, and nature.

5.11. To capture the ethos of transcendence in the process of transcending life for intersubjective valorization; to indicate the categorial intentions of these valorizations and concrete, historically conditioned modes in which the intentional impulse is enacted; to signal the risks to which the ethos of transcendence is exposed, both as it refers to its own principle and as it refers to single valorizations: all this is the task of a reformed ethnology or anthropology in which the ethos undertakes its greatest endeavor, becoming aware of itself and of its preeminence. In this perspective, the principle is neither "matter" nor "spirit," since both are constituted *within* the tension of transcendence. It is not intersubjective or individual, because transcendence entails an intersubjectivity that acts with all of the conditioning weight of a social tradition as well as individuals who freely open themselves to the intersubjective by renewing tradition. And above all, it is not the undue privilege and fetishistic absolutization of a particular categorial valorization (e.g., scientist naturalism, technicism, aestheticism, legalism, moralism, economism, mythologism, ritualism). The discovery of the ethos of transcendence as a fundamental anthropological principle—a founding category of categorizing and the continuous center for the localization, inspection, and redistribution of categorizing energy—is called to clarify the existentialist question of the "human condition" as *Weltverlorenheit*, "being-to-the-world" (*esserci al mondo*) (or "in" the world) and being lost in it.

Glossary

anabasis. From ancient Greek, de Martino uses *anabasis* (ascent) in contrast to *catabasis* (descent). These are technical terms in comparative religious history to designate, on the one hand, the hero's descent to the underworld, the kingdom of the dead; and on the other hand, the terrestrial return and ritual or spiritual ascent toward the celestial world.

anxiety (*angoscia*). *Angoscia* is the common translation in Italian for *Angst* as it appears in Heidegger's work. Here *angoscia* is rendered with "anxiety," the usual English translation for Heidegger's *Angst*, since this is consistently the context to which de Martino is referring rather than a psychological meaning of the term. While the subjective experience of anxiety is negative, for de Martino anxiety per se is not negative in that it is a signal that can stimulate the positive reactivity of a **presence** in crisis.

at hand/handiness (*utilizzabile*/*utilizzazione*). These terms refer to what Heidegger denotes with *zuhanden/Zuhandenheit*, words that are notoriously difficult to translate in English. The solution adopted here follows Joan Stambaugh's translation of *Being and Time*: some readers may be more familiar with Macquarrie and Robinson's "ready-to-hand" and "readiness-to-hand," which would have appeared too awkward within de Martino's text. The general sense of the terms relates to the unproblematic perception of nonhuman entities in terms of their usability. It should be noted that de Martino almost always diverges from Pietro Chiodi's authoritative Italian translation of Heidegger in using *utilizzazione* instead of *utilizzabilità* for *Zuhandenheit*.

being-acted-upon (*essere-agito-da*). This concept describes a common feature of what de Martino calls **crisis of presence**. Whether in an ethnological context dominated by magical practices or in contemporary Western psychiatry, individual agency in being-in-the-world may come under attack: sufferers may sense that an external force is acting on them, or else (as in possession) they may not be aware of such a force, though the effects on their agency is visible to the observer. See also de Martino's monographs *Il mondo magico* (The magical world; de Martino 1948) and *Sud e magia* (*Magic: A Theory from the South*) (de Martino 2015).

being-in-the-world (*esserci-nel-mondo*). De Martino borrows this expression from Heidegger's terminology: *in-der-Welt-sein*, a concept in close relation to Dasein to characterize human existence (as opposed to that of nonhuman entities).

being-there (*esserci*). *Esserci* is Pietro Chiodi's Italian translation for Heidegger's central concept of Dasein, which is commonly rendered "being-there" in English. De Martino uses the term almost interchangeably with **presence** and occasionally uses the German *Dasein*.

catabasis. See **anabasis**.

communitarian project of things at hand (*progetto comunitario dell'utilizzabile*). Formulated in various ways in de Martino's notes, his expression "communitarian project of things at hand" draws on the Italian translation of Heidegger's *Zuhandenes/Zuhandenheit* (see **at hand**). He mostly uses this as a synonym for "the economic" with the aim of confuting the vulgar materialist Marxist view that cultural life is merely a mechanical reflex of economic forces. The expression radically affirms the collective dimension as fundamental to being human and the dynamic quality of the Heideggerian "project" of goal-oriented action.

crisis of presence. This is fundamental notion in de Martino's oeuvre that captures the problematization of presence during critical events (e.g., mourning) or in conditions of extreme material precarity in which the sufferer typically suffers from a loss of agency: it is a "permanent anthropological risk." Despite its negative resonances, the crisis is nonetheless a signal of the presence's capacity for reactivity and should be understood in a broader framework as part of the process leading to (therapeutic) action that can restore presence.

cultural reintegration (*reintegrazione culturale*). This expression refers to both the means and the therapeutic outcome of culturally shared and transmitted mechanisms (rituals, symbols) that are employed to assist the presence in crisis. The shared quality of cultural reintegration distinguishes it from individual rituals and symbols, as seen, for example, in magical thinking in psychopathology.

Dasein. See **being-there**.

deworlding (*demondanizzazione*). Drawing initially on *Entweltlichung* in Heidegger, where it is discussed in terms of things at hand in space, de Martino instead uses this term to characterize one aspect of the loss of presence. Whereas Heidegger implies the existence of a "pure" Nature of things that are deworlded, in de Martino's conception there is no such precultural Nature, but the presence in crisis loses its world, inevitably and in toto culturally conditioned. De Martino marks his rethinking of Heidegger by not utilizing Pietro Chiodi's standard translation of *demondificazione*.

duty-to-be/duty-to-be-in-the-world (*dover essere, dover esserci / doverci-essere-nel-mondo*). Storch and Kulenkampff (1950) speak of a duty-to-be as a *Seinmüssen*, and together with a Crocean emphasis on ethics, de Martino draws on this to complement Heidegger's *Seinsollen*. De Martino's insistence on this "obligation to be" is a fundamental element of his notion of the ethos of transcendence.

entities within-the-world (entità intramondane). The expression is a direct borrowing from Heidegger's *innerweltlich Seindes*, to denote entities that Dasein encounters in the world, revealing themselves according to Dasein's projects and needs, especially entities with which Dasein proximally dwells.

eschaton. The ancient Greek "last" refers to the day at the end of time, but de Martino uses it as equivalent to "redemption," distinguishing apocalypses with and without eschaton. This redemption is to be understood in a Christian sense, suggesting a "fulfillment" that implies a theological conception of time.

ethos of transcendence (ethos del trascendimento). De Martino offers various formulations of this notion in *The End of the World*, including "transcendental ethos of transcendence" and "ethos of transcendence of life in (intersubjective) value." His notes for the book and his philosophical writings (de Martino 2005b) reveal his efforts to hammer out the concept. The ethos of transcendence is the valorizing energy that transcends the given situation, thereby founding and reaffirming presence and the world.

ganz Andere. See **wholly other**.

handy/handiness (utilizzabile/utilizzazione). See **at hand**.

hierogenetic (ierogenetico). See **hierogonic**.

hierogonic (ierogonico). This is a neologism by de Martino, who uses the Greek roots *iero* (sacred) and *gonia* (genesis) as a way of signaling the historical genesis of the sacred. According to historian of religion Marcello Massenzio (personal communication), this terminology reflects the novelty of de Martino's thought vis-à-vis that of Mircea Eliade: for de Martino, the sacred does not exist per se but is a product of history. Together with *theogenetic* and *hierogenetic* (the latter an established term in Italian religious studies), *hierogonic* is part of a family of similar terms that de Martino uses with this same intent of underlining historicity.

in illo tempore. Literally "at that time," the phrase refers to mythical time.

koinonia (coinonia). De Martino uses the Greek term to indicate a fusion of elements that should be kept distinct, a "con-fusion," to refer to the risk of losing the self/world distinction. He uses the term frequently in his monograph *Il mondo magico* to describe situations of loss of presence.

Parousia. The coming of Christ.

pia fraus. Literally, "pious fraud." In de Martino's theorization of ritual dehistorification, it refers to how ritual offers a protected space for being in history "as if" one were not, by following ritual's metahistorical time.

potentiality of being (poter essere). "Potentiality of being" is another borrowing from Heidegger (*Seinkönnen*), adopting here the Stambaugh translation (Macquarrie and Robinson use "potentiality-for-Being"). It describes the fundamental nature of Dasein as one of possible being along with its actual being.

presence (*presenza*). This key term is de Martino's reformulation of Heideggerian Dasein. As we see in this and other works by de Martino, his focus is on presence—against Kant's unity of apperception—as not to be considered given once and for all but as subject to being threatened with loss or a **crisis of presence**. De Martino looks at the ways in which culture, especially rituals and symbols, anchor and restore a presence at risk.

presentification (*presentificazione*). In part inspired by Pierre Janet's *présentification* (Janet 1928), de Martino often uses this term instead of **presence** in order to highlight the processual nature of presence, permanently at risk, dynamic, and in constant need of self-reaffirmation and configuration.

project (*progetto/progettazione*). De Martino's use of "project" is related to Heidegger's notion of *Entwurf*, and the translation here adopts Macquarrie and Robinson's usage in their English edition of *Being and Time*. De Martino's Italian often uses variations on the term, with *progettabile* (projectable), *progettabilità* (projectability), and *progettazione* (projecting, projection).

settled/settling (*appaesato/appaesamento*). The Italian terms *appaesato/appaesamento* are de Martino's invention to get at notions of domesticity, familiarity, and at-homeness. These must be understood in the context of their opposites, *spaesato/spaesamento* (see **unsettled/unsettling**). With these, he opens an innovative new arena for thinking about the role of culture in grounding existence. The Italian root *paese* does not have an exact English equivalent, but it can indicate an attachment to territory on different scales: a village or small town, but also a nation, a cultural homeland; landscape is *paesaggio*. The pair *settled/settling* does not directly embrace *paese* in the way the Italian terms do, but it does allude to a process of rooting in space.

Stimmung (pl. *Stimmungen*). *Stimmung* is a common German term meaning "mood" or "atmosphere," but it also forms part of Heidegger's lexicon and that of German phenomenological psychiatry. De Martino retains the German in many places as a nod to these thinkers.

theogenetic (*teogenetico*). See **hierogonic**.

tua res agitur. A citation from Horace, roughly "it is a matter that concerns you," sometimes associated with 1 Corinthians 6.

unsettled/unsettling (*spaesato/spaesamento*). De Martino uses *spaesato* extensively throughout the book, sometimes used intransitively as "unsettled" (disoriented) and at other times transitively as "unsettling" (uncanny). Although the standard Italian translation for *unheimlich* in the psychoanalytic thought is *perturbante*, at times de Martino places *spaesato* alongside the German as a gloss, suggesting that he is not using it strictly in its psychoanalytic sense. In English, of course, *unheimlich* is "uncanny." *Spaesamento*, which for de Martino suggests disorientation/alienation/*Unheimlichkeit*, has been translated here with the gerund "unsettling." The choice of "unsettled/unsettling" is an attempt to capture these various meanings along with their spatial connection and the sense of losing ground, visible in both the Italian and German etymologies. The terms form pairs with their opposites, **settled/settling**.

useful (*utile*). We can understand "the useful" in de Martino as a broad reference to the economic sphere, where he is adopting the language of Benedetto Croce's four categories of the Spirit (aesthetics, logic, economics, morals). The useful in Croce is the characteristic value of the economic domain, and it is a category that embraces other emanations of Spirit: science, technology, law, and politics.

vitality (*vitalità*). De Martino derives this term from the idealist philosophy of Croce, who used it a synonym of ***useful*** and *economic* as a basis for action. De Martino appropriates the term, distinguishing between biological (or animal) vitality and human vitality, constituted by **presence**. Presence, through the **ethos of transcendence**, detaches itself from biological vitality and constitutes culture in the various domains of its affirmation.

Weltuntergangserlebnis (abbr. WUE). A term coined in German psychiatry, *Weltuntergangserlebnis* is a lived experience of the end of the world in psychopathology.

wholly other (*tutt'altro*). De Martino draws this expression from the work of religious historian Rudolf Otto (*ganz Andere*). It refers to the experience of the radical alterity of the sacred.

worldhood (*mondanità*). With *worldhood*, de Martino refers to Heidegger's *Weltlichkeit* as an ontological structure of Dasein's world, but he introduces his own modifications deriving from his ethnological perspective. He almost always uses *mondanità* instead of *mondità*, Chiodi's canonical Italian translation of *Being and Time*.

worldly (*mondano*). While in some cases de Martino uses *mondano* in its conventional meaning as "secular," in most cases it appears in the volume as a gloss of Heidegger's *weltlich*.

Notes

Introduction

1. In this English edition, annotations have been kept to a minimum to maintain the book's length within established limits. For the same reason, the extensive commentaries by Charuty, Fabre, and Massenzio have regretfully been left out: though they do offer many useful observations to orient the reader, not all of them are pertinent for an English-language readership unfamiliar with de Martino. Furthermore, it was not possible to include the photographs from de Martino's fieldwork that accompany French and Italian editions. The essay in the appendix, "Cultural Apocalypses and Psychopathological Apocalypses," is being published separately.

2. Stanley Kubrick's film *Dr. Strangelove* came out in 1964, in Italy in the same year, while de Martino was preparing the book. However, Carlo Ginzburg (2017, 85) argues that Michelangelo Antonioni's *Eclisse* (The Eclipse) (1962) "may have sparked off the project on *La fine del mondo*."

3. In particular, see Lanternari's internationally influential monograph on the subject (English edition: Lanternari 1963).

4. As reconstructed, in this chapter de Martino does not actually treat Marxism so much as a new religion as he instead probes its perspective critically, rejecting vulgar materialism and Marxism's belittling of the importance of religion.

5. For a more thorough treatment in English, see de Martino (2012) and the translators' preface (Farnetti e Stewart 2012), as well as the intellectual biographies of de Martino by Ferrari (2012) and Geissheusler (2021). See also Saunders (1995) for an application of de Martino's framework to the ethnographic case of Italian Pentecostals.

6. The second section of chapter 1 ("*Mundus patet*") deals at length with the ancient Roman *mundus* ritual, giving a sense of how culture institutionally disciplines the process of world renewal.

7. That de Martino did not conceive of cultural homelands as exclusive was evident in his personal experience of adopting his own fieldwork area, Lucania, as a chosen homeland (*patria elettiva*). Even so, as I have noted elsewhere (Zinn 2020), despite this de Martino does not seem to go beyond a rather isomorphic conception of the connection between place and identity, with the attendant risk of producing essentializations and exclusions.

8. In English, see George Saunders's (1993) treatment of critical ethnocentrism but also Berrocal's (2009) discussion.

9. The US presents numerous other similar examples that are of interest (Stewart and Harding 1999; Harding and Stewart 2003).

Overture

1. Originally published as de Martino (1964).

2. The Italian term used by de Martino for "jinxing" is *iettatorio*. On the belief system of *jettatura*, see de Martino (2015) [trans.].

3. De Martino is referring to common Neapolitan apotropaic gestures: making a horn symbol with a hand or, for men, touching their genitals [trans.].

4. Lawrence (1931) 1966; the quotation is not verbatim [trans.].

5. Navel 1949, 201–2. De Martino attributes the citation to *Parcours*. It has been corrected here as *Travaux*.

6. Jean Rouch, dir., *Les maîtres fous* (1955).

7. It was not the Bambara but the Hauka sect that developed among the Songhay in the mid-1920s.

8. Of various possible titles for this essay, the editors selected the one cited by Vittorio Lanternari and in a summary present in the de Martino Archive, 23.16, pp. 98–100.

9. Thrupp 1962.

10. Centre d'étude des religions 1962.

11. De Martino is writing in the context of decolonization and the Second Vatican Council [trans.].

12. Gusdorf 1963.

13. Caruso 1963.

14. Caruso.

15. Dostoevsky 2009, 23–25 [trans.].

16. Mounier 1962.

17. Baumer 1954.

18. Franz Altheim, "Apokalyptik Heute," *Die Neue Rundschau* 1 (1954): 117–31.

19. See chap. 5, sec. 2.1.

20. Petriconi 1958.

21. "Apocalisse e Insecuritas," ed. Enrico Castelli, special issue, *Archivio di filosofia* 1 (1954).

22. Brandis and Dmitrevskij 1964 [trans.].

23. Schiff 1946.

24. Chap. 4, sec. 2.4, 2.5.

Chapter One

1. Bracketed comments are by de Martino [trans.].

2. Storch and Kulenkampff 1950, 103. The journal *Der Nervenarzt* was founded in

1930 to represent the phenomenological anthropology that developed around Ludwig Binswanger.

3. Alfred Storch (1888–1962) was one of the first psychiatrists to extend Heideggerian analysis to psychopathology.

4. Caspar Kulenkampff (1921–2002) was a central figure in the reform of German psychiatric institutions and considered a leading figure in "anthropological psychiatry".

5. De Martino paraphrases Storch and Kulenkampff [trans.].

6. Incomplete sentence.

7. Wetzel's use of *Unheimlichkeitstimmung* does not seem related to Freud's reelaboration of it.

8. Wetzel 1922.

9. "Eine wenigstens partielle radikale 'Entrückung' aus der gemeinsamen in eine private Welt." Kunz (1931, 697), mistakenly reported by de Martino as 1930 [trans.].

10. The expression is from Rudolf Otto, *ganz Andere*, in describing the alterity of the sacred.

11. This is an undated letter that de Martino planned to send to Kulenkampff; we do not know if ever arrived. In that period Kulenkampff was teaching at the University of Frankfurt am Main, but in the archives there is no trace of a reply.

12. De Martino mistakenly gave 81 as the volume number [trans.].

13. A cosmic tree in Nordic mythology.

14. De Martino paraphrases from the original text here.

15. In his translation, de Martino leaves the parenthetical matter in German but misspells *heimisch* as *heimlich* [trans.].

16. De Martino draws this concept from Binswanger to indicate a normative structuring underlying relations of sense that preside over behavior.

17. Nikolaus Lenau (1802–50), a post-Romantic Austrian writer.

18. A late elaboration of vitalist philosophy.

19. "ascending and surging life" [trans.].

20. "[E]verything that falls . . . becomes part of the void." Bachelard 1988, 74 [trans.].

21. "Eritis sicut Deus, scientes bonum et malum" (You will be like God, knowing good and evil; Genesis 3:5) [trans.].

22. "Gravity precedes light as its ever dark ground, which itself is not *actu* [actual], and flees into the night as the light (that which exists) dawns"; Schelling 2006, 27. Heidegger (1985, 114) critically rereads this quote [trans.].

23. Binswanger 1942.

24. Paris, 1943, 270; English edition: Bachelard 1988, 74 [trans.].

25. Zurich, 1949. English edition: *The Origins and History of Consciousness* (New York: Pantheon Books, 1954) [trans.].

26. Bachelard 1988, 74 [trans.].

27. De Martino uses the German edition (Heidegger 1935).

28. Rudolf Otto's concept indicating the impossibility of reducing to reason the religious experience of contact with the "wholly other."

29. Storch and Kulenkampff (1950, 108), erroneously noted as Wetzel. The original attributes the expressions "forgetfulness of being" and "belonging" to Heidegger, citations omitted in de Martino's Italian translation [trans.].

30. Plutarch 1914 [trans.].

31. "He" refers to Romulus [trans.].

32. Ovid 1931.

33. De Martino references Festus's text as established by Wallace Martin Lindsay (Festus 1965). No English version appears to be available [trans.].

34. Macrobius 1969, 108.

35. De Martino hired Glaesser to prepare a literature review on *mundus*, and it is Glaesser's voice that narrates section 2 of this chapter through excerpts from his report. The author at the center of his discussion is Henri Le Bonniec, whose monograph (Le Bonniec 1958) was of particular interest to de Martino: the passages underlined by de Martino are in italics [trans.].

36. He refers to data that allow the author to state that, as an Italic deity, Ceres belongs to the group of agrarian and underworld deities.

37. Sows sacrificed before the festival [trans.].

38. The Manes were the souls of the dead [trans.].

39. *Collection of Latin Inscriptions*, Mommsen 1863.

40. "with large and very ancient letters" [trans.].

41. "They used to think that the *manalis* stone was the opening of the Underworld, through which the souls of the dead who are called ghosts (manes) pass to the earthly world" [trans.].

42. Weinstock 1930.

43. Priest of Ceres [trans.].

44. "this being a sacred occasion dedicated to Father Dis and Proserpine, and men deemed it better to go out to battle when the jaws of Pluto are shut" [trans.].

45. "Some say that the *mundus* was placed in the shrine of Ceres and the sky was placed before the *mundus*" [trans.].

46. Deubner 1933.

47. Le Bonniec 1958 [trans.].

48. That the term *mundus* indicates a form of silo for storing seeds.

49. Piganiol 1923.

50. Turchi 1939.

51. Rose 1931.

52. Walde and Hofman 1938; Ernout and Meillet 1959.

53. Ernout 1946–65, 1:39.

54. The right of dead spirits [trans.].

55. Wissowa 1912.

56. Altheim 1931.

57. On ritual dehistorification in English, see de Martino 2012 [trans.].

58. De Martino writes, "del cosmificato e del cosmificabile," using the Greek root *cosmos* to indicate the attribution of culturally shaped order. I thank Marcello Massenzio for this information [trans.].

59. Pavese 1952.

60. *Incolta*, which also means "uncultured," "uncultivated" [trans.].

61. De Martino reformulates Marx's famous quote from "The Eighteenth Brumaire of Louis Bonaparte" [trans.].

62. De Martino's reference to "Spirit" should be understood as deriving from Benedetto Croce's "Philosophy of Spirit." See Croce 1909, 1917a, 1917b [trans.].

63. A Kierkegaardian theme; Kierkegaard 2014.

64. Kerényi 1963, 4.

65. The page reference is for the English translation; van der Leeuw 1957 [trans.].

66. Van der Leeuw 1957, 338. De Martino includes van der Leeuw's reference for this last line: Lietzmann 1936, 196 [trans.].

67. Zechariah 14:7, "And there shall be continuous day (it is known to the Lord), not day and not night, for at evening time there shall be light" [trans.].

68. Page references are for the English edition; Eliade (1957) 1960 [trans.].

69. De Martino is referring to "dreamtime" among numerous Indigenous peoples of Australia [trans.].

70. A divinatory practice in ancient Greece and Egypt [trans.].

71. Jensen 1951.

72. A collection of aphorisms from Indian philosophy compiled from 200 BCE to 500 CE.

73. See the English edition; Eliade 1958. Page numbers are for the Italian edition from which de Martino was working. There is not an exact correspondence in the citations of Eliade: either de Martino is paraphrasing Eliade or the English edition revised the French original [trans.].

74. Page references are for the English edition; Eliade 1961 [trans.].

75. Eliade's expression: "terror of history" [trans.].

76. English translation: Otto 1924.

77. Dilthey 1931.

78. Jacob Wilhelm Hauer (1881–1962).

79. Rosenberg 2011.

80. English edition: Coomaraswamy 1959 [trans.].

81. De Martino borrows this term from Heidegger.

82. "And until you learn the best, / This: Die, and become! / You are but a sullen guest, / Earth is dull and glum." From Goethe's poem "Blessed Longing"; Goethe 2010, 16–17.

83. St. Teresa of Avila 1985, 375–76 [trans.].

Chapter Two

1. The concept of *Dasein-Umwandlung*, developed from Heidegger's notion of *Umwandlung des Daseins*, was introduced by Alfred Storch in this article.

It was used by German existential psychiatrists at least until the end of the 1960s.

2. In Greek mythology, the metamorphosis of a thing, person, or hero into a constellation, or the transfer of the soul to heaven or among the stars.

3. Binswanger translated these categories from Heideggerian philosophy to the clinical context, adding a third dimension, the *Eigenwelt*, the private dimension of the relation to self.

4. See Jung (2000) (English ed.). The note in Storch's article lists several works on the subject [trans.].

5. De Martino's addition [trans.].

6. Here, de Martino cites Storch's work closely but shifts some of the sentences around; while it is not an exact quotation, it is more than a close paraphrase [trans.].

7. Storch cites the German poet Hölderlin from Rehm (1943).

8. Pages are for the English edition, Jaspers (1997, vol. 1). Emphases in direct citations are Jaspers's [trans.].

9. Carl Westphal (1833–1890), neurologist, neuranatomist, and psychiatrist representing intellectualist theory within the German school.

10. Sandberg 1895, 619.

11. This is the English translation of Jaspers: de Martino glosses this as "unfamiliar," followed in parentheses by "*spaesato, Unheimlich*" [trans.].

12. Hagen 1870.

13. A student of Karl Jaspers, in 1955 Kurt Schneider (1897–1967) described the "principal symptoms" for diagnosing schizophrenia.

14. De Martino's translation from German: "non familiare, spaesati (*unheimlich*)" [trans.].

15. The English edition of Jaspers speaks of the patient's "awareness of illness" as opposed to "judgement" or "insight" regarding the illness (Jaspers 1997, 419) [trans.].

16. "It is a matter that concerns you" [trans.].

17. Mayer-Gross, Slater, and Roth 1956. De Martino cites the British edition, while the US edition was consulted for the quotation [trans.]. Between 1920 and 1930, Wilhelm Mayer-Gross (1889–1961) was part of a small group of phenomenologists who formed the Heidelberg school, along with Karl Jaspers, Hans Walter Gruhle, and Kurt Beringer. His textbook of clinical psychiatry, used by de Martino, trained entire generations of doctors.

18. The gerund form here, rather than "end," is justified by de Martino's own use (*finire* vs. *fine*), drawing from an observation by his collaborator Bruno Callieri pointing to the need for a more dynamic translation for the German word *Untergang* [trans.].

19. Rhythmic, repetitive movements or vocalizations [trans.].

20. A religious concept of Eastern Melanesia that became a central category in debates on religion, magic, and symbolic efficacy between the 1880s and 1950s.

21. Lévi-Strauss 1987.

22. Page numbers refer to the English edition, Jaspers (1997). Emphasis in the quotes is Jaspers's [trans.].

23. De Martino's translation features this from the German original, which is not in the English edition: "or whose history he attempts to reconstruct" [trans.].

24. Karl Willhelm Ideler (1795–1860) was a representative of German Romantic psychiatry that introduced the distinction between disorders that strike affectivity (mania, melancholy) and disorders that strike thinking (paranoia); he was particularly interested in "religious delusions."

25. Ey 1954. De Martino dedicated many notes to his reading of Ey's *Études psychiatriques*, vol. 3. French psychiatrist Henri Ey (1900–1977) looks to John H. Jackson's and Pierre Janet's phenomenological notions of intentionality, and he draws on Binswanger's existential analysis to develop his original theory of structuration and destructuration of consciousness.

26. Ey 1954.

27. All page numbers are for the English edition, Jaspers (1997, vol. 2).

28. See chap. 1, n. 62.

29. De Martino's translation of Jaspers's *bildhafte Denken* is *pensiero simbolico* (symbolic thinking) [trans.].

30. "Such evil deeds could religion prompt"; Lucretius (1910), *On the Nature of Things* 1.101 [trans.].

31. Danilo Cargnello (1911–98) introduced German phenomenological psychopathology in Italy.

32. World-forming. The expression is Heidegger's, indicating a quality that distinguishes humans from animals.

33. Binswanger adopted this term in the 1940s to designate an original knowledge of "being human," both inspired by and critical of Freudian, Husserlian, and Heideggerian thought; with it, he refounded psychiatry starting from an analysis of the structure of existence.

34. Eugène Minkowski (1885–1972) introduced the concept of structure into French psychiatry.

35. In this public/private opposition, de Martino reformulates Heidegger's themes of the everydayness of being-in-the-world and thrownness in the publicness of the "they."

36. Janet frequently refers to Teresa of Avila in discussing the medicalization of religious ecstasy as a neurotic pathology.

37. In de Martino's monograph on tarantism, he refutes various reductive interpretations of the phenomenon [trans.].

38. Also known as "delusion of control": "A delusion that one's actions or thoughts are being controlled by an external agent" (Colman 2009, 198) [trans.].

39. Dumas 1946.

40. For an extensive treatment of Lucanian magic and its psychological aspects, see de Martino (2015) [trans.].

41. Callieri 1955.

42. Storch 1949.

43. *Weltuntergangserlebnis*: a psychiatric abbreviation for "end-of-the-world experience."
44. Albrecht Wetzel's (1922) article "Das Weltuntergangserlebnis in der Schizophrenie" [End-of-the-world experience in schizophrenia] was the first to identify this syndrome.
45. Anders 1959. According to Anders, the explosion of the atomic bomb on 6 August 1945 inaugurated a new era in which the possibility of humanity's self-destruction can only end with its disappearance, and we are incapable of representing to ourselves the apocalyptic danger we have produced.
46. Wetzel actually speaks of Catholic missions [trans.].
47. De Martino is paraphrasing Wetzel [trans.]. The Latin citation is Wetzel's allusion to Hagen's study of the "idée fixe" (Hagen 1870).
48. Here and below, Wetzel's emphasis [trans.].
49. Totally different: de Martino leaves the German *ganz andere* in his text, also suggesting an emphasis that connects this use, again, with Rudolf Otto's *ganz andere* as "wholly other" [trans.].
50. De Martino's comment [trans.].
51. Wetzel's exact original is *ganz anders*, not *ganz andere*, as de Martino notes here.
52. Volmat 1956.
53. A reference to sacred, mythical time in Eliade's thought [trans.].
54. Binswanger 1960.
55. Binswanger 1957.
56. Kranz 1955.
57. Gruhle 1915.
58. Storch 1930.
59. The second of two second points by de Martino [trans.].
60. *Geisteskranken*. De Martino's translation is *psicotici* [trans.].

Chapter Three

1. From Benedetto Croce: *res gestae* (things done), *historia rerum gestarum* (history of things done, or history of great deeds), *res gerendae* (things to be done) [trans.].
2. The expression is also from Croce's framework: "history in the making" [trans.].
3. Oscar Cullman (1902–99), historian, theologian and Protestant biblical exegete, specialist in the New Testament and the history of salvation. He set off a long debate among German-speaking Protestant theologians with his thesis that the New Testament places Christ "at the center of time."
4. An allusion to the work of theologian Rudolf Bultmann (1884–1976), who defined *demythologization* as the first step toward resolving the theological problem of the Christian message adapted to modernity.
5. Cullmann 1964 [trans.].

6. Bultmann 1955 [trans.].

7. In 1953–54 Jaspers and Bultmann engaged in a debate over "demythologization" (Jaspers and Bultmann 1954).

8. Page references are for the English edition, Eliade 1961 [trans.].

9. Eliade 1961, 31.

10. Viano 1960.

11. This paragraph ends with the beginning of a sentence: "If, for example, one . . ."

12. An expression de Martino uses to critique excessive identification with the object of study: he cites German concert halls where the audience is warned that "singing along is forbidden" [trans.].

13. The term *historicism* has two principal meanings: (1) a period of German historiography that dominated the second half of the nineteenth century: to define the rules of historical method in order to make it a rigorous science; and (2) the assertion that all human products are the result of a historical process, a sense that gained favor in the twentieth century as "relativist historicism." The postwar debate in Italy featured a critique of Croce's notion of "absolute historicism"— a philosophy of immanence that strongly criticized German historians in the attempt to resolve the tension between philosophy and history; it also figures into a debate between de Martino and Croce.

14. De Martino speaks of "actuality" in an Aristotelian sense [trans.].

15. The Italian edition gives 1954 as the date of publication, but the correct date is 1953. Page references are for the English edition, Eliade (1957) 1960 [trans.].

16. Eliade borrows the Vedic expression for "cosmic illusion" to describe the ontological irreality of the world and human experience.

17. Eliade borrows this Hasidic story, published by Martin Buber (1947), from the Indianist Heinrich Zimmer, without a reference.

18. De Martino paraphrases Eliade here (237) [trans.].

19. Page numbers reference the English edition, Eliade (1957) 1960 [trans.].

20. A term based on the ancient Greek *parousia* that designates, in the Greco-Roman world, the official visit of a prince. For theologists this term refers to the return of Christ at End-Times.

21. From the Greek *parakletos*, "one called to help," the term indicates the Holy Spirit's function of intercession in Christian tradition.

22. Acts of the Apostles.

23. The two poles of "already" and "not yet" are at the center of Cullmann's theology, treated here by de Martino. *Pistis, elpis,* and *agape* denote the three theological virtues of faith, hope, and charity.

24. Linforth 1941; Dodds 1951.

25. "End-times": an expression in apocalyptic literature whose interpretation has given rise to numerous debates.

26. De Martino 1958.

27. Page numbers refer to the English edition, Cullmann 1964 [trans.].

28. Incomplete sentence.

29. Cullmann 1964, 218–19, emphasis. Cullmann's [trans.].

30. Kierkegaard expounds the thesis that through imitation every believer becomes a contemporary of Christ.
31. Mark 1:15 and Matthew 4:17, "the Kingdom [of God] has come near" [trans.].
32. In this passage, de Martino paraphrases Cullmann (1964, 101–2) [trans.].
33. The reference corresponds to Epistle to the Colossians 1:16.
34. A geochronological interval of time.
35. Cullmann's expression (1964, 141–2) [trans.].
36. 1 Corinthians 7:31: "For the present form of this world is passing away."
37. The biblical passage cited by de Martino begins at 7:29.
38. Zoroastrianism.
39. Kittel 1935.
40. De Martino refers in a footnote to a series of Italian works on Rudolf Bultmann and the 1962 Italian translation of Bultmann (1955) [trans.].
41. Collingwood 1946.
42. Eliade 1954.
43. Benedict 1934.
44. Beginning, origin [trans.].
45. Spengler 1926.
46. Paul, 1 Corinthians 9:22: "To the weak I became weak, so that I might win the weak. I have become all things to all people, so that I might by any means save some." On de Martino's concept of critical ethnocentrism, see Saunders (1993).
47. See n. 21 above.
48. A reference to the work of Cebes of Thebes cited in Plato.

Chapter Four

1. De Martino's repetition [trans.].
2. Suspension of judgment [trans.].
3. "Race of savage people." Early modern thinkers borrowed this expression from medieval biblical exegesis in the attempt to categorize the new peoples they encountered [trans.].
4. Incomplete sentence.
5. Mühlmann 1962.
6. K. Jaspers, *Allegemeine Psychopathologie* (in English, Jaspers 1997).
7. "Pathological lying"; expression introduced by Ernest Dupré in the early twentieth century to describe a feature of hysteria.
8. Subsequent page numbers are for the English edition (Lommel 1997). The two English works by Lommel present different transcriptions for Unambal terms and names; usage in the 1950 text has been adopted here [trans.].
9. Elkin 1938.
10. Vittorio Lanternari (1960) dedicates several pages to this cult as an effect of "Euro-Australian cultural contact" and to its tolerance by missionaries and to the absence of local prophetism in hunter society: *Movimenti religiosi di libertà*

e di salvezza dei popoli oppressi (Milan: Feltrinelli, 1960), 217–22. [English edition, Lanternari (1963)—trans.]

11. Also *tjuringa*: ritual boards or tablets in wood or stone of the Aboriginal peoples of the central Australian desert; they are decorated with carved, nonfigurative designs; Lommel also calls them "slabs." They materialize the connection between individuals and totemic ancestors and between a local group and its territory. Lévi-Strauss has compared them to our historical archives.

12. Petri 1950.

13. Page numbers are for the English edition (Lommel 1997) [trans.].

14. De Martino mistakenly uses the feminine form in this sentence [trans.].

15. Page number in the English edition [trans.].

16. The emphasis in the citation is de Martino's, not in Lommel's original text [trans.].

17. English edition (Knox 1950, 149) [trans.].

18. Festinger, Riecken, and Schachter 1956.

19. "I believe it because it is absurd" [trans.].

20. Uniqueness [trans.].

21. A reference to the dispute between Guglielmo Guariglia, a Catholic priest connected to the Viennese school of cultural history, and Vittorio Lanternari, regarding the latter's book (Lanternari 1963).

22. Page numbers for citations are from the English edition (Petri 2014) [trans.].

23. Parker 1905 [trans.].

24. Parker uses the term "blacks" throughout, as does the English edition of Petri; de Martino uses *neri* [trans.].

25. The Boorah were initiation ceremonies. For this and other Euahlayi terms, Parker's transcriptions are adopted here [trans.].

26. The translation of Petri uses "half-caste"; de Martino renders it *meticci*.

27. The italics are de Martino's [trans.].

28. Aboriginal Australian nocturnal celebrations featuring sacred dances.

Chapter Five

1. An allusion to Lanternari 1960.

2. Lanternari 1963.

3. Cohn (1957) 1962.

4. De Martino refers to key themes in existentialist literature.

5. Italian writer Alberto Moravia's expression.

6. This paragraph ironically transposes Heidegger's analysis of "curiosity" (*Neugier*) as "being everywhere and nowhere" to Baudelaire ("Le Voyage") and Rimbaud.

7. Eatherly was a reconnaissance pilot in the Hiroshima bombing; Anders, who also wrote about Eichmann, corresponded with Eatherly and reconstructed his story (Eatherly and Anders 1962).

8. A citation from Nietzsche [trans.].

9. A reference to Jean Rouch's film *Les mâitres fous* (1955), which depicts the possession rituals of Accra's Hauka (Ghana).

10. From the English translation: Albino Pierro (2002, 55) "Le porte scritte nfàcce / It's Written on my Face [trans.].

11. De Martino interpreted Cesare Pavese's suicide in Turin in 1950 as the tragic consequence of an unresolved unsettlement.

12. A small town in the province of Catanzaro.

13. The original Italian *terra* has multiple meanings: the name of planet Earth, but also "land" and "homeland."

14. Emmanuel Mounier (1905–50), a leading French journalist, wrote extensively about the crisis of modern society. Page numbers refer to the English edition, Mounier 1962 [trans.].

15. In the passage de Martino emphasizes "lost"; he cites in French: "without rhyme or reason" [trans.].

16. Sedlmayr 1958 [trans.].

17. A note by de Martino lists a number of other publications dealing with apocalypse without eschaton in contemporary Western art.

18. Huyghe 1935.

19. "It is its abuses that give the best indication of trends" (Sedlmayr 1958, 4).

20. References are for the English edition (Friedrich 1974). De Martino paraphrases Friedrich, inserting his own terminology [trans.]. A student of Karl Jaspers and Ernest Robert Curtius, Friedrich (1904–78) was a scholar of Romance languages and a literary theorist.

21. Cited here in English (Rimbaud 2005) [trans.].

22. Today we know that Rimbaud's conversion to Catholicism was invented by his sister Isabelle and her husband, editors of the *Oeuvres* used by de Martino.

23. English edition (Friedrich 1974, 67) [trans.].

24. "The Sleeper in the Valley" (Rimbaud 2005, 46–49) [trans.].

25. "Tear" (Rimbaud 2005, 182–83. [trans.].

26. "The Drunken Boat" (Rimbaud 2005, 128–35) [trans.].

27. Emphasis in Rimbaud (2005, 377) [trans.].

28. (Rimbaud 2005, 371) [trans.].

29. (Rimbaud 2005, 215) [trans.].

30. From "Morning of Drunkenness" (Rimbaud 2005, 320–23) [trans.].

31. From "Farewell" (Rimbaud 2005, 302–5) [trans.].

32. Mann 2007.

33. Actually 1885; probably a typographical error on de Martino's part [trans.].

34. Leo Frobenius (1873–1938), noted German ethnologist and archaeologist who researched extensively in Africa.

35. Lawrence (1931) 1966, 40; Lawrence's emphasis [trans.].

36. Lawrence's emphasis.

37. Kerényi 1944. De Martino quotes from the Italian translation; no English edition is available [trans.].

38. Lawrence's introduction to Carter's book has been reprinted in Lawrence (1980); page numbers are for this volume [trans.].

39. De Martino's emphasis.

40. *La nausée*: pages refer to the English edition (Sartre 1964) [trans.].

41. The term comes from Heidegger [trans.].

42. See chap. 4, sec. 1.9.

43. Here and below, the reference is actually to the Self-Taught Man (Ogier P.), not a custodian [trans.].

44. Here and in the citations below, the emphasis is de Martino's [trans.].

45. "I felt surrounded . . . ," "the world was waiting," "feeble barriers," and "change" are all de Martino's emphasis; "anything, anything" is Sartre's emphasis [trans.].

46. All emphasis is de Martino's except for "everything" [trans.].

47. Page numbers refer to the English edition (Sartre 2007), discussing Camus's *The Stranger* [trans.].

48. An allusion to Dostoevsky's *The Idiot*.

49. Page numbers refer to the English edition (Camus [1942] 1955). De Martino cites several lines from Camus in French [trans.].

50. De Martino's emphasis.

51. Léon Chestov (1866–1938), Russian intellectual in exile in France who worked within Christian existentialism. Max Scheler (1874–1928) oriented phenomenological thought toward the analysis of values and affect.

52. Janet and Raymond 1903.

53. Moravia (1949) 2000 and 1950.

54. Alberto Moravia, *Disubbedienza* (1948) (Moravia 1950) [trans.].

55. Citations are from the English edition (Moravia (1960) 1999) [trans.].

56. Page references and citations are from the English edition (Moravia 1950) [trans.].

57. Page references and citations are from the English edition (Beckett 1954) [trans.].

58. This line does not exist: Beckett writes parenthetically, "Estragon says nothing."

59. Page references and citations are from the English edition (Robbe-Grillet 1989) [trans.].

60. Title of a mystical work by Saint Bonaventura (1259).

61. Emphasis is Robbe-Grillet's [trans.].

62. De Martino develops this anthropological redefinition of Husserl's *epoché* in chapter 7.

Chapter Six

1. Croce 1922, 22–24. This essay discusses the need to forget the deceased, to "make the dead die within us," as de Martino comments in his introduction to *Morte e pianto rituale* (de Martino 1958).

2. Croce 1949. There is no English edition, but the titles would be, respectively, "The end of civilization," "The antichrist within us," "Progress as a state of mind and progress as a philosophical concept," "Current historical experiences and conclusions for historiography," and "Truth and error in pessimistic predictions," in *Philosophy and Historiography* [trans.].

3. Date of the elections that ended with the overwhelming victory of the Christian Democrats, opposing the Popular Democratic Front.

4. "L'umanità e la natura" [trans.].

5. Croce 1945.

6. A secular religion of nationalism connected to the political ideals of Giuseppe Mazzini (1805–1872).

7. Croce's expression.

8. According to Marcello Massenzio (personal communication), in disagreement with Sartre's pessimism, de Martino constructs a dialectic between *securitas* as the inherited basis of our domesticity in the world—in short, tradition— and *securitas* as an existential security or anchoring that forms the basis from which we can move in history, innovating from that tradition [trans.].

9. Croce's categories of Spirit [trans.].

10. From Dante Alighieri's *Divine Comedy*, 26.l.119: "Consider your origins: you were not made to live as brutes, but to follow virtue and knowledge."

11. Mühlmann 1962.

12. Löwith 1949.

13. Manichaeism was founded in the third century in the Near East; Bogomilism arose in tenth-century Bulgaria. Both were dualistic systems based on the opposition of light and darkness, equivalent to the opposition of Good and Evil.

14. Wilhelm Weitling (1808–1871) founded the League of the Just (1836), which he defined as a religiously inspired communist system. The Hussite social and religious movement developed in Bohemia in the first half of the fifteenth century based on the doctrine of Czech reformer Jan Hus (1369–1415). The Taborites were a radical group of Hussites.

15. Thomas Müntzer (1489–1525), a preacher who initially sided with Martin Luther, became the religious leader of an armed revolt of peasants and workers against the clergy and nobility across Germany in 1525. For historians today he is both the last great representative of medieval-type Christian messianism and the one who introduced the modern need for transformation of social and political relations.

16. Later editions of Cohn's book do not make reference to Nazism and Communism [trans.].

17. The young Hegelians of the left anchored a critique of the Hegelian system to the analysis of Christianity, rejecting the identity between theology and philosophy as well as the objective superiority of the Christian religion.

18. Marx 1844a.

19. Second draft of this fragment.

20. "Religion is precisely the recognition of man in a roundabout way, through an intermediary", Marx 1844b [trans.].
21. Engels 1968.
22. The speech by Engels at Highgate Cemetery, 17 May 1883, https://www.marx ists.org/archive/marx/works/1883/death/burial.htm.
23. The citation is the beginning of the first thesis on Feuerbach (Marx 1969).
24. Expression created by psychologist Kurt Lewin from the Greek *hodos*—road or path—to define the concrete experience of the world as the whole of long and circuitous paths connected to the individual's psychic investments.
25. Marx 1968.
26. "Men have history, because they must produce it moreover in a certain way: this is determined by their physical organisation; their consciousness is determined in just the same way." English edition (Marx and Engels 1976, 70 and 86) [trans.].
27. Here and below, the page references are for Marx and Engels (1976), their emphasis. [trans.].
28. Marx 1969.
29. Marx and Engels 1976, 67.
30. Marx and Engels, 68.
31. Marx and Engels, 67.
32. Cornu 1934. Auguste Cornu (1888–1981) was a French historian and expert on the development and history of Marxist thought.
33. Philosophical term designating what has its own principle in itself.
34. Moses Hess (1812–1875) introduced the young Marx to economic and social problems.
35. Page numbers from Marx (1959) [trans.].
36. In 1963.
37. Engels 1946.
38. Engels and Marx 1956.
39. Karl Grün (1817–1887), a leading member of the Young Hegelians. He joined the "True Socialists" group around Hess, sharply criticized by Marx and Engels, who defined them as "crypto-idealists."
40. Page numbers are for the English edition (Gramsci 1971); de Martino's emphasis [trans.].
41. Q11§37, Gramsci 1995, 292.
42. Marx 1969, Marx's emphasis [trans.].
43. Page numbers refer to the English edition (Merleau-Ponty 1964) [trans.].

Chapter Seven

1. Abbagnano 1939, 1942. It is through his reading of that "positive" existentialist philosopher Nicola Abbagnano (1901–90) that de Martino constructs the figure below.
2. *Coesistenza*, a term emphasized in Abbagnano's reading; compare Heidegger's *Mitsein*. De Martino gives a culturalist meaning to "being-with."

3. Existentialist philosopher Enzo Paci (1911–76).
4. In the preceding entries de Martino traces the debate from 1941 to 1951 over the use of the categories "matter," "form," and the Crocean notion of "vitality."
5. Cf. chap. 6.
6. In Croce the category of the "vital" encompasses that of the "useful" to think of the articulation of nature and culture. In the early 1940s Paci attempted to assimilate Croce's "useful" to Heidegger's Dasein as a precategorial unity.
7. As understood in Croce's framework: see chap. 1, n. 62 [trans.].
8. Paci poses the question of the articulation of time and historicity with the transcendental as a structure.
9. The essay is a commentary on de Martino's book *The Magical World* (1948) [trans.].
10. Not really a citation. Paci describes anxiety as "The risk of losing oneself in nothingness, losing the relationship that constitutes him, the relationship between the practical and the theoretical, between the economic and moral law, between acting and knowing" (Paci 1950, 126).
11. De Martino used the term *naturalism* in his pungent critique of dominant ethnology (de Martino 1941) to indicate an ahistorical, positivist stance that applies the techniques of the natural sciences to the study of human society [trans.].
12. *Utilizzazioni.* Here, de Martino opens Heideggerian *Zuhandenheit* to a plurality [trans.].
13. An allusion to a theme treated by D. H. Lawrence.
14. In English: Merleau-Ponty 1962.
15. Here and below, "emergence" is used in the sense of Merleau-Ponty's phenomenology.
16. De Martino translated directly from the 1959 French edition. All quotes and page references here are from Lydia Davis's translation (Proust 2003) [trans.].
17. The analysis that follows is inspired by Mauss's notion of techniques of the body from a 1936 article (English translation: Mauss 1973).
18. Proust 2003, 5.
19. De Martino means the Self-Taught Man, not an employee.
20. Page references are for the English edition (Sartre 1956) [trans.]. In this book Sartre modifies Heidegger's analysis of *Zuhandenheit*, lacking in intentionality, by articulating it with the analysis of "one's own body," avoiding the distinction of consciousness and object.
21. See chap. 6, n. 24.
22. Italics and paraphrase in brackets are de Martino's [trans.].
23. Page references are for the English edition (Sartre 1956) [trans.].
24. Incomplete sentence.
25. Page references are for the English edition (Sartre 1948) [trans.].
26. De Martino's italics [trans.].
27. For Abbagnano "the individual is never alone"; de Martino makes this into an ethical imperative.
28. In English: Croce 1990, 148 [trans.].

29. This fragment begins with long annotation of Robert Hertz's famous essay from 1909, reprinted in English in 2013.
30. Georges Navel (1904–93) wrote about the workers' condition. In English: Navel 1949, 201–2. [trans.].
31. From Virgil: "Begin, sweet babe, to distinguish thy mother from her smiles" [trans.].
32. Inspired by stoic doctrine, the expression "eternal return" is from the late work of Nietzsche. Plato's *Timaeus* reflected on the theme of the diversity of cosmic times and the eternal return of a "great year."
33. The fragments in this section come from Binder 22.8 of the de Martino Archive, published in de Martino 2005b.
34. The Macquarrie and Robinson translation: Heidegger (1962) 2001, 114. [trans.].
35. Cf. Heidegger, 164 [trans.].
36. Mauss 1973.
37. Page references are for the English edition (Lévi-Strauss 1987) [trans.].
38. Storch 1924.
39. Heinz Werner (1890–1964) worked on the psychology of child development and theories of symbolic thought.
40. Croce 1938.
41. *L'appagante*: de Martino is referring to the Italian translation of Heidegger's *Bewandtnis* [trans.].
42. Heidegger (1962) 2001, 296ff, "Being-towards-death and the everydayness of Dasein."
43. Page references are for the Macquarrie and Robinson translation (Heidegger [1962] 2001); de Martino's emphasis [trans.].
44. A term from Heidegger's lexicon referring to the givenness of individual circumstances in "thrownness."
45. This definition of presence as "in decision" was introduced by Italian positive existentialism.
46. Incomplete sentence.
47. Incomplete sentence.
48. De Martino is referring to Croce's categories (forms) of Spirit: aesthetics, logic, economics, and ethics [trans.].

References

Abbagnano, Nicola. 1939. *La struttura dell'esistenza*. Turin: Paravia.

————. 1942. *Introduzione all'esistenzialismo*. Milan: Bompiani.

Adler, Gerhard. 1952. *Zur analytischen Psychologie*. Zurich: Rascher.

Anders, Günther. 1959. *Der Mann auf der Brücke: Tagesbuch aus Hiroshima und Nagasaki*. Munich: C. H. Beck.

Altheim, Franz. 1931 *Terra Mater: Untersuchungen zur altitalische Religionsgeschichte*. Giessen: Töpelman.

Bachelard, Gaston. 1988. *Air and Dreams: An Essay on the Imagination of Movements*. Translated by Edith R. Farrell and C. Frederick Farrell. Dallas, TX: Dallas Institute Publications.

Barnett, H. G. 1953. *Innovation: The Basis of Cultural Change*. New York: McGraw Hill.

————. 1957. *Indian Shakers: A Messianic Cult of the Pacific Northwest*. Carbondale: Southern Illinois University Press.

Baumer, Franklin L. 1954. "Twentieth-Century Version of the Apocalypse" *Cahiers d'histoire mondiale/Journal of World History* 1 (3): 623.

Beckett, Samuel. 1954. *Waiting for Godot*. New York: Random House.

Benedict, Ruth. 1934. *Patterns of Culture*. New York: Houghton Mifflin.

Berrocal, Emilio Giacomo. 2009. "The Post-colonialism of Ernesto De Martino: The Principle of Critical Ethnocentrism as a Failed Attempt to Reconstruct Ethnographic Authority." *History and Anthropology* 20 (2): 123–38.

Binswanger, Ludwig. 1942. *Grundformen und Erkenntnis menschlichen Dasein*. Zurich: Niehaus.

————. 1957. *Schizophrenie*. Pfullingen: Günther Neske.

————. 1960. *Melancholie und Manie: Phänomenologische Studien*. Pfullingen: Günther Neske.

Brandis, E., and V. Dmitrevskij. 1964. "Il futuro e i suoi precursori e i suoi falsi profeti." *Comunicazioni di massa* 2 (3/4): 105–20.

Buber, Martin. 1947. *Tales of the Hasidim*. New York: Schocken.

Bultmann, Rudolf. 1955. *History and Eschatology*. Edinburgh: Edinburgh University Press.

Callieri, Bruno. 1955. "Contributo allo studio psicopatologico dell'esperienza schiz-ofrenica di fine del mondo." *Archivio di psicologia, neurologia e psichiatria* 16 (4/5): 379–407.

Camus, Albert. (1942) 1955. *The Myth of Sisyphus and Other Essays.* Translated by Justin O'Brien. New York: Vintage Books.

———. (1942) 1988. *The Stranger.* Translated by Matthew Ward. New York: Vintage Books.

Cargnello, Danilo. "Dal naturalismo psicoanalitico alla fenomenologia antropologica della 'Daseinanalyse.'" In *Filosofia della alienazione e analisi esistenziale,* Archivio di filosofia, 127–89. Padua: CEDAM, 1961.

Caruso, Paolo. 1963. "Intervista a C. Lévi-Strauss." *Aut-Aut* 77 (September): 27–45.

Centre d'étude des religions. 1962. "Religions de salut." *Annales du Centre d'étude des religions* 2.

Cohn, Norman. (1957) 1962. *The Pursuit of the Millennium.* London: Mercury Books.

Collingwood, R. G. 1946. *The Idea of History.* Oxford: Clarendon Press.

Colman, Andrew M. 2009. *A Dictionary of Psychology.* 3rd ed. Oxford: Oxford University Press.

Coomaraswamy, Ananda K. 1959. *Hinduism and Buddhism.* New York: Philosophical Library.

Cornu, Auguste. 1934. *Karl Marx: L'homme et l'oeuvre.* Paris: Librarie Félix Alcan.

Corrodi, Heinrich. 1781–94. *Kritische Geschichte des Chiliasmus.* 4 vols. Frankfurt.

Croce, Benedetto. 1909. *Aesthetic: As Science of Expression and General Linguistic.* Translated by Douglas Ainslie. New York: Noonday.

———. 1917a. *Logic as the Science of the Pure Concept.* Translated by Douglas Ainslie. London: Macmillan

———. 1917b. *Philosophy of the Practical, Economic and Ethic.* Translated by Douglas Ainslie. London: Macmillan

———. 1922. *Frammenti di etica.* Bari: Laterza.

———. 1935. *Ultimi saggi.* Bari: Laterza.

———. 1938. *La storia come pensiero e come azione.* Bari: Laterza.

———. 1945. *Il carattere della filosofia moderna.* Bari: Laterza.

———. 1949. *Filosofia e storiografia.* Bari: Latera.

———. (1945) 1990. "Marcel Proust: A Case of Decadent Historicism." In *Essays on Literature and Literary Criticism,* translated by M. E. Moss, 145–49. Albany: State University of New York Press.

Cullmann, Oscar. 1964. *Christ and Time: The Primitive Christian Conception of Time and History,* translated by Floyd V. Filson. Philadelphia: Westminster Press.

Delling, Gerhard. 1940. *Das Zeitverständnis des Neuen Testaments.* Gütersloh: Bertelsmann.

de Martino, Ernesto 1941. *Naturalismo e storicismo nell'etnologia.* Bari: Laterza.

———. 1948. *Il mondo magico.* Turin: Einaudi.

———. 1958. *Morte e pianto rituale.* Turin: Einaudi.

———. 1959: *Sud e magia.* Milan: Feltrinelli.

———. 1961. *La terra del rimorso*. Milan: Saggiatore.

———. 1964. "Il problema della fine del mondo." In *Il mondo di domani*, edited by P. Prini, 225–31. Rome: Abete.

———. 2005a. *The Land of Remorse*. Translated by Dorothy L. Zinn. London: Free Association Books.

———. 2005b. *Scritti filosofici*. Edited by Roberto Pàstina. Bologna: Il Mulino.

———. 2012. "Crisis of Presence and Religious Reintegration." Translated by Tobia Farnetti and Charles Stewart. *HAU* 2 (2): 434–50.

———. 2015. *Magic: A Theory from the South*. Translated by Dorothy L. Zinn. Chicago: HAU Books.

Deubner, L. 1933. "Mundus." *Hermes* 68:226–87.

Dilthey, Wilhelm. 1931. *Weltanschauungslehre: Abhandlungen zur Philosophie der Philosophie*. Stuttgart: Teubner; Göttingen: Vandenhoeck & Ruprecht.

Dodds, Eric R. 1951. *The Greeks and the Irrational*. Berkeley: University of California Press.

Dostoevsky, Feodor. 2009. *Notes from Underground*. Translated by Constance Garnett. Indianapolis: Hackett.

Dumas, Georges. 1946. *Le surnaturel et les dieux d'après les maladies mentales*. Paris: Presses universitaires de France.

Eatherly, Claude, and Günther Anders. 1962. *Burning Conscience: The Case of the Hiroshima Pilot, Claude Eatherly, Told in His Letters to Günther Anders*. New York: Monthly Review Press.

Eliade, Mircea. 1954. *The Myth of the Eternal Return*. Translated by Willard R. Trask. New York: Pantheon.

———. (1957) 1960. *Myths, Dreams and Mysteries*. Translated by Philip Mairet. New York: Harper and Row.

———. 1958. *Patterns in Comparative Religion*. Translated by Rosemary Sheed. New York: Meridian.

———. 1961. *Images and Symbols*. Translated by Philip Mairet. New York: Sheed & Ward.

Elkin A. P. 1938. *The Australian Aborigines: How to Understand Them*. Sydney: Angus and Robertson.

Engels, Friedrich. 1946. *Ludwig Feuerbach and the End of Classical German Philosophy*. Moscow: Progress Publishers. https://www.marxists.org/archive/marx/works/1886/ludwig-feuerbach/index.htm.

———. 1968 Letter to Conrad Schmidt, trans. Donna Torr, in Marx and Engels Correspondence. https://www.marxists.org/archive/marx/works/1890/letters/90_10_27.htm.

Engels, Friedrich, and Karl Marx. 1956. "The Holy Family." Translated by Richard Dixon. Moscow: Foreign Languages Publishing House. https://www.marxists.org/archive/marx/works/1845/holy-family/index.htm.

Ernout, A. 1946–65. *Philologica*. 3 vols. Paris: Klincksieck.

Ernout, A., and A. Meillet. 1959. *Dictionnaire étymologique de la langue latine*. 4th ed. Paris: Klincksieck.

Ey, Henri. 1954. *Études psychiatriques*. Vol. 3. Paris: Desclée de Brower.

Fernandez, Dominique. 1960. *Il romanzo italiano e la crisi della coscienza moderna*. Milan: Lerici.

Ferrari, Fabrizio. 2012. *Ernesto de Martino on Religion: The Crisis and the Presence*. London: Routledge.

Festinger, Leon, Henry Riecken, and Stanley Schachter. 1956. *When Prophecy Fails: A Social and Psychological Study of a Modern Group That Predicted the Destruction of the World*. Minneapolis: University of Minnesota Press.

Festus, Sextus Pompeius. 1965. *De verborum significatu quae supersunt cum Pauli epitome*. Edited by Wallace Martin Lindsay. Hildesheim: Olms.

Friedrich, Hugo. 1974. *The Structure of Modern Poetry*. Translated by Joachim Neugroschel. Evanston, IL: Northwestern University Press.

Geissheusler, Flavio A. 2021. *The Life and Work of Ernesto de Martino: Italian Perspectives on Apocalypse and Rebirth in the Modern Study of Religion*. Leiden: Brill.

Ginzburg, Carlo. 2017. "On Ernesto de Martino's 'The End of the World' and Its Genesis." *Chicago Review* 60/61 (4/1): 77–91.

Goethe, Johann Wolfgang von. 2010. *The West-East Divan*. Translated by Martin Bidney. Binghamton, NY: Global Academic.

Gramsci, Antonio. 1971. *Selections from the Prison Notebooks of Antonio Gramsci*. Edited and translated by Quentin Hoare and Geoffrey Nowell Smith. New York: International.

———. 1995. *Further Selections from the Prison Notebooks*. Edited and translated by Derek Boothman. London: Lawrence & Wishart.

Gruhle, Hans W. 1915. "Selbstschilderung und Einfühlung." *Zeitschrift für die gesamte Neurologie und Psychiatrie*, no. 28, 148–231.

Gusdorf, Georges. 1963. "Projet de recherche interdisciplinaire dans les sciences humaines." *Diogène* 42 (April–June): 128–29.

Hagen, Friedrich Wilhelm. 1870. *Studien auf dem Gebiete der ärtzlichen Seelenkunde: Gemeinfassliche Vorträge*. Erlangen: Besold.

Harding, Susan, and Kathleen Stewart. 2003. "Anxieties of Influence: Conspiracy Theory and Therapeutic Culture in Millennial America." In *Transparency and Conspiracy: Ethnographies of Suspicion in the New World Order*, edited by Harry G. West and Todd Sanders, 258–86. Durham, NC: Duke University Press.

Heidegger, Martin. 1935. *Sein und Zeit*. Halle: Niemeyer.

———. (1962) 2001. *Being and Time*. Translated by John Macquarrie and Edward Robinson. Oxford: Blackwell.

———. 1985. *Schelling's Treatise on the Essence of Human Freedom*. Translated by Joan Stambaugh. Athens: Ohio University Press.

———. 1996. *Being and Time*. Translated by Joan Stambaugh. Albany: State University of New York Press.

Hertz, Robert. (1973) 2013. "The Pre-eminence of the Right Hand." Translated by Rodney Needham and Claudia Needham. *HAU* 3 (2): 335–57.

Huyghe, René. 1935. *Histoire de l'art contemporain*. Paris: Alcan.

Janet, Pierre. 1928. *De l'angoisse è l'extase*. Paris: Alcan.

Janet, Pierre, and Fulgence Raymond. 1903. *Les obsessions et la psychasthénie*. Paris: Alcan.

Jaspers, Karl, 1997, *General Psychopathology*. 2 vols. Translated by J. Hoenig and Marian W. Hamilton. Baltimore: Johns Hopkins University Press.

Jaspers, Karl, and Rudolf Bultmann. 1954. *Die Frage der Entmythologisierung*. Munich: Piper.

Jensen, Adolf Ellegard. 1951. *Mythos und Kult bei Naturvölkern*. Wiesbaden: F. Steiner.

Jung, Karl Gustav. 2000. "A Psychological Commentary on the Tibetan Book of the Dead." In *Collected Works of C.G. Jung*, translated by R. F. C. Hull, 509–26. Princeton, NJ: Princeton University Press.

Kerényi, Karl. 1944. *Töchter der Sonne*. Zurich: Rascher.

———. 1963. "Prolegomena." In *Essays on a Science of Mythology*, by C. G. Jung and K. Kerényi, translated by R. F. C. Hull, 1–24. New York: Harper and Row.

Kierkegaard, Søren. 2014. *The Concept of Anxiety*. Translated by Alistair Hannay. New York: Liveright.

Kittel, Gerhard. 1935. *Theologisches Wörterbuch zum Neuen Testament*. Stuttgart: Kohlhammer.

Klages, Ludwig. 1932. *Der Geist als Widersacher der Seele*. Leipzig: J. A. Barth.

Knox, Ronald A. 1950. *Enthusiasm: A Chapter in the History of Religion*. Oxford: Oxford University Press.

Kranz. Heinrich. 1955. "Mythos und Psychose." *Studium Generale* 8 (6): 370–78.

Kunz, Hans. 1931. "Die Grenze der psychopathologischen Wahninterpretationen." *Zeitschrift für die gesamte Neurologie und Psychiatrie* 135:671–715.

Lanternari, Vittorio. 1960. *La grande festa*. Milan: Il Saggiatore.

———. 1963. *The Religions of the Oppressed: A Study of Modern Messianic Cults*. New York: Alfred A. Knopf.

Lawrence, D. H. (1931) 1966. *Apocalypse*. New York: Viking Press.

———. 1980. "Introduction to *The Dragon of the Apocalypse* by Frederick Carter." In *Apocalypse and the Writings on Revelation*, edited by Mara Kalnins, 45–56. Cambridge: Cambridge University Press.

Le Bonniec, Henri. 1958. *Le culte de Cérès à Rome: Des origines à la fin de la république*. Paris: Klincksieck.

Lévi-Strauss, Claude. 1987. *Introduction to the Work of Marcel Mauss*. Translated by Felicity Baker. London: Routledge & Kegan Paul.

Lietzmann, Hans. 1936. *Geschichte der alten Kirche*. Vol. 2. Berlin: W. de Gruyter.

Linforth, Ivan M. 1941. *The Arts of Orpheus*. Berkeley: University of California Press.

Lommel, Andreas. 1950. "Modern Culture Influences on the Aborigines." *Oceania* 21:14–24

———. 1997 *The Unambal: A Tribe in Northwest Australia*. Translated by Ian Campbell. Carnavon Gorge: Takarakka Nowan Kas.

Löwith, Karl. 1949. *Meaning in History*. Chicago: University of Chicago Press.

Lucretius. 1910. *On the Nature of Things*. Translated by Cyril Bailey. Oxford: Clarendon Press.

Macrobius, Ambrosius Aurelius Theodosius. 1969. *The Saturnalia*. Translated by Percival Vaughan Davies. New York: Columbia University Press.

Mann, Thomas. 2007 *Death in Venice*. Translated by Martin Doege. https://archive.org/details/DeathInVenice.

Marx, Karl. 1844a. "Introduction: A Contribution to the Critique of Hegel's Philosophy of Right." Works of Karl Marx 1844. https://www.marxists.org/archive/marx/works/1843/critique-hpr/intro.htm.

———. 1844b. "On The Jewish Question." In Works of Karl Marx 1844. https://www.marxists.org/archive/marx/works/1844/jewish-question/.

———1959. *Economic and Philosophical Manuscripts of 1844*. Translated by Mark Milligan. Moscow: Progress. https://www.marxists.org/archive/marx/works/1844/manuscripts/preface.htm.

———. 1968. "A Critique of the German Ideology." https://www.marxists.org/archive/marx/works/1845/german-ideology/ch01a.htm.

———.1969. "Theses on Feuerbach." Translated W. Lough. Moscow: Progress. https://www.marxists.org/archive/marx/works/1845/theses/theses.htm.

Marx, Karl, and Friedrich Engels. 1976. *Collected Works*. Vol. 5, *Marx and Engels: 1845–1847*. New York: International.

Mauss, Marcel 1973. "Techniques of the Body." *Economy and Society* 2 (1): 70–88.

Mayer-Gross, Wilhelm, Eliot Slater, and Martin Roth. 1956. *Clinical Psychiatry*. Baltimore: Williams and Wilkins.

Merleau-Ponty, Maurice. 1962. *Phenomenology of Perception*. Translated by Colin Smith. New York: Routledge.

———. 1964. *Sense and Non-Sense*. Translated by Hubert L. Dreyfus and Patricia Allen Dreyfus. Evanston, IL: Northwestern University Press.

Mignolo, Walter D., and Catherine E. Walsh 2018. *On Decoloniality: Concepts, Analytics, Praxis*. Durham, NC: Duke University Press.

Mommsen, Theodor. 1863. *Corpus inscriptionum latinarum*. Berlin: Reimer.

Moravia, Alberto. (1949) 2000. *The Time of Indifference*. Translated Tami Calliope. South Royalton, VT: Steerforth Italia.

———. 1950. *Disobedience*. Translated by Angus Davidson. London: Secker & Warburg.

———. (1960) 1999. *Boredom*. Translated by Angus Davidson. New York: New York Review Books.

Mounier, Emmanuel. 1962. *Be Not Afraid: A Denunciation of Despair*. Translated by Cynthia Rowland. New York: Sheed & Ward.

Mühlmann, Wilhelm E. 1962. *Chilismus und Nativismus: Studien zur Psychologie, Soziologie und Kasuistik der Umsturzbewegungen*. Berlin: Dietrich Reiner.

Navel, Georges. 1949. *Man at Work*. Translated by George Reavey. London: Dennis Dobson.

Nicolini, Fausto. 1962. *Benedetto Croce*. Turin: Unione Tipografico-Editrice Torinese.

Otto, Rudolf. 1924. *The Idea of the Holy*. Translated by John W. Harvey. London: Oxford University Press.

Ovid. 1931. *Fasti*. Translated by James G. Frazer. Revised by G. P. Goold. Loeb Classical Library 253. Cambridge, MA: Harvard University Press.

Paci, Enzo. 1950. *Il nulla e il problema dell'uomo*. Turin: Taylor.

Parker, Katie Langloh. 1905. *The Eualayi Tribe: A Study of Aboriginal Life in Australia*. London: Archibald Constable.

Pavese, Cesare. 1952. *Il mestiere di vivere: Diario 1935–1950*. Edited by Massimo Mila, Italo Calvino, and Natalia Ginzburg. Turin: Einaudi.

Petri, Helmut. 1950. "Kuràngara: Neue magische Kulte in Nordwest-Australien." *Zeitschrift für Ethnologie*, no. 75, 43–51.

———. 2014. *The Australian Medicine Man*. Translated by Ian Campbell. Carlisle: Hesperian Press.

Petriconi, Hellmuth. 1958. *Das Reich des Untergangs: Bemerkungen über ein mythologisches Thema*. Hamburg: Hoffman und Campe.

Pierro, Albino. 2002. *Selected Poems*. Translated by Luigi Bonaffini. Toronto: Guernica.

Piganiol, A. 1923. *Recherches sur les jeux romains: Notes d'archéologie et d'histoire religieuse*. Strasbourg: Istra.

Plutarch. 1914. *Plutarch's Lives*. Translated by Bernadotte Perrin. Cambridge, MA: Harvard University Press. http://www.perseus.tufts.edu/hopper/text?doc =Perseus%3Atext%3A2008.01.0061%3Achapter%3D11%3Asection%3D1.

Proust, Marcel. 2003. *Swann's Way*. Translated by Lydia Davis. New York: Viking.

Rehm, Walther. 1943. "Tiefe und Abgrund in Hölderlins Dichtung." In *Hölderlin: Gedenkschrift zu seinem 100. Todestag, 7. Juni 1943*, edited by Paul Kluckhohn, 70–133. Tübingen: Mohr.

Rimbaud, Arthur. 2005. *Rimbaud: Complete Works, Selected Letters*. Translated by Wallace Fowlie. Chicago: University of Chicago Press.

Robbe-Grillet, Alain. 1989. *For a New Novel: Essays on Fiction*. Translated by Richard Howard. Evanston, IL: Northwestern University Press.

Rose, H. J. 1931. "The Mundus." *Studi e materiali di storia delle religioni* 7:115–27.

Rosenberg, Alfred 2011. *The Myth of the Twentieth Century*. Wentzville, MO: Invictus.

Sandberg, R. 1895. "Zur Psychopathologie der chronischen Paranoia." *Allgemeine Zeitschrift für Psychiatrie* 52 (3): 619–54.

Sartre, Jean-Paul. 1948. *The Emotions: Outline of a Theory*. Translated by Bernard Frechtman. New York: Philosophical Library.

———. 1956. *Being and Nothingness*. Translated by Hazel E. Barnes. New York: Philosophical Library.

———. 1964. *Nausea*, trans. Lloyd Alexander. New York: New Directions.

———. 2007. "A Commentary on *The Stranger*." In *Existentialism Is a Humanism*, translated by Carol Macomber, 73–98. New Haven, CT: Yale University Press.

Saunders, George R. 1993. "'Critical Ethnocentrism' and the Ethnology of Ernesto De Martino." *American Anthropologist* 95 (4): 875–95.

————. 1995. "The Crisis of Presence in Italian Pentacostal Conversion." *American Ethnologist* 22 (2): 324–40.

Schelling, F. W. J. 2006. *Philosophical Investigations into the Essence of Human Freedom.* Translated by Jeff Love and Johannes Schmidt. Albany: State University of New York Press.

Schiff, P. 1946. "La paranoïa de destruction: Réaction de Samson et phantasme de la fin du monde." *Annales médico-psychologiques,* 104 (3): 279–89.

Sedelmayr, Hans. 1958. *Art in Crisis: The Lost Center.* Chicago: Henry Regnery.

Signorelli, Amalia. 1997. "Presenza individuale e presenze collettive." In *Ernesto De Martino nella cultura europea,* edited by Clara Gallini, Marcello Massenzio, 121–30. Naples: Liguori.

Spengler, Oswald. 1926. *The Decline of the West.* New York: A. A. Knopf.

Stewart, Kathleen, and Susan Harding. 1999. "Bad Endings: American Apocalypsis." *Annual Review of Anthropology* 28 (1): 285–310.

Storch, Alfred. 1924. *The Primitive Archaic Forms of Inner Experiences and Thought in Schizophrenia: A Genetic and Clinical Study of Schizophrenia.* Translated by Clara Willard. Nervous and Mental Disease Monograph Series no. 36. New York: Nervous and Mental Disease Publishing.

————. 1930. "Die Welt der beginnenden Schizophrenie und die archaische Welt: Ein existential-analytischer Versuch." *Zeitschrift für die gesamte Neurologie und Psychiatrie* 127 (1): 799–810.

————. 1949. "Tod und Erneuerung in der schizophrenen Daseins-Umwandlung." *Archiv für Psychiatrie und Nervenkrankheiten* 181 (3): 275–93.

Storch, Alfred, and Caspar Kulenkampff. 1950. "Zum Verständnis des Weltungergangs bei den Schizophrenen." *Der Nervenarzt* 21:102–8.

St. Teresa of Avila. 1985. "Poetry." Translated by Adrian J. Cooney in *The Collected Works of St. Teresa of Avila,* 3:375–410. Washington, DC: Institute of Carmelite Studies.

Thrupp, Sylvia L. 1962. *Millennial Dreams in Action: Studies in Revolutionary Religious Movements.* The Hague: Mouton.

Turchi, N. 1939. *La religione di Roma antica.* Bologna: Cappelli.

van den Berg, J. H. 1955. *The Phenomenological Approach to Psychiatry: An Introduction to Recent Phenomenological Psychopathology.* Springfield, IL: Charles C. Thomas.

van der Leeuw, Gerardus. 1957. "Primordial Time and Final Time." In *Papers from the Eranos Yearbooks,* 324–52. New York: Pantheon.

Viano, C. A. 1960. *John Locke: Dal nazionalismo all'illuminismo.* Turin: Einaudi.

Virno, Paolo. 2006. "Promemoria su Ernesto de Martino." *Studi culturali* 3 (1): 147–58.

Volmat, Robert. 1956. *L'art psychopathologique.* Paris: Presses universitaires de France.

Wagenvoort, M. H. 1948. "Initia Cereris." *Mededelingen van de koniklijke Vlaamse Aacademie van België, Kl. De. Letteren* 10 (4). Translated into English in *Studies in Roman Literature: Culture and Religion.* Leiden: E. J. Brill, 1956.

Walde, A., and J. B. Hofmann. 1938. *Lateinisches Etymologisches Wörterbuch*. Heidelberg: Winter.

Weinstock, Stefan. 1930. "Mundus patet." *Mitteilungen des Deutschen Archäologischen Instituts* (Römische Abteilung) 45:111–23.

Wetzel, Albrecht. 1922. "Das Weltuntergangserlebnis in der Schizophrenie." *Zeitschrift für die gesamte Neurologie und Psychiatrie* 78:403–28.

Wissowa, Georg. 1912. *Religion und Kultus des Römer*. 2nd ed. Munich: Beck.

Zinn, Dorothy L. 2020. "Patrimonio culturale e inclusione sociale: alcune riflessioni demartiniane." In *Ernesto de Martino e il folklore*. Atti del Convegno Matera-Galatina, 24–25 giugno 2019, edited by Eugenio Imbriani, 79–99. Bari: Progedit.

Index

Abbagnano, Nicola, 277, 281, 345nn1–2, 346n27

absolutization, 85, 101, 261, 282–83, 297, 323–24

Abu-Lughod, Lila, xvi

Adler, Gerhard, 120

Alchera (dreamtime), 48, 335n69

alienation: of being-there, 312; crisis of, 52, 166; of the domestic, 191; end of the world as a product of, 94; fundamental moments of, 77, 166; Marxian theory of, 268–69; mental, 89; of presence, 53, 248; of reality from humankind, 202; religious, 254, 260, 268; risk of, 11, 13, 260, 275; self-, 260; technicist, 95; unsettled/unsettling and, 328; of the world, 26, 28

Altheim, Franz, 12, 38

anabasis/catabasis, 127, 193–94, 325

Anders, Günther, 103, 195, 338n45, 341n7

anxiety (*angoscia*), 310–16, 325; astronauts suffering from, 198; of becoming, 97, 115–16; existential, 318; feelings of, 101–2, 106, 113, 115; of freedom, 43, 316; as a fundamental mode of existence, 108; of history, 53, 117, 120, 132–33; inability to have, 107; incommunicability of, 91; modern, 131–33; nothingness and, 244; Paci's description of, 346n10; threat of, 167

apocalypse: Christian (*see* Christian apocalypse/eschatology); comparative study of Third World and European, 7–15; contradictions in apocalyptic thought, 177–78; Croce on the Antichrist and, 239–41; cultural (*see* cultural apocalypse); individual/collective levels of, xvi–xvii; Marxist (*see* Marxist apocalypse); modern, 9–15, 198–99; as mythical-ritual symbol, xiv (*see also* mythical-ritual, the); psychopathological (*see* psychopathological apocalypse); of the West (*see* crisis of the modern/contemporary West; West, apocalypse of the); without eschaton, eschatological perspective distinguished from, 191–92

art: the crisis in Western, 193–94; symptoms of the crisis in modern, 200–201

Ateius Capito, Gaius, 32–33

at hand / handiness, 325; the body's, 304, 307; communitarian project of things, 41, 203, 243, 261, 266, 269, 277, 282, 299–300; crisis of, 203, 218; current, 79; "going beyond," disappearance of, 222; horizon of, cultural/domestic, 217, 222, 243, 280, 294; human world, as basis of, 277; of life, 266, 283–86, 297–98, 307; new, 261, 284; rebellion against, 284;

at hand / handiness (*cont.*)
  risk from restrictions on, 41; science
  of, 81; sphere of, 203; transcendental
  principle and, 269; world of, 218–19,
  281, 284
atomic/nuclear catastrophe, 95, 191,
  195–96, 199
Augustine of Hippo, Saint, 30

Bachelard, Gaston, 29, 333n20
Bakhtin, Mikhail, xiii
Barnett, H. G., 177
Baudelaire, Charles, 30, 202, 341n6
Bauer, Bruno, 252, 271
Baumer, Franklin Le Van, 12
Beckett, Samuel, 11, 233–36, 343n58
Beck-Kleist, Gerta, 178
becoming, moments of, 96–97
being-acted-upon, 325–26; catastrophe
  of the ethos of transcendence and,
  71; crisis/loss of presentification
  and, 217–19, 222; experience of, 61;
  experience of alienation and, 77, 98,
  102; experience of the world and,
  102; modality of, 109; passivity, the
  subconscious, and, 204; positive
  dynamism of, 120; protagonist of
  Sartre's *Nausea* and, 14
being-in-the-world, 326; annihilation/
  obliteration of, 43, 219; catastrophe
  of, 14, 41, 71; culture and, 89–90;
  disclosure of, 39, 42, 140–41; duty-
  to-be-in-the-world and, 77–78; evidence of, 218; human condition as,
  223; human vitality, 244; modality
  of, 26; moral power rendering possible, 58; necessary route for, 256;
  not-, incoherence of, 90; "presence"
  as, 84, 89–90; restoring, 73
being-there, 326; of agency, 40, 243; in
  Beckett, 233, 235; catastrophe of, 71;
  consciousness of, 141; as Dasein, xiv,
  77, 100, 326 (*see also* Dasein); duty-
  to-be-in-the-world and, 76–77, 281;
  everydayness of, 306; *Geworfenheit*
  of, 2; homeland for, 288; the human
  condition and, 235; loss/risk of los-
  ing/not, 14, 40, 53, 98, 100, 108, 248;
  as presence, 233, 244, 248 (*see also*
  presence); in society, 321; socioeconomic, 243; symbolic order and, 43;
  in the world, 102, 108, 215, 219, 244;
  worldhood of, 78
Benedict, Ruth, 161, 307
Bergson, Henri, 55
Beringer, Kurt, 336n17
Bible, the, 139; Acts, 137–39; Acts
  1:7, 158; Colossians 1:16, 340n33;
  Colossians 1:19, 153; Colossians 1:25,
  157; 1 Corinthians, 95; 1 Corinthians 7:30, 156; 1 Corinthians 7:31,
  340n36; 1 Corinthians 9:22, 340n46;
  Ephesians 1:10, 157; Ephesians 3:2,
  157; Ephesians 3:9, 157; Genesis 3:5,
  333n21; Hebrews 7:27, 157; Hebrews
  9:12, 157; Hebrews 10:10, 157; Joel
  3:1–5, 139; Luke 23:45, 153; Mark
  1:15, 340n31; Matthew 4:17, 340n31;
  Matthew 27:51, 153; New Testament
  as historical document, 135–36, 147;
  2 Peter 3:8, 152; Psalm 74:13, 153;
  Revelations 1:3, 158; Revelations
  11:18, 158; Romans 6:10, 157; Romans
  8:19, 153; 1 Thessalonians 2:8, 182;
  1 Thessalonians 5:1, 158; Zechariah
  14:7, 335n67
Binswanger, Ludwig: commentary
  on the case of Roos, 112–14; Dasein
  of, 29, 308; existential analysis of,
  337n25; existentialism of, xiv, 84;
  existential psychopathology of, 89,
  308; normative structuring of sense
  presiding over behavior, concept of,
  333n16; phenomenological anthropology developed around, 333n2;
  private dimension of the relation to
  self added by, 336n3; problem of the
  structures of psychotics' abnormal

worlds outlined by, 74; refounding of psychiatry by, 337n33

body, the: alterations of position of, 116; animal, 79; of Christ, 137, 152; dead/lived, 57, 64, 211, 288; denial of, 210; lived heart of, 302; maternal, 304; one's own, 218, 289, 291–93, 302, 307, 346n20; reawakening of, 289–90; Sartre on, 293–96; techniques of, 301, 302–3, 304–6, 307–8

Brandis, E., 12

Buber, Martin, 131

Buddha, the, 50

Bultmann, Rudolf, 124, 158–62, 338n4, 339n7

Callieri, Bruno, 21, 100, 107, 336n18

Camus, Albert: the "absurd" in, 11; *Le mythe de Sisyphe* (*The Myth of Sisyphus*), 223, 225–28; *The Stranger*, 223–25

Cargnello, Danilo, 87–88, 337n31

catabasis. *See* anabasis/catabasis

Cato, Marcus Porcius, 32, 34

Charuty, Giordana, xi

Chestov, Léon, 343n51

children/infants, 37, 44, 89, 286–87

Chiodi, Pietro, 325–26

Choisy, Auguste, 201

Christian apocalypse/eschatology, 137–40, 156–58; Christ event, centrality of, 154, 157, 160–61 (*see also* Parousia); Christian and Judaic eschatology, distinction between, 154; ending as an eschaton, 199–200; as historical object, 133–42; historicity and, xiii; historiographic-anthropological problem of, 133–37; history and, 158–62; limits of Protestant theology, 142–62; time, conception and problem of, 142–58; *Weltuntergangserlebnis* (WUE), xiv–xv, 2, 13, 19, 94, 100–101, 103–4, 140–42, 318, 329; "world denial" of

early Christians, 155. *See also* Bible, the; eschaton; history; Parousia

Christianity, 159, 182, 199, 212. *See also* Bible, the; Christian apocalypse/eschatology; religion

Cohn, Norman, 250–52

Collingwood, R. G., 159

colonialism, xiii, 4–6, 173–74

Columella, Lucius Junius Moderatus, 36

communitarian project of things at hand, 277, 326; cultural history, as part of, 203; disintegration and collapse of, 77; as economic activity, Marxian theory and, 269–70; in fieri status of, xv; as a handiness, 269, 300; as a human order, 79; the individual and, 314, 322; nature as a horizon according to, 284; transcendence of, 263; valorizing activity and, 273, 307, 322; the "world" and, 261, 299

Coomaraswamy, Ananda K., 57

Cornu, Auguste, 266–67, 345n32

Corrodi, Heinrich, 248–49

crisis of presence, 326; being-acted-upon, 325 (*see also* being-acted-upon); the "end" of a world and, 96; as a fundamental hermeneutic principle, 68; incomplete articulation of, xvi; inversion of movement toward, 85; myth and, 45; needs and, 84; as a permanent anthropological risk, xiv, 326; symptomatic behaviors of in cultural apocalypse, 176

crisis of the modern/contemporary West: as apocalypse without eschaton, 191–92; atomic/nuclear catastrophe, 95, 191, 195–96, 199; in Beckett, 233–36; Camus and, 226–28; contradictory terrors of, 194–95; cultural homelands, 196–97; Friedrich on, 201–2; in Lawrence, 208–15; in Mann, 205–8; in Moravia, crisis of the modern/contemporary West (*cont.*) 228–33; Mounier's thesis on the modern apocalypse, 198–99; Rimbaud on, 202–5; in Sartre, 215–25; symptoms of the crisis in modern art, 200–201; theme of apocalypse in literature, visual arts, music, poetry, and philosophy, 192–94

critical ethnocentrism, xvi, 9, 162, 164, 174

Croce, Benedetto: "absolute historicism" of, critique of, 339n13; on the apocalypse, 239–41; biographical accounts, 237–39; "Current historical experiences and conclusions for historiography," 240–41; de Martino and, xii–xiii, xv, 339n13; dialectic of pleasure/pain, 242; ethics and the duty-to-be, 326; and ethos founded by *in-der-Welt-sein-sollen*, 309; historicity of, Bultmann and, 159; idealistic exorcism of, 273; legacy of, 237; on Proust, 301; "The Antichrist within us," 240; the useful/vital/ economic for, 278–80, 282, 329, 346n6; walking, style of, 306

Cullmann, Oscar, 124, 142–47, 150–55, 338n3, 339n23

cultural apocalypse: in the ancient world, xiii; comparative approach to, 13–15; institutionalization as a fundamental feature of, 176; Marxist (*see* Marxist apocalypse); millenarian and prophetic movements as, xiii; psychopathological apocalypse and, 13, 21–31; the West, apocalypse of (*see* crisis of the modern/contemporary West; West, apocalypse of the)

cultural homeland(s), xv, 3–4, 6, 196–98, 293, 328

cultural psychiatry, 83

cultural reintegration, 326; as a distinct type of problem, 86; the

mythical-ritual, symbolism and, 86, 259; psychopathological risk, fighting against, 75; restraint on as a fundamental hermeneutic principle, 68

cultural relativism: crisis of order/ historicism/coherence and, 132, 171, 194; as the danger facing ethnographic humanism, 174; horizonless, 161; literary roots of, 210–11; misunderstanding and, 83; perspective-free, 8; positive element represented by, 76

culture(s): as an ethos of order, 194; being-in-the-world and, 89; comparisons of, 8; detachment from natural vitality is, 244–46; dispersion of, 162–63, 171–72; "end of the world" as a torment for, 319; eternal return and, 42–43; ethos of transcendence and, 323; historical philosophy of, need for, 76; mythical-ritual symbolism and, 119–20; nature and, 41–42, 84, 165, 242, 244–47, 259, 261, 263, 284; normal/abnormal distinction and, 91; presence and, 244, 316, 328–29; prophetic (*see* millenarian/ prophetic movements); psychic disorders/mental health and, 81, 83–85, 87–89; religious, 165 (*see also* religion); rethinking of the concept of, xv–xvi; traditional Indigenous (*see* Indigenous/"primitive" peoples and Indians); Western (*see* crisis of the modern/contemporary West). *See also* communitarian project of things at hand

Dasein: destruction/negation in experience of, 25, 27–28, 61–63; entities within-the-world and, 327; hungering for, 64; *in-der-Welt-sein* of, 308–9 (see also *in-der-Welt-sein*); presence and, xiv, 89, 328 (*see also* presence); *Weltuntergangserlebnis* and, 19, 100–101. *See also* potentiality of being

decolonization, xiii, 173–74. *See also* colonialism

De Gaulle, Charles, 270

dehistorification: of the future in the eschaton, 157; history's, 42; horizon of, 57; mythical-ritual, 51, 53–54, 127, 156, 162, 256, 299 (*see also* mythical-ritual, the); mythical "step-back" as a technique of, 45; of the proliferation of social becoming, 52; radical, 116, 149; religion as a technique of, 247–48; religious, 41; ritual, xiv, 248, 327; of time, 149, 158

Delling, G., 157

Demeny, P., 203–5

depresentification, 88, 90–91, 96, 309, 310

Deubner, L., 35

deworlding, 326; "being-acted-upon" entailed by, 102; the delusional world and, 90–91; experience of the "end of the world" and, 96, 98; the threat of not being in any possible cultural world and, 309–10; as a threat to the ethos of valorizing transcendence, 88

Dilthey, Wilhelm, 55

Dmitrevskij, V., 12

Dodds, Eric R., 139

domesticity: as "backdrop"/background, 70, 78–79, 289, 293; cultural, 70; intersubjective, 98; loss / falling apart of, 17, 26, 69, 197, 286, 293; of/in the world, 11, 197, 280, 282, 286, 292, 344n8; settled/settling and, 328 (*see also* settled/settling)

Dostoevsky, Fyodor, 10

Dumézil, G., 37

Dupré, Ernest, 340n7

duty-to-be/duty-to-be-in-the-world, 326–27; as the basis of human existence, 318; being-there as, 77–78, 281; in the cultural world, 39; ethos of transcendence and, xv, 77, 203, 269, 301, 323; the individual, realization through, 301; for the intersubjective valorization of life, 323; manifestation in the mode of production of material goods, 269; melancholy and overturning / the catastrophe of, 76–77; risk of not being there, retreat in the face of, 203; unfree, 31; for value, 269

Dvořák, Max, 200

Eatherly, Claude, 195, 341n7

economy / the economic: dialectic of pleasure and pain, cannot be reduced to, 242–43; Marxism and, 257–58, 269–70; as the *value of securitas*, 243

Eichmann, Adolf, 195

Einaudi, Giulio, xii

Eliade, Mircea: as a historian of religion, 55; *Images et symboles*, 53–54, 124–26; influence of, 264; *Le mythe de l'éternel retour*, 160; *Mythes, rêves et mystères*, 47–51; *Symbolisme religieux et valorisation de l'angoisse*, 131–33; "The Morphology and Function of Myths," 51–53

Elkin, A. P., 178, 188

end of the world: among "primitive" peoples, 182–84; as a cultural theme, 87; death and, 57–59; different perspectives on, 195; experience of, examples of, 17–28 (see also *Weltuntergangserlebnis* [WUE]); experience of defined as pathological, question of, 94–103; hermeneutic perspective of the, 108–9; lived experiences of, 61–75; as a possibility, 299, 319; prophecies of among aborigines, 185–89; schizophrenia and experiences of, 101–12; two distinct senses for consideration of, 38–39. *See also* apocalypse

Engels, Friedrich: concept of order
mediated by, 194; cult of Müntzer
initiated by, 251; Feurbach, on influence of, 271; interpretation of
Marxism by, 253, 257, 273; religion, dismissal of, 256, 271; "True
Socialists" group, criticism of,
345n39
entities within-the-world, 77, 99, 261,
327
Ernout, A., 37
eschaton, 327; apocalypse with and
without, xiii; apocalypse without,
9–15, 191–97; Christian, 151, 200;
cultural apocalypses with, redemptive quality of, xiv; as elimination of
the negative, 177; the eschatological
moment of in history, 161; ethical
principle associated with, 151; the
future and, 157, 159; individual/
collective levels and, xvi–xvii; in
mythical-ritual consciousness, 184;
progress in human history, as the
end of, 320; as salvation, 75; unilinearity of development from an *arché*
to an, 162–63
eternal return: for the Buddha, 50;
cosmic rhythms of, 304; of the
identical, 162–63; in Lawrence, 208;
mythical-ritual symbolism and, 38–
59; myth/theory of, 38–41, 46, 87,
103, 163; natural, 41–43; in Nietzsche
and Plato, 347n32; struggle against,
43; time and, 47, 148
ethnocentrism, xvi, 9, 162, 164, 174. *See
also* Eurocentrism
ethnographic encounter, concept of,
xvi, 169–73
ethnographic humanism: cultural
relativism and, 174; cultural unification and, 236; as the difficult path
for modern humanism, 172–73; as
ethnology suited to modern humanism, 169; philological-classicist

humanism and, 173–74. *See also*
humanism
ethnological humanism. *See* ethnographic humanism
ethnology: distance between Western
and Indigenous cultures, shorten-
ing the, 171–73; methodology for,
169–71; reestablishing cultural-
historical coherence as a task of, 178;
as a science comparing oneself with
the foreign, 171; without philosophical options, 184–85. *See also*
Indigenous/"primitive" peoples and
Indians
ethos of transcendence: beginning
with, 75–76; being-there and, 321;
catastrophe/collapse/crisis of, 71,
76–77, 218, 281, 314, 316, 319, 322;
degrees of, 309; duty-to-be-in-the-
world and, 77, 203, 269, 283, 310,
318–19, 321–23; in fieri status of, xv;
as a fundamental anthropological
principle, 324; Gramsci and, 273–
74; human culture and, 323–24;
the individual and, 301; the intersubjective and, 216, 260, 313, 322–
24; manifestations of, 2; Marxist materialism and, 263, 269; not
exhausted in a particular value,
243, 299; "obligation to be" as a
fundamental element of, 327; as a
precategorial value, 321; primacy
of, 214–15, 230, 237, 318; as quintessential human experience, 320;
relationship to other values/forms,
278–80; risk of anxiety and, 313–14,
316; risk/retreat of, 2, 203, 281–82,
321–22, 324; three moments articulating, 79, 98; transcendental in a
dual sense, 267–68, 277
Eurocentrism, 162, 171. *See also*
ethnocentrism
existentialism: aberration of, 315;
Christian, 343n51; Croce, targeted

by, 237; Heideggerian, xv, 77, 319; human condition under, 235; negative, 11, 163, 318; positive, xiii, 281, 318, 347n45

Ey, Henri, 75–76, 337n25

Fabre, Daniel, xi
Fernandez, Dominique, 229
Festinger, Leon, 182
Festus, Sextus Pompeius, 32–35
Feuerbach, Ludwig, 265–68, 271, 274
foreign, the. *See* ethnographic encounter, concept of; Indigenous/ "primitive" peoples and Indians
Fowler, W. Warde, 35–38
Fox, D. C., 178
Frazer, James George, 208
freedom: anxiety of, 43, 313, 316; eternal return as threat to, 42; finitude as the condition of, 295; as a gift from God, 160–61; initial form of human, 291–93; psychiatry as a pathology of, 75; religious, observations of, 168; social boundedness of, 315; "terrible" destructive, 203–4
Freud, Sigmund, 2, 48, 55, 208, 333n7
Friedrich, Hugo, 201–3, 342n20
Friedrich Wilhelm IV (king of Prussia), 271
Frobenius, Leo, 208, 342n34

Gallini, Clara, xi–xii
Gandolfi, Antonio, 238
Geworfenheit, 315
Ginzburg, Carlo, 331n2
Glaesser, Gustav, 33–38, 334n35
Goethe, Johann Wolfgang von, 30, 335n82
Gramsci, Antonio, xv, 271–74
Gruhle, Hans Walter, 118, 336n17
Grün, Karl, 271, 345n39
Guariglia, Guglielmo, 184, 341n21
Gusdorf, Georges, 8

Hagen, Friedrich Wilhelm, 66, 105, 338n47
handy/handiness. *See* at hand / handiness
Hauer, Jacob Wilhelm, 55
Hegel, Georg Wilhelm Friedrich, 74, 250, 252, 259, 268, 274–75
Heidegger, Martin: *angst*, translation of, 325; anxiety in, 311–13; *Being and Time*, 306; "being thrown in the world," 160; Dasein, presence and, xiv, 328; Dasein as central concept for, 326 (*see also* Dasein); *das Man*, 306–7; death in, analysis of, 313–14; *Entweltlichung* and deworlding in, 326; *Entwurf*, project and, xvi, 328; everydayness of being-there, 306, 309, 313; existentialism of, xv, 77, 318–19; *Geworfenheit* of being-there, 2; *in-der-Welt-sein*, translation of, 326; *innerweltich Seindes*, entities within-the-world and, 327; no-longer-being-able-to-be-there of, 29; *Seinkönnen*, potentiality of being and, 327; *Seinsollen* and duty-to-be, 327; *weltlich*, worldly and, 329; world of things at hand for, 277; *zuhanden/Zuhandenheit*, translation of, 325–26
Herder, Johann Gottfried, 250
Hess, Moses, 268, 345n34, 345n39
hierogonic, 254–55, 327
historians, 124–25, 128–30, 145–47, 155, 256, 258–59. *See also* historiography
historical materialism, 230, 240, 250, 252–53, 279
historicism: antihistoricism, 208; crisis of, 132; Croce's "absolute," 339n13; Eurocentric/Western, 124, 132; history means, 128, 130; idealist, xii; Italian, 278; meanings of, 339n13
historicity: of becoming, 40, 45, 77, 183; Christianity and, xiii; cyclical consciousness of time and, 39–40;

historicity (*cont.*)
of the Dasein, 63; disguising/
concealing, 183, 188, 247–48; of
economic matter, 279; the "hier-
gonic," 327; of the human condition/
existence/situation, 52, 95, 116, 127,
131–33, 148, 159–61, 164–66, 246–
47, 282; loss of, 20; in the modern
world, 164; of the moment, 292;
myth and, 45–46, 96; possibility
of a valorizing decision within, 161;
of a regime of existence, 156; of a
religious phenomenon, 125
historiography: of apostolic Christianity, 132; conceptions of, 50; of
cultural life, 244, 258–59; idealist,
128; Marxist, 252–54, 259, 264–
65; methods/structure of, 121,
129–30; modern passion for, 132;
religious, 121, 129, 135, 252–54,
259, 264–65
history: as a dialectic, 125; emergence
of within the Christian symbol,
145; escape from, 54; eschatology
and, 158–62; experience of, 127;
humankind in, 123, 130–31; images
of, 162–65; living in, 164; Marxian
conception of, 263–64; meaning of
the term, 127–28; myth and, distinction between, 146; one's own and
foreign, dual thematization of, 171;
problem of, 124; reconstruction of
history in, 126–27; redemptive, 137,
143–45, 149, 151–52, 154–59, 161, 191,
250; of religion, 54, 246; sacred,
46–47, 111, 158, 327 (*see also* time,
Christian conception of); scriptures as, 147; as a unilinear process,
modern conception of, 161; without
philosophical options, 184–85. *See
also* time
Hitler, Adolf, 249, 251
Hofmann, J. B., 37
Hölderlin, Friedrich, 64, 74

Horace, 328
human condition: absurdity of, 223;
Beckett on, 233–35; existentialist
question of, 324; historicity of, 52, 95,
131–32, 148, 159–61, 246–47; image
of God-man as necessary to imagine, 195; polarity of, 228; presence
and, 246–47; reality of, 166; Sartre's
Nausea and, 216; transcendence and,
50, 80–81, 246
humanism: Bultmann and, 162; classical, 124, 164, 239; classicist, 172–
73; ethnographic (*see* ethnographic
humanism); ethnological, 173;
historicist, 166; integral, 6, 164–
65, 167–68; limits of, 163; modern,
168–69, 172; new/broader, 131,
162, 173
humanity, 13, 165, 171–72, 241
Huyghe, René, 200

Ideler, Karl Willhelm, 74, 337n24
in-der-Welt-sein, 77, 89, 266, 298, 308–
9, 311–12. *See also* being-in-the-
world
Indigenous/"primitive" peoples and
Indians: aborigines of Australia, 14,
178–81, 185–89, 341n11; collapse of
the world among, working hypotheses regarding, 182–84; conceptions
of time held by, 49–50; the human
condition's historicity and, 131–33;
modern culture influences on, 178–
79, 181; myth among, 179–81; prophecies of the end of the world among,
185–89; prophetic movements, comparison of Judeo-Christian millenarian movements and, 7–14; risks of
catastrophe for, 12–13; symbolism of
time for, 53–54; Western civilization
and, distance between, 171–73
individual, the: abstracted from
society, 260, 265, 267; biological,
130; as body, 75; the collective and,

xvi–xvii; concrete world of, 73, 265, 267; culture/community, rooted in, xvi, 81, 84; death of, 58; existence of, 125; finiteness of, 1, 301, 314; psychoanalysis/psychopathology of, 85, 102; salvation of, 40
in illo tempore, 40, 48–49, 55, 148, 156, 164, 166, 184, 188, 327
Izambard, Georges, 203, 205

Jackson, John H., 337n25
Janet, Pierre, 75, 228, 328, 337n25, 337n36
Jaspers, Karl: *Allgemeine Psychopathologie*, 73–74, 79–83; debate over "demythologization" with Bultmann, 124, 339n7; on delusion, 64–68; de Martino's familiarity with, xiv; Heidelberg school, association with, 336n17; Mühlmann reference to, 175; negative existentialism of, 318; as a philosopher participating in the *Stimmung* of the period, 55
Jensen, Adolf Ellegard, 49
Jervis, Giovanni, 21
Jones, Jim, xvii
Judaism: Christian and Judaic eschatology, distinction between, 154; conception of time in, 144; valorization of time in, 157; waiting for the future *telos*, 154
Jung, Carl Gustav, 51, 55, 63, 79–80, 85, 172, 264

Kant, Immanuel, 281, 328
karma, 50
Kerényi, Karl, 55, 210, 264
Kierkegaard, Søren, 228, 340n30
Kittel, Gerhard, 157
Klages, Ludwig, 28
Knox, Ronald A., 181–82
koinonia, 108, 218, 327
Kranz, Heinrich, 118, 120
Kretschmer, Ernst, 36–37

Kulenkampff, Caspar, 19–26, 29, 326, 333n4, 333n11
Kunz, Hans, 74

Lactantius, Lucius Caecilius Firmianus, 182
Lamenais (Félicité Robert de la Mennais), 252
Lanternari, Vittorio, xiii, 184, 332n1, 340n10, 341n21
Lawrence, David Herbert, 2, 208–15
Le Bonniec, Henri, 35, 334n35
Leibniz, Gottfried Wilhelm, 250
Lenau, Nikolaus, 28
Lenin, Vladimir Ilyich, 249, 273
Lévi-Strauss, Claude, 8–9, 72–73, 307–8, 341n11
Lévy-Bruhl, Lucien, 55, 93
Lewin, Kurt, 345n24
Linforth, Ivan M., 139
literature: Beckett, 233–36; Camus, 223, 225–28; the crisis in Western, 192–94; existentialist, themes of, 197; Lawrence, 208–15; Mann, 205–8; Moravia, 228–33; Sartre, 215–25
Locke, John, 126
Lommel, Andreas, 14, 178–81, 341n11
Löwith, Karl, 250

Macquarrie, John, vii, 325
Macrobius, Ambrosius Aurelius Theodosius, 32–34, 38
magic: of Aboriginal/"primitive" peoples, 179–81, 185; agricultural, 36–37; black, 6, 179, 303; as a category in ethnographic observation, 170; the collective unconscious and, 80; cultural life and, 247; delusion and, 92–94; of Good Friday, 153; the human condition and, 166–67, 246; linguistic, 201–2; psychopathology and, xvii, 61–62, 82–83, 86, 118–20, 326; in Sartre, 297–99
Mallarmé, Stéphane, 202

Mann, Thomas, 44, 205–8

Marcellinara, bell tower of, xv, 4, 6, 198, 216

Marx, Karl: alienation, theory of, 268–69; analysis of, 261–69; Cohn on, 252; *Economic and Philosophical Manuscripts of 1844*, 269, 273; Engels's interpretation of, 253, 257; Feuerbach, influence of, 271; *The German Ideology*, 262–65; Merleau-Ponty and, 274–75; predictions by, 259–60; on religion, 167, 345n20; rethinking of, xii; Slavic line of eschatology, place in, 250; "Theses on Feuerbach," 265–67, 273–74; "True Socialists" group, criticism of, 345n39

Marxism: Croce's concerns about, 240; religion and, 248–60, 264–65

Marxist apocalypse, xiii, 248–75

Massenzio, Marcello, xi, 344n8

Mauss, Marcel, 72, 307–8, 346n17

Mayer-Gross, Wilhem, 70, 336n17

Mazzini, Giuseppe, 344n6

Meillet, A., 37

Merleau-Ponty, Maurice, 275, 286, 290

millenarian/prophetic movements: among the Jacobins, 249; disastrous conditions that favor, 252; failed prophesies, impact of, 181–82; institutionalization and control of psychopathological risks in, 176–77; Judeo-Christian eschatological tradition and Third World, 7–8; psychopathology and, 175–76

Minkowski, Eugène, 89, 286, 337n34

Mommsen, Theodor, 33

Moravia, Alberto, 2, 11, 197, 228–33

Moreau, Jacques-Joseph, 76

Mounier, Emmanuel, 12, 198–99, 342n14

Mühlmann, Wilhelm E., xvii, 175–77, 181–82, 248–49

mundus (*patet*): agricultural interpretations of, 36–37; analysis of ancient accounts of, 33–38; ancient accounts of, 31–33

Müntzer, Thomas, 251, 344n15

mythical-ritual, the: apparatus of, xiv, xvi, 83; behaviors of, 189; consciousness and, 39, 43, 46, 57, 184, 259; dehistorification and, 51; horizon of, xiii, 30, 53–54, 102, 246, 254; metahistory and, 246; nexus of, 96, 247; resolution, xiv; symbols/symbolism, xiv, 38–43, 47, 52, 56, 78, 83–84, 94, 99–100, 118–21, 196, 254–55, 257–58

myth(s): among Australian aborigines, 179–81; dreams and, 48; dual protective function performed by, 45; of eternal return (*see* eternal return); as metahistory, 46; of origins, 46; of "primitive" man, 49, 51–52; what is?, 55–57

naturalism, 194, 214–15, 282–83, 324, 346n11

nature: antithesis of history and, 264; eternal return and, 41, 43; as incapable of culture, 242; Marx's vision of, 262–63; "per se," 262, 283–84

Navel, Georges, 2–3, 303

Neumann, Erich, 29

Nicolini, Fausto, 237–39

Nietzsche, Friedrich, 29, 347n32

Novalis, Georg Friedrich Philipp von Hardenberg, 201

objectivity: absolute/pure, 130, 296–97; claims of, 184–85; decided through worldly/human action, 265, 272; scientific ideal of, "God's point of view" as, 8–9; struggle for, 272, 274; temporal, 113

Otto, Rudolf: *Das Heilige*, movement beginning with the publication of, 55; *ganz Andere* in the work of, 329, 333n10, 338n49; as historian of religion, 55; influence of, 264;

religious experience of contact with the "wholly other," impossibility of reducing to reason, 334n28
Otto, Walter, 264
Ovid, 32, 35

Paci, Enzo, 278–82, 346n6, 346n8, 346n10
Parker, K. Langloh, 185
Parousia: in Cullman's perspective/ thesis, 143–45, 152; deferral/delay of, 136, 181–82; eschatological, 151; first, 139, 145; glossary definition of, 327; *parousia* as ancient Greek term, 339n20; period from first to second, 145, 149–50, 155–56, 164; placement in Judaic and Christian time/history, 145, 152, 154–55; second, 137–38, 140–41, 145, 154, 158–59
Pascal, Blaise, 30
Pástina, Roberto, xii
Pavese, Cesare, 41, 197, 342n11
Pentony, Patrick, 178
Petri, Helmut, 178–79, 185–88
Petriconi, Helmuth, 12
pia fraus, 40, 42, 57, 166, 327
Pierro, Albino, 196–97
Piganiol, A., 35
Plato, 50, 55, 58, 139, 249, 347n32
Pliny, 36
Plutarch, 31–32, 35
poetry, 201–5
potentiality of being, 28, 311–12, 314, 327
presence: alienation of, 53, 248; annihilation of is the loss of culture, 244; being-in-the-world, 316; crisis of (*see* crisis of presence); Dasein and, xiv, 328 (*see also* Dasein); as detachment from nature, 247; development of the notion of, xiv; ethical time of, 45–46; the human condition and, 246–47; human vitality is, 241–42, 244; illustrated by Beckett's *Waiting*

for Godot, 233–35; *in-der-Welt-sein* of, 89; individual/collective levels of, xvi; loss of, 309; mythical-ritual resolution and, xiv (*see also* mythical-ritual, the); nonbeing of, 243; "norm" of, 318; process of (*see* presentification); resistant, inert world of body instruments with respect to, 218; risk of losing, 118–19, 281–82, 316; as the synthetic power that conditions all cultural life, 242, 244. *See also* being-there
presentification, 328; anxiety and, 311, 313; being-there and, 71, 96, 219, 288, 308, 310; ceaseless, enactment of, 322; collapse of the world and, 286; in cyclical time, 40; domesticity and, 282, 285–86, 288; ethos of presence as an energy of, 257; ethos of transcendence and, 214; inaugural value of, 218; individual, transcendence of, 79, 257, 316; intentional, 71, 219, 310; inversion of, 318–20; loss/collapse/obliteration of, 20, 56, 59, 154, 219, 222–23, 310, 311, 317–20; as presence in action, 310; primordial ethos of, 39; risk of absence, combat against, 316; valorizing, 40, 56, 59, 71, 215–16, 278, 305, 316–17, 322; walking and, 305–6; as worlding/being-in-the-world, 88, 90, 310. *See also* depresentification
"primitive" peoples. *See* Indigenous/"primitive" peoples and Indians
progress: of civilization, 319–20; of the ethos of transcendence, 281; Marxian/Gramscian, 269, 273; positivistic ideology of, 159, 163; of religious ethnology, 55; of science, 296; technological, 3, 11; in transcendence, 85; "unilinear," concept of, 124
projection/projectability, 119, 120, 316, 328; of actions, 219, 294, 297;

projection/projectability (*cont.*)
of becoming, 57–58, 102; being-in-the-world as, 11, 311; the body as, 295–96; communitarian, xvii, 39, 41, 78, 194, 243, 266, 269, 278, 281–82, 293, 303, 307, 318, 322 (*see also* communitarian project of things at hand); Croce's, 237; economic, 278; handiness as/and, 277, 282, 284, 307; historical limits of, 299; as a horizon for the potential of being, xvi; human/humanity, 284, 315; of images, 110; intersubjectivity, 20, 71, 78, 266; lack of in single perceptive spheres, 108; of life, 95, 200; of objects, 219, 222; of/in the world, 27, 88–89; onto a foreign culture, 170; in the other, 62; of "others," 218; presentification and, 282 (*see also* presentification); of self in the world, 110–11; of value, 233; of worldly becoming, 102; of world unification, limit and irony of, 194, 320

prophetic movements. *See* millenarian/prophetic movements

Proust, Marcel, 288–89, 291–92, 300–301

psychoanalysis, 50–51, 85, 88, 172, 266, 287

psychopathological apocalypse, xiv; cultural apocalypses and, 13, 21–31; death and schizophrenia, 61–64; ethos of transcendence, beginning with, 75–76; lived experiences of the end of the world, 61–75; religious apocalypses and, 14. *See also* schizophrenia; *Weltuntergangserlebnis* (WUE)

psychopathological document(ation), 13, 192

psychopathology: ambivalence, 118–19; anthropoanalysis, 87–89; catatonia and ritualism, 115–18; concrete and abnormal worlds, 73–75; crisis of objectivization, 114–15; critical moments of Christian apocalypse and, 134; cultural psychiatry, 83–84; delusional experiences, 64–72; delusional world, 90–91; delusion of influence, 92–94; ethos of transcendence and, 2; existential, 309; existential analysis in, 89–90; experience of the end of the world, 94–103; healthy, model of, 86–87; incipient schizophrenia, end of the world experiences and, 101–12; melancholy, 76–77; millenarian movements and, 175–76; mythical-ritual symbolism and, 119–21; normal/abnormal, distinguishing, 85–86, 91–92; "primitive" mentality and contemporary psychotic states, comparison between, 82; psychic disorders, division of, 81; religion and, interdependence of, 103–7; sociology/history and, 79–82; suicide, a case of, 112–14

Rehm, Walther, 30

reintegration: apparatuses, 148; cultural (*see* cultural reintegration); horizon of, 40–41, 140, 275; human / of humanity, 13, 256, 268; myth and, 45; of presence, 246; psychoanalysis and, 51, 83; public, 73; recovery and, 119, 121, 310; religion / religious cultural institutions and, 43, 253; risk, 91; risk of the end of the world and, 99, 102; into social reality, 91; symbolic/symbol of, 196, 255; unconscious objectives of, 178; into value, 53

religion: Christian (*See* Christian apocalypse/eschatology; Christianity); as a cultural institution, 42–43; as a detour, 255, 275; eschatological perspective, 191; fall of and the modern apocalypse, 199; historical reconstruction of, 126–27; historicity of, 125–26; historiography and, 129–30; history of, 54, 246; impact of Judeo-Christian eschatological tradition on Third World prophetic movements, 7–8; Judaism (*see* Judaism); Marxism and, 248–60, 264–65; as a mask for historicity of existence, 165–66; as mediation of detachment from nature of presence, 247; as myth, 259; psychopathology and, interdependence of, 103–7; question of the need for, 167–68; rationality of, 126; religious aspiration, 245–46; religious freedom, observations on, 168; unilinear image of historical development and, 162–64 (*see also* history; mythical-ritual, the; time)

Riecken, Henry, 182

Rimbaud, Jean-Arthur, 202–4, 341n6, 342n22

ritual: abolition of time through, 111; Aboriginal, 187–88, 341n11; agricultural, 36–37; of the Bambara, 5–6; calendrical, 142; cultural apocalypse and, xiii; dehistorification, xiv, 51, 248, 327; efficacy of, 97; foundational identity repeated through, 183; funerary, 140, 314; individual distinguished from cultural reintegration, 326; institutionalization through, 176–77; mental chaos, as a reaction to, 96–97; mundus, connected to, 34, 36, 38, 331n6; negligence of, 184; presence protected from an uncertain future by, xiv, 328; psychopathologies combatted by, 177; reappropriation of the other through, 260; recitation by a patient, 49, 82; repetition of a mythical order through, 39, 42, 44–47, 54–57, 148–49, 156, 183, 320; as a return to the past, 52; ritualism, 96–97,

117–18, 247, 324. *See also* mythical-ritual, the

Rivière, J., 203

Robbe-Grillet, Alain, 235

Robinson, Edward, vii, 325

Roos, Reto, 112–14

Rose, H. J., 36–37

Rosenberg, Alfred, 55, 251

Rouch, Jean, 4, 342n9

Ruskin, John, 249

Sandberg, R., 65

Sartre, Jean-Paul: "A Commentary on *The Stranger*," 223–25; on the body, 290, 293–96; bourgeois world, derision aimed at, 315–16; *Esquisse d'une théorie des émotions*, 297–98; Heidegger's analysis of *Zuhandenheit*, modification of, 346n20; *L'être et le néant*, 293–97; *Nausea*, xiii, 2, 11, 14, 291; nausea theme and the indigestibility of the world, 215–23; nausea theme and threat to cultural homelands, 197; on the world, 297–99

Schacter, Stanley, 182

Scheler, Max, 343n51

Schelling, Friedrich Wilhelm Joseph, 29, 250, 333n22

Schetz, Agnes, 178

Schiff, P., 13

schizophrenia: autistic feature of, 28; catastrophe / end of the world / *Weltuntergangserlebnis* and incipient, 13, 77, 100–105, 338n44 (see also *Weltuntergangserlebnis* [WUE]); diagnosis of, 336n13; modification of *in-der-Welt-sein* of Dasein in incipient, 308; as the most philosophical of mental illnesses, 112; revelation and the onset of, 74

Schlosser, Julius von, 200

Schmidt, Conrad, 256

Schmidt, G., 66

Schneider, Kurt, 66, 336n13

science(s): as an emanation of Spirit, 329; comparison of cultural histories and, 15, 164; establishment of culture and, 247; ethnocentrism of Western, 84; ethnology as a, xvi, 163, 169, 171–72, 184; ethos of transcendence and, 78, 323; European, 133; fear of losing the world to, 195; of handiness, 81; as a historical category / human relation, 272, 277; historiography as, 129–30, 258; literary perspective on, 202, 208; magic, polemic against, 170; as morally indifferent, potential for, 6, 196 (*see also* atomic/nuclear catastrophe); "naturalism" of, 215, 346n11; naturalistic valorization of, 284; of nature, Marxism and, 258, 262, 266; of nature, struggle against, 282; perspective of, 9–10; as the reduction of nature to culture, 42; religious, 183, 264–65; Sartre on, 296–97; truth clothed in, historical materialism and, 249–50

Sedlmayr, Hans, 12, 200–201, 342n19
Serra, Renato, 238
settled/settling, 328; as the backdrop of human history (being-in-the-world), 288; catastrophe of, 191; cultural homelands and phenomenological rootedness of, xv; human work to attain a world that is, 261, 288; unsettling of, 191; the world as, 192, 201, 215, 287–88. *See also* unsettled/unsettling
Signorelli, Amalia, xvi
Sophists, the, 55
Sorel, Georges, 56
Spengler, Oswald, 2, 159, 163, 239
Stalin, Josef, 273
Stambaugh, Joan, 325
Stimmung/Stimmungen, xvii, 2, 21, 55, 65, 192, 201, 306, 328
Stirner, Max, 252, 271
Storch, Alfred, 19–26, 29, 61–64, 100, 118, 308, 326, 333n3

Straus, E., 74
Strauss, David, 252, 271
strike, the, 270–71
symbols as complexes of emotional experience, 213. *See also* mythical-ritual, the

Teresa of Avila, Saint, 59, 212
theogenetic. *See* hierogonic
Thunberg, Greta, xvii
time: apostolic Christian apocalypse and, xiii; Christian conception of, 142–58; conceptions of held by "primitive" peoples, 49–50; cyclical, 39–41, 45–47 (*see also* eternal return); cyclical of the Greeks, 157; eschatological, 47; the eternal return and, 47, 148 (*see also* eternal return); ethical, 45–46; heartbeats participating in, 302; the incarnation as a privileged moment of, 163; Indian symbolism of, 53–54; Judaic valorization of, 157; *kairós*, 157–58; psychoanalysis and, 50–51; the schizophrenic experience of, 111–12; search for lost, 291–92; undoing, 49. *See also* history
transcendence. *See* ethos of transcendence
tua res agitur, 69, 105, 109, 156, 328
Turchi, N., 35

unsettled/unsettling, 328–29; another's death as provoking a feeling of, 314; anxiety and, 311–13; emigrant's life as, 196; examples of, xv, 17–19, 198; feeling of, 69, 105, 292, 311–12; manifested in art, poetry, and philosophy, 194, 201–2; our cultural homeland threatened by, 197; for Proust, 292; for Rimbaud, 203–4; for Sartre, 224; of the settled, 191. *See also* settled/settling
useful, the, 280, 329; as a category of ethnographic discourse, 169; for

Croce, 329, 346n6; distinction of the, opening the self to, 243–44; as economic forms, xv, 242–43; as the existential matter from which spiritual forms arise, 278–79; objects as, 217, 229, 233; sun as obviously, 285

value(s) of existence, 317–18. *See also* communitarian project of things at hand; ethos of transcendence
van den Berg, J. H., 300
van der Leeuw, Gerardus, 45, 47, 53
van Gogh, Vincent, 74
Varro, Marcus Terentius, 33–34
Verrius Flaccus, Marcus, 36
Viano, C. A., 126
Vico, Giambattista, 282
Virgil, 36, 38
Virno, Paolo, xii
vitality, 329; animal, 241–44, 247; cultural-historical, 136; dialectic of morality and, 240; economicity confused with, 282; human, presence and, 244; human distinguished from that of plants/animals or biological/natural, 241–44; loss of, 230; natural, culture as detachment from, 244–45; passing to humanity from, 75; "raw and green," 241, 244, 278–79; reembracing, 193; transcending of mere, 263, 269, 280
Volmat, Robert, 109, 111
von Baeyer, Walter Ritter, 74
von Gebsattel, Viktor Emil, 74

Wagenvoort, M. H., 36–37
Walde, A., 37
Weinstock, Stefan, 34–35
Weitling, Wilhelm, 250, 252, 344n14
Weltuntergangserlebnis (WUE), xiv–xv, 2, 13, 19, 94, 100–101, 103–4, 140–42, 318, 329. *See also* schizophrenia
Werner, Heinz, 308

West, apocalypse of the: as an apocalypse without eschaton, xiii, 9–15, 191–92 (*see also* crisis of the modern/contemporary West); questions circling around, xvii
Western culture, distance between Indigenous cultures and, 171–73. *See also* ethnographic encounter, concept of
Westphal, Carl, 64–65, 336n9
Wetzel, Albrecht, 19, 103–4, 333n7, 338n44
wholly other, 329; "Last Judgment" and, 106; making understandable, 20; other becoming a, 222, 299; presence and, 248; of the psychic functions, being-acted-upon and, 102; recovering the, 119; religious experience of contact with, Otto's concept and, 334n28; religious pretenses and the task of historiography, 125, 256, 265; risk of the catastrophe of the world and, 41; space, collective domestication of, 301; that upsets, 121; values, 43, 126, 255; values, religious life and, 245, 247; witnessing, the end of the world and, 138, 199; of the world that gets deworlded, 109
Wissowa, Georg, 38
world: as a backdrop, 287–88; as a cultural concept / culturally constructed, 297, 315; ending of, possibility of, 299, 319; as a given in its communitarian totality, 286; horizon of, the sun and, 284–86; magical, 298–99; of things at hand, 202, 217–18, 222, 277, 313, 321; of tomorrow and today, 1–6
worldhood, 329; of being-there, 78; chaos of for Camus, 228; coherence of, 90; as the duty to transcend in the presence that "overcomes" the situation, 108; of the entities

worldhood (*cont.*)
  within-the-world, 77; experiencing of, 109; Heidegger's anxiety and, 311, 314; human, 244–45; inner sign of, 19–20; of operating, history as, 128
worldly, the, 329; actions, objectivity decided by, 265; actions, process of reappropriation that mediates, 121; actions, restrictions of, 247; actions rendered intelligible by a transcendental sense of, 267; apocalypse of, 197; becoming, losing the practicability of, 58, 102–3; becoming, myth of origins and, 46; catastrophe/fall of, 13, 100, 108–9, 191, 195, 319; Christian apocalypse as beginnings of, 200; crisis of presentification and, 222; extraliturgical agency restored to the, 142; living, mythical-ritual consciousness and, 166; occurrence, supreme human responsibility in, 151; one's own corporeality penetrated by, 71; perception of, everyday occurrences altering the, 70; practicability, horizon of, 39, 56, 182; relationship, restabilizing, 115; in Rimbaud, 204

Zacharias, 47
Zimmer, Heinrich, 131
Zönd, Jarg, 113